RELIGION, DYNASTY, AND P
EARLY CHRISTIAN ROM

This collection of essays traces the central role played by aristocratic patronage in the transformation of the city of Rome at the end of antiquity. Rather than privileging the administrative and institutional developments related to the rise of papal authority as the paramount theme in the post-classical history of the city, as previous studies have tended to do, here the focus shifts to the networks of reciprocity between patrons and their dependants. Using material culture and social theory to challenge traditional readings of the textual sources, the volume undermines the teleological picture of ecclesiastical sources such as the *Liber Pontificalis*, and presents the lay, clerical and ascetic populations of the city of Rome at the end of antiquity as interacting in a fluid environment of alliance-building and status negotiation. Drawing on work by members of the Centre for Late Antiquity at the University of Manchester over the last decade, the collection focuses on a wide range of topics, from imperial policy, to the inheritance strategies of aristocratic households, to the rise of monastic foundations. By bringing the city whose aristocracy is the best documented of any ancient population squarely into the centre of discussion, the volume makes an important contribution to our understanding of the role played by elites across the end of antiquity.

KATE COOPER is Senior Lecturer in Early Christianity and Director of the Centre for Late Antiquity at the University of Manchester. Educated at Princeton, Harvard and Wesleyan universities, she has taught at Barnard College of Columbia University and the University of Padova, and has been a Visiting Research Fellow in the Austrian Academy of Sciences and a Rome Prize Fellow at the American Academy in Rome. Her books include *The Virgin and the Bride: Idealized Womanhood in Late Antiquity* (1996) and *The Fall of the Roman Household* (forthcoming from Cambridge).

JULIA HILLNER is a British Academy Postdoctoral Fellow in the Department of Classics and Ancient History and the Centre for Late Antiquity at the University of Manchester. Educated at the Rheinische Friedrich-Wilhelms Universität Bonn, she is an expert on the late Roman household and the author of *Jedes Haus ist eine Stadt: Privatimmobilien im spätantiken Rom* (2004).

RELIGION, DYNASTY, AND PATRONAGE IN EARLY CHRISTIAN ROME, 300–900

EDITED BY

KATE COOPER

and

JULIA HILLNER

CAMBRIDGE
UNIVERSITY PRESS

CAMBRIDGE UNIVERSITY PRESS
Cambridge, New York, Melbourne, Madrid, Cape Town, Singapore,
São Paulo, Delhi, Dubai, Tokyo

Cambridge University Press
The Edinburgh Building, Cambridge CB2 8RU, UK

Published in the United States of America by Cambridge University Press, New York

www.cambridge.org
Information on this title: www.cambridge.org/9780521131278

First published 2007
This digitally printed version 2010

A catalogue record for this publication is available from the British Library

ISBN 978-0-521-87641-4 Hardback
ISBN 978-0-521-13127-8 Paperback

PIGNORIBUS

Hester Leyser

Hildelith Leyser

Julian Peres

Karl Rausch

Madeleine Connor

Nicholas Otter

Antonia Rausch

Contents

Acknowledgements — *page* ix
List of contributors — xii
Abbreviations — xiv

Introduction
Kate Cooper and Julia Hillner — 1

PART I ICONS OF AUTHORITY: POPE AND EMPEROR — 19

1 From emperor to pope? Ceremonial, space, and authority at Rome from Constantine to Gregory the Great
Mark Humphries — 21

2 Memory and authority in sixth-century Rome: the *Liber Pontificalis* and the *Collectio Avellana*
Kate Blair-Dixon — 59

PART II LAY, CLERICAL, AND ASCETIC CONTEXTS FOR THE ROMAN *GESTA MARTYRUM* — 77

3 Domestic conversions: households and bishops in the late antique 'papal legends'
Kristina Sessa — 79

4 Agnes and Constantia: domesticity and cult patronage in the *Passion of Agnes*
Hannah Jones — 115

5 'A church in the house of the saints': property and power in the *Passion of John and Paul*
Conrad Leyser — 140

PART III RELIGION, DYNASTY, AND PATRONAGE 163

6 Poverty, obligation, and inheritance: Roman heiresses and the varieties of senatorial Christianity in fifth-century Rome
Kate Cooper 165

7 *Demetrias ancilla dei*: Anicia Demetrias and the problem of the missing patron
Anne Kurdock 190

8 Families, patronage, and the titular churches of Rome, *c.* 300–*c.* 600
Julia Hillner 225

9 To be the neighbour of St Stephen: patronage, martyr cult, and Roman monasteries, *c.* 600–*c.* 900
Marios Costambeys and Conrad Leyser 262

Bibliography 288
Index 317

Acknowledgements

This volume results from a series of collaborations in the Centre for Late Antiquity of the University of Manchester, going back to the spring of 1996. Over this period innumerable debts have been accumulated. A number of colleagues in addition to the volume contributors supported its development by contributing papers and discussion to our research colloquia on related themes, and by reading and responding to draft versions of the contributing essays. Thanks are due to Sam Barnish, Robert Coates-Stephens, Tim Cornell, Andy Fear, Paul Fouracre, Gavin Kelly, Stephen Todd, and Ian Wood, and especially to Lucy Grig and Clare Pilsworth for their generosity as readers. Michael Sharp and the anonymous readers of Cambridge University Press offered outstandingly careful and valuable help. Warm thanks indeed are due to the revered friends and mentors, Peter Brown, Gillian Clark, Robert Markus, Philip Rousseau, and Chris Wickham, who offered advice and encouragement during the very early stages of our thinking about how to think about Roman patronage. Readers will recognize our debt to their work on every page of the present volume, even if none lives up to the precipitous standard of their own.

There are also very practical contributions to record and to honour. In 1996 and 1997 the British Academy and the University of Manchester Research Support Fund made grants to sponsor the initial phase of what became, respectively, the Roman Martyrs Project and the Religion, Dynasty, and Patronage Project. Much is owed to Catherine Conybeare and Marios Costambeys, the Research Associates who began work on the two projects in September of 1996 and 1997 respectively, whose nous and hard work were in large measure responsible for the fruitful way in which the work subsequently developed. The peerless Mark Humphries, Clare Pilsworth, and Anne Kurdock served successively as Research Associates to the Roman Martyrs Project, supported by the British Academy (1997–99) and the University of Manchester Distributed Learning Fund (2004–5).

Clare Pilsworth and Julia Hillner both served as Research Associates to the Religion, Dynasty, and Patronage Project following a Major Research Grant made by the British Arts and Humanities Research Board in the spring of 1999. At the time of writing, web-searchable digital resources resulting from the work of both projects, including a digital index to the Roman *gesta martyrum* and *Religion, Dynasty, and Patronage in Rome, c.440–c.840*, a relational database of documentary and inscriptional evidence for Roman acts of patronage, can be found on the Centre for Late Antiquity website at www.arts.manchester.ac.uk/cla. (In addition, the latter database has been deposited in Microsoft Access form with the Arts and Humanities Data Service, www.ahds.uk.)

We are also grateful to the British Academy and the AHRC respectively for sponsoring two short conferences, in March 1999 and January 2003 respectively, to discuss and develop the work of the two projects. The first of these resulted in *Early Medieval Europe* 9.3 (2000), 'The Roman martyrs and the politics of memory', a special issue edited by Kate Cooper. The second has resulted in the present volume, which in many ways represents a further iteration of the thinking in the first. Contributors to the original colloquium and other collaborators have joined and left the volume as its theme came into focus. We are grateful to Franz-Alto Bauer, Adam Cohen, Jonathan Conant, Sumaiya Hamdani, Bill Klingshirn, Fred Paxton, Philip Rousseau, Antonio Sennis, Sarah Tatum, and Hannah Williams for invaluable contributions to the 2003 colloquium, and to Joanne Moran Cruz and the Medieval Studies Program at Georgetown University, Washington, DC, for hosting the colloquium in high style. Warm thanks are also due to Jim O'Donnell of Georgetown University and Alice-Mary Talbot of Dumbarton Oaks for generosity and inspiration during the work in Washington. The Departments of Classics and Ancient History, of History, and of Religions and Theology at the University of Manchester have throughout offered collegiality and invaluable support.

It remains to record our gratitude to the volume's contributors, who have showed rare intellectual stamina and generosity through the long process of revision, editing, and cross-referencing. We have been immensely fortunate to work with such a group, and would like in particular to thank Marios Costambeys, Mark Humphries, and Tina Sessa, who each went beyond the call of duty more than once in lending erudition and intelligence to the work of others in the group, a contribution which made all the difference to the editorial process. *Primus inter pares*, however, has been Conrad Leyser, who has directed the Religion, Dynasty, and Patronage project from its inception and has served as an informal mentor to more than one contributor. Warm thanks are due to Jamie Wood, who compiled the Index. Michael Sharp and his staff at Cambridge University Press shepherded the volume through the production process with wonderful intelligence and good humour.

Lastly, we record our thanks to a group of people who have done their best to slow the volume's progress, even as they struggled to impart wisdom to their parents. Every contributor to the present volume has, whether a parent or not, had the experience during the last decade of discussing late Roman patronage while juggling a baby on his or her knee, and though the babies got larger and had to hand on the job of wiggling on laps to younger siblings, they did their best to keep the grown-ups distracted but somehow also inspired. It is to Hester Leyser, Hildelith Leyser, Julian Peres, Karl Rausch, Madeleine Connor, Nicholas Otter, and Antonia Rausch, born in that order from 1997 to 2007, that we dedicate this book.

Contributors

KATE BLAIR-DIXON is an independent scholar living in Bad Homburg, Germany. Her contribution on the *Collectia Avellana* develops work begun in her 2004 Manchester PhD thesis, 'Schism and the politics of memory: constructing authority from Hippolytus through the Laurentian schism'.

KATE COOPER is Director of the Centre for Late Antiquity in the University of Manchester. Her publications include *The Virgin and the Bride: Idealized Womanhood in Late Antiquity* (1996) and *The Fall of the Roman Household* (2007); *Passion and Persuasion*, a volume on the Roman *gesta martyrum*, is currently in preparation.

MARIOS COSTAMBEYS is Lecturer in Medieval History at the University of Liverpool and Director of the Liverpool Centre for Medieval Studies. He served as research associate in the Centre for Late Antiquity for the pilot project on 'Roman Nobles in the Age of Theoderic and Justinian: Religion, Dynasty, and Civic Patronage'; and subsequently as Leverhulme Special Research Fellow in the University of Manchester. His publications include *Power and Patronage in Early Medieval Italy: Local Society and the Abbey of Farfa, c.700–c.900* (2007).

JULIA HILLNER is a British Academy Postdoctoral Fellow in the Centre for Late Antiquity and Department of Classics and Ancient History at the University of Manchester. She was previously a research associate on the project 'Religion, Dynasty and Patronage in Rome, *c.*440–*c.*840' in the University of Manchester. Her publications include *Jedes Haus ist eine Stadt: Privatimmobilien im spätantiken Rom* (2004).

MARK HUMPHRIES is Professor of Ancient History at the University of Swansea; he was previously a research associate on the Roman Martyrs Project in the University of Manchester. His publications include

Communities of the Blessed (1999) and *Early Christianity* (2006). He is general editor of the series Translated Texts for Historians.

HANNAH JONES is a writer, English teacher and Chinese-language student living in Shanghai. She completed her 1998 MA dissertation, 'The desert and desire: virginity, city and family in the Roman martyr-legends of Agnes and Eugenia', at the University of Manchester. The dissertation explored the relationship between the imagery of virginity in the legends of these two female saints and the social context of law patronage around their Roman cult sites.

ANNE KURDOCK is Teaching Fellow in the Department of Religions and Theology, University of Manchester. After completing her PhD in the University of Manchester in 2003, with a thesis entitled 'The Anician women: patronage and dynastic strategy in a late Roman domus, 350 CE–600 CE', she served as research associate on the Virtual Cities Project of the Centre for Late Antiquity in the University of Manchester.

CONRAD LEYSER is Senior Lecturer in Medieval History at the University of Manchester, and, at the time of writing, a Humboldt Fellow at the Monumenta Germaniae Historica in Munich. He is the author of *Authority and Asceticism from Augustine to Gregory the Great* (2000), and is currently working on a book provisionally entitled *Celibacy and the Priesthood, ca. 400–1100.*

KRISTINA SESSA is Assistant Professor of History at the Ohio State University. She has published articles on the Roman *gesta martyrum* and on late ancient conceptions of domestic space, and is currently completing a monograph entitled *The Household and the Bishop* on the relationship between Roman episcopal authority and the private household.

Abbreviations

AASS	*Acta Sanctorum quotquot toto urbe coluntur* (ed. J. Bollandius et al., Antwerp and Brussels, 1634–)
AB	*Analecta Bollandiana*
ACO	*Acta Conciliorum Oecumenicorum*
ACW	*Ancient Christian Writers*
AJA	*American Journal of Archaeology*
BAC	*Bulletino di Archeologia Cristiana*
BHG	*Bibliotheca Hagiographica Graeca* (ed. F. Halkin, 3rd edn, Brussels, 1957)
BHL	*Bibliotheca Hagiographica Latina* (Brussels, 1898–1901); *Supplementum* (1911); *Novum Supplementum* (1986)
CA	*Collectio Avellana*
CBCR	*Corpus Basilicarum Christianarum Romae*
CCSL	*Corpus Christianorum, Series Latina* (Turnhout, 1952–)
CIL	*Corpus Scriptionum Latinarum*
CJ	*Classical Journal*
CLA	*Codices Latini Antiquiores* (Oxford, 1935–71)
CP	*Classical Philology*
CPL	*Clavis Patrum Latinorum* (ed. E. Dekkers and A. Gaar, 3rd edn, Turnhout, 1955)
CSEL	*Corpus Scriptorum Ecclesiasticorum Latinorum* (Vienna, 1866–)
CTh	*Codex Theodosianus*
DACL	*Dictionnaire d'archéologie chrétienne et de liturgie* (ed. F. Cabrol and H. Leclercq, Paris, 1924–)
DOP	*Dumbarton Oaks Papers*
EHR	*English Historical Review*
EME	*Early Medieval Europe*
HEL	*Histoire, Epistémologie, Langage*
HN	Zosimus, *Historia Nova*

ICUR	*Inscriptiones Christianae Urbis Romae* (ed. J. B. De Rossi, A. Silvagni and A. Ferrua, Rome, 1922–)
ILCV	*Inscriptiones Latinae Christianae Veteres* (ed. E. Diehl, 1925–)
ILS	*Inscriptiones Latinae Selectae* (ed. H. Dessau, Berlin, 1892–)
JAChr	*Jahrbuch für Antike und Christentum*
JECS	*Journal of Early Christian Studies*
JRA	*Journal of Roman Archaeology*
JRS	*Journal of Roman Studies*
JTS	*Journal of Theological Studies*
LCL	Loeb Classical Library
LP	*Liber Pontificalis*
LTUR	*Lexicon Topographicum Urbis Romae* (ed. E. M. Steinby, Rome, 1993[2]–)
Meded	*Mededelingen van het Nederlandse Instituut te Rome*
MEFRA	*Mélange de l'Ecole Française de Rome, Antiquité*
MEFRM	*Mélange de l'Ecole Française de Rome, Moyen Age*
MGH	*Monumenta Germaniae Historica*
AA	*Auctores Antiquissimi*
Epp.	*Epistolae*
SRL	*Scriptores Rerum Langobardicarum et Italicarum*
SRM	*Scriptores Rerum Merovingicarum*
NCMH	*New Cambridge Medieval History*
NPNF	*Nicene and Post-Nicene Fathers*
PBSR	*Papers of the British School at Rome*
PCBE	*Prosopographie chrétienne du Bas-Empire* (ed. C. Pietri and L. Pietri, Rome, 1982–)
PG	*Patrologiae Cursus Completus, Series Graeca* (ed. J.-P. Migne, Paris 1857–66)
PL	*Patrologiae cursus completus, Series latina* (ed. J.-P. Migne, Paris 1844–55)
PLRE	*Prosopography of the Later Roman Empire* (ed. A. H. M. Jones and J. R. Martindale, Cambridge 1971–)
PLS	*Patrologia Latina, Supplementum*
RivAC	*Rivista di Archeologia Cristiana*
RE	*Paulys Realencyclopädie der classischen Alterthumswissenschaften*
RM	*Regula Magistri*
SC	Sources Chrétiennes
SCH	*Studies in Church History*
ZKG	*Zeitschrift für Kirchengeschichte*

Introduction

Kate Cooper and Julia Hillner

'In all ages, whatever the form or name of government, be it monarchy, republic, or democracy, an oligarchy lurks behind the façade.'[1] With these words Sir Ronald Syme began his landmark investigation into the lively political networks of the late Republican noble families of the city of Rome, families who drew their power from ancestry and landed wealth as much as from the political process. This statement holds gradually less true for their successors at the end of antiquity, who struggled to maintain their position in the face of set-backs such as civil war in Italy in the 470s and 480s, and again from 534 to 554. The fifth and sixth centuries saw a progressive erosion of the landed wealth of Rome's aristocratic families. While they had long resisted the centralizing instincts of Rome's principal land-owner, the emperor, new pressures and opportunities led the Roman aristocracy to seek a more cooperative relationship with Rome's bishop, whose ever greater *ex officio* holdings came to rival those of the emperor, and were more secure in the face of political upheaval. If this strategy of cooperation was largely successful, however, its success brought with it the eventual waning of Roman memory where the aristocracy was concerned.

During late antiquity, the urban fabric of the city of Rome was the result of efforts by three categories of patron: senators, emperors, and bishops (although individual patrons could belong to more than one category). The western senatorial elite based in Rome were the principal beneficiaries, along with the emperor himself, not only of Italy's status as a destination for tax revenue, but also of their own standing as international land-owners. Unlike their Constantinopolitan counterparts (or later aristocracies in Italy), Roman senatorial families often owned land right across the span of the empire. This meant that rents collected, along with other private business interests, allowed them to skim the surplus off the economies of the imperial provinces. Since the senatorial aristocrats based in

[1] Syme 1939: 7.

Rome were second only to the emperor in the extent of their land-holdings, the progressive loss of access to wealth situated beyond their Italian base had far-reaching repercussions in both east and west in addition to Rome itself.

If Rome stood as the emblem of their power, the city was also the principal stage upon which the wealth of empire could most visibly be displayed. Three factors altered the balance of this economy of senatorial consumption at the end of antiquity. The loss of the provinces, especially Africa in 439 (with its private and tax revenues and above all the grain ships which brought the *annona* every autumn to feed Rome's *plebs*), had already meant that Rome no longer benefited from the same surplus and could no longer sustain the accustomed magnificence. Indeed, the population of Rome seems to have declined dramatically in the fifth and early sixth centuries, probably as a result of the loss of the *annona*,[2] compounded by disease (such as the arrival of the plague in 541–2 and again later in the century).[3] Yet worse, however, was the destruction of the infrastructure which might have allowed Rome and other cities of the peninsula to rebuild economic networks.

Senatorial families had always sought to sustain and enhance the city's health and splendour, and at the same time to leave a trace of their own role in doing so. But the old habits of senatorial self-commemoration had been challenged. In an important article of 1997, Werner Eck showed that once the *princeps* had appropriated the prerogative of public building it was virtually impossible for families to achieve a lasting impact on the urban landscape of Rome. Furthermore the life-cycle of senatorial dynasties was short: families on the wane were replaced by a constant influx of *homines novi*, a process which lent vitality to the city's economy[4] at the same time as it made self-commemoration difficult for the families themselves. Across the empire, senatorial families were required to maintain a residence in the imperial city, and up to the time of Theodosius II (d. 450) they were also required to request explicit permission from the emperor when they wished to be absent from the city.[5] Their persistent presence, and their requirement for lavish premises, gave Rome a specific character as the city of the Senate, but under the Empire this character was overlaid by the more visible interventions signifying imperial *praesentia*.[6]

[2] Wickham 2005: 34. [3] Christie 2006: 500–2; Liebeschuetz 2001: 53–4.
[4] Eck 1997: 189–90. [5] Salzman 2002: 72.
[6] Veyne 1990: 386–92; Garnsey and Saller 1987: 149–50. For repercussions of this monopoly on the classical patronage system see Johnson and Dandeker 1989: 238–9.

The waning of the emperor's involvement in Rome brought opportunities for the city's aristocracy, though the blessing was never unmixed.

With the rise of legal privilege granted to Christian bishops, the urban landscape acquired yet another layer of symbolic meaning. The increasingly Christian senatorial class probably saw the powers granted to the church in the fourth and fifth centuries as a new opportunity to establish continuity for their acts of patronage.[7] In this they were more than successful, since many of the foundations in question still stand today, and are still actively in use. But there is an irony: the price of continuity was the virtual disappearance, over time, of the evidence of the lay acts of patronage so crucial to the development of early Christian Rome. Once the patronal families had died off, their memory was eroded in favour of a grand narrative of the emerging Roman episcopacy, even where their foundations had in fact survived.

Up until 534, the senatorial aristocracy in Italy were able to continue more or less as they always had where the eternal city was concerned. This year marks the beginning of Justinian's attempt to recapture Italy from Theodahad, the Amal ruler of Italy who had murdered the Amal princess and imperial protégée Amalasuintha. The Gothic Wars, as they came to be known thanks to Procopius' account, marked a watershed in Italy. Up through the reign of Theoderic the Great (d. 526) and the regency (brought into jeopardy by her son's death in 533) of his daughter Amalasuintha, Ostrogothic rule had offered a peaceful end to the Italian wars of succession of the early 470s;[8] with the invasion of Belisarius on Justinian's behalf in 534, destruction and disease began, swiftly and decisively, to erode the infrastructure of the Italian cities.[9] As Chris Wickham has put it, 'Italy thus fits the old storyline of "the barbarian invasion destroying the Roman world" better than most regions do, with the proviso that it was the *Roman* invasion that caused the Gothic war.'[10]

Although the scope of the present volume extends from 300 to 900, it pivots on this single dramatic phase of change in the sixth century. It is one of its contentions that the relationship between the city and her aristocracy changed dramatically as a result of the failure of the Ostrogothic experiment, and the resulting Gothic Wars. At the same time, this period sees a new experiment, one with far-reaching consequences: a 'media revolution'

7 Ward-Perkins 1984: 239–41; Smith 2003: 151.

8 Moorhead 1992: 78–80 on the *civitas* ideology of Theoderic; see also Amory 1997: 112–20 on the comparatively peaceful cohabitation of Goths and Romans up to the death of Athalaric.

9 Brown 1984: 6–7. 10 Wickham 2005: 36.

centred on the rise of the Roman bishop as the central mediator of Rome's memory. Some time ago Michael Clanchy argued in an influential study that in England immediately following the Norman Conquest[11] new relationships of authority and obedience, and new technologies for defending older claims to autonomy, were articulated through new kinds of record-keeping. A similar process, we suggest, was in play in early sixth-century Rome.[12]

The bishop of Rome, implausibly, emerged the winner from the Ostrogothic–Byzantine crisis. Up to the death of Theoderic, a pivotally important group of popes found themselves having to navigate between the Scylla of an Arian king and the Charybdis of a succession of theologically demanding Eastern emperors along with their senatorial supporters in the city of Rome. The Gothic Wars did not improve this situation: popes were imprisoned and assassinated as a result of the escalating chaos. At the same time, inspired improvisation by successive sixth-century bishops led to the development of a new vision of episcopal authority and new forms of documentation and self-presentation. In the second half of the sixth century, during the last period of imperial rule in central Italy, these gains were consolidated on terms appropriate to Italy's (and Europe's) post-Roman future.

The sixth century was the 'tipping point' connecting two processes: the waning of imperial and aristocratic gestures of 'conspicuous consumption', and the waxing of ecclesiastical institutions as a mechanism through which bishops could establish continuity of culture and historical memory. From this point forward, the evidentiary record becomes increasingly coloured by the initiative of the city's bishop. Put simply, the principal reason for this is a book. The first half of the sixth century witnessed the production of a collection of popes' lives, the *Liber Pontificalis*, from Peter up to Felix IV (526–530). Compiled initially around 530 during the regency of Amalasuintha, according to its most distinguished analyst, Louis Duchesne, the *Liber Pontificalis* was to be regularly continued until the late ninth century and came to dominate the narrative landscape of this period.[13] We suggest that it is no accident that the precious but immensely

[11] Clanchy 1979.

[12] Other scholars of late antiquity, Charles Hedrick and Doron Mendels, have published important studies involving technologies of memory and information management in late antiquity while this collection was in preparation, and we have benefited from their insights although our source material and method differ in points of detail. Hedrick 2000; Mendels 1999.

[13] For the composition context of the *Liber Pontificalis* see Duchesne 1955: xxxiii–xlviii and 7–9; Davis 2000: xii–xvi. For an alternative view of the dating of the first part, attributed to not earlier than the seventh century, see Mommsen 1898: xviii. On the dating problem see also Geertman 2003.

problematic sources produced in the early sixth century – especially the *Liber Pontificalis*, but also the *Collectio Avellana*, a collection of papal and imperial letters of the fourth to sixth centuries[14] – record an intense effort on the part of the Roman bishops to establish the Roman episcopacy as an autonomous institution free of control by emperor or senate, at the same time as they record a largely successful attempt to control the shape of Roman memory.

The waning of aristocratic visibility has to be reassessed on the following lines: does it simply reflect a decline in the *production* of the sources, such as letters and inscriptions, on which study of aristocratic strategies traditionally depends? Or does it reflect selective *transmission* of the sources? Since the libraries which survived the end of antiquity were all based in ecclesiastical institutions, the relationship between the narrowing of aristocratic source production on the one hand, and the ecclesiastically biased preservation of texts on the other, is of course virtually impossible to establish.

Up to the late fourth century, the agency of the aristocratic families based in Rome is still widely documented and has consequently attracted much attention.[15] It is perhaps not surprising that scholarship for this period often has focused on either the continuities of secular munificence, most notably games, or Christian withdrawal from social expectations, but less on aristocratic material support for Rome's Christian community.[16] Some of these fourth-century figures may in fact have been 'picked up' by monastic librarians because of their role as characters in the pageant of ecclesiastical history. Quintus Aurelius Symmachus, for example, *praefectus urbi* in 384, whose letter-collection has come down to us, was an antagonist of Ambrose and the target of a diatribe by Prudentius – the *Contra Symmachum* – as well as being the ancestor of a dynasty whose power did not diminish in Rome until the Gothic Wars at the earliest, and who were known for supporting the early Roman monasteries.

In the succeeding generations, however, our evidence – particularly epigraphy – becomes thinner and thinner.[17] By the eighth century, we have only three secure epigraphical records of lay patronage in the city of Rome: a donation of rural estates to the church of S. Maria in Cosmedin by the *dux* Eusthatius, the foundation of the church of S. Paulus (today's S. Angelo in Pescheria) by the *primicerius* Theodotus, and a donation to the

[14] Ed. O. Günther (1895) *Epistulae imperatorum pontificium aliorum*, 1. CSEL 35. Leipzig.

[15] Arnheim 1972; Matthews 1990; Näf 1995; Schlinkert 1996; Niquet 2000; Salzman 2002.

[16] See for example Smith 2003; Lim 1999: 265–81; Curran 2000: esp. 260–320.

[17] See Barnish 1988. On epigraphy see De Rubeis 2001.

church of S. Maria in Cosmedin by the *notarius* Gregorius.[18] Again, it is not clear whether this decline in epigraphic production reflects simultaneous decline in aristocratic patronage, or is simply an expression of the changes in epigraphic habit due to economic hardship and rising illiteracy. It seems, however, that at least the area of monumental inscriptions, alongside the according scriptural pattern, was gradually appropriated by the Roman bishop.[19]

As a result of the uneven availability of textual sources, reciprocal influence between archaeologists and historians is an urgent desideratum. An increase in the quantity and quality of archaeological data since the 1980s, especially thanks to the excavation of the Crypta Balbi in the southern Campus Martius, has revolutionized, and in a way 'normalized', our understanding of Rome's evolving urban fabric in this period.[20] We now know that Rome's civic infrastructure supported a surprising continuity of daily life and economic activity through the disruptions of the fifth, sixth, and seventh centuries.[21] New interest in infrastructural elements such as residential building, trade and manufacture, and the road network can only be welcome. Rome has historically been viewed as virtually *sui generis*, with the declining economic activity of urban elites, and new organization of urban space accounted for almost entirely in terms of the rise of the bishop, rather than with refeence to issues which help us to understand late Roman urbanism in general, such as the decline of institutions of civic self-government, new forms of urban finances, or the changes in the importance and locations of trade and manufacture.[22] On these grounds it has been argued, for example, that Rome was the exception to a general rule that ecclesiastical building projects usually had to rely on accessible space rather than 'driving' late Roman and early medieval urbanism.[23]

Owing to the rapid turnover of new discoveries we will probably lack a synthetic survey of Rome's material culture in this period for years to come, although Neil Christie's *From Constantine to Charlemagne* (2006) now offers a valuable starting-point for historians wishing to navigate the ever richer archaeological scholarship. For the analysis of Christian polity, a

[18] De Rubeis 2001: 118–19, n. 10; 119, n. 11 a, b; 118, n. 9.

[19] De Rubeis 2001: 108. [20] Arena and Delogu (2000).

[21] See, for example, Coates-Stephens 1996, 1997; Meneghini and Santangeli Valenziani 2001a; Santangeli Valenziani 2000; Augenti 2000; Manacorda 2001.

[22] For similar and related questions on late antique and early medieval urbanism see e.g. Rich 1992; Christie and Loseby 1996; Lepelly 1996; Brogiolo and Ward-Perkins 1999; Brogiolo, Gauthier, and Christie 2000; Burns and Eadie 2001; Lavan 2001; Liebeschuetz 2001.

[23] Gauthier 1999.

number of excellent comprehensive studies exist, most notably Charles Pietri's masterly *Roma Christiana* and Richard Krautheimer's influential *Rome: Profile of a City, 312–1308*,[24] though both are now well out of date.[25] The prime concern of these studies was to chart the growth of Christian Rome's primary institution, the papacy, and to a greater or lesser degree they are guided by the teleological paradigm of the *Liber Pontificalis.* Still uncharted, therefore, is the role of lay elites and institutions in the Christianization of the city, and the often lively collaboration between lay and ascetic or clerical institutions.

In seeking to move beyond papal teleology, the present volume will centre on two questions. The first concerns the sources: how do the specific needs of the Roman bishops, as evidenced in the texts they generated in the sixth century – the *Liber Pontificalis* and the *Collectio Avellana* – distort our understanding of the relationship between Rome's three principal sources of patronage – emperor, bishop, and aristocratic laity – during our period? Second, what role can we uncover for the aristocratic laity themselves? Our study of the role of the Roman aristocracy in effecting the urban fabric of Rome draws on methodological premises that also underlie, for example, Michele Salzman's study exploring the Christianization of the late Roman aristocracy not as a top-down process originating from the emperor, but as a more diffuse development generated by the aristocrats themselves.[26]

In responding to both of these questions, we must resurrect a debate about the private ownership of church land. While a German tradition following Stutz, and made popular by Friedrich Prinz, saw the *Eigenkirche* or lay-owned ecclesiastical foundation as tending to result from Germanic influence after 476, French twentieth-century scholarship, following Lesne and Gaudemet, tended to lay emphasis on private foundations in the Roman period as the starting-point for ecclesiastical property.[27] Our own work tends to support the 'Roman' view of private foundations.[28] By comparison to the well-known contributions of Pietri and Krautheimer, our starting-point therefore has been to look at the needs and forms of lay patronage from the perspective of the aristocrats themselves rather than seeking antecedents for medieval forms and institutions. Where direct

24 Pietri 1976; Krautheimer 1980. See also Llewellyn 1971; Ullmann 1970.

25 An interim update to the territory covered by Krautheimer is now available in the collaborative volume Pani Ermini 2000.

26 Salzman 2002. Salzman's study is a response, above all, to Barnes 1995.

27 Davis 1976; Stutz 1895, 1938; Prinz 1965; Thomas 1906; Lesne 1910–43; Gaudemet 1958. For a recent treatment in the tradition of Stutz, see now Wood 2006.

28 Bowes 2002.

evidence is lacking, as it often is, we have sought to understand how both the bishop and lay patrons would have acted according to traditional Roman norms and within traditional social networks. Our guiding assumption has been that where no evidence compels us to do otherwise, we should imagine that Roman aristocrats tended to err in the direction of a self-aggrandizing cultural conservatism, rather than towards slavish anticipation of the possible needs of future popes.

At the same time, in the absence of transmitted lay archives for our period, the evidentiary basis for the precise study of lay ownership of Christian institutions and lay strategies for transmitting those institutions to heirs, whether lay or institutional, poses many problems. The lack of lay archives deposited with the Roman monasteries (such as those donated to Bobbio in northern Italy for example), along with the even more surprising lack of a rich source base for the Roman monasteries themselves in the period before 1100, will always stand as a daunting obstacle, but we must at least think our way around it. Why, for example, did a city so rich in monasteries emerge as so poor in monastic librarianship for the early medieval period? Both the abundance of early monasteries in Rome and the real poverty of the evidence for Roman monasticism emerge clearly in Guy Ferrari's classic compendium *Early Roman Monasteries*, now fifty years old but still indispensable.[29] Ferrari's work brings us to a roadblock.

The disappearance of Roman monastic archives probably does not mean they never existed: this is a point which must be repeated over and over again. Most of our charter evidence for early medieval monasteries elsewhere in Europe is transmitted not through the original *chartae*, often copied onto friable papyrus up to the Carolingian period where Rome is concerned, but through cartularies dating from the eleventh century and even later. Why such collections for Roman institutions either were not produced or do not survive remains an important question.[30] There is almost surely a story of nineteenth-century destruction of archives to be told in the case of at least some of the Roman monasteries.[31]

This last point leads, of course, to the wider problem of the role of laity in our period. It is some years since, in an important article on the ubiquitous early sixth-century political and military figure Liberius the patrician, J. J. O'Donnell called for a new approach to the history of the laity in our period, one which would reach behind the monumentalizing instincts of monastic librarians to the multiplicity of players and points of

[29] Ferrari 1957. [30] Guyotjeanin, Morelle, and Parisse 1993.
[31] See e.g. Bartòla 1989 and 2003. For further discussion, see Costambeys and Leyser in this volume.

view in the sixth-century west.[32] During his own well-documented lifetime, Cassiodorus Senator, chancellor to the Ostrogothic kings and after the Gothic Wars founder of an important monastery, may not, O'Donnell argued, have been so visible or influential a figure as his contemporary the patrician Liberius, a figure about whom we now know very little. The key difference, of course, is that Liberius was not possessed of the historical foresight – or sheer luck – which led Cassiodorus to found a monastic library to preserve his own book collection, and indeed in no small part his own writings, at just the historical moment when other means of transmission were becoming perilously unreliable. But to do justice to the challenge posed by O'Donnell's painstaking reinvestigation of source materials, a conceptual shift is required.

It has taken a figure of the intellectual stature of Robert Markus to establish a vocabulary, drawn from the patristic sources themselves, through which a problem of this magnitude can be approached. In a chain of publications from *Saeculum* in 1970[33] to *The End of Ancient Christianity* in 1990, Markus developed a radical rereading of the works of Augustine of Hippo which could lay the foundation for an understanding of what Markus somewhat alarmingly called 'a defence of Christian mediocrity'.[34] Thus the role within the church of non-ascetic householders, whether married or unmarried, was a critical pastoral topic during the fifth and sixth centuries, and one central to an appreciation of the lines of tension within the polity of any major Christian city. The 'core values' of the laity, on this reading, centred on an idea of *mediocritas* as a virtuous temperance in the pursuit of excellence. This lay Christianity dismissed the excesses of the ascetic movement as a sign of moral imbalance rather than excellence in virtue.[35] The senatorial Roman laity can only be understood if this deep commitment to *temperantia* is appreciated.[36]

Fundamental to the Markus reading of Augustine is a watershed in Augustine thinking, based on his rereading, in the 390s, of the letters of St Paul. This 'watershed' led the bishop to reject the increasingly popular late fourth-century idea of a 'two-tiered' church, in which an elite of one kind or another (whether ascetic or Donatist, Pelagian, or Manichaean) tolerated the 'excess baggage' of its patent spiritual inferiors. This 'intellectual landslide' – Peter Brown's vivid phrase for the same development[37] – led

[32] O'Donnell 1981. [33] Markus 1970, 2nd edn 1988. [34] Markus 1990: 45.

[35] See, for example, the classical attitudes to virtue without moderation as intrinsically invalid, discussed in Francis 1995 and North 1966.

[36] Central here is Hunter 1987. [37] Brown 1967, cited in Markus 1990: 50.

Augustine to re-evaluate the place of the married in the Christian polity, arguing that the ascetic elitism of a Jerome or an Ambrose could only be counter-productive. When learned aristocrats resisted the agenda of bishops or of the ascetic party, they tended to do so not out of cold-footedness or because they preferred 'paganism' to 'Christianity', but rather because they believed, along with Augustine, that a Christianity out of step with the philosophical tradition on *temperantia* could not be true to Christian values.

Thus, Markus reminds us, Augustine comes to assert that 'Both sorts of faithful belong within the one Church and both are called to serve God in faith and love. All who seek to follow the Lord are within his flock: "and the married are certainly able to follow His footsteps [*vestigia*], even if their feet do not fit perfectly into the footprints, yet following the same path".'[38] This was Augustine's re-affirmation of the central Christian tradition. We will see below that Augustine's view of the relationship between ascetics and the married played a concrete role in the ascetic decision-making of aristocratic Roman women such as Demetrias and Melania the Younger.[39]

The present volume draws on recent work by members of the Centre for Late Antiquity at the University of Manchester. This work has sought to understand the lay, clerical, and ascetic populations of the city of Rome at the end of antiquity as interacting in an atmosphere more fluid than the institutional teleology claimed by the official ecclesiastical sources. Most importantly, we have aimed at re-establishing the link between the Roman church's resources and the local elites. The difficulty, hitherto, of synthesizing the fragmentary and arcane evidence has encouraged historians to assume that the ascetic tendency that rose to prominence within Christianity in this period was hostile to the worldly family and, by extension, to its property, that to be 'authentic' in their vocation ascetics could only reject, and never collaborate with, the 'earthly' institution of the biological family. One of our starting-points has been to try to move beyond the reductionist view that sees lay patrons as acting *either* out of faith *or* in accord with social or other objectives, and ascetics as *either* genuinely ascetic *or* closely associated with the continued possession of wealth. We will see below in Kate Cooper's chapter that at least some senatorial ascetics saw property ownership as a form of stewardship on behalf of the church.[40]

38 Markus 1990: 46.

39 See the contributions of Anne Kurdock and Kate Cooper in this volume, and in addition Cooper 2006.

40 On the 'false problem' of reductionism see Cooper 2005a.

Our challenge to the traditional overreliance on papal sources has a firm foundation in two major collaborative projects reassessing the evidentiary base for lay religious and patronal agency in late ancient and early medieval Rome. Our British Academy-sponsored Roman Martyrs Project has produced a systematic survey of the *gesta martyrum*, the little-understood hagiographical texts produced from the fifth century onwards purporting to describe the lives and passions of the martyrs.[41] At the same time, another Centre for Late Antiquity project, 'Religion, Dynasty, and Patronage in Rome, *c.*440–*c.*840', funded by the University of Manchester and the AHRC, has developed a relational database of the evidence for patronage in the city of Rome drawn from documentary, literary, and epigraphic sources.[42] This tool allows us new flexibility in assembling and analysing the evidence for how the Roman church acquired its wealth, against the evidence for other enterprises which individuals and families chose to finance, a comparison which is central to understanding how the various ecclesiastical, ascetic, and civic agendas for investment of resources competed and collaborated with one another.

A word or two should be said about the principal hagiographical sources for Rome in this period, the *gesta martyrum*. Even their collective title is a mystification, a term coined by the *Liber Pontificalis*, a text which seems to bear a pointed interest in according legitimacy to at least some Roman martyr narratives, probably shortly after the majority of the texts were written.[43] The *Liber Pontificalis* claimed, spuriously, that the texts were of great antiquity, dating from the age of persecutions, when popes from Fabian (pope from 236–250) onwards had begun to keep archives documenting the heroic deeds (*gesta*) of the city's martyrs.[44] The second edition of the *Liber Pontificalis* (produced after 530 and before 546) links these archives to the emerging diaconal structure of the city, praising the same Fabian 'who appointed seven subdeacons who directed seven clerks to faithfully gather the deeds of the martyrs (*gesta martyrum*) in their entirety'.[45] These passages tell us a great deal about the early sixth century, and probably nothing at all about the third.

[41] See www.arts.manchester.ac.uk/cla/projects/romanmartyrsproject/.

[42] A web-searchable interface for this database is available at www.arts.manchester.ac.uk/cla/projects/patronageproject/ at the time of writing, and will be maintained for the foreseeable future.

[43] The following two paragraphs summarize a more detailed discussion in Cooper 1999: 297–301. On the external parameters for dating of the *gesta*, see Pilsworth 2000.

[44] *LP*, ed. Duchesne, I, 148.

[45] *LP*, ed. Duchesne, I, 148: 'Hic regiones divisit diaconibus et fecit VII subdiaconos qui VII notariis inminerent, ut gestas martyrum in integro fideliter colligerent, et multas fabricas per cymiteria praecipit.' Cited here is the translation of Davis 1989: 8. This is probably an expansion of the entry in the fourth-century Liberian Catalogue preserved in the so-called Calendar of 354, which credits Fabian with instituting the city's diaconal structure along with a system of care for the cemeteries: 'Hic regiones divisit diaconibus et multas fabricas per cymiteria fieri iussit', *LP*, ed. Duchesne, I, 4–5.

Albert Dufourcq, whose eccentric *Étude sur les gesta martyrum romains* saw the *gesta* as vehicles for the concerns of the Roman *ecclesia* of the fifth and sixth centuries,[46] gave rise to an energetic industry during the first decades of the twentieth century.[47] A century later, the Roman topography of dynasty and allegiance has yet to be established conclusively, though in an important 1989 article Charles Pietri attempted to account for how the sevenfold Roman diaconal structure followed on from the fourteen civil regions of the time of Augustus.[48] Pietri sought to develop Dufourcq's approach, mining the *gesta martyrum* for clues to the social tensions of the fifth and sixth centuries, the period in which the bulk of the *gesta* are presumed to have been written,[49] while the British scholar Peter Llewelyn[50] and the Italian Giovanni Nino Verrando[51] have tentatively found among the *gesta* apologetic texts for the Laurentian and Symmachan parties of the Laurentian schism of *c.* 498 to 507 or 508. These writers have tended to give substantial weight to the lay–clerical binary: seeing the *gesta martyrum* as reflecting an ever more acute tension between the senatorial aristocracy and the increasingly centralized, and increasingly ambitious, clerical hierarchy of the city of Rome. Our own approach, by contrast, has returned to an earlier paradigm, following the ideas suggested by G. B. De Rossi's *Roma Sotteranea* over a century ago, that competition for resources and prestige among aristocrat-led coalitions involving lay and clerical participants, rather than competition between the clergy and laity per se, should be the guiding principle of work on Rome's Christian topography.[52]

The *gesta* offer an invaluable insight into the interaction of the laity and the clergy in the context of a 'lay' urban landscape, with a focus on 'lay' institutions such as the aristocratic household, and into the role of cult sites as geographical arenas for the competition for resources, not between laity and clergy, but among lay–clerical coalitions, often driven by the dynastic interest of lay aristocrats. These texts are notoriously difficult to date, and our starting-point has been to assume that their dating is an open question. Our view is that the attempt to assign dates to the *gesta*, more precise than a general frame from roughly 410 to 540 for the majority of texts, can only be

[46] Dufourcq (1910, 1988).

[47] Kirsch 1918 and Lanzoni 1925; both developed Dufourcq's interest in the *gesta* as foundation myths for the Roman churches. For subsequent bibliography on individual cults, see Amore 1975.

[48] Pietri 1989.

[49] Among the more important contributions by Pietri are: Pietri 1978b, 1981a, 1981b.

[50] Llewellyn 1976a, 1977. [51] Verrando 1987: 354. [52] De Rossi (1864–77); here III: xxii.

speculative.[53] Nonetheless, there are reasons to suspect that a number of the *gesta* were written in the second quarter of the sixth century, at roughly the same time as the *Liber Pontificalis*,[54] a point which will be explored by the contribution of Conrad Leyser below.

The chapters of the present volume focus on a wide range of topics relating to manifestations of lay patronage, from imperial policies, to the property strategies of aristocratic households, to monastic foundations. The first two chapters (Humphries and Blair-Dixon) and the last (Leyser/Costambeys) offer a framework that is both chronological and conceptual, viewing the role of the papacy in its relationship with the most significant lay authorities at either end of the period covered by this volume, the Roman emperor on the one hand and the Carolingian dynasty on the other.

The second group of chapters (Sessa, Jones, Leyser) highlights the role of the *gesta martyrum* for our understanding of lay, clerical, and ascetic groups in late antique and early medieval Rome, by offering a variety of approaches to this highly complex source material, leading us from the *gesta*'s original Roman context of production to the transmission (and mutation) of their contents north of the Alps. The next set of chapters (Cooper, Kurdock, Hillner) shifts the focus away from the literary representation of patronage to the historical contexts of the activities of the great Roman families, both within Rome and in their areas of influence beyond the city walls.

In his chapter on papal ceremonial space, Mark Humphries examines the transformation of ceremonial expressions of authority in the city of Rome in the centuries from Constantine to Gregory the Great by focusing on an account of imperial *adventus*. He shows that at the outset of this period ceremonial underpinned the authority of the emperor, his representatives, and Rome's aristocratic elite, the senate. By the end of the period, we can see how Rome's clergy began to appropriate to themselves vehicles of authority that had hitherto been in lay hands. However, Humphries argues, drastic as this transformation may seem, the process through which change was wrought was a gradual one. Humphries shows that the bishop was only one of several forces shaping ceremony in the late antique city. Christian space was as much open to exploitation by powerful

[53] The only absolute point of reference is the date of their first attestation in manuscript: see Franklin 2001 and Pilsworth 2000.

[54] Cooper 1999: 305–8.

members of the laity for the display of status as was secular ceremonial space to the clergy.

Our perception of the tension between pope and emperor is complicated by Kate Blair-Dixon's study of the *Liber Pontificalis* and *Collectio Avellana*, two sixth-century collections of material relating to the Roman episcopacy which reflect very different agendas. Attention to the dynamics which a comparatively rich tradition of scholarship has begun to uncover with respect to the *Liber Pontificalis*, Blair-Dixon argues, can help to make visible the process of patronage and competition for authority which lies behind the more problematic *Collectio Avellana*.

With Kristina Sessa's chapter the volume turns to give closer attention to the complex history of lay–clerical relationships from the point of view of the Roman aristocracy, considering in particular the spatial imaginary of the late ancient city of Rome. In a vivid exploration of the representation of what might be called the bishop's pastoral visits to the *domus* of the Roman aristocrats, Sessa addresses the social, political, and material significance of domestic space for the negotiation of clerical authority within the city at large. Alongside the better-known contemporary literary texts, such as the *Gesta de Xysti purgatione*, that display a coercive relationship between bishop and lay household, Sessa offers a number of texts drawn from the *gesta martyrum*. These, she argues, offer a different strategy of representing the formation of clerical authority in the household that resembles the mechanisms of ancient patronage. Here, bishop and householder engage in a dialogue of cooperation and exchange, as shown, most importantly, in the liturgy of baptism performed in the private household. Although the bishop is represented as ultimately the more powerful figure – since he is able to act as a supernatural agent in baptism – the householder retains his agency by being able to offer resources in support of the church. Ultimately, the civic position of both bishop and lay householder are strengthened by collaboration and mutual acknowledgement. Sessa's chapter refutes a traditional understanding of the lay household as a 'casualty' of Rome's papalization. Instead she shows that the household was not just a proto-church, but continued to play a decisive role in Rome's Christian landscape in its own right.

In the next chapter Hannah Jones turns to the examination of one individual text among the *gesta martyrum*, the *passio* of the virgin martyr Agnes. Jones investigates both the evidence for Agnes' cult site in the city of Rome and the textual traditions concerning her passion. She shows that the memory of Agnes is mobilized in cult building and production of texts by both clerical and lay groups in support of authority throughout the fourth, fifth, and sixth centuries. In the *passio Agnetis* the rich tradition of motifs regarding her virginity and her martyrdom are reworked in order to make of Agnes a powerful symbol of lay patronage. With its strong focus on the theme of familial continuity the *passio*, Jones argues, can be positioned in the traditions of ancient civic rhetoric, rather than in the context of the rejection of family and city in early Christian literature. At the end of antiquity, the virgin heroine, in this way, once again became a civic icon.

Conrad Leyser's chapter also concentrates on one individual text, the *passio* of John and Paul. However, where Jones is interested in an immediate aristocratic audience in the city of Rome, Leyser turns his attention also to the implications of the transmission of the text, or one particular version of it, from an urban ecclesial to a rural monastic context. He investigates the passion of John and Paul, patrons of a fifth-century church in Rome, as it appears in a codex from the monastery of Corbie in northern Francia. In this manuscript, copied *c.* AD 600 in southern Italian monastic circles, the *passio* appears alongside monastic rules and works of ascetic instruction. The codex may be viewed as an artfully assembled monastic miscellany, and the choice of the particular version of the passion of John and Paul, Leyser argues, was not taken at random. The *passio*'s claustrophobic focus on the domestic setting of the martyrdom was a way of dramatizing the moral imperative of stability, both physical and spiritual, in a monastic context. Meanwhile, the martyrs' defiance of the emperor spoke to the independence of the monastery as an institution, and, conceivably, to the involvement of Italian monasticism in the anti-imperial stance adopted by the Roman church in the course of the sixth century. Rural monastic founders such as Eugippius of Lucullanum and Benedict of Nursia will have lived through the widening tension after the death of Theoderic no less than their Roman sponsors and commemorators, the Roman matron Proba and Pope Gregory the Great.

Kate Cooper's contribution links the part of the volume that focuses on literary representation of lay patronage to the part dealing with the wider basis of evidence, by taking up the problem of our literary sources for lay patronage of ecclesiastical institutions. Concentrating principally on two fifth-century sources, the *Epistula ad Demetriadem de vera humilitate* and the *Ad Ecclesiam* of Salvian of Marseilles, Cooper argues that Rome was a stronghold of an approach to wealth which saw the aristocratic laity as stewards of wealth on behalf of the church – retaining both control of, and responsibility for, their estates even as they sought to draw on their revenues to assist the church. This approach, of course, tended to slow the process by which the bishop of Rome was fast becoming the city's principal land-owner, and eventually lost out to a view which favoured assignment of wealth to the control of the bishop.

In the next chapter Anne Kurdock looks in detail at one of the most famous among these lay patrons of the Roman church in the fifth century. Anicia Demetrias is known to history primarily as the addressee of treatises of spiritual direction by the leading Christian authorities of the time. No writings of her own survive, and in recent modern scholarship Demetrias has accordingly been treated as a woman whose 'voice' is veiled by layers of patristic moralizing. Kurdock's approach is rather to call attention to the considerable power that Demetrias is recorded as having exerted. An analysis of the literary strategies of the letters in the light of the familial network surrounding Demetrias demonstrates that the aim of their authors was mainly to cultivate Demetrias, and by extension the *domus Anicia*, as an influential patron. While her spiritual leaders may have differed considerably in their theological positions, they shared similar motivations and fears vis-à-vis their lay patrons. Most importantly, they agreed in advising Demetrias to exercise a cautious management of her wealth on behalf of the church.

Julia Hillner's chapter confirms that bishops were anxious to ensure use of lay wealth that ultimately benefited the Christian community, but also shows the difficulties of these enterprises. Hillner turns her attention to the evidence for the titular churches in Rome. These churches are traditionally interpreted as a particular type of institution in the Roman dioceses, namely an independent church endowed by its lay founder with a patrimony to permanently maintain the building and its clergy. They are, in consequence, usually cited as icons of lay patronage and lay/papal estrangement. Hillner suggests a different understanding of titular churches. She argues that titular churches were endowed not by their lay founders, but by the bishop with ecclesiastical property, either at the time of their foundation or at a later date. What this means is that lay control over church property in late antique Rome may have been far less focused on endowment than is often presumed. Lay patrons, it is argued, did not endow their foundations, or preferred one-off donations to foundations altogether, since they did not want to concede control over endowments to the bishop. The bishops of Rome, however, saw this reluctance as unnecessarily burdensome to the diocese, which – like modern universities – sometimes found itself in the position of footing expensive maintenance bills for inconvenient or inessential holdings, and thus encouraged lay patrons to endow their foundations.

Conrad Leyser and Marios Costambeys' chapter concludes the volume by focusing our attention on questions already raised by other chapters. In particular, the chapter returns to the evidence for monasteries in early medieval Rome. The evidence for the enmeshment of Roman monasteries in lay dynastic interests differs from that widely available elsewhere in Europe and in rural Italy, as there are no surviving early charters. Yet, we know that a lively monastic movement existed in early medieval Rome, although it is traditionally seen as a vehicle of papal authority. The chapter surveys other kinds of evidence available for lay patronage of Roman monasteries from the seventh to the ninth centuries, working from the *Liber Pontificalis* outwards to martyr narratives. By tracking particularly the cult of Anicia Demetrias' patron St Stephen, Leyser and Costambeys suggest that Rome is a site of continuity of a variety of late ancient practice of benefaction and of creativity within these traditions. These indicators for a strong self-confidence of Roman monasteries encourage us to rethink both the traditional picture of Rome as a passive recipient of monastic reform in the Carolingian period and beyond, and, on a more universal level, the apparently unique status of Roman monasticism in the early Middle Ages.

Our contributors insist upon the centrality of the lay household to social and religious life in the city of Rome. As Sessa, Jones, and Cooper show, the façade of oligarchy drops altogether in fact in such essentially Roman texts as the *gesta martyrum*, where we cannot miss the prominence of the lay family as a source of spiritual and material support. The household, as Leyser illustrates, could become a model of stability even beyond the city, owing not only to the actual provision of resources, but also to the lay household's embodiment of civic traditions. The rural monasteries of Lazio and Campania, which were in turn to become the template for religious houses north of the Alps, looked to the dwellings on the hills of Rome for their template. When SS. Peter and Paul at Corbie, or later still the St Peter's at Cluny, claimed to be new Romes, and sought the special protection of the papacy, these were not or not only pious fictions: they appealed to a historical genealogy.

Where does all of this leave us regarding the dominance of the *Liber Pontificalis* in the source landscape of late antique and early medieval Rome? First of all, the volume shows that the public celebration of the papacy in ecclesiastical texts may have been, in reality, less a statement of power than an expression of competition with a self-confident laity who, as Leyser and Costambeys show, may simply not have needed documentary records of their actions. Yet, while it is true that the authors of the *Liber*

Pontificalis pursued a highly selective agenda, it is also not necessary always to presume on these grounds an incompatibility of clerical and lay concerns and deliberate suppression of the latter. As Hillner shows, for example, the sixth-century authors of the *Liber Pontificalis* may have shown a deeper understanding of lay patronage behaviour than modern scholarship has managed to grasp.

Bishop and clergy were, in short, dependent on lay disposition. While this dependence can doubtless be overstated, Kurdock shows the value of admitting that, as in the case of Demetrias and her spiritual advisors, the Roman church may have benefited as much, if not more, from the association with a powerful and wealthy family than the family did, in the long run, from the association with the Roman church. It is through their connections with lay circles, for example, as both Sessa and Humphries argue, that the bishop's authoritative position in the city was enhanced. Put bluntly, the papacy was successful because both patronage of and competition with lay people, including the emperor, allowed it to be. For the same reasons, as Kurdock, Cooper, and Hillner show, Christian authorities strove actively to cultivate sometimes reluctant lay patronage. One of the ways they did this was by integration of the biological family into a morally cohesive Christian lifestyle. Another one was to encourage not complete disposal of wealth, but its reasonable and lasting use, in order to cast lay families into a leading role in the church. Perhaps most importantly, however, we hope to have shown how attention to the patronage and narrative of martyr cult can help scholars to overcome the limitations of monastic and lay sources for Rome. Perhaps the importance of the Roman martyrs should not surprise us, since the martyr exemplum in late antiquity served as a model open to imitation both by ascetics and by non-ascetics, an invitation to unity in a religious landscape characterized as much by competition as by collaboration.

PART I

Icons of authority: pope and emperor

I

From emperor to pope? Ceremonial, space, and authority at Rome from Constantine to Gregory the Great

Mark Humphries

INTRODUCTION: DISCOURSES AND SOURCES

On 25 April 603 the Lateran basilica in Rome was the venue for a splendid ceremonial occasion. Rome's clergy and senate assembled there, together with the city's bishop, Pope Gregory the Great (590–604), for the reception of images, newly arrived from Constantinople, of the emperor Phocas (602–610) and his consort Leontia. The images were acclaimed in the basilica with chants of 'Christ hear us! Long live Phocas Augustus and Leontia Augusta!' After the gathering at the Lateran, Gregory oversaw the placing of the images in the chapel of St Caesarius within the old imperial palace on the Palatine hill.[1] This striking episode is described in a document preserved in manuscripts of Gregory's *Registrum*. By the standards of our sources for early seventh-century Rome, it presents us with a very comprehensive account: it gives details not only of the date, location, and participants, but also of the ritual performed.

In an important respect, the events of 25 April 603 call into question some central assumptions about the history of the city of Rome in late antiquity. It is a feature of conventional descriptions of Rome in this period to stress how the place in society once occupied by emperor, senate, and imperial officials was taken over by the pope and the Roman clergy. This transformation from one dispensation to another is often regarded as having been mirrored by other shifts, most obviously in the city's religious profile, but also in terms of its physical fabric. Such was the thrust, for example, of the influential analysis offered by Richard Krautheimer a quarter of a century ago. For him, the process of change was inexorable

[1] Greg. Mag., *Reg.* App. VIII: 'venit autem icona suprascriptorum Focae et Leontiae Augustorum Romae septimo Kalendarum Maiarum, et acclamatum est eis in Lateranis in basilica Iulii ab omni clero uel senatu: "Exaudi Christe! Focae Augusto et Leontiae Augustae vita!" Tunc iussit ipsam iconam domnus [*sic*] beatissimus et apostolicus Gregorius papa reponi eam in oratorio sancti Caesarii intra palatio.'

from the beginning of the fourth century, when various policies of the emperor Constantine (306–337) 'left Rome in a power vacuum: she was no longer an active capital. The administrative focus of the empire was at the emperor's headquarters, which was quickly [*sic*] stabilized at Constantinople.'[2] Thereafter, he argued, the rise of Christian, papal Rome was inevitable, and any obstacles were soon overcome:

> To the end of the [fourth] century, Rome remained a stronghold of paganism, supported by a powerful group of local aristocrats. The Church, though backed by the imperial court and by the urban masses inside the city, had a hard time asserting her position. The struggle, at times bitter, ended early in the fifth century with the triumph of the Church, no longer contested. Only from then on does the map of Rome increasingly reflect the city's Christian character, and this remains so until 1870.[3]

The actors in Krautheimer's drama after Constantine are popes, not emperors. For him – and indeed for other scholars – late antiquity ushered in a new era in the history of the city: Rome became the stage upon which the popes acted the leading part, and this was a role that they were to continue to play until they were shunted aside by the forces of the nascent modern Italian state.[4]

At first sight, it might seem that such a view is endorsed by sources from late antiquity itself. One of the figures often associated with the watershed between antiquity and the middle ages is the aforementioned Pope Gregory the Great. Although he lived nearly three centuries after Constantine, Gregory's experiences and writings would appear to confirm Krautheimer's thesis about the demise of the imperial city and the rise of a papal one.[5] The scion of a wealthy (but probably not noble) Roman family, and a former prefect of the city,[6] Gregory came to the papacy at a time of profound crisis,

[2] Krautheimer 1980: 33. For a recent restatement of this view, see Benoist 2005: 4, describing 'la fondation de Constantinople et son corollaire, l'abandon de Rome'.

[3] Krautheimer 1980: 33. For other problems with Krautheimer's analysis, see below nn. 18, 89, 91, 145, 160.

[4] The idea that Rome's imperial significance was a thing of the past already by the time of Diocletian was remarked upon by Jones (1964: 687). The analysis of Charles Pietri (1976), while it prioritizes ecclesiastical affairs, seeks to locate them in a broader context including secular politics. Nevertheless, Pietri states that when Leo I assumed the papacy in 440, 'l'Eglise de Rome s'établit déjà en capitale chrétienne', a process that he regards as having accelerated under Damasus I (366–388), and having resulted in 'la conquête du temps et de l'espace urbain' (Pietri 1976: 1653).

[5] For a penetrating analysis of this trope, and the problems it presents, see Delogu 2001: 9–11.

[6] See Markus 1997: 8–10 on Gregory's background and early career. Markus argues that Gregory's family was not noble; other scholars, however, have trusted the tradition (attested by Gregory of Tours, *Hist.* 10. 1) that Gregory's family was descended from a distinguished senatorial lineage. This view is accepted, for example, in *PCBE, Italie* 1.945 (Gregorius 9).

and in his writings, especially his letters, he depicted a society undergoing radical change, where the church was fast replacing the imperial administration and the old senatorial aristocracy as the city's dominant social institution. In a famous and oft-quoted homily, Gregory gave a bleak depiction of the fortunes of Rome and its inhabitants at the end of the sixth century. The city, he said, had become a desert, abandoned by its citizens, oppressed by its enemies, and filled with ruins. 'Where is the senate? And where are the people?', he asked; his answer was that the senate was no more and the people had gone away as Rome's troubles increased.[7] In this context, it was the spiritual guidance offered by Gregory's preaching and not the city's ancient institutions upon which contemporary Romans would depend for succour in times of stress. Modern scholars have often endorsed this portrait. Some suggest that Gregory's depiction is articulated with such force that it cannot simply be explained away as rhetorical exaggeration.[8] Others have seized upon it as a striking pivotal reference to the demise of the city's ancient institutions, particularly the senate, in the years around 600.[9]

Gregory's account is open to debate from a number of perspectives, however. Not the least of these is the sometimes discounted question of rhetorical exaggeration. Consider the biblical text upon which Gregory was preaching: the Old Testament prophet Ezekiel was giving an apocalyptic portrait of the woes that would overcome an impious Israel as it felt the wrath of God.[10] Consider too the circumstances in which Gregory was preaching: the year was 593, when the Lombard Agilulf had scored a number of victories over the Byzantine imperial armies in Italy and was now marching his forces on Rome.[11] We are told by another source that, in this threatening atmosphere, Gregory was transfixed by terror and broke off from his preaching.[12] We should be wary of an account written in such emotive circumstances: as Robert Markus has observed, 'Moments of acute crisis were apt to prompt some of the most powerful of Gregory's

[7] Greg. Mag, *Hom. Ezech.* 2.6.22: 'Ipsa autem quae aliquando mundi domina esse videbatur qualis remanserit Roma conspicimus: immensis doloribus multipliciter attrita desolatione civium, impressione hostium, frequentia ruinarum . . . Ubi enim senatus? Ubi iam populus? . . . Quia enim senatus deest, populus interiit et tamen in paucis qui sunt dolores et gemitus quotidie multiplicantur, iam vacua ardet Roma.'

[8] Thus Arnaldi 1982: 36 ('l'accenno a "Roma vuota" nell'omelia del 583 non era solo un'iperbole'). Cf. Brown 1984: 31.

[9] E.g. Arnaldi 1982: 34–6; Burgarella 2001: 169–71; Chastagnol 1996: 349–50.

[10] Ezek. 24.4–11.

[11] For the Lombard threat to Rome, see Bavant 1979: 56–8.

[12] Paul. Diac., *Hist. Lang.* 4.8: 'Huius regis adventum in tantum beatus Gregorius papa exterritus est, ut ab expositione templo, de quo in Ezechiele legitur, desisteret, sic ut ipse quoque in suis homeliis refert.' Gregory refers to the context in the preface to book 2 of his homilies.

apocalyptic expositions of scriptural imagery.'[13] This is not to deny that Rome, and Italy more generally, experienced profound dislocation in the late sixth century in the wake of the debilitating effects of the Byzantine wars against the Goths and the subsequent Lombard invasions, or that the city's institutions were undergoing profound transformations.[14] That is not the same, however, as accepting Gregory's grimly apocalyptic account at face value, and seeing the demise of the city's ancient institutions as a swift, cataclysmic event, leaving a vacuum into which stepped the papacy. Other sources suggest that the demise of the senate, one of the key factors in many analyses of Rome's transformation, was a piecemeal process. Agnellus of Ravenna, writing in the ninth century, preserves a notice perhaps from an earlier chronicle that describes how, after the appointment in Italy of the Byzantine praetorian prefect Longinus in 568, 'the Roman senate disappeared gradually (*paulatim*)'.[15] The reasons for the senate's disappearance as an active institution, as we will see later, are varied and extend over a long period. A further problem with Gregory's analysis is that ten years after he asked 'Where is the senate?', we know that he would himself have been able to give a clear answer, when he and his clergy joined the senators for the ritual welcome of the portraits of the eastern emperor and empress on 25 April 603.

Thus the evidence connected with Gregory the Great presents us with something of a paradox. On the one hand, he wrote practically an obituary for the ancient institutions of Rome; on the other, he was witness to some of those institutions still functioning, as the senate participated in the quite traditional ritual of acclaiming the supremacy of its imperial overlords. Such a paradox highlights the importance of not allowing sweeping teleological interpretations to overcome our understanding of Rome's transformation in late antiquity.[16] Indeed, as a consequence of much of the new archaeological data that have become available recently, a picture of more subtle transformation – involving factors such as economic and demographic change – is coming to light that confounds expectations that Rome's late antique transformation was structured around a simple shift in authority from emperor to pope.[17] It is beginning to look as if the self-conscious creation of a papal Rome was a much later development than Krautheimer (who was writing, of course, before these new data became

[13] Markus 1997: 52. [14] Cf. Humphries 2000: esp. 533–8.

[15] Agnellus, *Liber Pontificalis Ecclesiae Ravennatis* 95: 'Deinde paulatim Romanus deficit senatus.' The suggestion that this text is extracted from an earlier annal is made by its editor, O. Holder-Egger, MGH SRL (1878), 338 n. 8.

[16] See also the chapter by Kristina Sessa in this volume. [17] Delogu 2000: 83–108.

available) tended to think;[18] rather than belonging to the fifth, sixth, or even seventh century, the project of creating a 'papal' Rome only came to fruition in the eighth and ninth centuries.[19] Thus late antiquity (and the early middle ages) was a period when the authority of the bishop of Rome was only one of several shaping the city: however much the institutional power of the church increased after the fourth century, Rome did not swiftly become the pope's to mould as he pleased.

It is the purpose of this chapter to examine the forces shaping Rome between the mid-fourth and early seventh century by focusing on rituals concerned with the political authority of emperors (and, for a time, Ostrogothic kings). Rulers obviously asserted their pre-eminence in the city at times of *adventus*. As we will see, however, they remained an important influence in Roman society down to the seventh century, albeit in varied ways, even when they were not physically present in the city. Thus rulers provide a useful focus for an enquiry into the development of Rome in late antiquity, not least because by placing them at the centre of discussion we can seek to comprehend the changing roles played by institutions such as the senate and the church in the context of the city's relationship with its political masters. Furthermore, by focusing on the role played by the city's rulers, we can aim to distance ourselves from the discourse (implicit in the words of Krautheimer quoted above) that treats Rome's secular and ecclesiastical history in late antiquity as, effectively, two discrete, and indeed discontinuous, narratives.[20]

The ritual framework that I will analyse takes its lead from the events of 25 April 603. The senators' participation in welcoming imperial images to Rome mirrored their involvement in earlier structured celebrations of welcoming, such as imperial *adventus* in the fourth century. Of course, there are striking differences between the earlier and later rituals. For example, fourth-century *adventus* focused on the arrival of the emperor in person, whereas in 603 it was imperial portraits, not persons, that arrived.[21] Also, the prominence of pope and clergy in the early seventh century represents a significant change from the ceremonial of earlier centuries. One of my central concerns, therefore, will be to assess the extent

[18] For example, Krautheimer (1980: 58) argues that building projects in the area around the Lateran 'hint at a conscious attempt of the fifth century papacy to change the map of Rome'. Later he states that the process had its roots earlier: 'The physical collapse of the [secular, classical] city from the fourth century built Christian Rome' (66).

[19] Noble 2001: 217–41. This had already been sensed, on the basis of papal restorations of church buildings, by Delogu (1988) and by Llewellyn (1986), on the basis of institutional history.

[20] See the remarks (and *desiderata*) of Marazzi 2000: 40–1.

[21] I suggest below, pp. 44–5, that the difference was more apparent than real.

of continuity and change in the period under discussion. A recent study of the emergence of medieval papal ceremonial at Rome, for instance, has argued for continuity between late antique imperial *adventus* and the emergence of rituals to serve the needs of the early papacy.[22] Towards the end of the chapter, therefore, I will address the extent to which any continuity in political rituals performed at Rome throughout late antiquity might have prompted the popes to emulate them in the development of their own ceremonial repertoire.

The period under discussion, stretching from Constantine to Gregory, is a long one. My aim is to examine developments in terms of the *longue durée*, thereby offering a perspective that might be precluded by an analysis of a much shorter period. Given that my study will range over a period of three centuries, I have had to be selective in terms of what I do, and do not, discuss. But I hope to provide enough representative evidence on the processes at work to suggest an account of the interrelationships between different interest groups – rulers, senators, and the church – in late antique Rome that is a viable alternative to the precipitous shift from classical/secular to papal/ecclesiastical propounded in traditional descriptions.

SEARCHING FOR RITUALS AND CONTEXTS: SOURCES AGAIN

It is no easy task to trace these developments, given the state of the evidence. The important archaeological discoveries made in recent decades, however much they may throw light on aspects of Rome's late antique physical fabric or economic life, are often less revealing on matters of public ceremonial. The continuous history of settlement at Rome means that many aspects of the city's late antique and early medieval appearance are difficult for us to imagine in precisely such a way that would allow us to visualize the impact of political ritual and the spaces within which it was performed. Throughout the middle ages, the Renaissance, and beyond, ancient edifices have been demolished or have been swallowed up in more recent building projects, while churches have been continually renovated and rebuilt. The explosion of Rome's population since the nineteenth century, and the consequent swamping of the urban area with residential building, means that the urban context within which ceremonial occurred in late antiquity and the early middle ages has largely disappeared.[23]

[22] Twyman 2002: 41–87; however, Miller (2003) argues that such continuities are less certain.

[23] The best guide to this process remains Krautheimer 1980: 231–59.

Similarly, the literary sources for Rome's late antique and early medieval ceremonial life can be stubbornly silent on many of the questions that modern historians of this topic are prone to ask. For instance, the ceremony of imperial *adventus*, which is narrated in great detail by authors of the fourth and early fifth century, is much less prominent in texts later than the panegyrics of Claudian, whose last work is datable to 404.[24] Moreover, some literary sources demonstrably pass over in silence issues about which we might want to know more. For example, the classic description of late antique *adventus* at Rome is Ammianus Marcellinus' account of the ceremonial entry into the city by the emperor Constantius II (337–361) on 28 April 357.[25] Many analyses both of *adventus* and of late antique Rome routinely exploit it, and with good reason. Like much of Ammianus' narrative, this episode is recounted in vivid detail, describing both the imperial procession and the monuments of Rome visited by Constantius. Detailed as it is, however, the account remains deeply problematic. Ammianus' description of Rome's monuments is highly selective. While he devotes much energy to describing the Colosseum, the Pantheon, and the Forum of Trajan, the pagan historian has nothing to say of the city's various Christian buildings. By 357, Rome would have been graced by two particularly enormous basilicas, both begun by members of Constantius' family: on the eastern edge of the city stood St John Lateran, begun by his father, Constantine the Great, while on the Vatican hill across the river Tiber rose St Peter's, probably begun by Constantius' brother and erstwhile co-emperor Constans (337–350).[26] But as scholars have begun to realize in recent years, Ammianus is a historian prone to significant, often distorting, silences.[27] It is possible too that Ammianus' presentation omits references to events as well as buildings. He tells us that Constantius hosted games in the Circus Maximus,[28] but missing from his account is a detail provided by another source, the fifth-century ecclesiastical historian Theodoret, who states that these games were the occasion for a public protest by Rome's population, demanding the return of their bishop

[24] For the absence of *adventus* from fifth-century texts, see MacCormack 1972: 742–3; reiterated, with some modification, in MacCormack 1981: 62–3. See further pp. 43–5 below.

[25] Amm. Marc. 16.10; for further analysis, see Klein 1979.

[26] I am tempted to accept the arguments against seeing St Peter's as a Constantinian foundation advanced by Bowersock (2002); note, however, that this theory is rejected (without cogent explanation) by Johnson (2006: 297 n. 27). For the Lateran, see Curran 2000: 93–6.

[27] Barnes 1998: esp. 43–53; also, with specific reference to Rome, Kelly 2003. Ammianus is persuasive, and misleading: for example, Noble (2001: 46), states, on the strength of the historian's account, that Constantius 'ignored both the Christian sites and ecclesiastical personnel of the city'.

[28] Amm. Marc. 16.10.13.

Liberius, whom Constantius had sent into exile for his refusal to adhere to imperial religious policy.[29]

A quite different, but no less serious, set of problems is presented by one of the main ecclesiastical sources for Rome, the papal chronicle known as the *Liber Pontificalis*. The complexities of this text have been well rehearsed by scholars,[30] but a few pertinent points may be made here. The *Liber Pontificalis*' description of papal ceremonial provides in no way a comprehensive account. Its allusions to ceremonies associated with papal election and consecration before the eighth century, for example, are generally only found at moments of conflict and crisis.[31] Thus, in recording the contested election of 498, it notes that one candidate, Symmachus, was installed in the Lateran, while his rival Laurentius seized control of S. Maria Maggiore.[32] Similarly detailed topographical information is offered of the conflicts surrounding the election of Sergius I in 687.[33] But this feature is not universal: of the disputed election of 366, the text simply notes that there was rivalry between Damasus and Ursinus, and that a council of *sacerdotes* (bishops, presumably) found in favour of the former; for details of the violence that attended this election, however, we must turn instead to other sources.[34] In general, it is only from the last decades of the seventh century that the *Liber Pontificalis* begins to recount the specifics of papal successions and ceremonies associated with them.[35] Even then, however, its notices can be frustratingly allusive. On the accession of John V in 685, it states that he was elected in the Lateran and conducted to the papal residence there 'after the passing of many years and popes, according to ancient custom' – but does not make explicit *why* this old practice was

[29] Thdt., *HE* 2.14. Now Theodoret is a notoriously unreliable source, often inventing attractive set pieces to enliven his narrative, most notably the famous (if implausible) encounter between Theodosius I and Bishop Ambrose at the doors of the cathedral in Milan (*HE* 5.18; cf. McLynn 2004: 268–70). However, another source suggests that Constantius was indeed the recipient of a public protest on behalf of Liberius (*Collectio Avellana* 1.3: 'post annos duos venit Romam Constantius imperator; pro Liberio rogatur a populo'). This makes it clear that the protest was publicly staged, even if it does not specify the venue in which this confrontation between emperor and populace occurred. The historicity of the incident is defended by (e.g.) Barnes (1992: 260) and Curran (2000: 134–5, 233).

[30] The most important discussion remains the introduction in Duchesne 1886: I, esp. xxxiii–lxvii. For more recent analyses of the problems, see Noble 1985, and Davis 2000: esp. xii–xxvii, xlvi–xlviii.

[31] For the period before 731, see Daileader 1993: 12–14.

[32] *LP* 53.2 (I, 260): 'Hic sub intentione ordinates est uno die cum Laurentio, Symmachus in basilica Constantiniana, Laurentius in basilica beatae Mariae.' For an important rereading of the evidence for this dispute, see the chapter by Julia Hillner in this volume.

[33] *LP* 86.2-3 (I, 371–2).

[34] *LP* 39.1 (I, 212). Amm. Marc. 27.3 gives details of the strife in which 137 souls lost their lives.

[35] Twyman 2002: 59–62; cf. Daileader 1993: 14, which places the shift later, after 731.

re-established, or *when* it had fallen into abeyance.[36] We can only assume that the procedures for pontifical election and installation would have been self-evident to the early medieval compilers of the *Liber Pontificalis*; but they are much less clear to us.

These examples highlight the various difficulties involved in trying to reconstruct the history of ceremonial in late antique Rome. The authors of our sources – narrative sources in particular – may omit detail either because it did not suit their broader agenda (as in the case of Ammianus) or because it may have been so obvious to them that it was deemed unnecessary to recount it (thus certain passages of the *Liber Pontificalis*). It will become apparent in what follows that a holistic approach is necessary: in addition to narratives, we need to press into service a wide variety of sources, such as letters, panegyrics, laws, and inscriptions. For all that, there is a clear imbalance in the quantity of the source material, in that we are much less well informed about the fifth, sixth, and seventh centuries than we are about the fourth. In what follows, therefore, the fourth century will receive a rather more detailed treatment than succeeding periods. Yet this has value in itself, in that it will provide a framework against which we can judge the changes that occurred in later centuries.

ADVENTUS, AUTHORITY, AND SPACE FROM CONSTANTINE TO HONORIUS

I noted earlier how it is often observed that, after Constantine, Rome became, effectively, a city without an emperor, that this led to an inevitable decline in the city's traditional imperial institutions, and that into this gap there stepped, with something of an air of inevitability, the papacy. We will see below, however, that in the fifth century Rome once again became, albeit intermittently, a city with a strong imperial presence. For the fourth century, of course, imperial residence at Rome was certainly infrequent. At the beginning of the fourth century, Constantine's rival for power in the west, Maxentius, had made Rome his capital for six years (306–312). During this period, he embellished the city – not least its central areas, around the Via Sacra – with new buildings, some of them subsequently usurped by Constantine.[37] In a very real sense, however, Maxentius'

[36] *LP* 84.1 (1, 366): 'Hic post multorum pontificum tempora vel annorum, iuxta priscam consuetudinem'. The change was undoubtedly occasioned by the end of imperial confirmation of papal elections: see below p. 55.

[37] Cullhed 1994: 49–60; for the Via Appia complex, see also Pisani Sartorio 2000.

lengthy presence in the city was unusual: since the time of Marcus Aurelius (161–180), emperors had often been absent from the city, fighting wars in frontier provinces, and under Diocletian (284–305) and his tetrarchic system of government (from 293), new permanent imperial residences had sprung up in provincial cities.[38] The pattern that was becoming established was for Rome to see the emperor only during short and sporadic visits. After the defeat and death of Maxentius at the battle of the Milvian Bridge on 28 October 312, this pattern of imperial presence at Rome was reasserted. From then until the early fifth century, Rome only saw the emperor for, at most, a few months, or even weeks, and then maybe only once or twice in a reign.[39] Even so, the notion that Rome had become somehow peripheral to the concerns of emperors, or indeed that emperors had become peripheral to the concerns of Rome, should be rejected. In terms of both ritual life and the articulation of space, the emperor still exercised a profound influence on the city.

Rome, the emperor, and adventus

The basic contours of *adventus* ritual, in terms of its participants and procedures, have been well established from analyses of texts such as the Gallic corpus of panegyrics, Ammianus, and Claudian.[40] The emperor's arrival, usually in the company of his army, was anticipated by the senate and people of Rome. A delegation would leave the city to greet the emperor at a pre-arranged location outside its walls. After this formal salutation, the emperor processed into the city in splendid array, his advent resounding to the chanted acclamations of the populace. Upon entering the city centre, the emperor would address the senate, often in the curia in the Forum Romanum, and then the people, again usually in the Forum. He would take up residence in the imperial palace on the Palatine hill. Later, he would give a display of generosity to the people, through the gift of games in the Circus Maximus. Often there would be the erection of

[38] Benoist 2005: 61–101; Millar 1992: 40–53. This is not to say that emperors did not seek to have an impact on life in the city. For some third-century examples, see Curran 2000: 5–26, and Dimitriev 2004.

[39] Demandt 1989: 376 n. 7 gives a list of imperial visits to Rome in the period from 284 to 476, generally culled from Seeck 1919. These details require some modification. That there was a visit by Gratian in 376 is no longer tenable: see Barnes 1999. For the usurper Nepotianus in 350 and his Roman supporters, see Lizzi Testa 2004: 43–5. See n. 73 below on the putative visit of Honorius in 414.

[40] In addition to the basic studies of late antique *adventus* by Sabine MacCormack (1972 and 1981), see also the following, which examine the ceremony also under the principate: Benoist 2005: 25–101; Dufraigne 1994; Lehnen 1997.

commemorative monuments, sometimes the renovation of existing buildings or the construction of new ones. By his presence, speech, and munificence, the emperor advertised in a tangible manner his authority over a city that, for the most part, rarely witnessed the physical presence of its ruler.

The general description just offered is an inadequate guide to the dynamics of *adventus* for various reasons. Such ceremonies were often associated with other manifestations of imperial power. Thus the entry of Honorius (395–423) into Rome at the beginning of 404 was not simply the arrival of an otherwise absent emperor, but also celebrated his consulship in that year.[41] Such subtle manipulations of *adventus* could articulate changes in imperial policy. When Constantine arrived in Rome on 29 October 312, he did so as the victor over Maxentius at the battle of the Milvian Bridge the previous day. His *adventus* had about it the air of a triumph: it was commemorated, after all, by the erection of a triumphal arch, and Maxentius' head was paraded around the city as a gruesome trophy.[42] But whereas triumphant generals and emperors in the past routinely ascended the Capitoline hill and offered sacrifice at the temple of Jupiter Optimus Maximus, it seems that Constantine did not do this. Although this must be assumed on the basis of an *argumentum ex silentio*, the total absence of references in all the extant sources to any such sacrifice would appear to be persuasive.[43] The omission of sacrifices to Jupiter from Constantine's triumphal *adventus* articulated a significant shift in the character of the emperor's rule. Constantine had defeated Maxentius with the aid of the Christian God, and his troops had carried a Christian standard into battle: when previous pagan emperors sacrificed to Jupiter, they attributed their victories to the gods; when Constantine did not, he showed his allegiance to a wholly different divinity.

Furthermore, reducing the description of *adventus* to a basic formula also obscures the potent political significance of individual imperial arrivals. *Adventus* at Rome in the fourth and early fifth centuries were not simply about the arrival of a usually absent emperor; often they were also an

[41] Explicit at Claudian, *VI cons. Hon.* 638–41, with its allusions to Janus; cf. Dufraigne 1994: 217.

[42] The arch will be discussed presently. For Maxentius' head (which after its tour of Rome was sent to Africa, which had been formerly under his jurisdiction), see Pan. Lat. 9 (12) 18.3 and 10 (4) 31.5; Zos., *HN* 2.17.1.

[43] The most forceful recent proponent of Constantine's refusal to sacrifice is Fraschetti (1999: 9–63), reviewing earlier discussions. Fraschetti comments (76) that 'in base alla più assoluta mancanza di ogni positiva documentazione è difficile, molto difficile, supporre che nel 312 in occasione del suo primo *adventus* a Roma Costantino fosse asceso fino al tempio di Giove Ottimo Massimo'. For the changes wrought by Christianity to *adventus* ritual more broadly: Dufraigne 1994: 74–83, 249–325.

ostentatious reassertion of legitimate imperial authority over the city.[44] Constantine's arrival in 312 signalled the end of Maxentius' regime. The point was articulated with particular force on the triumphal arch that the senate erected in honour of Constantine's *decennalia* in 315. However much the expressions in the attic inscriptions sought to achieve a studied religious neutrality in ascribing the emperor's victory to 'the inspiration of (the) divinity' (*instinctu divinitatis*), there was no such ambiguity about the political message contained in the rest of these texts. Maxentius and his associates were not named, but were reduced to the formula 'the tyrant and all his faction' (*tam de tyranno quam de omni eius factione*). On the central passageway of the arch, further inscriptions hailed Constantine as the liberator of the city (*liberatori urbis*) and the founder of peace (*fundatori quietis*).[45] As depicted on the arch, the *adventus* of 312 was all about establishing Maxentius as an illegitimate usurper, and Constantine as the legitimate Augustus.

Other *adventus* in this period emphasized similar points. Ammianus satirized the vast military retinue that accompanied Constantius II to Rome in 357, suggesting that the size of the emperor's entourage was more appropriate to a frontier campaign than to a visit to Rome.[46] But it is likely that this show of strength was part of Constantius' intention. His *adventus* to Rome, like that of his father in 312, was a statement of triumph and a reassertion of legitimate rule. As a panegyric delivered in Rome at this time on behalf of the senate of Constantinople by the eastern orator Themistius makes clear, Constantius' journey to Rome was the occasion for a celebration both of his recent victories over barbarians on the frontiers and of his vanquishing of the usurper Magnentius.[47] So too the *adventus* of Theodosius I (379–395) in 389 was a celebration of victory over the usurper Magnus Maximus (383–388, in control of Italy from 387) the previous year; again a surviving panegyric, by the Gallic orator Pacatus, celebrated the re-establishment of legitimate rule.[48] What does not survive, unfortunately, is another panegyric delivered around this time by the distinguished senator Q. Aurelius Symmachus. He had previously pronounced an oration in honour of the usurper Maximus, presumably pledging the allegiance of the

44 For *adventus* and legitimation, see Benoist 2005: 66–79.

45 *CIL* 6.1139. The language of the inscription probably echoes deliberately that of Augustus': Averil Cameron 2005: 96. For the potency of the term *factio* in the Roman political lexicon, there remains much of profit in Syme 1939: 149–61. See also Bruggisser 2002: esp. 86–91, on the symbolism of the arch and the imposition of the new regime.

46 Amm. Marc. 16.10.6; cf. Kelly 2003: 594–604.

47 Them., *Or.* 3.41d–42a and 43a–c.

48 Pan. Lat. 12 (2) 45–7.

senate to him; at the news of Theodosius' impending arrival, he was abandoned by his fellow senators, but was forgiven for his transgression by Theodosius.[49] His new panegyric, then, set the seal not only on his personal rehabilitation, but on the status of Theodosius, not Maximus, as the legitimate emperor. Thus the interrelationship between *adventus* and imperial power will have been made very forcefully.[50] In the early fifth century, a visit by Honorius similarly underscored the legitimacy of his administration. In the events leading up to the sack of the city by the Goths in 410, their leader Alaric had presented the Romans with a rival emperor, Priscus Attalus, in opposition to Honorius: his scheme was that while Honorius seemed to have little care for the privations of the besieged Romans, Attalus would provide a figurehead more amenable to the concerns of both the people of Rome and the Goths.[51] In 416, however, Honorius gave a potent demonstration of his own reasserted legitimacy by celebrating an *adventus*-cum-triumph at Rome, with Attalus, now a prisoner, walking in front of the imperial carriage.[52]

The presence of the absent emperor

While the power of the emperor over Rome was most potently expressed during such *adventus*, it would be erroneous to assume that his influence in civic affairs disappeared once he and his retinue left the city. The emperor's symbolic presence was constantly invoked in the rhythms of life in the city. As the *Codex Calendar of 354* shows, the year in Rome was punctuated by festivals honouring the emperor: imperial birthdays, anniversaries (both of accessions to the throne and, interestingly, of *adventus* to Rome), and victories were all celebrated.[53] The importance attached to such celebrations should not be underestimated: they were not ephemeral, passing expressions of popular devotion to the throne. Instead, their place in the calendar was enshrined in law, which decreed that imperial anniversaries should be observed as public holidays.[54] Moreover, at a time when the

49 Soc., *HE* 5.14.6; Symm., *Ep.* 2.13 and 31.

50 Humphries 2003: 36–7.

51 Olympiodorus, frr. 10.1 and 3 Blockley.

52 Prosper, *Chron.* c. 1263 (*Chron. Min.* 1, 468): 'Honorius Romam cum triumpho ingreditur praeunte currum eius Attalo.' Prosper lists the event under the consuls for 417, but most modern scholars, following Seeck 1919: 332, favour 416.

53 Salzman 1990: 137–57, 181–2. So too the arrival of news concerning the emperor could be the occasion for some public demonstration of loyalty. For instance, Eusebius (*Vit. Const.* 4.69) asserts that when news of Constantine's death reached Rome, there was a period of public mourning; cf. Curran 2000: 218.

54 *CTh* 2.8.19 (Valentinian II, Theodosius I, and Arcadius to the urban prefect Albinus, 7 Aug. 389).

population of Rome was increasingly divided along religious lines, between pagans and Christians, celebrations in honour of the emperor provided a ceremonial common ground that could be commemorated by *all* Romans, regardless of religious affiliation. There should be no doubt that Christians were in regular attendance at games in various venues: the complaint of Pope Leo I (440–461) that many Christians preferred the blandishments of circus to attendance at church may well be a trope, but one that only makes sense if the issue at the heart of his grievance was true.[55] One of the prime locations for such celebrations was the Circus Maximus, lying in the shadow of the imperial palace on the Palatine hill.[56] Games were celebrated here, and while the sponsors of such spectacles might well be Rome's senatorial aristocrats, the ideological supremacy of the emperor was not forgotten. In his official communications to court in the year of his urban prefecture (384–385), Symmachus conveyed to his imperial masters the acclamations offered in their honour by the assembled *populus* in the Circus.[57] He also records how captured barbarians might be paraded here (and despatched by gladiators or thrown to beasts), a sign of the emperor's dutiful defence of the empire.[58]

Urban space, as well as the rhythms of life, attested to the emperor's supremacy. Rome had long been the focus of grandiose building projects aimed at glorifying individual emperors and their dynasties. At the end of the third century and the beginning of the fourth, the trend had continued. Following a fire that had destroyed substantial areas of the Forum Romanum and the adjacent Forum of Caesar, a redevelopment had reconfigured space, particularly in the Forum Romanum, in such a way as to glorify the tetrarchic emperors under whom it was pursued. The Forum piazza was enclosed by a series of monuments: a new senatorial curia, two new rostra at either end of the square (one replacing the pre-existing rostra), and a series of columns dedicated to the Augusti and Caesars and their tutelary deities.[59] On the Viminal, overlooking the city, a massive set of baths was built in honour of Diocletian and Maximian.[60] In the years following, Maxentius built his complex of buildings in the urban centre, as well as a large suburban palace on the Via Appia.[61] When Maxentius was defeated by Constantine, the new emperor usurped some of his building projects in the city centre, and in so doing asserted his

[55] Leo, *Sermo* 84.1; for Christian attendance at games in late antique Rome, see Lim 1999: 279–81.

[56] See esp. Curran 2000: 218–59.

[57] Symm., *Rel.* 9.4 and 10.2. For the complexities of senatorial benefaction, and how it was interwoven with imperial interests, see Lim 1999: 267–75.

[58] Symm., *Rel.* 47.2. [59] Coarelli 1999: 23–33. [60] *CIL* 6.1130–1. [61] See above n. 37.

legitimate claim on the throne and the city just as he had done through his *adventus* in October 312. The vast basilica to the north of the Via Sacra begun by Maxentius was now completed in Constantine's name, and at its heart sat a colossal statue of the new emperor. Even his interventions on behalf of Christianity were inextricably linked to this assertion of his legitimacy. The new basilica of St John Lateran rose above the demolished camp of the *equites singulares*, the horse guards who had fought valiantly on Maxentius' side at the Milvian Bridge.[62] Together with ritual, architecture and the command of space were mobilized to achieve the political obliteration of Maxentius and his minions, establishing Constantine alone as the legitimate imperial authority.

Throughout the fourth century, and into the fifth, other building projects similarly focused attention on the emperor and his dynasty.[63] This was true even of emperors who never visited Rome, such as Valentinian I (364–375), his brother and eastern co-emperor Valens (364–378), and his son Gratian (western co-Augustus from 367). These were hardly happy times at Rome: as is well known from the pages of Ammianus, the period from 369 to 375 saw a number of magic and treason trials in the city, directed against senators and commoners alike.[64] Nevertheless, several building projects were initiated to honour Valentinian and his dynasty. The Pons Aurelius, where the *Via Triumphalis* entered the city, was renovated and dedicated to Valentinian and Valens at the beginning of their reign, and a few years later a new bridge built further downstream was bedecked with inscriptions commemorating all three joint-rulers (Valentinian I, Valens, and Gratian) as victorious generals.[65] Such architectural projects and their dedications gave physical form to the senate's loyalty to its emperors, also expressed by the senator Q. Aurelius Symmachus during a visit to Valentinian and Gratian's court at Trier in Gaul in 369–370.[66] Emperors after Constantine were also associated with the construction of churches, although such Christian imperial monuments seem to have been less numerous than secular ones. Constans (probably) began construction of

[62] Curran 2000: 93.

[63] As well they might, given that a law of 394 stated that the failure of any magistrate to list the emperor's name on a building was treason: *CTh* 15.1.31. For a sensitive analysis of the significance of such building projects in the Forum Romanum, see Machado forthcoming.

[64] Amm. Marc. 28.1; for analysis, see Matthews 1989: 209–17; and now esp. Lenski 2002: 220–3 and 232–3, arguing cogently against seeing the trials as an anti-senatorial purge.

[65] Pons Aurelius: *ILS* 769, with Amm. Marc. 27.3.3. Pons Valentiniani: *CIL* 6.1175–6, 31402–12; see further Bertinetti 2000; Lizzi Testa 2004: 447–54.

[66] Symm., *Orr.* 1–3; cf. Humphries 2003: 34–6.

St Peter's on the Vatican in the 340s,[67] while, at the end of the century, Valentinian II and Theodosius I initiated reconstruction of another vast extramural basilica, St Paul's on the Via Ostiensis.[68]

The extent to which space could be used to express loyalty to the emperor is shown most effectively by a series of monuments that can be linked to episodes of imperial *adventus*. Constantius II's visit in 357 was, as we have seen, the occasion for celebration both of his victories over barbarians and of his defeat of the usurper Magnentius. Monuments erected at Rome between Magnentius' initial defeat at Mursa in 351 and Constantius' arrival in 357 commemorated the emperor in precisely these terms. By the Via Sacra, between the arch of Septimius Severus and the senate house, stood an equestrian statue of Constantius, erected in 352/3; the inscription on its base acclaimed him as 'restorer of the city of Rome and the world and suppressor of wretched tyranny' (*restitutori urbis Romae adque orb* [*is*] *et extinctori pestiferae tyrannidis*) and as 'victorious and triumphant' (*victori ac triumfatori*).[69] Other inscriptions attest to similar monuments elsewhere in the city.[70] That they were consonant with the emperor's own goals is confirmed by the inscription on the base of the obelisk that Constantius himself erected in the Circus Maximus.[71] So too the arrival of Theodosius in 389 after the defeat of Magnus Maximus prompted a flurry of monuments. We have seen that Theodosius' visit provided an opportunity for Symmachus to repent of his former allegiance to the usurper. The legitimacy of Theodosius and his then fellow emperors Valentinian II and Arcadius was underscored by a triad of statues erected near the curia, each bearing an identical inscription (save for the imperial name) that extolled each emperor as the 'suppressor of usurpers' (*extinctori tyrannorum*).[72]

After Theodosius' death in January 395, imperial visits to Rome became more frequent. His son Honorius visited the city on perhaps as many as six occasions.[73] Again, such visits were accompanied by the erection of

[67] See above n. 26.

[68] Krautheimer, *CBCR* V, 97–8, 161–2. The imperial dedication and splendour (*regia pompa*) were recalled soon afterwards by Prudentius (*Peristeph.* 12.45–54): a sure indication that the project emphasized not only the emperors' piety, but also their authority.

[69] *CIL* 6.1158. [70] Humphries 2003: 38–40.

[71] *CIL* 6.1163 c–d. For the significance of this project, see the excellent analysis of Henck 2001: 281–3.

[72] *CIL* 6.3791 a–b, 31413–31414, 36959.

[73] Demandt (1989: 376 n. 7, following Seeck 1919: 328) suggests that Honorius visited Rome on 30 August 414 on the strength of the dating clause of *CTh* 16.5.55 (*dat. III kal. September Rom.*). However, laws of 8 August (*CJ* 1.33.3) and 17 September that year were issued from Ravenna. While a swift visit to Rome in the interim is not impossible, it is equally likely that the dating formula of *CTh* 16.5.55 has become corrupt, with *Rom.* being written in place of *Rav.*: thus Mommsen and Meyer 1954: 874, app. crit. ad loc.

monuments that stressed the benefits of the emperor's rule. In the Forum Romanum, beside the Via Sacra, and facing the senate house, a statue and inscription were erected to honour the general Stilicho for his victory over the Goths at the battle of Pollentia in 403; when Honorius visited Rome in 404, Stilicho was at his side.[74] The sack of Rome in 410, and the events leading up to it (including the ephemeral reign of Priscus Attalus), seem to have provoked from Honorius' government a more emphatic statement of imperial presence in the city. Perhaps because the imperial residence on the Palatine had been damaged in the sack, a new palace rose on the Pincian hill to the north of the city. Its chief feature was a semi-circular pavilion, sumptuously decorated in *opus sectile*, oriented south to look out over the city. If the excavators are right in identifying this building as an imperial construction of the 410s on land acquired by the imperial fisc from the Anicii family (one of whom, Anicia Faltonia Proba, had been accused of admitting the Goths to the city), then this new palace may have been built in anticipation of the emperor's visit in 416 (with its ceremonial humiliation of Attalus).[75] Around the same time, either in anticipation of this same imperial visit or in its immediate aftermath, other restoration work was also undertaken. A fragmentary inscription records activity in Honorius' name in the Colosseum.[76] More substantial works seem to have been carried out in the Forum Romanum, particularly in the vicinity of the senate house, probably to restore damage caused in 410.[77] Such projects, taken together with Honorius' visit, will have eloquently symbolized the emperor's care for, and the restoration of his authority over, the city after the trauma, and treachery, of the Gothic assault.

Emperor, senate, church

Of course, emperors were not the only individuals involved in the deployment of ritual and space to their advantage; senators and bishops too were active. Ammianus provides a famous (and hostile) depiction of the luxury of senatorial *domus* that demonstrates how domestic space was used by

74 *CIL* 6.31987; for the positioning, see Giuliani and Verducchi 1987: 77–8. On Stilicho's presence by Honorius' side in 404, see Claudian, *VI Cons. Hon.* 578–83.

75 Broise, Dewailly, and Jolivet 1999 and 2000. Claire Sotinel (pers. comm.) suggests to me that construction is equally likely under Valentinian III (425–455), since any Anician abandonment under Honorius provides only a *terminus post quem* for the construction.

76 Full analysis (with texts) in Orlandi 2004: 70–2, 74, 76, 81–6.

77 *CIL* 6.1718 and 41386–7; cf. Fraschetti 1999: 218–19. For other work in the Forum at this time, see Machado forthcoming.

aristocrats to display their status and wealth.[78] In addition, senators were active in areas where the emperors had little interest in becoming involved. A celebrated example is the maintenance by pagan aristocrats of Rome's ancient pagan cults, which had been progressively deprived of state funding.[79] Meanwhile, Rome's bishops were also active sponsors of architectural and liturgical projects that advertised their authority within the city's Christian community. For example, Pope Liberius (352–366) built a basilica that bore his name (the *basilica Liberiana*) on the Esquiline hill, on the site later occupied by S. Maria Maggiore,[80] while his successor Damasus (366–384), perhaps in an effort to heal rifts in his congregation following his disputed election, did much to foster and give shape to the cult of the Roman martyrs.[81] We should resist the temptation to see these patterns of patronage by emperors, senators, and bishops as entirely separate; rather, systems of patronage and display of status were interwoven. For example, senatorial aristocrats could act as patrons of ecclesiastical building projects, donating land or paying for their construction, or funding their renovation.[82] Senators could also be buried in prominent locations in, or near, churches, as were Iunius Bassus and Sextus Petronius Probus at the Vatican.[83] Thus the activities by and in honour of emperors need to be viewed in the context of a wider web of patronage and status display.[84]

It might be objected, furthermore, that such statements of imperial authority as were found in dedications to the emperors were merely reflections at Rome of their glorification found in inscriptions and monuments across the empire. At Rome, however, it seems to me that there is a compelling correlation between the dedication of monuments expressing loyalty and occasions for the periodic presence of the emperor. Moreover, many of these monuments and imperial presences clustered around moments when the loyalty of Rome might have seemed to be in doubt. Thus Theodosius' visit in 389 after the usurpation of Magnus Maximus provided the opportunity to reassert legitimate authority in a number of ways: first, the *adventus* expressly celebrated Theodosius' victory; secondly,

78 Amm. Marc. 28.6.13. 79 Lizzi Testa 2004: 412–24.

80 Liberius' foundation is recorded to this day in the beautiful singing of the *capella Liberiana* at S. Maria Maggiore. Another example of a basilica perpetuating the name of its founder is offered by the Lateran, frequently referred to (not least in the *Liber Pontificalis*) as the *basilica Constantiniana*. In Milan, the memory of Bishop Ambrose (374–397) was recalled by the *basilica Ambrosiana*.

81 Curran 2000: 142–55; Sághy 2000.

82 For senatorial benefaction at Rome, see Ward-Perkins 1984: 239–41; cf. Lim 1999: 275–9, for the broader context.

83 Iunius Bassus: *CIL* 6.1737; Petronius Probus: *ICUR* ns 2.4219 a–b.

84 For the intersection of senatorial patronage with that of others, see Alföldy 2001.

the panegyric of Pacatus underscored the perfidy of Maximus and his supporters and, in contrast, the justness of Theodosius' cause; thirdly, Symmachus, who had previously pronounced a panegyric on Maximus, was forgiven his transgression, and now delivered a speech expressing loyalty to the re-established legitimate regime; finally, statues celebrating the ruling dynasty as the suppressors of usurpers rose near the senate house.

Such actions were necessary given the propensity of various sections of the Roman population, not least its senators, to support usurpers. Nepotianus in 350, Magnentius in 350–351, Magnus Maximus in 387–388, Eugenius in 393–394, and Priscus Attalus before the sack of 410 had all received support from groups within the city. Imperial presences in the city, whether in person through *adventus* or through the erection of monuments, were key to maintaining legitimate authority over Rome. Moreover, such presences could also be used to advertise the penalties of rebellion. The parading of Maxentius' head in 312 and of Priscus Attalus before Honorius' carriage in 416 are obvious examples. Other lessons could be taught through the mechanism of *damnatio memoriae.* During the period of Magnentius' ascendancy in Italy, the urban prefect had set up dedications in his honour; once Magnentius was ousted, however, the names of both usurper and prefect were erased from the inscriptions.[85] A similar fate was suffered by an inscription (on a statue base) honouring the distinguished senator Nicomachus Flavianus following his ill-advised support of Eugenius.[86] Any form of perceived treason was enough: after Stilicho was removed in 408, his name was erased from the large monument standing opposite the senate house. In each of these cases, the blocks bearing the mutilated inscriptions, and presumably denuded of any statues they may have borne, were left *in situ*; each stood as 'a mute reminder of . . . disgrace',[87] and a testimony to the authority of legitimate rulers. The emperor might largely be absent from Rome, but signs of his power were everywhere to be sensed and seen.

URBS REGIA: FROM VALENTINIAN III TO THE GOTHIC WARS

Under Honorius the security and integrity of the western empire was repeatedly undermined by civil war and barbarian invasion. The century

[85] *CIL* 6.1166.

[86] The block survives, with an inscription recording Flavianus' rehabilitation in 431: *CIL* 6.1783. For commentary, see the subtle analysis of Hedrick 2000: esp. 89–130 on the dynamics of *damnatio memoriae.*

[87] The elegant formulation of Hedrick 2000: 110.

or so that followed his death in 423 witnessed further disruption, as the Roman empire in the west crumbled and disappeared. These events were to have a significant impact on the city of Rome. Some episodes are well known: the sack of Alaric was followed forty-five years later by another, perpetrated by the Vandals who had carved out a kingdom for themselves in what had once been Roman north Africa. Later, in 476, the last western emperor was deposed and, in 493, Rome, with the rest of Italy, came under the domination of the Ostrogothic kings. An exclusive concentration on such episodes, and the unquestioning construction of them as moments of crisis,[88] serves to buttress the notion that there was a precipitous shift in Rome's fortunes in late antiquity. If we adopt such a view, then the lingering elements of the city's imperial past can appear as nothing more than pathetic anachronisms.[89] Such an analysis is misleading for various reasons. As we will see, Rome remained an important focus for the activities of emperors in the fifth century, and under the Ostrogothic kings who succeeded them this trend continued. In other words, even in a period when Rome's ancient institutions appeared to be crumbling, the city remained a venue for the expression of secular authority in a way that would limit the ability of the papacy to dominate affairs there.

Rome and the last western emperors

If, in the fourth and early fifth centuries, actual imperial presence in Rome was sporadic and temporary, in the last decades of the western empire, particularly after 440, it became much more common. In part, this was a consequence of the disintegration of Roman rule over former provinces: as Africa, Gaul, and Spain all passed into the hands of barbarian kings, Italy was soon all that was left for western emperors to rule. Of course, other centres remained important, notably Ravenna in northern Italy and, for as long as Roman power held sway there, Arles in southern Gaul. Even so, certain Roman emperors chose to spend often lengthy periods at Rome.[90] Valentinian III (425–455), for example, was there for nearly eight of the last fifteen years of his reign – or, to put it another way, for over a quarter of his

88 See Croke 1983, for the re-evaluation of the deposition of Romulus Augustulus in the context of Justinian's planned reconquests.

89 Thus Krautheimer 1980: 33: 'No emperor ever returned to take up permanent residence there, but fragments of the administration remained and Rome *continued to cling* to her claim of being a legitimate capital of the empire and the center of civilized mankind' (emphasis added). For Krautheimer's reiteration of this sense of anachronism for the sixth century, see below at n. 160.

90 For what follows, see now Gillett 2001: esp. 148–57 for details of emperors residing at Rome; this updates the catalogue in Seeck 1919.

entire reign.[91] His short-lived successor Petronius Maximus seemingly resided there for all of his few months as emperor (March–May 455). Avitus (455–6) and Majorian (457–61) both seem to have regarded Rome as important: Avitus travelled to the city for the inauguration of his consulship in 456, while Majorian was probably making for the city at the moment he was deposed. Thereafter, Anthemius (467–472), Olybrius (472), and Glycerius (473–474) were at Rome for almost all of their reigns. At the very end of imperial rule, Julius Nepos spent nearly a year at Rome (474–475), whence he fled to Dalmatia. Such comparatively long residences of emperors at Rome call for comment.

In one respect, the presence of the emperor in the city meant that Rome became the venue for court politics in a way that had not been possible since the second and early third centuries. In 455, for example, court intrigues led to the murders first of the general Aëtius and then of Valentinian III. Later, in 472, Rome was embroiled in civil strife, when the patrician Ricimer laid siege to the city, captured it, and hunted down Anthemius. The senatorial aristocracy were deeply implicated in such events: it was members of their order, Petronius Maximus and Olybrius, who succeeded to the throne after the assassinations of 455 and 472.[92] Such senatorial treachery was recognized by the eastern emperor Zeno. An embassy of Roman senators came to Constantinople after the deposition of Romulus Augustulus in 476 to inform Zeno that it would be sufficient for the general Odovacer to govern Italy in the eastern emperor's name. Zeno took the opportunity, however, to upbraid the senators for their involvement in Anthemius' murder and Julius Nepos' expulsion.[93] The embassy of 476 also foreshadows an important role that senators were to perform under the Ostrogothic kings, as a conduit of communication between Italy's new barbarian rulers and the imperial court at Constantinople.[94]

The dynamic role of the senate in imperial politics at this period was mirrored, in the opposite direction, by signs from the emperors of care for the city of Rome, not least for its senatorial aristocrats. The best-known

[91] The evidence of dating clauses in imperial laws shows that Valentinian was continuously at Rome in the periods 24 Jan. to 20 March 440, 18 Jan. 445 to 3 June 447, and 21 Feb. 450 to 16 March 455. He had previously spent four months (23 Oct. 425 to 24 Feb. 426) there at the beginning of his reign, and is also recorded in Rome in August 442 and March 443. In spite of this, he does not appear at all in Krautheimer 1980. Pietri (1976: 956) surely underestimates Valentinian's presence when he states that the emperor 's'attache beaucoup plus à Rome que son oncle Honorius à la fin de son règne', but that 'la Cour réside très rarement dans la vieille capitale'. In part, of course, this is true of the period treated by Pietri, which ends in 440.

[92] For details of their early careers, see *PLRE* 2.749–51 (Maximus 22), and 796–8 (Olybrius 6).

[93] Malchus, fr. 14 Blockley; cf. Burgarella 2001: 121–6. [94] Burgarella 2001: *passim*.

example is the fourth *Novella* of Majorian (457–461), issued in 458, which ordered that Rome's buildings, including its temples, be preserved as *ornamenta*. Apart from this, however, Majorian's legislation showed little direct concern for the city of Rome.[95] A more cogent display of solicitude is to be found amongst the laws of Valentinian III issued during his periods of residence in the city. These show the emperor legislating for a variety of problems confronting the city, such as its provisioning,[96] problems of currency fluctuations,[97] and the rights of freedmen and the status of resident foreigners.[98] Senatorial concerns also commanded the emperor's attention: two laws responded to cases involving disputes over senators' testaments.[99] Indeed, Valentinian's legislative activity was sometimes conducted before the senate: a law of 24 February 426, on the partial remission of the *aurum oblaticum*, was read before the senate by the *primicerius notariorum* Theodosius;[100] another, of 5 March 450, was cast in the form of an oration to the consuls, praetors, tribunes, and the senate, and was read before it on 14 March by the official Postumianus.[101] In 440, Valentinian had begun a law on various aspects of Rome's administration with the grandiloquent statement: 'Our constant care for the city of Rome, which we justly venerate as the head of our empire, abides with us, to such an extent that we make wise provision in all ways for her peace and abundance.'[102] At times, it must have seemed that the emperor's actions were matching his rhetoric.

As had been the case in the fourth and early fifth centuries, the period from Valentinian III onwards saw the emperor's power reflected also in building projects. A series of inscriptions from the Colosseum attests to a number of interventions there in honour of Valentinian and his eastern co-emperor Theodosius II (408–450). These renovations must predate Theodosius' death in 450, but apart from that their chronology is uncertain. It is possible, however, that the interventions in question were provoked by earthquakes known to have hit the city in 429 and 443.[103]

95 Only two other laws are concerned with the city. *Nov. Maj.* 1 was issued at the beginning of his reign and to coincide with his consulship in 458: it was addressed to the senate, but from Ravenna, and its contents extend to no more than conventional platitudes about the desire for harmony between emperor and senate. The other law – *Nov. Maj.* 10 – was on senators' testamentary rights: but its text has been lost and it is known only from its title.

96 Here, and in the following notes, I append the year of issue of such laws in parentheses: *Nov. Val.* 5 (440), 29 (450), and 36, esp. §§ 2 and 9 (452).

97 *Nov. Val.* 16 (445). 98 *Nov. Val.* 25 (447) and 31 (451).

99 *Nov. Val.* 21.1 and 21.2 (both 446). 100 *CTh* 6.2.25. 101 *Nov. Val.* 1.3.

102 *Nov. Val.* 5: 'Urbis Romae, quam merito caput nostri veneamur imperii, in tantum nos cura non deserit, ut quieti eius atque abundantiae modis omnibus consulamus.'

103 For discussion and texts, see now Orlandi 2004: 42–6, 67–81, 86–159; cf. Chastagnol 1966: 5–23, 64–6.

Further works in the amphitheatre are attested under Anthemius; inscriptions record that they were dedicated by Fl. Messius Phoebus Severus, apparently one of the emperor's closest associates in the senate.[104] Emperors and members of their retinues continued to be involved in the building and renovation of churches also: Licinia Eudoxia, wife of Valentinian III, made donations to S. Pietro in Vincoli;[105] Valentinian and his mother Galla Placidia renovated a chapel at S. Croce in Gerusalemme;[106] and Ricimer dedicated S. Agata dei Goti.[107] Under the last western emperors, then, Rome remained a stage upon which their power was advertised. Indeed, given the more frequent presence of the court in the city after 440, it could be argued that in the fifth century the display of imperial authority and munificence at Rome was more prominent than it had been at any time since the reign of Maxentius.

Ritual, authority, and space in fifth-century Rome

In addition to such concrete manifestations of the ruler's power, Rome was also witness to various ritualized expressions of his authority. Much has been made of the apparent disappearance of *adventus* ritual in the fifth century. Sabine MacCormack has drawn attention to the absence of the theme of *adventus* in the panegyrics pronounced by Sidonius Apollinaris on the consular inaugurations at Rome of Avitus in 456 and Anthemius in 468 – an omission that is especially noteworthy given Sidonius' close dependence on Claudian, whose panegyrics are replete with descriptions of *adventus*, as literary model.[108] MacCormack speculates that 'the ceremony survived, but the associations surrounding it had either fallen silent or found expression through other means'.[109] For this period, our sources for Rome itself are often brief, forcing us to build much of our picture on bald notices in annals and chronicles.[110] In spite of this, however, there are some indications that rituals concerned with political authority continued to occur.

It is hard to imagine, for instance, that ceremonial did not attend the arrival in Italy in autumn 467 of Anthemius, despatched as ruler of the west

[104] Reconstruction and discussion of the texts (*CIL* 6.32091–2) in Orlandi 2004: 47–51; cf. *PLRE* 2.1005–6 (Severus 17) for Severus' investment in Anthemius' regime.

[105] Krautheimer, *CBCR* III, 181, 226–7. [106] Krautheimer, *CBCR* I, 168.

[107] Krautheimer, *CBCR* I, 3, 11–12. [108] MacCormack 1981: 62–4. [109] MacCormack 1981: 64.

[110] Often the same word can be used of an imperial arrival as of some other event. For example, the continuation to Prosper of Aquitaine's *Chronicle* in the Codex Reichenaviensis uses *ingressus* to describe both the sack by the Vandal king Geiseric (c. 29, in *Chron. Min.* 1.490) and the arrival of icons of the emperor Marcian (see n. 113 below).

by the eastern Augustus Leo. To be sure (and as MacCormack has noted), Sidonius says nothing about any *adventus* in his panegyric for Anthemius' consulship the following year – but then he says very little about the *precise* circumstances of Anthemius' accession at all. An entry in Cassiodorus' *Chronicle*, however, notes that Anthemius 'received the imperial power at Brontotae, at the third milestone from the city'.[111] The account is tantalizingly brief, and even the precise whereabouts of Brontotae is unknown.[112] Its location a few miles outside the city, however, invites comparisons with the initial greeting of an emperor beyond Rome's walls that initiated *adventus* ceremonies. Is it possible that some form of coronation ritual for Anthemius occurred there, followed by a procession into the city?

Rather more, perhaps, can be made of an event recorded in 452. Our source again is a brief entry in a chronicle: 'Images of the emperor Marcian entered Rome on the third day before the Kalends of April (i.e. 30 March).'[113] Evidence from elsewhere in the empire, however, suggests a ceremonial context for this event. The use of images of emperors is well attested in late antiquity (we noted at the beginning of this chapter the arrival in Rome of portraits of Phocas and Leontia; we will return to them in due course). A law of 425 noted that images should be regarded as representing the presence of the emperor when he was otherwise absent.[114] Zosimus provides two vignettes that show them being displayed as a means of asserting the legitimacy of an emperor. First, before the final breach between Maxentius and Constantine in 312, images of the latter were paraded about Rome 'as was customary'.[115] Secondly, in 386, at a time when Theodosius I was compelled to negotiate with Magnus Maximus, the emperor despatched an image of the usurper to Alexandria, where it was to be set up in public and the legitimacy of Maximus was to be proclaimed.[116] Various other texts expand on the theme. Constantine Porphyrogenitus' *Liber de Caeremoniis* excerpts a protocol for the reception of portraits of Anthemius at Constantinople in 468. Like the *adventus* of an emperor in person, this was to be the occasion for the performance of panegyrics.[117]

111 Cassiodorus, *Chron.* c. 1283 (*Chron. Min.* 2.158): 'His conss. Anthemius a Leone imp. ad Italiam mittitur, qui tertio miliario in loco Brontotas suscepit imperio.'

112 Hülsen 1903.

113 Continuation to Prosper in the Codex Reichenaviensis, c. 21 (*Chron. Min.* 1.490): 'iconica Marciani imperatoris Romam ingressa III kal. Aprilis'.

114 *CTh* 15.4.1. For a general discussion of imperial icons, see MacCormack 1981: 67–73; also Bruun 1976, reviewing numismatic evidence. Neither study, however, mentions either the law or the arrival of Marcian's images at Rome.

115 Zos., *HN* 2.9.2: κατὰ τὸ σύνηθες.

116 Zos., *HN* 4.37.3; cf. MacCormack 1981: 67.

117 Const. Porph., *De Caer.* 1.87; MacCormack 1981: 68.

Just such a speech survives from Procopius of Gaza, honouring the arrival in his city of an image of the emperor Anastasius I (491–518).[118] It does not seem unreasonable to suppose that Marcian's image was sent to Rome in the expectation that it would receive a ceremonial welcome, and that precisely this occurred when it arrived there: why else should the chronicler have noted it?

For one event at least, there can be no ambiguity about the rituals performed or their significance. On 25 December 438, the senate gathered for a special session in the Roman home of Anicius Acilius Glabrio Faustus, then praetorian prefect and consul, and formerly urban prefect at Rome on three occasions. The purpose of the meeting was to mark the arrival of the Theodosian Code, the great compilation of law ordered by Theodosius II in 429 and published at Constantinople in the autumn of 437. At its initial publication in the east – an event that had coincided with the wedding of Theodosius' daughter Licinia Eudoxia to the western emperor Valentinian III – the senate had been represented by two envoys, one of whom was the self-same Faustus in whose house the assembly now gathered.[119] The senators listened as he recounted the history of the Code's publication, shouting acclamations at appropriate junctures. The meeting as a whole concluded with yet more acclamations – 748 in total! – some in honour of the chief imperial officials in the west (Faustus included), but the bulk of them in honour of the emperors. In their rhythmical chanting of the emperors' virtues, with the bound volumes of imperial law sitting in their midst, the senators gave voice to their loyalty to a united empire of east and west under the guidance of Theodosius and Valentinian.[120]

Continuity and change

The picture just presented, of Rome as a stage upon which the emperor still acted a leading part, risks misleading if it gives the impression that all continued to be well in the city, and that the fifth century saw no changes at all. In fact there are signs of change to be seen in many aspects of urban life

118 MacCormack 1981: 68–70, with texts given at 305 nn. 273–4.

119 For what follows, see the *Gesta Senatus* in Mommsen and Meyer 1954: 1–4; I rely substantially on the analysis of Matthews 2000: 31–54.

120 For the mechanics and purpose of these acclamations, see Matthews 2000: 39–49. Harries (1999: 65) describes the whole meeting as 'carefully structured', and suggests that the account in *Gesta Senatus* 1 that the senators and imperial officers 'had gathered together and held deliberations among themselves for a considerable time (*convenissent habuissentque inter se aliquamdiu tractatum*)' reflected a preliminary meeting at which the ceremonial protocol for the subsequent part of the assembly was arranged (66 n. 37).

and at many locations within the city in the last decades of imperial rule and, later, under the Ostrogothic kings. Some of them hint at decay. If we may extrapolate from the decreasing amounts of cash allocated in laws to provisioning Rome with food, then it seems incontestable that the city's population was shrinking.[121] Such decline extended to parts of Rome's urban fabric. By the end of the fifth century (or the middle of the sixth) it appears that the Forum of Augustus was already in a ruinous condition and being used as a quarry for building material; since the fourth century, there had also been changes afoot in the Templum Pacis, which was being transformed from a public space to some more utilitarian function.[122]

Not all areas were experiencing decline, however. A striking feature of late antique Rome is that the Forum of Trajan became a major centre for the display of prestige and authority. It was here, for example, that the mutilated statue base of Nicomachus Flavianus stood for nearly forty years before his *damnatio memoriae* was revoked.[123] Many other statues of local and imperial dignitaries were placed in this precinct, including, most famously, one in honour of the court poet Claudian.[124] The rising importance of Trajan's Forum seems to have begun in the fourth century, but accelerated in the course of the fifth. It was one of the main venues too for one of the more routine means of displaying imperial authority in the city: many of the texts of laws that we have from Rome were taken down from copies posted in this Forum.[125] Any picture of Rome in the fifth and sixth centuries must account, then, for topographical changes occurring at different rates in different locations.

We have already noted the patronage of church construction by emperors throughout the fourth and fifth centuries. This may have been mirrored by the adoption of churches as venues for the display of authority through ceremonial. In the east, the fifth century saw the emperor succeed 'in appropriating the ceremonial spotlight of the church in Constantinople'.[126] For Rome, our sources, predominantly ecclesiastical, are much less clear, and

[121] Lo Cascio 2000: 58–61, citing anterior bibliography.

[122] Meneghini and Santangeli Valenzani 1996: 77–91; summary in their 2001b: 34–5.

[123] See above p. 39.

[124] In general, see Packer 1997:1, 8–10. Claudian: *CIL* 6.1710.

[125] Again, there is a notable concentration with Valentinian III: *Nov. Val.* 11, 19, 21.1 and 2, 23, 25, and 31 were all posted here. Laws were posted there in the fourth century, but in other venues also. This much is clear from the two surviving versions of Theodosius I's law of 390 on the public burning of homosexual prostitutes: we have a heavily edited version from the Forum of Trajan (*CTh* 9.7.6), as well as a more extensive text from the atrium of Minerva (*Coll. leg. Rom. et Mos.* 5.3); see Matthews 2000: 277–9, for commentary.

[126] McLynn 2004: 270.

tend to focus on the prominence of the bishop: as such, they accord well with the discourse of a shift in authority from emperor to pope. But they may conceal attempts by emperors to use the spaces of the Roman church for their own ceremonial ends. How early this process began is similarly difficult to gauge. Honorius may have visited St Peter's on the occasion of his *adventus* to the city in 404, but the evidence for such a visit must be adduced from a vague allusion in a sermon delivered by Augustine in north Africa.[127]

Clearer evidence for the presence of the emperor in church is found during the Roman residences of Valentinian III. A series of letters from the western imperial family to their eastern counterparts in 450 show that the emperor, together with his mother Galla Placidia and his wife Licinia Eudoxia, attended a vigil in St Peter's, perhaps on the night of 21 February, but in any case only a day after the imperial entourage had arrived in the city.[128] Apart from their presence we know nothing, but it is not hard to imagine the *visual* impact that the imperial family (and presumably its attendants) might have had on other members of the congregation. Valentinian's family also used the spaces of the Roman church for state funerals. An entry in an anonymous fifth-century chronicle relates that in 450 '[the body of] Theodosius was led in splendid array by [Galla] Placidia and [Pope] Leo and the whole senate and buried in the mausoleum by the Apostle Peter'.[129] The Theodosius in question was not the emperor of the east (who died that year), but the son of Galla Placidia by her first marriage to the Gothic leader Athaulf. He had previously been interred at Barcelona, but was now brought to Rome for reburial. The location of the mausoleum mentioned in the text would appear to be the former chapel of S. Petronilla, which stood beside the old St Peter's, but was pulled down during the construction works of the present basilica. A number of impressive burials were found there in 1458 and 1544, making it a likely candidate for an imperial mausoleum.[130]

Another instance of the use of ecclesiastical space as a venue for the display of secular authority comes from late in the period of Ostrogothic rule. A letter penned by Cassiodorus on behalf of King Athalaric (526–534) to Pope John II (533–535) addressed problems of strife within the Roman

[127] Fraschetti 1999: 261–3.

[128] Texts in *PL* 54.857–66: they are preserved among the letters of Pope Leo I. Valentinian himself wrote: 'Cum advenissem in urbem Romam . . . sequenti die ad basilicam apostoli Petri.' Discussion of chronology in Susman 1961 [1964]: 21–6.

[129] Continuation to Prosper in the Codex Reichenaviensis, c. 12 (*Chron. Min.* 1.489): 'Theodosius cum magna pompa a Placidia et Leone et omni senatu deductus et in mausoleo ad apostulum Petrum depositus est.'

[130] Johnson 1991: 330–8.

church, and a consequent recourse to bribery at pontifical elections, that had plagued the papacy of Boniface II (530–532).[131] This had already commanded the attention of the senate, who had passed a *senatus consultum* on the matter.[132] Now the king added his weight in support of the senate's decree. Most importantly, Athalaric sent careful instructions to Salventius, the prefect of Rome, ordering that both the royal judgement on the matter and the decree of the senate should be inscribed on marble tablets and be erected in front of the atrium of St Peter's (*ante atrium beati Petri apostoli*), a practice that recalls the use of secular public spaces, notably the Forum of Trajan, for the display of laws; he also sent a functionary to report back to him that this had been carried out.[133] Here we have an instance not only of a secular ruler seeking to stamp a sign of his authority on the space of the church, but also of his keen desire to make certain that this was achieved according to his instructions.

These various themes of continuity and change cohere in the Roman *adventus* of the first Ostrogothic king, Theoderic, in 500.[134] Many of the traditional elements are present and correct: the king was greeted outside the city by a delegation of senators; their reception of him was an occasion for rejoicing; Theoderic progressed into the city, gave speeches to the senate and the people, took up residence in the imperial palace, and showed his generosity through games in the circus, distributions of grain and wine, and restorations of buildings.[135] Theoderic himself was aware of the symbolic nature of his visit, and proclaimed to the people that he would maintain the privileges granted to them previously by the emperors.[136] At the same time, however, Theoderic's arrival also indicated changes that had occurred. Prominent among the delegation that greeted the king outside the city was Pope Symmachus (498–514), whose contested election two years earlier had been ratified by royal dictate.[137] Like Valentinian III before him, Theoderic's *adventus* also included a visit to St Peter's.[138] That the church could be used to signal the authority of a secular ruler – and a heterodox one at that – had already been signalled at a church council held under Symmachus' presidency in 499. The meeting ended with

[131] Sotinel 1992: 442–3. [132] Cass., *Var.* 9.15.3; 9.16.1. [133] Cass., *Var.* 9.16.3.

[134] The most recent discussion, citing all relevant sources and the pertinent modern bibliography, is Vitiello 2004.

[135] *Anon. Val.* 65–7.

[136] *Anon. Val.* 66: 'se omnia . . . quod retro principes Romani ordinaverunt, inviolabiliter servaturum promittit'.

[137] *Anon. Val.* 65; *L P* 53.3 (I, 260).

[138] *Anon. Val.* 65: 'ambulavit rex Theodericus Romam et occurrit beato Petro'.

acclamations: prominent among them, and chanted thirty times, was 'Christ hear us! Long life to Theoderic!'[139]

Under the last emperors and the Ostrogothic kings, then, the ceremonial life of Rome remained focused on its rulers. Both emperors and kings sought to demonstrate their authority at Rome, either through their actual presence or through the display of laws. Even when rulers were absent, their authority was granted ceremonial recognition, for example with the acclamations of the emperors at the proclamation of the Theodosian Code in 438, or those for Theoderic at the church council of 499. That said, the fifth and sixth centuries did not see a simple continuity of the situation that had obtained in the fourth century. In some respects, the last decades of imperial rule in the fifth century represent something of an anomaly since, with the emperor and his court in the city for long periods, Rome became, much more than at any time since the early third century, a venue for the display of an actively present imperial authority. Also, while many traditional topographical sites of ceremonial and authority remained important, there was an increased tendency to use the spaces of the church for such displays by secular rulers. This latter phenomenon demonstrates above all that however much the fifth and sixth centuries might be regarded as witnessing the collapse and disappearance of traditional institutions in the west, the city of Rome did not swiftly fall under the dominance of the church; indeed, even in church buildings, the secular authority could continue to display its supremacy in Roman life.

SPACE, CEREMONY, AND AUTHORITY IN THE AGE OF GREGORY THE GREAT

During the Ostrogothic period, moreover, Rome retained its significance in the politics of empire. Although Italy had ceased to be ruled directly by the emperor, the city's aristocracy provided an important link between the imperial court at Constantinople and that of Theoderic and his successors at Ravenna. Again, however, we need to be wary of seeing continuity in simplistic terms. The decades of Ostrogothic rule coincided with a gradual erosion of the central place of the senate in Italian affairs. While many senators occupied positions in the Ostrogothic government, other posts, not least in the military, devolved upon the Goths themselves. At the same time, the senate's numbers dwindled as aristocratic families left Rome and

139 *Acta synodi a. CCCCXCVIIII*, § 6 (MGH AA 12 (1894), 405): 'Exaudi, Christe! Theoderico vitam! Dictum XXX.' The other acclamations were only repeated ten times.

relocated, above all to Constantinople. The gravitational pull of the eastern imperial capital, with its fund of honour and promise of greater security, undoubtedly played a part. But the leeching away of Rome's senators also reflected more deep-seated problems facing the old elite, problems which had begun to make an impact already in the last decades of imperial rule in the fifth century. A crucial factor was the erosion of the economic base of the ruling class. Among the important causes of this was the dismemberment of the western empire, which robbed many senators of their estates in the provinces.[140]

Such factors were exacerbated by the Byzantine reconquest initiated by Justinian in 536. Here was a cruel irony: senatorial émigrés at Constantinople had been among the leading advocates of the restoration of direct imperial rule to Italy. The attacks of the Lombards after 568 made matters worse, not least because they provoked from the Byzantine government an administrative solution that sidelined the senate. With Italy increasingly divided up into Byzantine frontier marches and Lombard duchies, the imperial administration prioritized the appointment of military commanders from within the ranks of its own army.[141] Any senators who had anticipated a restoration of their fortunes with the reintegration of Italy into the empire were to be bitterly disappointed, as the institution of the senate became increasingly irrelevant in a society dominated instead by military commanders and churchmen.[142] None of this is to say that the senate suddenly ceased to be an institution of any importance. It remained active – if only sporadically so – in the life of the city down to *c.* 600. Two successive late-sixth-century embassies sent from Rome to Constantinople to ask for assistance against the Lombards throw the changes into high relief: the first was apparently led only by a member of the senate; the second, however, involved clergy as well as senators, and our source tells us that the pope had been involved in their selection.[143] After the early seventh century, however, and even though individual members of the senatorial aristocracy can still occasionally be identified in our sources, the senate finally disappears from view as a corporate body.[144] In general, then, the senate, as an institution, was coming to play a less significant role in Roman affairs after Justinian's wars. This would inevitably have an impact on the groups involved in the interplay between ceremonial and authority in the

[140] Brown 1984: 21–37, esp. 25–30. [141] Bavant 1979: *passim.* [142] Humphries 2000: 538–44.

[143] Men. Prot., frr. 22 and 24 Blockley; cf. Bavant 1979: 47–9.

[144] For this late transformation of the senatorial aristocracy, seen in broader perspective, see Barnish 1988.

city of Rome; but it is important to see developments there in context, lest the changes appear too precipitous.

The emergence of papal ritual

At first sight, it might seem that the events of the sixth century, such as the waning fortunes of the senate, coincided with (and perhaps were a cause of) the establishment of papal power over the city. It was in this period, after all, that church buildings began to encroach on the city's ancient seats of secular power, with the construction of SS. Cosmas and Damian and S. Maria Antiqua in close proximity to Rome's ancient heart, the Forum Romanum.[145] As we have seen, however, the appearance of these buildings needs to be seen as part of a longer process whereby the church of Rome made its presence felt in the city. Evidence for the emergence of papal ceremonial similarly points to its evolution occurring over a considerable period. Already in the third century, we can catch glimpses of the formation of rituals for such episodes as the consecration of Rome's bishop.[146] Only with Constantine's legalization of Christianity did it become easier (or at least less dangerous!) for bishops, both in Rome and throughout the empire, to perform grand public rituals as an expression of their authority.[147] In neither case, architecturally or ceremonially, did Rome swiftly become a city dominated by the church.

At Rome, from the mid-fourth century onwards, we begin to get tantalizing references to processions marking important moments in particular pontificates, such as consecrations and funerals, and also when bishops, such as Liberius, who had been exiled from the city returned to Rome and were greeted by the faithful.[148] Precise topographical details that might allow us to see these and other types of processions in their urban context are lacking, however, before the fifth century.[149] A letter from the

[145] Again, Krautheimer stresses a teleological picture of change: 'In the urban fabric of the city, the interplay of secular government and ecclesiastical administration and the gradual replacement of the former by the latter are first reflected in the Church takeover of public buildings'; of these, the Forum 'was a showplace, then largely deprived of its former administrative and representative functions, and had thus fallen into disuse' (1980: 71 and 75 respectively).

[146] Eus., *HE* 6.43.8. This was part of a gradual consolidation of episcopal authority in the third century: Humphries 2006: 153–4.

[147] Dufraigne 1994: 268–84.

[148] On consecrations and the return of exiled popes, see Twyman 2002: 46–52. For an example of papal funeral ceremonial, see *LP* 67.2 (I, 315): the cortège of Sabinian in 606 leaves Rome by the gate at St John Lateran, proceeds to the Milvian Bridge, and concludes with his entombment at St Peter's.

[149] Cf. Lim 1999: 279, noting '[t]he continued absence (well into the 5th c.) of large-scale Christian events in the recognized public space of the city'.

urban prefect to the emperor Honorius records that in 418 Pope Boniface I was elected at the *titulus Marcelli* and was then conducted in procession to St Peter's.[150] Church buildings could be used for other displays of episcopal authority. Writings of the Manichaeans were burned before the doors of S. Maria Maggiore by Gelasius I (492–496) and before those of the Lateran by Symmachus (498–514), thereby demonstrating the popes as arbiters of orthodoxy and heresy.[151] Boniface II (530–532) sought to calm dissension in his congregation by burning, in front of the *confessio* of St Peter's, the document in which he sought to arrange for his designated successor to ascend to the Roman see.[152] In a related episode, Agapetus (535–536) had the anathemas previously secured by Boniface against his opponents burned 'in the middle of the church' (*in medio ecclesiae*).[153]

In their search for ceremonial means to assert their authority, it seems that the bishops of Rome looked to precedents from imperial practice. The burning of heretical writings and other documents seems to be an adaptation of a conventional display of authority deployed by emperors: Hadrian, Marcus Aurelius, and Aurelian had burned debtors' records in public, while Christian books had regularly been consigned to the flames during persecutions.[154] Processions too were probably inspired by secular models. In yet another of his more notorious passages, Ammianus Marcellinus excoriated Rome's bishops for their attachment to various worldly extravagances, including their riding around Rome in a carriage.[155] It is worth noting that the use of carriages was associated also with high imperial officials, as is reflected in a law of 386 and in the illustrated insignia of the praetorian prefects of Illyricum and Italy and the urban prefect of Rome in the *Notitia Dignitatum* of *c.* 400.[156]

The appropriation of secular models by the papacy in the development of their own ritual repertoire does not reflect a simple ecclesiastical ascendancy over ceremonial life in the city. Secular and clerical elites can be seen acting side by side for some considerable time. For example, when Boniface II (as described above) publicly burned documents concerning the papal succession in St Peter's, he did so in the presence of not only the clergy, but also the entire senate.[157] Other evidence points to a similar co-existence

150 *CA* 14.6. 151 *LP* 51.1 (1, 255), and 53.5 (1, 261). 152 *LP* 57.4 (1, 281).

153 *LP* 59.1 (1, 287). For the historical context, see above at n. 131.

154 Debtors' records: Dmitriev 2004: 571, with refs. For Christian books see (e.g.) Lact., *De Mort. Pers.* 12.1–5; references to this practice are common in sources for Diocletian's persecution initiated in 303, and indeed featured in his measures against the Manichaeans: see further Humphries forthcoming.

155 Amm. Marc. 27.3.14: 'procedantque uehiculis insidentes'. 156 Alföldi 1970: 109–10.

157 *LP* 57.4 (1, 281): 'praesentia omnium sacerdotum et cleri et senatus'.

between the needs of laity and clergy in Roman ceremonies. By the time we get a fully detailed account of Rome's stational liturgy in the eighth-century *Ordo Romanus* I, the laity are present, and are arranged, moreover, according to social rank: thus papal processions could be used to convey an impression of the structure of Christian society in the city and of the place within it occupied by secular as well as ecclesiastical elites.[158] Although we can postulate the origins of Rome's stational liturgy in the fourth or fifth century,[159] precise evidence is lacking for how the laity might have participated in it at that time. Nevertheless, the interweaving of Christian liturgical space with the demands of lay elites is apparent from various factors. We have seen how church buildings at Rome, not least St Peter's, were exploited by powerful members of the laity (emperors, kings, and senators) for displays of status by a variety of means (patronage, burial, and presence during the liturgy). Efforts to assert the prominence of the pope through ceremonial and ceremonial space were enmeshed, therefore, in circumstances whereby churches were also used by lay elites to emphasize their position in society.

The continuing relevance of the emperor

Such factors are a reminder that, however much the evidence from Rome might imply a 'rise of the papacy' or a transition 'from emperor to pope', we should resist the temptation to regard the popes as the only authority in the city by the second half of the sixth century.[160] This is an easy assumption to make, especially in light of Gregory I's letters, which show him involving himself in areas of administration (such as the provisioning of Rome and the upkeep of its buildings) that might otherwise seem to be the preserve of the secular government.[161] Part of the problem, however, is that we have little other evidence to provide a context against which to read Gregory's statements, with the consequent risk that they may distort our understanding of Roman (and Italian) society in the years around 600.[162] Of course, there can be no denying that the material resources of the

158 *Ordo Romanus Primus* 69, 75, ed. Andrieu 1948: 91–2; cf. Mathews 1962: 73–95, arguing that such arrangements are visible already in the planning of Roman churches in the fifth century.

159 Baldovin 1987: 143–66.

160 Again, the assumption underpins Krautheimer's analysis. Of the sixth century he remarks that '[t]he Church was the only *efficient* organization left to maintain the economic, social, and indeed the political fabric of Rome' (Krautheimer 1980: 70, emphasis added). Of Gregory the Great's pontificate, he states: 'The Church rather than the Byzantine state, *nominally still the legitimate government*, was responsible for providing for the urban population' (1980: 71, emphasis added).

161 Markus 1997: 112–24.

162 See n. 5 above.

church now constituted the most substantial financial patrimony in the city.[163] In spite of this, an examination of the (admittedly scattered and sparse) evidence for Rome suggests that the emperor, however remote he may have been physically, remained an important figure of authority in the city.

While inscriptions of fourth- and fifth-century emperors and the Ostrogothic kings (particularly Theoderic) are found in some numbers at Rome, by the time we reach the period after Justinian's reconquest, the numbers fall off sharply: that is surely an indication that changes were occurring in terms of the means through which authority was expressed – but it would be going too far, I think, to infer from it that Rome had become a papal city. Nevertheless, such texts as survive show a concern to display imperial authority in traditional form. In 565, Justinian's general in Italy, Narses, placed an inscription on a restored bridge along the Via Salaria just outside Rome. It celebrated the end of the Gothic Wars and the restoration of freedom to Rome and the whole of Italy, and honoured the emperor as 'forever triumphant'.[164] Four decades later, in 608, the Byzantine exarch of Italy, Smaragdus, renovated a column in the Forum Romanum. He gave the gilded statue that stood on top of it a face lift so that it resembled the ruling emperor Phocas (602–610) and constructed a new set of steps around its base. On the plinth, and (perhaps significantly) on the side facing the entrance to the senate house, he placed an inscription extolling Phocas' virtues and the restoration of peace and liberty in Italy.[165] There can be little doubt that, in shattered post-war Italy, the sentiments expressed in such inscriptions were effectively meaningless. In spite of this, they were still considered appropriate gestures by the imperial administration.

Even the transition to a Christian city involved the emperor, and it is important not to overlook this. The case of the conversion of ancient buildings into churches is a pertinent case, not least because many modern accounts treat it as emblematic of the demise of the ancient city and its institutions.[166] The conversion of the Pantheon into a church under Boniface IV (608–615) only proceeded once permission had been secured from Phocas.[167] Similarly, the removal of roof tiles by Honorius I (625–638) from a building that the *Liber Pontificalis* calls the 'templum

[163] Marazzi 2000: 37–8. [164] *CIL* 6.1199.

[165] *CIL* 6.1200. It might be as well not to make too much of the orientation of the inscription, since it was carved over the erasure of an earlier inscription: Giuliani and Verducchi 1987: 174–7, esp. 176.

[166] E.g. Brown 1984: 22, on the conversion of the curia: '[t]he fate of the Senate is *neatly reflected* in the physical fortunes of its meeting hall' (emphasis added).

[167] *LP* 69.1 (1, 317).

Romae', and their use for roofing St Peter's, required permission from Heraclius (610–641).[168] Pope Honorius was also responsible for the conversion of the senatorial curia into the church of S. Adriano. Here the *Liber Pontificalis* makes no mention of an imperial grant of permission (but then it also claims that Honorius 'built' (*fecit*) the church, rather than converted an existing building),[169] yet such a grant is possible given the rededication in Phocas' honour of the column in front of the curia only a few decades earlier. Imperial control over the physical fabric of Rome was demonstrated emphatically, if more negatively, during the visit there by Constans II in 663. He proceeded to remove a number of the city's bronze ornaments – including some from the former Pantheon – and send them off to Constantinople.[170]

It is important not to forget either that popes like Gregory the Great and Honorius I, so often associated with the watershed between antiquity and the middle ages, were treated effectively as imperial officials. Until the pontificate of Agatho (678–681), newly elected popes had to pay induction fees like other officers of the empire.[171] Imperial ratification of a papal election was required before the new pontiff could be installed until the time of Benedict II (684–685), with the result that the vacancies between pontificates often lasted months.[172] Even after that, confirmation was still required from the exarch at Ravenna.[173] It is surely no coincidence that, in the sixth and seventh centuries, several popes previously served as *apocrisarius*, a representative of the western church at the imperial court in Constantinople: already by the time of their election, therefore, these men will have been well known to the eastern emperor and his palatine officials.[174] Other aspects of the imperial administration of Italy demonstrated how the church was subservient to the emperor. For example, taxes on the lands of the Roman church were paid to the imperial fisc until the eastern emperor Constantine IV (668–685) abolished them.[175] Of course, relations between Constantinople and Rome did not always run smoothly. Justinian had had to strive hard to secure the compliance of Pope Vigilius (537–555) in the doctrinal dispute of the Three Chapters.[176] While popes certainly sought to maintain some measure of autonomy from the

[168] *LP* 72.2 (I, 323). The question of the identity of the 'templum Romae' is discussed by Duchesne (1886: I, 279 n. 3), who favours the basilica of Maxentius, against the natural assumption that the adjacent temple of Venus and Rome is meant.

[169] *LP* 72.6 (I, 324). [170] *LP* 78.3 (I, 343); Paul. Diac. *Hist. Lang.* 5.11. [171] *LP* 81.2 (I, 354).

[172] *LP* 83.3 (I, 363). Length of vacancies: Llewellyn 1986: 43 n. 2.

[173] Implicit in *LP* 85.2 (I, 368) and 86.3 (I, 372). [174] Llewellyn 1986: 42–3. [175] *LP* 84.2 (I, 366).

[176] Sotinel 1992: 457–63. For developments in the late sixth century, see Markus 1997: 83–96. The perspective of Constantinople is examined in Magi 1972.

emperor, especially in doctrinal affairs,[177] emperors nevertheless assumed that they were the superior authority until well into the seventh century. Pope Martin I (649–653) was arrested by the exarch Theodore, indicted on charges of subverting the authority of the Constantinopolitan church, and sent into exile in the Crimea; a similar effort was made to dislodge Sergius I (687–701), but the attempt failed.[178]

The superior authority and enduring relevance of the emperor was asserted above all during Constans II's visit to Rome in July 663. He attended stational liturgies at St Peter's (where he also presented a *pallium* of golden cloth) and bathed and dined with Pope Vitalian (657–671) at the Lateran. Such actions should not be misconstrued as reflecting the emperor honouring the pope. When Vitalian acted as host, he did so as a dutiful imperial servant. He had done so already at the beginning of Constans' visit, when the pope and clergy (and probably also a delegation of the Roman laity) went out to greet the emperor at the sixth milestone outside the city. Here we have the last *adventus* of a Roman emperor – a successor of Constantine, Theodosius, and the rest – to the old imperial capital.[179] Throughout his visit, moreover, Constans resided in the imperial palace on the Palatine hill; indeed, an official charged with the care of the palace is attested as late as 687.[180]

PHOCAS AT THE LATERAN

It is in this context of the emperor's enduring relevance that the events of 25 April 603 make sense. It is likely that the reception of imperial icons at the Lateran was the occasion for a liturgical celebration: that was by now the pattern for imperial ceremonies at Constantinople.[181] But it is important not to assume that it was an event of purely ecclesiastical rather than political significance: the icons were received in a church, but they were also acclaimed; later they were installed in another church, that of St Caesarius, but it was located on the Palatine, within the precincts of

177 Sotinel 2005 provides excellent analysis.

178 *LP* 76.8 (I, 338), on Martin; 86.7–9 (I, 373–4), on Sergius.

179 The presence of the people is noted in Paul. Diac., *Hist. Lang.* 5.11: 'Cui [*sc.* Constans II] sexto miliario Vitalianus papa cum sacerdotibus et Romano populo'; *LP* 78.3 (I, 343) records the reception committee as comprising 'Apostolicus cum clero suo'. For Constans' impact generally, see Llewellyn 1976a.

180 The tombstone of 'Plato v[ir] ill[ustris] cura palatii urbis Romae', father of the later pope John VII: text in Duchesne 1886: I, 386 n. I.

181 McCormick 1986: 69–78; for the fully developed Byzantine imperial liturgy, see Dagron 2003: 84–124.

the old imperial residence.[182] Thus the proceedings on that spring day represent the confluence of two trends. First, there was the maintenance of tradition, reflected in the role of the senate, the act of acclamation of the imperial images as representing the presence of the emperor and his wife, and the installation of the portraits in the imperial palace. That such traditions remained strong is suggested also by Smaragdus' renovation of the column in the Forum in honour of Phocas: its location in front of the curia showed that the old *loci* of power could still be exploited and considered relevant.

Secondly, the ceremony in the Lateran indicates how Rome was changing. The presence of Gregory, who directed the ceremonies on the day, and his clergy, together with the location of the reception in a church, are indicative of the transformations of power that were occurring in the city. Where once the senate had been the primary representative body in the city's dealings with its imperial masters, this was a role in which bishop and clergy had become important participants. None of this means, however, that the pope, even if he was the liturgical impresario on the day, was now in total control of Rome. It is crucial to see the events of 603 in terms of their wider political context. Phocas had seized power in a brutal coup at Constantinople the previous year. It was important for him both to assert his authority over outlying regions of the empire, and to have local elites there make ostentatious signs of their allegiance to him. That was what Gregory, the clergy, and the senate were doing in 603: as the elite of the city of Rome, they were signalling their submission to the new regime. The ceremony on 25 April 603 was necessary, above all for the emperor and the assertion of his authority. In other parts of the west, however, resentment against the new ruler seethed, and it was to be from Africa that Heraclius would set sail for Constantinople to depose Phocas in 610.[183]

It is important to keep in mind a fine balance between continuity and change. Throughout this chapter, I have argued that the teleological view of ancient Rome as doomed in the time of Gregory the Great, if not that of Constantine, is a distortion, which risks foreshortening our vision of the resilience of the city's ancient institutions through late antiquity. I would be guilty of gross distortion also if I were to insist, on the basis of what I have said, that Rome experienced *no* change at all in the centuries between Constantine and Gregory, or if I maintained that Rome's traditional institutions were as vital in the early seventh century as they had been in the early fourth. This, plainly, was not the case. The senate did, after all,

[182] See n. 1 above. [183] For mounting discontent against Phocas, see Kaegi 2003: 37–45.

disappear as a functioning assembly shortly after their grand day out with Gregory and the clergy in 603, and no senators are recorded as having been in attendance at Constans II's reception sixty years later. Direct imperial control over Rome was also changing: emperors living at Constantinople could not hope to assert their authority over Rome in quite the same way as emperors who visited, and even resided, in the old capital. By the seventh century too, much of Rome's ancient fabric was becoming dilapidated. In stark contrast to these trends, meanwhile, the material resources and local authority of the church were increasing.

What I hope to have shown is that the transformations of Rome in late antiquity were a complex process that cannot simply be understood as the result of an inevitable shift in authority from imperial institutions to ecclesiastical ones. On a number of occasions – not least on 25 April 603 – we have seen the two operating side by side. The reasons for Rome's metamorphosis were more complex and deep rooted, and were worked out gradually over centuries. That Rome *did* become a papal city rather than an imperial one is not in doubt, but the reasons for it cannot be explained by appealing to the foundation of Constantinople, seeing that as naturally leading to an imperial abandonment of Rome, and regarding the papacy's assumption of authority over the city as inevitable. From the fourth century through to the seventh, the emperor continued to exercise influence over the city. Only in the later seventh century and the eighth did Rome throw off imperial hegemony, but this was for reasons particular to the time and place.[184] It is, perhaps, not too extreme to suggest that if the popes did ultimately become Rome's undisputed leaders, they were able to do so in no small measure because, as the city's traditional administrative institutions (such as the senate) decayed, the emperors increasingly invested responsibility for the city's governance in its bishop and clergy.[185]

184 Llewellyn 1986.

185 I have incurred many debts in writing this chapter. Kate Cooper and Julia Hillner have been exemplary editors, being both encouraging and critical, while other contributors to the volume and the two anonymous readers for the Press have suggested numerous useful improvements. Earlier versions have benefited from having been read to perceptive audiences at Birmingham and Maynooth. Without generous input, in various ways, from Robert Coates-Stephens, Marios Costambeys, Carlos Machado and Claire Sotinel, the final product would have been much poorer.

2

Memory and authority in sixth-century Rome: the Liber Pontificalis *and the* Collectio Avellana

Kate Blair-Dixon

> Then Damasus sent in the gladiators, the charioteers, the gravediggers, and all the clergy armed to the teeth with swords and clubs to besiege the basilica. And they joined battle in earnest . . . From all sides the Damasans broke into the basilica and killed a hundred and sixty people, women as well as men. They wounded several more, many of whom were to die later. On the Damasan side, there was not one casualty.[1]

Historians of late Roman Christianity, especially those of a Gibbonian stripe, take delight from this extraordinary account of the no-holds-barred contest for the papacy in 366, and the resulting massacre in the Liberian basilica of the supporters of Ursinus.[2] But they rarely take heed of their source. The text stands at the opening of the *Collectio Avellana*, a mid-sixth-century collection of nearly 250 documents relating to the bishopric of Rome in the fourth, fifth, and sixth centuries. While its account of Damasus is frequently cited, the *Collectio* as a whole is something of a backwater, in both medieval and modern scholarship.[3] This obscurity is surely undeserved, and it obtains only because we have asked the wrong question. As an early medieval canon law collection the *Collectio* is indeed a virtual dead end – far less successful and important than the near-contemporary collection of Dionysius Exiguus. As a dossier presenting a view of papal history, however, the *Collectio* is a striking witness in itself, and an invaluable supplement to the familiar testimony of the *Liber Pontificalis*. Our dependence on the *Liber Pontificalis* as a narrative source for papal history in this period is worrying at best. No less heavily do we

[1] *CA* 1 (CSEL 35.3). Cf. Amm. Marc. 27.3, where the total casualties are reckoned at 137. My thanks to the editors and to fellow contributors for help, advice, and editorial input that went beyond the call of duty. In particular, Kate Cooper and Conrad Leyser each offered substantive suggestions at a number of stages in the development of the piece. Thanks also to Claire Sotinel for her advice and generosity in the final stages. Responsibility for any errors remains my own.

[2] See further McLynn 1992. [3] See Kéry 1999: 37–8 for a summary bibliography.

rely on the *Collectio Avellana* for our account of the papal schisms of the mid-fourth and early fifth centuries, but scholars have tended not to consider closely how the *Collectio*'s perspective may colour the evidence it offers. Here, we will suggest that if the *Liber Pontificalis* and the *Collectio Avellana* are read in light of each other, then the contrasting strategies of each text with regard to the problem of authority and memory will allow us to correct, at least in part, for their often ignored distortions.

The distinctive profile of the *Collectio Avellana* – and the most obvious point of contrast with the account of the papacy proposed by the *Liber Pontificalis* – is nowhere clearer than in the depiction of Pope Damasus. The *Liber Pontificalis*, we may recall, opens with a (fictive) request from none other than Damasus to Jerome, to compile a record of papal history.

> My respectful request is that you may oblige me with an orderly account of the history enacted in your see from the reign of the apostle Peter down to your own time, so that in humility I may learn which of the bishops of your see deserved the crown of martyrdom, and which of them is reckoned to have transgressed against the canons of the apostles.[4]

The *Liber Pontificalis* celebrates Damasus as the faithful guardian of Petrine tradition. In contrast, the *Collectio Avellana* seeks to heap infamy on Damasus' head, recording his ruthless ambition and his treacherous complicity with the Arian emperor, Constantius. It would be going too far to claim that the *Collectio* represents a polemical response to the *Liber Pontificalis*. We know too little about the composition and audience of both texts to be able to make claims about direct contact between the two. What we can say is that their authors and readers were dealing with the same set of problems. In the era of the Arian king Theoderic and of Justinian's wars of reconquest, questions of loyalty and betrayal came to a head for the bishop of Rome. For the Roman church at this juncture, the representation of Damasus and the history of papal/imperial relations were far from academic issues.

THE UNITY OF THE *COLLECTIO AVELLANA*

Research interest in the *Collectio Avellana* (hereafter *CA*) peaked briefly in the late nineteenth century, with the discovery of a new manuscript copy of the text. It had been known as 'the Avellana' since the pioneering work in the eighteenth century of the Ballerini brothers, who edited the text

[4] *LP* I, 117, trans. Davis 1989: 1.

using primarily an eleventh-century copy from the library of St Romuald's foundation at Fonte Avellana (Vat. Reg. Lat. 4961). In the 1880s, however, Paul Ewald identified another, slightly earlier copy (Vat. Reg. Lat. 3787, from Nonantola), from which, he suspected, the Avellana copy was derived. Ewald's work was brought to fruition in the following decade by Otto Günther, who re-edited the text and analysed its composition with a thoroughness that remains unsurpassed.[5]

Günther confirmed the traditional dating of *CA* to the mid-sixth century.[6] The collection as transmitted in the two eleventh-century manuscripts was, in his view, compiled shortly after the date of its last dated letter, from Pope Vigilius (537–555) to the emperor Justinian in 553. This letter, number 83, along with letters of bishops Agapetus and John II (Letters 82–93), is out of chronological place in the collection – a feature to which we return below – but it all the same established a clear *terminus post quem* for *CA*. The only certain *terminus ante quem* is provided by the two eleventh-century manuscripts: in the intervening centuries between the sixth and the eleventh, the collection may of course have been reworked. Our only point of reference here is the use of some *CA* material in other collections, such as the ninth-century *Collectio Berolinensis* in particular, to which Günther devotes due attention. Further consideration of the early medieval transmission and use of *CA* and its reception in the eleventh century is beyond the scope of this study. Suffice it to note that there is reason to revisit this topic; just as *CA*'s compiler in Ostrogothic/Byzantine Italy may have found reason to recall earlier tensions between pope and emperor, so also may *CA*'s eleventh-century readers in the era of Gregory VII and Henry IV.

Our discussion here is focused on the composition of *CA* in the sixth century, and on the question of the unity of the collection. In general, scholars have regarded *CA* as a somewhat random assemblage of papal correspondence. Frederick Maassen, the late nineteenth-century authority on Latin canonical collections, regarded *CA* as a miscellany in six separate parts, separated according to the time and topic of the papal letters. Günther, however, divided the collection into five sections, and, more importantly, saw signs of a controlling editorial hand. Günther's five sections are as follows:[7]

[5] Günther 1895 and 1896. [6] Günther 1896: 2.
[7] Günther 1895: iii; also Günther 1896: 2–66, a reworking of the six sections in Maassen 1877. This order follows the eleventh-century Vat. Reg. Lat. 3787. Early modern copies placed the Greek letters 71–78, 140, and 237 in different locations.

1 Letters 1–40, comprising material on the Ursinian schism (Letters 1–13), the schism between Boniface and Eulalius in 418–419 (Letters 14–37), and three letters (38–40) from Roman emperors (Honorius in 404, and Maximus in 385–387).
2 Letters 41–50 regarding the church in Africa and its condemnation of Pelagius under popes Innocent (401–417) and Zosimus (417–418).
3 Letters 51–55 from Pope Leo I (440–461), otherwise unattested, all from 460.
4 Letters 56–104 regarding the Acacian schism (470–519) from popes Simplicius (468–483), Felix (483–492), Gelasius (492–496), and Symmachus (498–514). Letters 82 to 93, featuring Justinian and the bishops of Rome, date from 536 to 553, so interrupting the collection's chronological sequence.
5 Letters 105–243, from Pope Hormisdas (514–523) between 514 and 521. These letters comprise over half of the collection.[8]

In Günther's view, *CA* was more than an accidental miscellany: it was a careful collection of materials made by a learned clerical archivist in 550s Rome.[9] He suggested that there were at least two layers to be discerned in the composition of *CA*. First came the opening section (Letters 1–40), with its unique witness to the schisms of Ursinus and Boniface. Günther suggested that this was compiled from the archives of the prefect of the city of Rome, and existed as a collection prior to its incorporation in *CA*.[10] Then, according to Günther, the enthusiastic archivist took this collection as the starting-point for the addition of the other documents which make *CA*. At various points across the whole collection Günther discerned a coherent editorial policy of organization and comment. In the section containing Hormisdas' letters, for example, the oldest copy transmits a note that the *gesta* of a Bishop Abundantius of Traianopolis *habemus in scrinio*.[11] From this and similar observations elsewhere in the collection, it appears that the compiler was taking care not to duplicate copies of texts to which he already had access. The compiler evidently regarded *CA* as a

[8] Added to the end of the *Collectio* was a letter from Epiphanius of Constantia to Bishop Dioscorus of Tyre, in which he explains seven different types of precious stone, ranging from lapis to amethyst. Günther (1895: iii) asserts that this letter probably circulated on its own and was later added to the collection. Amory (1997: 112 n. 18, 130 n. 131) mentions that Constantia is in the province of Scythia. A number of the letters in *CA* are concerned with Scythian monks. The letter was cited by Facundius of Hermiane in *Pro defensione trium capit.* IV, 2 (*PL* 67.617–18).

[9] Günther 1896: 66: 'Die Avellana ist vielmehr nichts als eine Materialsammlung, die wir dem Sammeleifer eines Gelehrtes verdanken, der um die Zeit des Vigilius in Rom lebte und aus diesen und anderen Quellen die Sammlung zusammenschrieb, die uns heute vorliegt.'

[10] Günther 1896: 3–19. [11] Günther 1896: 63 (see also 23).

vehicle for conveniently bringing together material which the existing archives did not contain.

While Günther saw more of a guiding hand at work in *CA* than had other scholars, he nonetheless did not hesitate to distinguish *CA* from contemporary canonical collections, and above all the work of Dionysius Exiguus, the Scythian monk who gathered and translated the accounts of the Greek councils in a form that would become definitive for the Latin west.[12] *CA* does overlap once with the Dionysian collection. (The document the collections have in common is Letter 37 in *CA*. This letter records Honorius' intervention in the schism of 418 in favour of Boniface.) Günther dismissed the possibility of a substantial connection between *CA* and the *Dionysiana*.[13] The compiler was a private scholar, making a collection of raw material. Dionysius, by contrast, worked with papal sponsorship over two decades in compiling three editions of his collection.

Günther's analysis of *CA* as a whole has not been substantially challenged. Scholars have tended to focus on the first section (Letters 1–40), confirming Günther's suggestion that this existed prior to the compilation of *CA*. Thus in his 1993 study of the Laurentian schism, Erich Wirbelauer argued that the pronounced interest in schism of this section of *CA* finds a *Sitz im Leben* in the bitter dispute between the supporters of Symmachus and those of Laurentius in early sixth-century Rome.[14] Wirbelauer points to a revealing aside from one of the Symmachan party, Ennodius of Pavia, who remarks that there should be no talk of the 'times of Boniface and Eulalius'.[15] *CA*, as we have seen, includes a thorough dossier on Boniface and Eulalius, and this prompts Wirbelauer to suggest that the opening section of *CA* was a Laurentian compilation. Developing Günther's suggestion that the compiler of this section had access to municipal archives, Wirbelauer further suggests that the compiler of this dossier may have operated under Anicius Faustus Junior Albus, prefect of the city for the second time in 502/3, and a supporter of Laurentius.

The collection as a whole, however, Wirbelauer regards as a series of disparate elements. While he observes that sections of *CA*, such as the material on the Acacian schism, could also have served a Laurentian agenda, he sees no overall logic to the bringing together of the sections in a manuscript after 553. Where Günther compared *CA* to the Dionysian collection,

[12] See Wirbelauer 1993: 129–34 and Kéry 1999: 9–13 for further references.

[13] Günther 1896: 66. Wirbelauer (1993: 138) sees the absence of overlap as evidence of a degree of collaboration between the Dionysian and the Avellana collectors.

[14] Wirbelauer 1993: 134–8. [15] Ennodius, *Libellus pro synodo* (MGH AA VII, 63).

Wirbelauer compares it to the much more systematic *Collectio Italica* (also known as the *Sanblasiana*).[16] This was a full-blown Symmachan production, containing a number of *gesta*, or historical narratives concerning Roman bishops from the fourth to the early sixth century, in particular the fictional accounts of bishops Silvester, Liberius and Damasus, and Xystus, known as the Symmachan apocrypha. These narratives were *roman-à-clef* propaganda for the Symmachan side of the Laurentian schism. Now, as Wirbelauer notes, *CA* does share one document with the *Italica*. This is the letter of Honorius (*CA* Letter 37), shared also with the Dionysian collection.[17] In sum, however, although a similar theme of schism can be traced in both collections, *CA* does not include any material from the Symmachan apocrypha. The interest of CA, according to Wirbelauer, is that its first section is a precious record of 'loser's history'.[18] But he has nothing to add to Günther's analysis of the transmission of this record – the incorporation of the opening section into the larger collection that is *CA*.

Our approach looks to return to Günther's insight into *CA* as a unified composition of the 550s. Its sections may appear dissociated, but this should not preclude examination of the whole collection as a deliberate assemblage. If we turn to what, according to Wirbelauer, are the 'non-Laurentian' sections, we see something of the ambition of our compiler. *CA* holds correspondence between Roman bishops in a number of sees across a vast geographical area. Some letters were to or from bishops of Africa or Antioch, while others are known to have circulated in Gaul (Letters 41–50). A group of letters between bishops in the 530s and 540s were sent to Constantinople. Patrick Amory observes in passing that the Mediterranean scope of *CA* amounted in fact to an editorial policy: one might have expected to see in *CA* a concern for comprehensive coverage, to include letters from popes Felix (526–530) and Boniface (530–532); instead, they are omitted because, if we follow Amory, 'they did not address any broader issues'.[19]

To appreciate the unifying purpose of *CA*, we should compare it not with other canonical collections, but with the *Liber Pontificalis* (hereafter *LP*), to which we now turn. The compiler of *CA* seems to have used a similar source base as the author of *LP*, but it presented a divergent history of the Roman bishops. The introductory letter in *CA* condemning

[16] Wirbelauer 1993: 122–8; see further Kéry 1999: 29–31 and *LP* I, cxxxiv–cxli.

[17] This is the only letter that appears in the *Dionysiana*, the *Italica*, and the *Avellana*. See *LP* I, cxxxiv–v for Duchesne's comment on its use by the compiler of *LP*.

[18] Wirbelauer 1993: 138. [19] Amory 1997: 221.

Damasus was only one of a series of documents which contrasts with the image of the papacy projected by *LP*. As we now see, referring to the letters from Justinian's reign, and the figure of Vigilius in particular, it is possible to suggest that the author of *CA* deliberately chose or excluded letters which fit with the overarching themes of his collection. No less than *LP*, *CA* participated in the effort of self-definition of the papacy in the mid-sixth century.

THE PAST AND THE PRESENT IN THE *LIBER PONTIFICALIS* AND THE *COLLECTIO AVELLANA*

The most important contribution toward understanding *LP* is still Duchesne's critical edition and discussion.[20] Duchesne's chronology for the composition is widely deferred to, but rarely set out in its full complexity.[21] His basic contention is that there were two editions of *LP*, each of which was supplemented by continuators. Duchesne's reconstruction is as follows:

1 The first edition, now lost (although reflected in two extant epitomes), was composed shortly after 530 following the death of Pope Felix IV (526–530).[22]

2 This edition was then continued by a contemporary who wrote the lives of Boniface II, John II, and Agapetus and the first half of the entry for Silverius (536–537).

3 The second edition, the basis for the *LP* that has come down to us, involved an overhaul of the material in the first. It was composed under Pope Vigilius (537–555).[23] Its author, suggested Duchesne, may have been the continuator of the first edition; or the writer who sewed a second half (a *Passio Silverii*) onto the incomplete entry for Silverius. (The join between the two halves remains obvious, however, not least because the second Silverius author is as sympathetic to his subject as the first author is hostile.)[24]

4 Then came a break of some three or four decades before continuators of the second edition got to work.[25] Duchesne suggested the 580s as the

[20] See the summary in Vogel 1975.

[21] Cf. the summary in Davis 1989: xxxvii. Noble (1985) puts the case for an earlier date of 518–520.

[22] *LP* I, xxii–lxviii, esp. xlii–xliii. [23] *LP* I, xxxviii–xl, ccxxx–ccxxxi.

[24] *LP* I, ccxxx. On the complexities of the Silverius entry, see further Hildebrand 1922, Bertolini 1924, and Sotinel 2000a.

[25] *LP* I, ccxxxi–ccxxxiii.

moment at which the life of Vigilius was composed, along with the lives down to Pope Benedict (575–579).

5 In the final phase, begun under Pope Honorius onwards (625–638), the *LP* continuators filled in the notices since Benedict, and began the practice of completing the notices for each pope immediately after his death, down until the late ninth century.

LP was written, re-edited, and continued with an interest in schisms. Duchesne traces the origins of *LP* back to the Laurentian schism (502–514). The first edition's notice for Symmachus seems to have been written as a response to the so-called *Laurentian Fragment*, a *Vita* of Laurentius, Symmachus' rival. This text was the last life from an earlier collection of papal *vitae* (and it is the only surviving document from this collection). According to Duchesne, the *Laurentian Fragment* was probably written after Symmachus' death in 514.[26] Its author clearly supported Laurentius; the *Vita* for Symmachus in *LP*, however, reflects support for the Symmachan party. Likewise, some of the other biographies, particularly in the late fifth and early sixth centuries, seem to be tied to the schismatic biases of the author.[27] *LP*'s dependence on a number of pro-Symmachan texts, including the *Symmachan Apocrypha*,[28] further indicates that the author was interested in presenting a version of the schisms that supported his own sympathies.[29]

The *CA* compiler was no less interested in schisms. In fact, comparison of *LP* with *CA* shows that there was by no means unanimity regarding papal history in clerical circles in Rome. Two striking examples demonstrate the divergence between the *LP* and *CA* perspectives. Let us look first at their treatments of the fifth-century schism between Boniface and Eulalius, both ordained on the same day in 418. *LP*'s author states that the emperors Honorius and Valentinian III made a ruling in Boniface's favour, but it omits to mention that Honorius intervened to remove Boniface and Eulalius for a time, and favoured a third party, Achilleus. *LP* also overlooks other information in the imperial decree. The decree regretfully accepts Boniface as bishop, and at the same time states that no bishop of contested election shall ever hold the See after Boniface. The author of *LP* certainly knew the imperial decree, but the information he extracted from it was pithy and out of context. The *CA* compiler, however,

[26] *LP* I, xxx–xxxvii.

[27] The author of the second edition, for example, shows support for Dioscorus, the opponent of Boniface II in 530, as emphasized by Davis 1989: xiv–xvi.

[28] *LP* I, cxx–cxxvii and cxxxiii–cxli.

[29] On this technique with other Laurentian sources see Fowden 1994.

not only provided the imperial decree to Boniface, mentioned in *LP*, but also chose to assemble the letters surrounding the controversy, thus adding context to *LP*'s description of Boniface's papacy.[30]

Secondly, we may note a contrast in our texts' descriptions of the Acacian schism which divided Rome and Constantinople from the 470s. The author of *LP* states that Pope Simplicius never sent a reply to the patriarch Acacius' letters. *CA*, however, provides thirteen letters of reply from Simplicius to Acacius and Zeno concerning the Acacian schism. Whether the *CA* compiler knew this reference in *LP* cannot be certain, but the information contained within clearly contradicts the *LP Vita*. In these important instances, then, *CA* attempts to present a more complete picture of the papacy, which at times directly contradicts the history recorded in *LP*.[31]

The key area of contrast between *CA* and *LP* concerns not the past, but what would have been contemporary history, and in particular the controversial papacy of Vigilius.[32] If we abide by Duchesne's chronology, we can see that *LP*'s testimony for Vigilius is a complicated one. Vigilius features in the notices for Boniface and Silverius, both composed (in stages) in the mid-sixth century, but his own *LP* entry is not written until the 580s. With this caution stated, we may review the *LP*'s account, which runs as follows. In 536, the Goths invaded Rome, and Pope Agapetus took refuge in Constantinople. There he died, and Silverius assumed the see. Vigilius meanwhile made a deal with the empress Theodora, a strict monophysite and supporter of the deposed bishop Anthimus. He agreed to restore Anthimus in Constantinople if she helped him to take the see of Rome. Forthwith, Theodora commissioned Belisarius and Vigilius to travel to Rome and take Silverius into custody, thus opening the way for Vigilius' ascension. Thus far, Vigilius as represented in what Duchesne called the *LP*'s *Passio Silverii*. The *Vita* of Vigilius then records that once he had ascended to the bishopric, he sent a letter to Theodora rescinding his initial offer. On account of his position as bishop he was duty bound to uphold the orthodox faith. Shortly thereafter, Theodora and Justinian kidnapped Vigilius and brought him to Constantinople.[33] Of the dispute between Justinian and Vigilius over the Three Chapters, where Vigilius seems to have tried to defy the emperor, *LP* has nothing to say.

[30] *LP* I, 227–8; *CA* 14–37 (CSEL 35.59–85). [31] *LP* I, 249; *CA* 56–69 (CSEL 35.124–55).

[32] See Sotinel 1992 and 2000b.

[33] For detailed discussion of the secular and theological politics involved in these events, see Amory 1997: 221–7 and Gray 1979: 344ff.

The politics of these years and the figure of Vigilius appear different in *CA*. We must refer in particular to the section comprising Letters 82–93, dropped into the letters concerning the Acacian schism. These letters may provide the greatest clues to the overarching theme of *CA*, its relationship to *LP*, and its argument for papal history.

CA 82 Agapetus to Justinian, 18 March 536
CA 83 Vigilius to Justinian, 14 May 553, the *Constitutum de tribus capitulis*
CA 84 John II to Justinian,[34] 25 May 534
CA 85 Reparatus of Carthage to John, May 535
CA 86 Agapetus to Reparatus, 9 September 535
CA 87 Agapetus to Reparatus, 9 September 535
CA 88 Agapetus to Justinian, 15 October 535
CA 89 Justinian to Agapetus, 16 March 536
CA 90 Menas of Constantinople to Agapetus, 16 March 536
CA 91 Agapetus to Justinian, 18 March 536
CA 92 Vigilius to Justinian, 17 September 540
CA 93 Vigilius to Menas, 17 September 540

The letters from bishops John II (533–535), Agapetus, and Vigilius, during the reign of Justinian, exhibit a concern for Rome's theological opposition to monophysitism and the concern aroused by Justinian's efforts to look for compromise with the monophysite position.[35] Pope John II's letter to Justinian, number 84, for example, stresses Justinian's willingness to subject Constantinople to Rome, and implies Rome's interest in establishing a view of the imperial throne as subjected to the bishop of Rome. John's reply maintains the Roman bishop's concern about imperial intervention into ecclesiastical affairs.[36] The main concern of this section is Justinian's subordination to Agapetus, and the bishop's intervention into Constantinopolitan affairs. Letter 89, for example, anathematizes the monophysites, who were promptly exiled from the city, and decrees that a confession of Chalcedonian theology is required. It was followed by Justinian's imperial decree. Letter 91, on the other hand, shows some tension between the emperor and the west. Agapetus suggests in this letter that secular rulers should not involve themselves in theological concerns.[37]

[34] With insertions of other letters between John and Justinian.
[35] For a brief overview, see for example Frend 1984: 841–2.
[36] Note that John here in fact conceded to Justinian's decree of 533, accepting the Theopaschite formula proposed a decade before by the Scythian monks, but rejected by Pope Hormisdas. See Amory 1997: 222 and Gray 1979: 65.
[37] See Chastagnol 1960: 382–5; also Amory 1997: 226ff.

But by far the most important of the letters in this section of *CA* is number 83, the *Constitutum* Pope Vigilius wrote in May 553 condeming Justinian's decree on the Three Chapters.[38] Justinian had convoked the second Council of Constantinople, in which the eastern patriarchs met to reaffirm the decisions of Chalcedon, while anathematizing the Antiochene, anti-Cyrillian writers Theodore of Mopsuesta, Ibas of Edessa, and Theoderet. Vigilius, who had once conceded to Justinian on this matter, refused to attend the council, and out of frustration with his torn position between the western bishops and the emperor, the Roman bishop set forth a series of canons criticizing Justinian's anathematization of the Three Chapters. He was subsequently forced to accept the condemnation. *CA*, then, presents Vigilius in what, as far as Latin audiences were concerned, was his best light. The compiler could have chosen either of two other letters by Vigilius to the emperor: either Vigilius' acceptance of Justinian's edict against the Three Chapters in 544 which circulated in 548 as the *Judicatum*, or his official acceptance of the condemnation. Instead, the compiler of *CA* inserted a strong critique of the emperor's entrance into church affairs and Vigilius' concern for the precedents set forth in earlier councils. It seems that the compiler deliberately overlooked the two documents that the bishops of Illyricum, northern Italy, and Africa so vehemently rejected.

CA then gives us a contemporary picture of Vigilius, with which we may compare *LP*'s later version. Rather than presenting him as the emperor's pawn, though he very well may have been, *CA* provides only three letters, all of which suggest his concern for Roman primacy. Letters 91 and 92 seem to be those alluded to in *LP*, in which Vigilius upheld the orthodoxy of Rome, and stuck strongly to the precedent set by Agapetus. The former letter to Justinian reaffirms the four councils and his own orthodoxy. At nearly the same time, Vigilius also sent the latter letter to Menas, confirming him as bishop of the see of Constantinople and acknowledging his orthodoxy. The only other letter contained in the collection is the *Institutum*, or critique of Justinian's decisions at the Council of Constantinople. The compiler's preservation of Vigilius' letter that critiques Justinian's theology, and its placement at the beginning of an entire section on the Roman bishops under Justinianic reign, functions to increase the moral standing of Bishop Vigilius, and to strengthen further the *CA*'s overarching theme of Rome's primacy. These bishops are deliberately depicted positively, and as actors

[38] See Sotinel 1992 and 2000b for a judicious account (and further references). Chazelle and Cubitt (forthcoming) will set the study of the little-understood phenomenon of the Three Chapters on a new footing.

independent of imperial intervention. All the letters of Vigilius, as with those of Agapetus and John II, portray the bishop as a keeper of the orthodox faith and defender to Roman primacy, while eliminating any suggestion that the bishop was politically manipulative, as he appears in *LP*.

LP and *CA* were agreed on presenting papacy in the best-possible light, but they differed widely in how to go about this. *LP* authors, it should be remembered, differed among themselves. The first edition, now lost, is reflected in two extant epitomes, the Felician and the Cononian. The Felician document records years and durations of the bishops' tenure of office and provided minimal historical details of bishops up until Felix IV in 530. This version was critical of the senate.[39] The Cononian author places more emphasis on the details of patronage, dedications of basilicas, and the Roman *tituli*, mentioning very specific numbers of donations until just after 530. To this scenario of discussion should be added the reinterpretation of the lives and deeds of the bishops of Rome offered by *CA*.

THE FIGURE OF DAMASUS

We may return now to the figure of Damasus with whom we began. The negative portrayal of Bishop Damasus is striking in the *Collectio Avellana*, because it is so condemning of a bishop whom other literature presents in quite a positive light. Damasus had become an iconic figure, remembered particularly for his remarkable collection of inscriptions documenting Rome's Christian history in inscriptions.[40] He was believed to be a man elected by his people, a supporter for the poor, and an immensely important bishop for subsequent development of the see of Rome.

Not so in *CA*. The first two items of *CA* stand out as being particularly polemical and perhaps of tendentious reliability for a history of the events they record. The anti-Damasan introductory letter of the collection, the *Praefatio*, may reflect the issues surrounding the compiler and a rhetoric of schism more closely associated with the time of the collection, rather than a true history of the events.[41] The *Praefatio* is a hostile letter from a pro-Ursinian cohort in Rome that gives a narrative of the conflicts between Liberius and Constantius, Felix's takeover of the see, and Damasus' election. This item is headed *Quae gesta sunt inter Liberium et Felicem episcopos*,

[39] Llewellyn 1976b. [40] See Fontaine 1981 and 1986.

[41] This letter is unusual in this collection not only as a pro-schismatic text, but also for its form as a narrative recording the events of a bishop's tenure. Except for items 99, the *Gesta de nomine Acaci*, and 103, the *Gesta de absolutione Miseni*, all other contents of *CA* are letters or canons.

but is more commonly referred to as the *Praefatio* or *Gesta Liberii*.[42] The compiler's choice of this letter at the beginning of the compilation provides a further clue to the role of *CA* as a whole and to the sixth-century recollection of Damasan politics.

The *Praefatio* presents the reader with a number of anachronisms that lead one to question its date and reliability. It is possible that the text may have been written later or may include interpolations from the fifth or sixth century. Archaeological evidence reveals that at least two of the buildings mentioned in this document had yet to be built, or at least formally recognized under the names given here. The first of these references is the mention of Damasus' election *in lucinis*, identified by many as S. Lorenzo in Lucina, and the second is the Basilica Liberii.

The *Praefatio* clearly states that Damasus was elected bishop by his supporters *in lucinis* in 366 on the same day as his competitor Ursinus was elected at *titulus Iulii*.[43] Using the text as the authoritative document, scholars have argued that *in lucinis* must be the *titulus Lucinae* mentioned in the synod list of 499,[44] which in turn must be the basilica of S. Lorenzo in Lucina.[45] The basilica is set in the north-west of the city near to the *horologium Augusti* and other important Roman monuments of the *Campus Martius*.[46] The biography of Xystus III in *LP* states that Xystus built a basilica with columns dedicated to Laurence with the permission of Valentinian III. Geertman suggested that the reference referred to S. Lorenzo *fuori le mura*. He drew his proposal from analysis of the literary evidence alone, and was heavily criticized.[47] Alchermes, however, argued that the basilica to which *LP* refers is in fact S. Lorenzo in Lucina.[48] With the exception of the *Praefatio*, literary references to the *titulus Lucinae*,

42 Both titles are a source for confusion. The title *Praefatio* has been used to suggest that this first letter is the preface to the second letter (described below), the *Libellus Praecum*, to which it has no definitive relationship other than its similar anti-Damasan sentiments. Pietri (1976: 407ff) gives the title *Gesta Liberii*, which has been a source of confusion for other scholars, as it is the same as the title used to describe a text of *Symmachan Apocrypha* from the early sixth century. Neither title is completely applicable, but for the sake of clarity it will henceforth be referred to as the *Praefatio*, following Curran 2000 and Trout 2001.

43 *CA* I (CSEL 35.2) 44 MGH AA XII, 410.

45 Ferrua 1952–54. Ferrua, however, gives only one partially preserved inscription of uncertain date and bases a large part of his discussion on the textual evidence of the *Praefatio*. Three scholars follow Ferrua's lead: Krautheimer 1937–80: 160, Pietri 1976: 95–6, and Bertoldi 1994: 22.

46 This site was important not only for its proximity to the *horologium*, but also to the obelisk. Bertoldi (1994: 22–4) notes that this is the site at which the senate met after Augustus returned from Gaul and Spain, which is noted on the *Ara Pacis*. The area was home to many wine vendors and an industry of marble production, as well as a largely Jewish population.

47 Geertman 1975: 146–7. 48 Alchermes 1989.

as in the lists of 499, or to the basilica of S. Lorenzo in Lucina mentioned in *LP*, all date to the late fifth and sixth centuries.

Recent excavations, however, have adequately demonstrated that the church did not exist until the early fifth century. It was probably constructed under the direction of Bishop Xystus III. Furthermore, the excavations suggest that there is no evidence for a Christian community on this location prior to Xystus' patronage. These campaigns suggest that the site underwent two distinct phases. They confirm that the first was probably a public or commercial one through the fourth century. The first indication of a Christian element is the baptistery of the 430s. A baptismal font was added to the site under Xystus III, as similarly occurred at Sta Maria Maggiore and Sta Sabina. Olaf Brandt records that in the first campaign of 1993 a fourth-century spoil mentioning a certain Flavia Hilarina was found. The spoil was reused in the building of a circular baptistery, and thus provides evidence for a second phase of building activity. More recently, Olaf Brandt has shown that there is archaeological evidence for a horse stable at this location during the late fourth century, further implying that the space did not function ecclesiastically during Damasus' pontificate.[49]

The *basilica Liberii* presents a second anachronism that raises a question about the date of the *Praefatio*. The basilica is mentioned in the *Praefatio* as the location of the second gathering and attack on Ursinian supporters following Damasus' election. This reference is the only extant so-called fourth-century reference to this location in the context of the schism. All other references to the *basilica Liberii* appear later in the sixth-century *LP*. Indeed contemporary discussions of the schisms by Ammianus and Jerome, or the fifth-century historians Socrates and Sozemen, do not mention a 'basilica Liberii'. According to these other datable sources, the Ursinians gathered in a 'basilica Sicinini' or 'in Sicininum'. These discrepancies between the texts and this isolated reference to this basilica until well into the sixth century further suggest that perhaps the *Praefatio* was written, or edited, at this later date. Both anachronisms in topographical references suggest that perhaps the *Praefatio* was written after the construction of S. Lorenzo in Lucina, if not later.

Like the *Praefatio*, the second letter, or the *Libellus Precum*, presents a hostile account of Damasus' pontificate. The authors of the letter identify themselves as pro-Luciferian supporters congregating in Rome and requesting the emperor's assistance against Damasus.[50] They oppose

49 Brandt 1994, 1995, and 1996.

50 Green 1971 argues that the authors were pro-Ursinian, not Luciferian, and that they were also the authors of the first letter, the *Praefatio*.

Bishop Damasus and seem sympathetic to his opponent Ursinus. This letter is the longest of the *gesta* on Damasus and is likely to date to approximately 368 on the basis of internal evidence in the text and its style.[51] The letter was seemingly selected to be part of the anti-Damasan section that begins *CA*.[52] Letters 3 to 7 and 13 similarly relate to the controversy between Damasus and Liberius.

There appears at first glance to be no particularly apparent reason for *CA* to include a negative portrayal of Damasus. According to the internal logic of the text, *CA* supports bishops who kept Roman sovereignty in the face of imperial intervention and condemns those who were weak. Thus Boniface was completely dependent on the emperor Honorius' favour during his papacy, and gave into Honorius' decisions on more than one occasion. The letters to Justinian all attempted to show the emperor as subjected to the Roman bishop, and the bishops of this period as acting in defence of this ideal.

We would thus expect to see Liberius and Ursinus as attracting opprobium because of their overt willingness to make compromise with Constantius and his successors, with their rivals Felix and Damasus emerging as the heroes of Roman independence. But as *CA* tells the story, it is Damasus who is too well connected to the emperor. Indeed, one of the main critiques of the *Praefatio* is that Damasus is inextricably entwined in Roman imperial politics and patronage structures. According to *CA*, Valentinian II was forced to exile Ursinus and his cohort from Rome in order to calm the city, with the result that Damasus was partly dependent on the emperor for his authority. *CA* finds in Damasus a bishop who did not defend Roman papal sovereignty, but rather depended too greatly on the emperor's intervention.

It is impossible to be certain what caused this volte-face regarding Damasus. It may well be that, from the fourth century forward, dependence on the emperor became a standard accusation among Roman churchmen, with the result that the party of one or another candidate would always seek to distance their own man from any grounds for suspicion on this point, while cultivating unpleasant detail about his rivals. It may also be the case, however, that the authors of the *Liber Pontificalis* were genuinely unaware of the accusations of imperial pandering preserved against Damasus in the fourth-century *Libellus Praecum*. However frustrating our

[51] See Pietri 1976: 408 for a full discussion of chronology. See also Caspar 1930: 199, Künzle 1961, and Lippold 1965. Künzle states that the latest date mentioned in the letter is for 367.

[52] But it also circulated on its own, and is attested in a sixth- or seventh-century manuscript, Paris 12097: see Maassen 1870: 556–9 and CSEL 35.lviii.

own incomplete knowledge of Roman ecclesiastical politics at the end of antiquity, we should remember that the churchmen of the early sixth century were even less well served than ourselves with regard to evidence. Indeed, they were only just developing the record-keeping strategies of which Damasus would become the patron saint, as it were.

CONCLUSION: MEMORY AND THE ARCHIVE IN SIXTH-CENTURY ROME

In exploring the contrast between the *Liber Pontificalis* and the *Collectio Avellana*, it is important to remember what they have in common as sources for papal self-understanding in the sixth century. The *Collectio* implicitly and the *Liber* explicitly share a commitment to the written record as the best guarantee of institutional identity. Organized as a composite biography of Roman bishops from St Peter forward, the *Liber Pontificalis* was clearly written at a time when the Roman church was newly interested in documenting, or indeed creating, the history of its own bureaucratic traditions. This point is evident in the notice on Fabian (d. 250), for example, who is credited with having organized the activity of seven deacons across seven ecclesiastical regions of the city, along with the seven notaries who 'would faithfully collect the acts of the martyrs' (trans. Davis, p. 8), or Marcellus (d. 308), who was remembered as establishing the twenty-five *tituli* within Rome.[53] Damasus was remembered as having erected verse inscriptions to the memory of the church's martyrs recording their history.

Whether Damasus was in fact the instigator of enhanced episcopal record-keeping remains a moot point. A number of scholars have argued that there is little evidence for a papal library or archive in the sixth century. Riché and Peterson admit that by the sixth century letter collections and other sources may have been gathered, but they do not accept the existence of a papal archive as the idea is commonly understood until about half way through the seventh century. Peterson concedes that perhaps an official library could have been established by 598, when Gregory refers to a *schola* of *notarii* at the Lateran.[54] Noble, on the other hand, has suggested that a papal archive existed from the period of Damasus and was eventually moved to the Lateran in 649.

53 *LP* I, 148, trans. Davis 1989: 8. See Cooper 1999.

54 Riché (1976) argues that there is no papal library before the seventh century, but does distinguish papal *scrinia* or archives of the Lateran and St Peter's collections of codices. Noble (1984: 219–21) suggests 649 as the date of the papal archives moving to the Lateran, and states that a *primicerius* was in charge of them; see also Noble 1990. Petersen (1987: 3) notes that this indicates the existence only of a *scrinia* and not of a library.

His more recent work suggests that there is evidence of papal archives, though scanty, but that there is no relationship between the earliest papal archive and S. Lorenzo in Damaso. It is difficult to prove that there is no connection, but the interest in Damasus in sixth-century collections is striking.

While this is not the place to revisit in full this discussion, we may note that the sixth-century memory may not have been entirely inaccurate. From the fourth century there is evidence of at least rudimentary record-keeping where papal correspondence was concerned. In his polemical treatise against Rufinus, Jerome defended himself from an accusation of epistolary forgery by arguing that the papal letter could be found in the *chartario* of the Roman church.[55] The exact meaning of the term *chartario* is unclear, but it does indicate that letters were being kept, and that at least some well-placed insiders in Rome could gain access to at least some letters. Damasus himself erected one inscription on the outside of the church S. Lorenzo in Damaso, which stated that he was erecting a new roof to the archive. This inscription has been a source of vast debate, and in 1953 Kunzle suggested that the inscription should not be read as a new roof *for the archive* (*archibis*) but as '*chrite tibi*', thus prompting most scholars to conclude that the papal archives could not have been in S. Lorenzo in Damaso.[56] The original inscription, unfortunately, has been lost, although its contents were recorded by a pilgrim a few centuries after its production. The inscription is thus only known by a late manuscript attestation, and it may be this element that prompts epigraphers to correct the words of the inscription. Although the epigraphic evidence is not conclusive, Damasus' systematization of church history along with his strong connection to papal history and letter collections in the sixth century indicate a need to reopen the question of whether Damasus did indeed renovate an archive, and if so, what its status was.

Perhaps it is more helpful to reconsider what sixth-century authors themselves meant by the term 'archive', as it is entirely possible that the compilers of *LP* may have accessed one or more private libraries, or one of a number of ecclesiastical collections existing in the city. What we can determine, however, is that by this point they understood these collections to serve an archival purpose. The first reference to a papal decree in *LP* is in the *Vita Siricii* at the end of the fourth century. The *LP* author mentions that Siricius issued a decree against Manichaean heretics that is kept in the archive. The compiler of *CA* included two letters from Siricius on the Manichaean and Arian heresies, Letters 39 and 40. The only other document relating to Siricius in *CA* is his ordination, Letter 4. The next reference

[55] *Epistula adversus Rufinum* 20 (CCSL 19.91). [56] Künzle 1953; see discussion in Ferrua 1953.

to an archive is in the *Life* of Leo. Here, the author of *LP* states that his letters are in 'archives' and then proceeds to list the contents of the archive: twelve letters to Marcian, thirteen to Leo, nine to Flavian, and eighteen to bishops of the east. According to *LP*, Leo confirmed earlier synods in these letters. *CA* holds five otherwise unknown letters of Leo to various bishops of the east. Many of these letters confirm the earlier synods. Yet another example is Gelasius' *Vita*. The *LP* author mentions that Gelasius wrote five books against Nestorius and Eutyches, which are kept in the church archive, and then adds that he also wrote tracts, hymns, and prayers. This last addition seems to indicate that the other records were not held in the archive. *CA* contains a few narrative accounts, supposedly written under Gelasius, which concern the Acacian schism.[57] One of the *CA*'s documents, the *Gesta de absolutione Miseni*, seems to share a source with *LP*, which has similar information regarding the episcopacy of Felix.[58]

LP and *CA* cannot be used as a wholly reliable source for the history of the papacy in the early centuries of the church, because of their persistent tendency to retroject their own visions of the Roman church into earlier periods. All the same, the allusions to archives, letters, and synods are not *necessarily* fictional detail. The specific mentions of archives or libraries in *LP* indicate that, by the time of the author, church historians had access to collections that they thought of as archives. When the author of *LP* mentions a hierarchy with deacons and notaries under the mid-third-century bishop Fabian, this is evidence that deacons and notaries were organized this way in the sixth century rather than in the third. Likewise, *LP*'s references to archives indicate their existence in the sixth century, though not in the third.

For all that they may differ over Damasus, then, *LP* and *CA* have more in common with each other than with other contemporary texts representing other strategies of memory and authority.[59] We may recall here the *Collectio Italica* of Symmachan forgeries, produced in the heat of the Laurentian schism; or other papal *gesta*, such as the *gesta Alexandrii*, as discussed by Kristina Sessa elsewhere in this volume. For all of their interest in schism, or their fierce commitment to the papal cause in the face of imperial pressure, neither *LP* nor *CA* fights shy of this legendary culture. They could be seen to represent the decision of Roman churchmen operating in the generation after the Laurentian schism to move towards less divisive techniques of memory. In the archive, in the properly arranged sequence of documents, lay the future of the past.

57 *CA* 99 and 103. 58 *CA* 103.

59 See more broadly Teitler 1985, Kelly 1994, Hedrick 2000, and Matthews 2000: 280–93.

PART II

Lay, clerical, and ascetic contexts for the Roman gesta martyrum

3

Domestic conversions: households and bishops in the late antique 'papal legends'

Kristina Sessa

> And what is more suitable to the Christian faith than that there should be a forgiveness of sins not only in the church but also in the homes of all men?
>
> Leo, *Sermo* 49.5. Lent, 457 AD[1]

The idea that Christianity orders a moral topography extending from *ecclesia* to *domus* figures prominently in the sermons of the Roman bishop Leo I (441–461). 'Rule your slaves and those who are subjected to you with fairness; let none of them be tortured by imprisonment or chains', he exhorted his congregation on the first Sunday of Lent in 444.[2] Elsewhere Leo urgently directed his congregation to search their homes for heretics, while his successor Gelasius (492–496) expressly targeted aristocratic households in an open letter to a leading Roman senator, in which he railed against their participation in the Lupercalia, an archaic Roman fertility rite that was still performed annually by Rome's elite residents as late as the 490s.[3] We might also consider anecdotes about financial assistance to impoverished *matronae*, stories of bishops helping to arrange marriages, and episcopal involvement in monastic foundations as evidence for the bishop's growing interest in, and sense of responsibility for, the city's various households.[4]

* I would like to thank the editors, Kate Cooper and Julia Hillner, as well as Kate Blair-Dixon, Kevin Uhalde, and the two anonymous readers for their perceptive and productive comments. All remaining errors are my own.

1 Leo, *Sermo* 49.5 (CCSL 138a, 289): 'Quid autem convenientius fidei Christianae quam ut non solum in ecclesia, sed etiam in omnium domibus fiat remissio peaccatorum?' All translations are my own unless noted otherwise.

2 Leo, *Sermo* 42.6 (CCSL 138a, 249): 'Servis et his qui vobis subiecti sunt, cum aequitate dominamini, nullus eorum aut claustris crucietur aut vinculis.'

3 Leo, *Sermo* 16.5 (CCSL 138a, 65–6). For Gelasius on the Lupercalia see *Ep.* 1 or *Adversum Andromachum et ceteros Romanos qui Lupercalia secundem morem pristinum colenda constituunt* (ed. Pomares 1959: 162).

4 For episcopal assistance to impoverished widows and involvement in the marrying of fatherless women see Gregory, *Epp.* I, 44, and II, 25, 29. We know from the *Liber Pontificalis* that several Roman bishops in the fifth and sixth centuries (including Gregory himself) founded suburban and urban monasteries. This is not to suggest, of course, that before the fifth century Christian bishops

Leo's demand for an ethical parity between household and church recalls a familiar paradigm in ancient political and biblical thought. Cicero's famous study of the ideal statesman emphasized the importance of a well-run *domus* as the foundation of a well-run *res publica*, while Xenophon and later Paul underlined household management (*oikonomia*) as constitutive of a man's duty to his family, to his community, and to his God.[5] Both the classical and the Christian models of the household as the cornerstone of social, economic, and religious life reflect the central place of the domestic sphere in the ancient and late ancient Mediterranean world.[6] A space that was at once public and private, the household was the site of child rearing, the disciplining of slaves, religious worship, business, and entertainment.[7] According to Andrew Wallace-Hadrill, the *domus* was where 'a public figure went ... not so much to shield himself from the public gaze as to present himself to it in the best light'.[8] The household, in other words, was a performative and ceremonial space, *the* site of the production and reproduction of the empire's most essential resources: bodies, property, and reputations.

Though by no means an exclusively male space, the household, ancient law and custom make clear, was typically characterized as the domain of the *paterfamilias*, the legal term for the male ascendant head of the household, who wielded extensive authority over most of those living under his roof.[9]

did not view certain domestic activities, like the extramarital sexual activities of married couples, within their pastoral purview. *Cf.* Ignatius of Antioch, *Letter to Polycarp* 4.3 and canons 5, 7, 9–10, 15, 17, 31, 54, 69–70, 72 of the Council of Elvira, *c.* 309.

[5] Cicero, *De officiis* 1.17.52–4, which should be compared with Augustine, *De civitate Dei* 19.16; Xenophon, *Oeconomicos* 2.5–8 (on the civic and religious expectations of households); for Paul and importance of household management in the Christian community, see 1 Cor. 4–5 and his letter to Philemon. The scholarly literature on the household and its relation to the city, social order, and religious community is vast. In addition to the contribution of Conrad Leyser in this volume, see Humphreys 1983; Joubert: 1995; Meyer 1998; and Shaw 1987: esp. 10–12.

[6] By 'domestic sphere' I refer collectively to the physical place, practices, and people who constituted a household in late antiquity. In no way do I mean to equate this 'domestic sphere' with what modern political theorists refer to as the 'private sphere', for the ancient and late ancient *domus* resists simple categorization as private or public.

[7] Legally speaking, the *domus* was owned by an individual and not by the state, and was in this technical sense a 'private' space. But as the ancients themselves acknowledged, the household was also a site of 'public' activities. Vitruvius, *De arch.* 6.5.2, for example, described the *domus* as a place for 'public meetings as well as private trials and proceedings before arbiters' (*publica consilia et privata iudicia arbitriaque*). Such fluidity between public and private within the household seems to have been the norm throughout Roman antiquity and the middle ages. See Wallace-Hadrill 1988: 50–8 and 1994; Riggsby 1997; and McSheffrey 2004.

[8] Wallace-Hadrill 1994: 5. See also Eck 1997. On the continuing centrality of the *domus* as a space of senatorial self-presentation in late antiquity, see Näf 1995 and Schlinkert 1996: esp. 132–44. On the late antique *domus* as a performative space, see Ellis 1988: 565–76 and 1991.

[9] A man's wife was often the exception to the rule, since in the late empire wives were typically subject not to their husbands' *patria potestas*, but to their fathers'. Many would have also been emancipated,

The public reputation of the *paterfamilias* was vested in his perceived ability to manage his household in a decorous manner.

To be sure, Roman emperors and kings occasionally interfered in the governing of the household by imposing legal strictures on certain domestic activities: Augustus famously made adultery a public crime, Constantine attempted to stamp out divorce, and Theoderic castigated lax *domini* for failing to control their more violent slaves in public venues.[10] But as historians of Roman family law have shown, these restrictions did not fundamentally erode the *paterfamilias'* extraordinary legal privilege and social power within his own household.[11] According to recent studies of the Christianization of the late Roman senatorial aristocracy, conversion to Christianity in the late fourth and early fifth centuries remained the distinct prerogative of the male head of house, and was neither thrust upon the *domus* by imperial pressure nor effected through the 'back door' of womanly influence.[12] Moreover, since there is good reason to believe that Christians also worshipped within their homes in late antiquity like their polytheist counterparts, it is likely that the traditional religious authority of the *paterfamilias* extended to Christian domestic rituals as well.[13]

In these respects, the late Roman household would seem to be the least likely space in which an outside male religious or social authority, like a bishop, might hope to have influence. But it is important to remember that the household also frequently appears in biblical and early Christian

and therefore legally independent. Consequently, women could be legally recognized as heads of households, own property, make wills, and conduct most aspects of domestic management. In following the emphasis of my sources and focusing on the *paterfamilias* in this essay, I in no way wish to elide the role of women in the *domus*. However, the fact that the late ancient household was *not*, like its modern counterpart, a space exclusively associated with female activities, and thus separate from and marginal to the 'public sphere', may demand that we privilege *male* activities and interests when we explore the relations of power that structured the late antique household. On women in the household, see Dixon, 1988 and Saller 1999. On *patria potestas* in late antiquity, see Shaw 1987; Arjava 1996: 41–52, 98–105, and 1998.

10 Under Augustus, the *lex Julia de adulteris* (18 BC) made sexual offences between the married and the unmarried punishable as a public crime for the first time. For Constantine's attempt to discourage unilateral divorce (divorce by mutual consent was never contested in antiquity or late antiquity, so Arjava 1996: 178–9) see *CTh* 3.16.1 (331 BC), and Evans Grubbs 1995). On Theoderic's reaction to unruly slaves in public, see Cassiodorus, *Variae* 1.27. For a general discussion of the social and legal limitations of *patria potestas*, see Crook 1967a.

11 Arjava (1996: 261–5 and 1998: 159–65) demonstrates that *patria potestas* remained legally viable well into the sixth century, though with some important changes like the increased practice of filial emancipation.

12 Salzman 2002: 155–61; Cooper 1992.

13 There is both textual and material evidence for Christian domestic liturgy in late antiquity. For a full treatment of the subject, see Bowes 2002. On domestic chapels in Rome see Brenk 1995; Cerrito 2002; Sotinel 2002. See also Brenk 1999 on possible liturgical vessels found among the ruins of the so-called House of the Valerii on the Caelian.

literature as a ritual space under the express direction of such an outsider.[14] In the New Testament, for example, there are examples of what scholars refer to as 'house Christianity' or '*oikos*-fellowships'.[15] Both Luke-Acts and the letters of Paul describe situations in which householders open up their homes to other Christians for assembly and worship under the direction of Peter or Paul.[16] We also find the household at the centre of religious interaction between householders and apostles in other pre-Nicene traditions, like the *Apocryphal Acts of the Apostles*. In texts like the *Acts of Thomas* and the *Acts of Andrew* apostles enter the homes of pagan families in order to convert certain members (typically wives and daughters) to a celibate Christian lifestyle. However, though in some cases (such as the *Acts of Peter*) liturgical activities ensue within the household with the householder's permission, the *Apocryphal Acts* more often depict the household as the primary battle ground on which apostles and *patresfamilias* wrestle for domestic resources, namely the allegiances of spouses and children.[17]

Roman social practice and Christian literary tradition thus underline the complex nature of the late Roman household, as a place that was socially and religiously autonomous on the one hand, but integral to Christian history and community on the other. It was, in other words, both the least and most natural space in which to find a bishop. This ambivalence ought to give us pause when considering the force and, more importantly, the reception of Leo's intrusion into the household from the pulpit. Did Christian householders in Rome too see their *domus* as an extension of the church and thus subject to the moral and social authority of their bishop? Or did they perceive their relationship to episcopal authority in a more complex and even agonistic manner? How exactly was the bishop's authority established within the domestic sphere?

Though scholars have long recognized the social and economic significance of private households in the process of Christianization, they have rarely considered the political and ethical implications of the late antique bishop's steadily expanding authority within the city for the householder's own power and status within his household. This is particularly true for the historiography of the Roman bishop, which remains dominated by traditional narratives of late antique and early medieval Rome as the

[14] Meyer 1998: 63–71. [15] Meeks 1983; Barclay 1997; White 1990.
[16] Cf. Acts 10 (Peter at the house of Cornelius); 18.9–11 (Paul at the house of Crispus); 19.8ff (Paul at the 'hall of Tyrannus'); Romans 16.3–5 and 1 Cor. 16.19 (the 'church' in the house of Prisca and Aquila).
[17] Much has been written on the social meaning of the *Apocryphal Acts*. See especially Perkins 1995; Cooper 1996: 45–67; and Jacobs 1999.

site of the 'rise of the papacy'. According to historians like Erich Caspar, P. A. B. Llewellyn, and Charles Pietri, it was precisely during the fourth to seventh centuries when Roman bishops came to wield an increasingly singular moral and civic authority, not only within Rome, but also beyond the city's walls.[18] In charting the Roman bishop's ascendancy, some scholars have posited the agency of the lay householder and the integrity of his house as apparent casualties of Rome's 'papalization'. The practice of patronage has received considerable attention in this respect. For example, Llewellyn concluded that the charges of fiscal misconduct directed at the bishop Symmachus (498–514) during the Laurentian schism (498–507) – a protracted ecclesiastical and political conflict that erupted following the simultaneous elections of two bishops in 498, the priest Laurentius and the deacon (and eventual pope) Symmachus – constituted the last stand of Rome's lay patrons to control the fate of their gifts to the church, especially those connected to the local neighbourhood foundations known as *tituli*.[19]

Not even the physical house itself, it seems, could resist the church's clutch. Since the earliest days of Christian archaeology in Rome, scholars like J. P. Kirsch, Richard Krautheimer, and now Federico Guidobaldi have drawn attention to the few, celebrated cases of topographical and architectural coincidences between late antique domestic reception spaces and early Christian churches, whereby *tituli* (like SS. Giovanni e Paolo and S. Clemente) were constructed either directly over or in structural relation to pre-existing Roman *domus*.[20] While noting that several of these houses had probably been donated to the church by their lay owners, most historians have nevertheless explained this remarkable slippage between *domus* and *ecclesia* from an ecclesiastical and teleological perspective; the Christian *domus* it seems was never really a *domus* at all,

[18] Caspar 1930–33; Llewellyn 1971; Pietri 1976. Of course, such claims are made about late antique bishops throughout the Mediterranean world. Cf. Hunt 1998: 263–76 and Rapp 2005:155–290.

[19] Llewellyn 1976b: 417–27. According to Llewellyn, Roman senators and priests who supported Laurentius in the schism sought to challenge Symmachus' legitimacy by accusing him of the improper alienation of properties conjoined to the *tituli*. Llewellyn argued that the charges were symptomatic of the laity's perceived loss of agency in controlling the fate of their donations. For the *tituli*, see below and the chapter by Julia Hillner in this volume.

[20] Kirsch (1918) and Lanzoni (1925) saw in many of Rome's early medieval *tituli* traces of the original, pre-Constantinian *domus ecclesia* or 'house church' (a sort of architectural hybrid in which pre-Constantinian Christians supposedly worshipped), while Richard Krautheimer (1965: 1–12) identified the *domus ecclesia* as the third-century stage of his model of architectural development for Roman churches. Their claims, however, were debunked by Pietri (1978a and 1981a: 435–53), who showed that all known late antique *tituli* were post-Constantinian establishments. Nevertheless, as Federico Guidobaldi points out, a number of Rome's *tituli* occupy areas on which large, aristocratic *domus* once stood. See Guidobaldi 1989 and 1993.

but a church inchoate.[21] What is more, the majority of late antique Roman houses did *not* become churches – a fact that is often overlooked by scholars.

Such studies have shaped our reading of late antique Rome as caught in the irreversible and ineluctable throes of becoming an ecclesiastical city centrally controlled by the pope. However, more recent work on late ancient and early medieval Rome, including the contributions in this volume, has called into question so totalizing and teleological a paradigm of the city's social, material, and religious history.[22] From the sobering comments of Paolo Delogu, who warns against the tendency to extrapolate sweeping models of institutional power and authority from the contingent actions of individual bishops (notably those of Gregory I, 590–604), to recent archaeological studies of early medieval domestic space by Riccardo Santangeli Valenzani and Robert Coates-Stephens, scholars have begun to re-evaluate many assumptions about the emergence of *Roma Christiana*, including the history of the *domus* and its place in late antique and early medieval urban life.[23]

The present chapter joins this discussion by exploring how the bishop's authority could have been mapped onto the already existing complex of relations and practices that structured the late Roman Christian household. It examines how a group of texts independently produced in Rome between the fifth and seventh centuries variously modelled the relationship between bishops and male householders, and how their authors imagined the presence of episcopal authority within the domestic sphere. Rather than view the urban *domus* as a blank slate onto which the bishop simply etched his power or built his church, we shall privilege the householder's agency and perspective in the process of establishing episcopal authority in the household. A shift in focus from bishop to householder and from *ecclesia* to *domus* will enable us to begin to reconstruct how, why, and to what extent Roman householders might have resisted, accepted, or even welcomed the bishop's participation in the practice of household affairs.

[21] Pietri, for example, consistently dismissed the multiple descriptions of *domus* as liturgical spaces in the Roman martyr narratives as 'anachronisms' (Pietri 1981a: 437–40), while Llewellyn (1976: esp. 418–19) discussed the *domus* of Pudens depicted in the *Passio SS. Praxedis et Pudentianae* exclusively as a *titulus*, despite the fact that it is also imagined in the narrative as a house where the virgin sisters Praxedis and Pudentiana lived.

[22] On the teleological framework typically adopted by historians of the papacy, see Costambeys 2000. Studies by scholars who work from an ancient perspective on the late Roman aristocracy, like Barnish 1988 and Näf 1995, offer important non-ecclesiastically orientated discussions of late Roman civic culture.

[23] Delogu 1993: 12–13 and 2001; Santangeli Valenzani 1997: 64–70 and 2000; Coates-Stephens 1996.

Just as there was no single model of the Christian household in late antiquity (lay-biological, clerical, monastic, and combinations thereof are all possibilities, as recent work has shown[24]), so there was no dominant paradigm of episcopal interaction with and within the domestic sphere. In the following pages, two different models will be explored. Some authors and audiences imagined the bishop's relation to the *domus* in litigious and ultimately coercive terms. In this first model, bishops and householders compete for domestic resources and authority in a zero-sum game that is played out in a juridical arena, through their participation in various legal and extra-legal practices. For others, the bishop's connection to the household and householder was ideally forged through more cooperative practices, namely the exchange of social and spiritual *beneficia*. In the second paradigm, liturgy (and baptism in particular) emerges as the ultimate ritual of exchange, through which the bishop's moral presence within the household is established, though in a manner that preserves the householder's private agency and elevates the civic position of his house. It is, of course, hardly surprising to find episcopal authority articulated in terms of law or liturgy. Nevertheless, it is remarkable to see how their imagined practice *within the household* not only recalibrated the *domus* and the householder's own domestic authority, but also shaped the bishop's own position within the city at large. Such 'domestic conversions' are the subject of this study.

HOUSEHOLDS AND BISHOPS IN THE 'PAPAL LEGENDS' OF LATE ANTIQUE ROME: APPROACHES OLD AND NEW

To explore these two contrasting paradigms of the bishop's authority from a domestic point of view, it is necessary to look outside the corpus of sources typically favoured by scholars of the papacy, such as the *Liber Pontificalis* and the decretals, to a still largely unexplored literature of biographical texts that represent the Roman bishop actively engaging with members of his community in spaces throughout the city, including the domestic sphere. Sources like the so-called Symmachan forgeries[25] (a small group of putatively fourth- and early fifth-century episcopal letters, conciliar proceedings, and eye-witness accounts of episcopal trials that were probably penned during the Laurentian schism in the early sixth century),

[24] See, for example, the essays by Jacobs and Krawiec 2003 as well as the contributions of Kate Cooper, Anne Kurdock and Conrad Leyser in this volume.

[25] For the so-called Symmachan forgeries, see now Wirbelauer 1993. Wirbelauer's is the most recent critical edition and provides a German translation.

and the episcopal passions of the fifth-, sixth- and seventh-century Roman *gesta martyrum* present us with alternative images of Rome's episcopal founding fathers, from Clement and Cornelius to Silvester.[26] It is the domestic orientation of these 'papal legends', that is, their thematic and topical emphasis on the household as a dynamic social space long overlooked by historians of Roman episcopal authority, that interests us here.[27]

Representative of the first, more coercive model of episcopal interaction with the household is one document typically grouped among the Symmachan forgeries known as *Gesta de Xysti purgatione*.[28] An anonymous 'historical re-creation' of the circumstances surrounding the trial of Pope Xystus III (432–441), the *Gesta de Xysti purgatione* weaves a tale about the bishop's involvement in two different domestic disputes with two different unethical but nevertheless Christian households. These disputes culminate in Xystus' own trial before the emperor Valentinian III, where the bishop is charged by the householders with sexual misconduct, only to be exonerated and declared, as pope, to be beyond all earthly judgement.[29]

For the second, more cooperative paradigm of domestic–episcopal exchange, we shall look to three of the episcopal *gesta martyrum*: the *Passio SS. Alexandri, Eventii, et Theodoli martyrum*, the *Passio S. Callisti papae et martyris*, and the *Passio S. Stephani papae et martyris*.[30] Like the *Gesta de Xysti purgatione*, these texts have also come down to us without authorial

[26] The episcopal *gesta martyrum* include: *Passio SS. Alexandri, Eventii, et Theodolii* (*BHL* 266–7); *Passio S. Callisti papae* (*BHL* 1523); *Passio S. Clementis martyris et episcopi* (*BHL* 1848–57); *Passio S. Cornelii papae* (*BHL* 1958–66); *Passio S. Marcelli papae et martyris ac sotiorum* [*sic*] *eius* (*BHL* 5234–9); *Passio S. Xysti* (*BHL* 7801–12, which is an episode of the *Passio S. Polychronii*); and the *Passio S. Stephani papae et martyris* (*BHL* 7845–7). I also consider the *Actus Silvestri* (*BHL* 7725–43), which is not technically a passion as Silvester is not remembered as a martyr, because of its close textual and rhetorical relationship to the *gesta martyrum*. There is no single modern, critical edition of the *gesta martyrum*. Scholars may consult the fifteenth-century edition of Boninus Mombritius, *Sanctuarium seu Vitae Sanctorum* (Milan, about 1480, reprinted Paris 1910, and reissued New York 1978, with some critical notes) or the versions published by the Bollandists in the volumes of the *Acta Sanctorum*. In certain individual cases, a modern critical edition with apparatus has been produced, such as for the *Passio S. Clementis*, edited by Funk and Diekamp 1913.

[27] One notable exception is Pietri 1981a, but see my critique below.

[28] I will not discuss the *Gesta Polychronii*, another document grouped among the Symmachan forgeries that is often described by scholars as an appendage to the *Gesta de Xysti purgatione*. It is true that the two are grouped together in most manuscripts, but I do not think this warrants treating them as a single text. See Wirbelauer 1993: 86–8 for a discussion of the issue.

[29] *Gesta de Xysti purgatione* (ed. Wirbelauer 1993: 262–71). Though the specific details surrounding Xystus' trial were probably fabricated by the sixth-century writers, the bishop does appear to have been actually involved in some kind of serious legal dispute during his tenure. See Xystus III's biography in the *Liber Pontificalis* (ed. Duchesne, I, 232), which alludes to a trial.

[30] *Passio SS. Alexandri, Eventii, et Theodoli martyrum* (ed. Mombritius 1978: I, 44–9); *Passio S. Callisti papae et martyris* (ed. Mombritius 1978: I, 268–71); *Passio S. Stephani papae et martyris* (ed. Mombritius 1978: II, 495–500).

attribution. In addition to the martyrdoms of the pre-Constantinian bishops Alexander (*c.* 110–115), Callistus (217–222), and Stephen (254–257), these three passions portray bishops and householders engaged in face-to-face encounters that bring about the household's transformation from a pious but unproductive pagan residence to a vital Christian *domus*. As mentioned above, this transformation is effected through the exchange of 'favours' between the householder and bishop, wherein the latter offers his powers to heal bodies and baptize souls and the former a share of his paternal authority.

Though the late antique compilers of the *Liber Pontificalis* drew upon several of these 'papal legends' as biographical sources for the Roman episcopacy, modern scholars have treated them with far greater suspicion.[31] Since the eighteenth century, scholars have recognized the complex relationship that both sets of texts bear to their production context. Pierre Coustant and later Louis Duchesne revealed the seemingly authentic *Gesta de Xysti purgatione* and other Symmachan documents to be forged, polemical 'pamphlets' penned by supporters of Symmachus or his rival Laurentius during the height of the Laurentian schism.[32] A similar discovery was made about the *gesta matyrum* when Duchesne's junior colleague Albert Dufourcq concluded that these dramatic, allegedly eye-witness accounts of the trials, torture, and deaths of Rome's martyrs were first composed not during the epoch of the persecutions (as the narratives themselves purport), but centuries later during the Ostrogothic period (476–523), and thus reflect a definitely post-Constantinian Christianity.[33]

Such revelations about the late antique dating of sources like the *Gesta de Xysti purgatione* and the *gesta martyrum* have orientated the historical inquiry. Building upon the chronologies suggested by Duchesne and Dufourcq, virtually all modern studies of these 'papal legends' have followed a contextualist approach, whereby authors begin with events or issues external to the texts (typically those dated to the late fifth and early sixth century) in order to shed light upon what the texts themselves are 'really'

[31] Duchesne, I, lxviii–cxli.

[32] Coustant (1721: 115–24) first suggested a Symmachan context, a hypothesis reiterated by Maassen (1870: 411–414 (537–9), 519 (557–9)) and further developed by Duchesne, I, cxxxiii–cxvi. The hypothetical Symmachan context for these sources – as we have no concrete, external evidence for such a reading, only a number of internal coincidences between details of the narratives and events/personages of the Laurentian schism – is widely accepted: Caspar 1930–33: II, 107–10; Townsend 1933: 172; Levison 1948: 409; Zecchini 1980; Pietri, 1981a: 440–1; Wirbelauer 1993: 5–7.

[33] Dufourcq 1900–10: I, 287–321. The reader should note that Dufourcq's claim to have identified a manuscript tradition for a single, late antique codex containing the Roman martyr narratives has been entirely debunked: Franklin 2001: 857–95 and Pilsworth 2000: 314–16.

about.[34] For example, as mentioned above, scholars have consistently invoked the Laurentian schism as the hermeneutic key to the Symmachan forgeries, consequently drawing upon the facts of Symmachus' life and episcopal tenure to explain specific narrative details.[35] The *gesta martyrum* have also been subject to a contextualist approach. In several independent studies P. A. B. Llewellyn and Charles Pietri underlined the domestic orientation of the *gesta martyrum* by drawing attention to the exchanges between bishops and householders that are presented in certain passions. Though they drew opposing conclusions as to the implications of these exchanges, both historians interpreted the narratives as reflecting rather specific late fifth-and early sixth-century historical debates between laymen and clergy over patronage, with particular emphasis placed upon the tenure of Symmachus and the Laurentian schism.[36] Moreover, those elements of the texts deemed inconsistent with their assumed early sixth-century context, such as their depiction of houses as spaces of private habitation *and* liturgical ritual, were dismissed as 'anachronisms' irrelevant to the 'true' historical significance of the text.[37]

Without denying the significance of these previous studies, the present chapter forges new ground in the study of the 'papal legends' and their importance for the history of Roman episcopal authority by investigating the very anachronisms that Pietri and others have pushed aside. In a manner that I hope complements these more contextualist studies, I shall take a narrative approach. A narrative approach focuses not on a text's hypothetical external context (for these are, after all, anonymous texts whose chronology remains at best approximate and open-ended), but on its internal, literary elements – elements which collectively and complexly delineate larger discourses about episcopal authority in the domestic sphere.[38] To a certain extent, it follows a path first forged in the early twentieth century by Hippolyte Delehaye, who sought to understand hagiographical texts as literary *and* historical sources, created and consumed

34 See, for example, Llewellyn 1976b; Pietri, 1981a; Verrando 1987; and Cooper 1999.

35 For example, Zecchini 1980: 60–74 and Wirbelauer 1993: 73–99.

36 Llewellyn 1976b: esp. 423–4. Llewellyn saw the *domus* of the *gesta martyrum* as a *titulus* and the passion an ecclesiastical foundation legend that served the apologetic interests of Roman priests and senators who wanted to protect their own ecclesiastical foundations from the encroaching arm of bishops like Symmachus. Pietri (1981a: 440–7) too maintained that the *gesta martyrum* must be read in light of late fifth- and sixth-century ecclesiastical politics, lay patronage, and the foundation of the *tituli*, but, contra Llewellyn, he argued that the texts shored up the bishop's position rather than subverted it.

37 Pietri 1981a: 437–40.

38 In this respect, the work of scholars like Verrando (see above, n. 34), who has attempted to create more precise relative chronologies for specific texts among the *gesta martyrum*, does not persuade.

within a context of Christian prose narrative traditions, from biblical narratives to authentic pre-Constantinian martyr *acta*.[39] Though I shall not apply Delehaye's 'scientific' method of sifting fact from fiction, my approach treats the 'papal legends' as complex and self-consciously *rhetorical* documents, and thus engages primarily with the topical features of the texts.[40] A focus upon *topoi* is a particularly fruitful way in to a group of anonymous narratives, whose characters I believe cannot be easily assimilated to 'real' historical figures and whose impressionistic relationship to an earlier era is an important facet of their meaning and collective force, and not an anachronism to be ignored or explained away. For it is important to remember that these sources were read in late antiquity and the early middle ages as authoritative (and no doubt entertaining) documents about the lives and deaths of Rome's early bishops, as their extensive and relatively early manuscript history attests.[41]

In conjunction with a narrative approach, we shall pay close attention to the intertextual dimensions of both the *Gesta de Xysti purgatione* and the episcopal *gesta martyrum*. Though these two sets of sources are of different genres (the former a putatively historical account of a trial, the latter a martyr narrative), their layered, literary topography reveals a number of shared models, from ancient romance to the *acta martyrum*.[42] In this essay, we shall attend especially to their biblical background and explore how they build upon and redirect expectations about households and Christian holy men that were originally forged in the *Apocryphal Acts of the Apostles*. In many respects, these 'papal legends' distinctly remember the bishop as a Romanized apostle, whose concerns for and interactions with the Roman *domus* are often modelled upon those of his apostolic avatar in sources like the *Acts of Paul and Thecla* or the *Acts of Peter* – two texts that were, not incidentally, read and subsequently reshaped in Rome during the fifth,

39 Delehaye 1921 and 1936: esp. 14–41, where he outlines many of the salient scenes, themes, and *dramatis personae* of the Roman *gesta martyrum*. For Delehaye, it was essential to determine the literary features of a hagiographical text in order to identify the more concretely 'historical' material about a saint's life. On the contributions of Delehaye to the study of hagiography, see Kitchen 1998: 3–22.

40 Cameron 1991 and Clark 2004 have emphasized the importance of attending to rhetorical strategy and the formation of discourses in Christian literature.

41 For the early manuscript history of the *gesta martyrum*, see the contribution of Conrad Leyser in this volume. For the Symmachan forgeries see Wirbelauer 1993: 172–225.

42 Cooper (1999: 305) identifies ancient romance as an important intertext for the *gesta martyrum*, to which one should add the model of the pre-Constantinian *acta martyrum*. I would suggest that the *Gesta de Xysti purgatione*, with its thematic emphasis on domestic conflict, its frequent use of direct speech, and its narrative reconstruction of Xystus' trial, bears a relationship to both of these genres.

sixth, and seventh centuries.[43] As we shall see, the writers of the 'papal legends' also altered these inherited stories in fundamental ways, emphasizing certain social and spiritual practices (like judicial process, patronage, and liturgy) while de-emphasizing others (like the call to a celibate lifestyle). The investigation of *how* texts like the *Gesta de Xysti purgatione* and the episcopal *gesta martyrum* created new paradigms of the relationship between bishop and householder constitutes the analytic aim of this study.

But before turning to an analysis of these texts and to our two different paradigms of episcopal interaction in the domestic sphere, a brief note on authorship is warranted. Although these narratives give voice to the memories of Rome's great episcopal founding fathers, they were almost certainly not composed by the bishops themselves, at least not directly. Clerical writers are often assumed, and given the degree of liturgical detail and polemical orientation of many of these texts, this is perhaps a reasonable hypothesis.[44] However, in the case of the narratives discussed here, this rather vague yet narrow identification of the texts' immediate social context can be both sharpened and broadened to include lay readers and perhaps even writers. While my argument to this effect is based largely on internal analysis, it is nevertheless grounded in recent work on the late Roman civic environment, which has critiqued the lay–clerical binary with which scholars have traditionally examined conflict in late antique cities.[45] Rather than view clerics and laypeople as partisans of separate camps who occasionally joined forces, we should adopt a more fluid model of social and political organization, in which clergy, laypeople and monks were often members of the same households, interconnected through ties of blood and/or bonds of friendship. Perhaps the most famous Roman

43 The *Acts of Peter* was among the sources used by the compilers of the *Liber Pontificalis* as Duchesne showed (I, cii); it was also the model for several Latin adaptations of the legend of Peter's death in Rome, like the *Martyrium beati Petri conscriptum a Lino episcopo*, which may have been written in Rome. See Verrando 1983. A distinctly Roman version of the *Acts of Paul and Thecla* was written in the sixth or seventh century, by which time Thecla's cult appears to have been thriving at Rome. See Dagron 1978: 49–50; Davis 2001: 46–7, and especially Cooper 1995: 13–20. However, earlier versions of the *Acts of Paul and Thecla* were in circulation in the western Mediterranean far earlier: cf. Tertullian, *De baptismo* 17.4; Jerome, *De vir. ill.* 7 for references to the narrative.

44 Historians typically characterize the writers of the Symmachan forgeries as 'supporters of Symmachus', and Wirbelauer (1993: 69–71) draws attention to their knowledge of conciliar canons (e.g. Nicaea and Chalcedon) and late antique ecclesiastical law as indicative of their clerical status. Such knowledge, however, was not the exclusive domain of clergymen, as the Roman career of the Scythian monk Dionysius Exiguus shows. For clerical authorship of (some of) the *gesta martyrum* see Dufourcq 1900–10: I, 318; 359–361. Delehaye suggested that the writers of the *gesta martyrum* collectively hailed from the same 'school' (1936: 12), but the manuscript histories of these texts render such a claim untenable.

45 Cooper 1999: 298–301.

example of such a *domus* is that of Gregory I;[46] but an inscription from the *titulus* of S. Clemente, which records a gift of an altar given by the titular priest Mercurius *cum sociis*, suggests a wider presence of such 'mixed' households in sixth-century Rome.[47] According to the *Liber Pontificalis*, the priest Mercurius, later known as Pope John II (533–535), was a member of a family with property on the Caelian, whose resources, along with those of his associates (*socii*), were probably used to procure the altar.[48] Mercurius' inscription and prosopographical record show that clergy and bishops were part of larger networks of family and friends, many of whom were *not* priests, like Mercurius' own father Proiectus.[49] Such historical households, I suggest, could have been the intended audience or perhaps even the authors of the narratives discussed here. At the very least, they constitute the sort of communities that the 'papal legends' imagine and whose conceptions of episcopal authority they endeavoured to shape.

NEMO ENIM IUDICAVIT DOMINUM IN CONSILIO SERVI[50] (CERTAINLY NO ONE JUDGES A *DOMINUS* IN HIS HANDLING A SLAVE)

The *Gesta de Xysti purgatione* opens with a property dispute: a Roman *patricius* named Marinianus learns from one of his slaves that his neighbour has willed some choice Sicilian property to the church that he had apparently hoped to procure for himself.[51] After hearing about the transaction, Marinianus rushes directly to the pope and asks for the land, but Xystus refuses to grant his request, saying that the property will go to the support of the poor.[52] On what basis Marinianus thought that he had been defrauded by his neighbour the text does not say, but it is clear that the *patricius*' desire for financial gain was a factor in Xystus' rejection of his

[46] For Gregory's household, see Markus 1997: 8–14;

[47] ALTARE TIBI DS SALVO HORMISDA PAPA MERCURIUS CUM SOCIIS OF ('Mercurius with his associates offered this altar to you Holy Lord, in the lifetime of Pope Hormisdas'). For the inscription, see De Rossi 1870a: 143.

[48] *Liber Pontificalis* (ed. Duchesne 1886–1957: I, 285). It is interesting to speculate about the social identities of the *socii* with whom Mercurius dedicated the altar at S. Clemente in the name of Pope Hormisdas. Were they his fellow priests and clergy at the *titulus*? Or were they members of his larger domestic network, brothers, sisters, patrons, and clients?

[49] Apart from his aristocratic name, there is no evidence that this Proiectus was of senatorial rank. Richards (1979: 243) explicitly denies Mercurius such a background.

[50] *Gesta de Xysti purgatione* 21–2 (ed. Wirbelauer 1993: 264).

[51] The text refers explicitly to the old man's naming of the church as his heir: 'Crescentio fully made and established the church as his heir.' (*Crescentio . . . in integro fecit ecclesiam heredam atque instituit*) *Gesta de Xysti purgatione* 4–5 (ed. Wirbelauer 1993: 262).

[52] *Gesta de Xysti purgatione* 1–14 (ed. Wirbelauer 1993: 262).

complaint: 'The Church does not become rich from my revenues, my dear son; it desires to relieve the old age of the poor, not to ruin them.'[53]

The story strives to paint the interaction between bishop and householder in bold class and spiritual colours, with Xystus and the church as the righteous champions of the elderly and the poor and Marinianus as an avaricious, aristocratic land-grabber.[54] And indeed a more 'Symmachan' reading of this passage would draw attention to Xystus' refusal to alienate church property upon Marinianus' request, a move that perhaps dramatizes Symmachus' own rearticulation of a law prohibiting the alienation of ecclesiastical property at the Roman council of 502, as Julia Hillner suggests in this volume.[55] But the domestic background of the scene is equally important to its rhetorical force: the economic success of a householder's *domus* is impeded (through the perceived loss of profit), and the indirect cause of the impediment is the Roman church, which appears in the narrative as the primary competitor to the aristocrat's domestic interests. The householder then attempts to rectify the perceived wrong by going to the bishop himself, who appears in this part of the story as the opposing party in a civil dispute over property. However, Xystus refuses to comply with Marinianus' bald attempt to circumvent the terms of a legitimate will through extra-legal negotiation.[56] The scene closes with the greedy *paterfamilias* walking off in a huff: *hoc audito Marinianus habuit in semetipsum et discessit ab eo* ('Hearing this, Marinianus contained himself and walked away from him').[57]

A second domestic altercation immediately follows, in which the tension between *dominus* and bishop is even more acute. Here we read not of a disputed will but of the disputed status of a ward and the illegal appropriation of his property by an unscrupulous guardian.[58] In this scene, a young, freeborn nobleman and man of wealth named Epifanius had been raised in

[53] *Gesta de Xysti purgatione* 11–12 (ed. Wirbelauer 1993: 262: *Nihil ex meis reditibus crevit ecclesiae, unde, carissime fili, pauperorum senecta sublevare desiderat ecclesia, non subvertere*).

[54] The bishop as 'friend of the poor' is a familiar model of late antique episcopal identity and authority. See Brown 1992 and 2002.

[55] MGH AA XII (ed. Mommsen 1894: 444). Hillner argues that Symmachus largely reiterated secular legislation passed under the direction of the praetorian prefect Caecina Decius Maximinus Basilius in 483 during the brief interim between the death of Simplicius and the election of Felix III. Basilius and his colleagues apparently attempted to put an end to the practice of clerics selling off church properties in order to raise money for bribes in episcopal elections. See also Pietri 1978b: 334.

[56] On this extra-legal practice of dispute resolution in late antiquity, see Harries 1999: 172.

[57] *Gesta de Xysti pugatione* 13–14 (ed. Wirbelauer 1993: 262).

[58] According to Roman law, fatherless children (male and female) were required to have a legal guardian up until they reached the age of adulthood, which in our period was twenty-five years. Arjava 1996: 112; Evans Grubbs 1995: 324.

the house of his guardian, another *patricius* and *exconsul* named Bassus.[59] According to the tale, Epifanius flees his guardian's house after being struck by one of the slaves and seeks refuge with Xystus, to whom he complains of his mistreatment in the *domus Bassi* despite his freeborn status.[60] Here the narrative plays upon broader Roman anxiety about guardian–ward relations as well as the increasingly frequent activity of the bishop as counsellor, spokesperson, or arbiter in legal affairs.[61]

For it is in his capacity as an advocate that Xystus visits Bassus in his home, where he questions the *paterfamilias* about Epifanius' charges.[62] However, rather than accepting Xystus' authority in the matter, Bassus rejects the bishop's presence in his *domus* outright: 'Certainly no one', he pronounces in the epigram cited above, 'judges a *dominus* in his handling of a slave.'[63] In response to the bishop's visit, Bassus throws Epifanius out of his house and illegally seizes his ward's property.[64] Recognizing perhaps the limitations of his own extra-legal authority in a domestic dispute, Xystus appeals directly to Valentinian III (depicted as residing in Rome), where he asks the emperor to uphold the young man's freeborn status and return his property.[65]

59 *Gesta de Xysti purgatione* 15 (ed. Wirbelauer 1993: 262): 'Thereupon the freeborn Epifanius had been begot of noble parents and raised with property here, as it were, in the *domus* of the ex-consul Bassus.' '*Epifanius igitur ingenuus ex nobilibus parentibus procreatus et facultatibus hic nutritus fuerat quasi in domum Bassi ex consule.*'

60 While not explicitly stated, the text implies that Epifanius sought asylum with Xystus. On ecclesiastical asylum in late antiquity, see Ducloux 1994 and Rapp 2005: 253–60, esp. 258–9, where she discusses how asylum was sometimes seen to derive from the personal authority of the bishop.

61 On the rise of the late antique bishop as a defender of citizens and legal arbiter, see Selb 1967; Humfress and Garnsey 2001: 72–7; Harries 1999: 191–216; Brown 1992; Rapp 2005: 260–273: and Uhalde 2007. I am especially grateful to Kevin Uhalde for his help in this section.

62 We might compare Xystus' visit to Bassus' home with Ambrose of Milan's far more convivial call on the home of an unnamed *matrona* in Trastevere, where, according to his biographer Paulinus, he performed a private mass for the woman and her *domus* (Paulinus, *Vita S. Ambrosii* 10.1; see also 4.1, where Ambrose recounts seeing the Roman bishop Liberius (354–366) make a similar visit). Hospitality is yet another dimension of the bishop's relationship to the household, and is explored in Sessa, *The Household and the Bishop: Space, Social Practice and Authority in Late Antique Rome* (in preparation).

63 *Gesta de Xysti purgatione* 21–2, cited above. Historically speaking, Bassus' statement is not entirely true. For example, emperors repeatedly attempted to limit the *dominus*' freedom to abuse or kill his slaves, and, in fact, among the judicial functions of the late Roman urban prefect was to hear cases made by slaves against their masters. For example, if the urban prefect determined that a master had seriously beaten a slave or denied him/her food, he could force the *dominus* to sell the slave. The urban prefect could also order a slave's immediate manumission were the master to have prostituted him/her. See Chastagnol 1960: 111 n. 3 for references to the legislation that dates from the reign of Septimius Severus to Justinian.

64 *Gesta de Xysti purgatione* 22–3 (ed. Wirbelauer 1993: 264).

65 *Gesta de Xysti purgatione* 22–5 (ed. Wirbelauer 1993: 264).

Lay households in the *Gesta de Xysti purgatione* are spaces of conflict and tension, wherein householders perversely exercise their paternal power. In the case of Marinianus, it is his unbalanced desire to increase the wealth of his *domus* that impels him to interfere in what is a pious act of lay patronage to the church. Bassus' crime is even more unconscionable: to deny a ward his rightful legal status and, in turn, to steal all of the very goods he was legally bound to protect.[66] The practice of household management is all but reduced in these scenes to the crass and impious material interests of the householder, who perceives his authority within this domain to be, as Bassus asserts, absolute. From the perspective of these *domini*, the bishop's interventions in their private affairs constitute unwelcome intrusions into the domestic sphere, even if they are performed within an (at least partially) accepted juridical framework. Xystus, by contrast, emerges as a prudent and exceedingly just Christian official. He exercises his authority within the household largely through extra-judicial means, through his refusal to abide by Marinianus' claim to his neighbour's property and through his advocacy on Epifanius' behalf, first before Bassus at the *dominus*' own home, and then in an unspecified location (an imperial palace?) before the emperor himself.

On the one hand, therefore, a late Roman audience of the *Gesta de Xysti purgatione* would have undoubtedly associated the actions of the fictionalized Xystus with the judicial activities of real Roman bishops that developed in conjunction with the traditional practice of private negotiation between parties and the rise of episcopal arbitration.[67] On the other, he or she might also have compared Xystus' agonistic relationship to these two *domus* with certain biblical and early Christian narratives that also depict the household as a space of conflict and the relationship between householders and holy men as sharply divisive.

Paul's letter to the householder Philemon concerning his slave Onesimus offers one such intertext.[68] In the biblical story, Onesimus escapes from his master Philemon in Phrygia and finds his way to Rome, where he meets Paul. There he is apparently converted and baptized by

[66] Guardianship was heavily regulated in Roman law: *CTh* 3.17.1 (319); 3.30.1 (314) and 3.30.2 (probably between 319 and 323) state that guardians are legally bound to make good on any property lost under their management for their ward; even 'superfluous animals' were not to be sold. *CTh* 3.30.3 (in 326). *CTh* 2.16.1 (326) and 3.32.1 (322) state expressly that the landed interests of minors (i.e. those under twenty-five years of age) cannot be alienated by their guardian.

[67] Note, however, that here Xystus is not portrayed as a third-party arbiter, since such an arrangement traditionally required the consent of both parties. This is distinctly *not* the situation represented in the *Gesta de Xysti purgatione*.

[68] On Paul's letter to Philemon and domestic management, see Joubert 1995.

the apostle, though this fact does not, as Paul tacitly admits, change the man's legal status: Onesimus is still Philemon's legal property and must return to his master at once. Nevertheless, Paul directs Philemon to treat his slave differently now that he is a Christian: 'So if you consider me your partner, receive him as you would receive me . . . Confident of your obedience, I write to you knowing that you will do even more than I say.'[69]

The stories are not identical: Epifanius is not actually a slave, and Paul, unlike Xystus, does not demand that Philemon relinquish his 'property'. Nor, obviously, does Paul petition the emperor for assistance in the dispute. But like Xystus, Paul directly interferes in the running of a man's *domus* when he instructs Philemon in the letter to treat Onesimus with special care in light of his spiritual transformation. There is, it would seem, biblical precedent for Xystus' unspoken assumption that his authority extends into the domestic sphere. Unfortunately, however, there is no record of Philemon's response to Paul's intrusion into his household affairs. Thus we are left to wonder: Did he welcome the apostle's attentions? Or did he respond to them with hostility and frustration, as did the imagined householders of the *Gesta de Xysti purgatione*?

Though the letters of Paul say little about the possibility of conflict between householder and holy man, texts like the *Acts of Paul and Thecla* make such conflict the main subject of the narrative. As discussed in a number of excellent studies, many of the second- and third-century *Apocryphal Acts of the Apostles* portray traditional Roman households at moments of acute crisis, when Christian apostles (like Paul) persuade key members of an elite pagan *domus* (often daughters and wives) to abandon their traditional domestic obligations of marriage and child-bearing, and to embrace a new set of Christian ethics grounded in the practice of celibacy.[70] In texts like the *Acts of Paul and Thecla* and the *Acts of Peter* the apostle's influence permanently sunders the *domus* and subverts the traditional interests of their fathers and husbands.

While the *Gesta de Xysti purgatione* recommends neither celibacy nor the destruction of the *domus*, it builds upon narratives like the *Acts of Paul and Thecla* and the *Acts of Peter* in striking ways. In both of the pre-Constantinian texts, embittered, lustful householders attempt to silence the apostle's blatant intrusion into their domestic affairs via legal recourse by taking the interloper to court. For example, in the *Acts of Paul and Thecla*, Thecla's fiancé Thamyris accuses Paul before the governor, who

[69] Philemon vv. 17–21. [70] Bibliography noted above, n. 17.

rules that Paul is to be thrown out of the city and Thecla burned alive.[71] In the *Acts of Peter*, a similar scenario is imagined following Peter's success in Rome at winning the hearts and minds of the wife of the aristocratic Albinus and the four concubines of the city's prefect Agrippa, who then takes justice into his own hands following consultation with Albinus and orders Peter's execution.[72]

Though distinctly redirected, all of these elements – wicked *domini*, a judicial context, and charges wielded against the 'nefarious' influence of the apostle within the *domus* – reappear in the account of Xystus' interactions with Marinianus and Bassus. In place of sexual desire, for example, the *Gesta de Xysti purgatione* substitutes avarice and materiality, but in both cases the householder's character is marred by his uncontrollable excess. Moreover, just as Albinus and Agippus unite to bring about Peter's earthly demise, so do Marinianus and Bassus join forces to destroy Xystus' reputation by accusing him before Valentinian III of sexually violating a consecrated Christian woman.[73] While in the *Apocryphal Acts* the apostle is charged with the crime of encouraging celibacy, here we find an updated version of the move: Xystus is accused not of preaching a continent life, but of defiling a woman already dedicated to such ascetic ideals.

Another early sixth-century text about Symmachus known as the 'Laurentian Fragment' preserves a similar charge of sexual misconduct, thus suggesting that Symmachus had actually been accused of such a crime.[74] To a certain extent one could interpret this narrative development as an aspect of the text's specific polemical context. But charges of sexual impropriety were frequently levelled against Roman clergy in late antiquity and we must also, therefore, read the detail as the introduction of a motif.[75]

71 *Acts of Paul and Thecla* 16–21 (ed. Lipsius and Bonnet 1990: 246–50).

72 *Acts of Peter* 34 (5)–35 (6) (ed. Lipsius and Bonnet 1990: 86–8).

73 *Gesta de Xysti purgatione* 27–9 (ed. Wirbelauer 1993: 264): 'Angered, however, over what had just been said, Marinianus came to Bassus, speaking, as it were, of Bishop Xystus's malice, and what he had heard through Peter, a slave of Bishop Xystus: that [Xystus] had defiled the consecrated Chrisogonites. After a plan was hatched, the two began to make a complaint against him to the emperor Valentinian' *Iratus autem Marinianus de quae supra dicta sunt, venit ad Bassum, dicens quasi de malitia Xysti episcopi, et quod per Petrum audierat servum episcopi Xysti, eo quod consecratam Chrisogonitem stuprasset. Consilio inito coeperunt ambo accusare eum augusto Valentiniano.*

74 For the Laurentian Fragment, see *Liber Pontificalis* I (ed. Duchesne, xxx–xxxii) and Richards 1979: 81.

75 Jerome (*Ep.* 22.28) pilloried Roman clerics for lining up outside the bedroom doors of wealthy Roman *matronae*. In this respect, the spectre of sexual misconduct was closely linked to financial scandals involving Christian women. This may have been precisely what Valentinian I tried to mitigate against when he passed a law in 370 forbidding ecclesiastics and monks to accept legacies from Roman women (*CTh* 16.2.20). On the *topos* of sexual dishonour and clerical authority, see Fontaine 1988.

What is more, a female 'love interest' is among the primary tropes mobilized by the authors of *Apocryphal Acts*, who used the heroine in order to highlight the tension between the two male contenders for her allegiance, the husband/betrothed and the apostle.[76] In both cases, the moral authority of the apostle/bishop is ironically called into question by unethical (and, in the case of the *Apocryphal Acts*, pagan) *domini*, whose obviously false accusations against their competitor paradoxically shore up the Christian holy man's moral authority within the community.

As noted above, the householder's resolve to punish the apostle for destroying his *domus* typically culminates in a final courtroom scene, where a Roman (and pagan) judge pronounces the apostle guilty as charged and orders his execution. The *Gesta de Xysti purgatione* too concludes outside of the householder's *domus* in a judicial setting, though in this later text the very institution that brings about the apostle's earthly demise exonerates Xystus and pronounces his authority to be beyond judgement.

Following Marinianus' and Bassus' appearance before Valentinian III, the emperor is moved by the clamouring of the *urbana plebs* to examine the householders' allegations in 'a single contest' (*in uno conflicto*).[77] The emperor convenes the trial (*probatio*) in the *basilica Heleniana, quod dicitur Sessorium*, the Constantinian church founded by the emperor's mother Helena that is now known as S. Croce in Gerusalemne. There a jury comprised of all of Rome's senators, presbyters, and monks sits with the emperor himself in judgement of the bishop of Rome.[78] However, the jury declines to hear Bassus' and Marinianus' evidence against the pope altogether, and moves to terminate the trial in the bishop's favour, declaring in the words of an *exconsul* named Maximus that 'it is not permitted to pass sentence against the *pontifex*'.[79] Indeed, while Bassus may have appealed to his *patria potestas* when he proclaimed that no one may judge a *dominus* in matters pertaining to slaves, the Roman citizenry trumped his claim when it

[76] A narrative device identified and discussed in detail by Cooper 1996: 51–62.

[77] *Gesta de Xysti purgatione* 37–42 (ed. Wirbelauer 1993: 264).

[78] Such a 'mixed' assembly may not be entirely the stuff of the authors' imagination. An assembly of senators and clergy met in Rome in 483 under the authority of the praetorian prefect Caecius Decius Maximus Basilius Iunior in order to block Felix III's attempt to alienate certain ecclesiastical properties. Cf. MGH AA XII (ed. Mommsen 1894: 444–51), as discussed by Pietri 1981a: 441. However, the *Gesta de Xysti purgatione* takes some poetic liberties when it places Xystus as a defendant before such a quasi-civil jury, since Roman law stated that bishops could only be judged in ecclesiastical courts. See *CTh* 16.2.12 (355), 16.2.41 (411 or 412) and Rapp 2005: 276.

[79] *Gesta de Xysti purgatione* 64 (ed. Wirbelauer 1993: 268): *non licet enim adversus pontificum dare sententiam*. Pronouncements similar to this appear in a number of the Symmachan forgeries. Cf. *Gesta Polychronii* 70–1 (ed. Wirbelauer 1993: 276) and the *Gesta Marcellini* 96–7 and 219–20 (ed. Wirbelauer 1993: 290 and 300).

unambiguously declared that the bishop of Rome is above civic judgement altogether. Here the logic of Roman law, which stipulated that bishops could only be tried in ecclesiastical courts, is brutally applied to a case that involves episcopal meddling in the domestic affairs of Roman householders.[80]

This imposition of episcopal authority upon the city and its households is further conveyed in the *Gesta de Xysti purgatione* is spatial terms, through the situation of Xystus' trial in the *basilica Sessoriana*. To be sure, the use of an *ecclesia* as a place of arbitration and judgement was commonplace and, in fact, this particular church was the site of Symmachus' first trial on 1 September 502 before a group of bishops and clergy – an event that, in some scholars' view, explains its appearance in the *Gesta de Xysti purgatione*.[81] Yet, the *basilica Sessoriana* was not only the site of Symmachus' trial; it was also a church used by members of the imperial family as a veritable private chapel.[82] In other words, Xystus is tried and his authority proclaimed absolute within the emperor's own *domus*. In this respect the *Gesta de Xysti purgatione* shares with other texts among the Symmachan forgeries and with related sources like the *Actus Silvestri* an interest in manufacturing a history of a relationship between the Roman bishop and the emperor that perhaps had never existed. But it is important to point out that this relationship is presented in distinctly domestic terms: the emperor's house has also become God's house (*domus Dei*), the care of which has been transferred to the bishop. For in the very next scene Xystus takes on the emperor's role of conciliar convener and judge when he calls for a second assembly in the church, this time with only Roman priests invited, in order to determine the punishments of the two incorrigible householders. Depicted as meting out justice literally from the emperor's own place (*sedit in eodem loco, quia ibidem consistebat augustus*) Xystus calls for the householders' damnation and excommunication.[83] And though both men beg to be received back into communion with their bishop (with Bassus even offering the church all of his property), Xystus categorically denies their appeal, and the two men die banished from the Church.[84]

In the *Gesta de Xysti purgatione* episcopal authority is not subtly insinuated into the household. It is legally thrust upon it through a proclamation

80 For the legislation, see above, n. 78. Technically, of course, the fictional case against Xystus involved only the sexual allegations, but the larger narrative context closely connects the trumped-up charges to Xystus' interference in the two men's management of their households.

81 Pietri 1981a: 441; Richards 1979: 81; Moorhead 1992: 123.

82 Colli 1996: 771–815.

83 *Gesta de Xysti purgatione* 75–6 (ed. Wirbelauer 1993: 268): 'And he sat in the same place, since the emperor used to stand just there.'

84 *Gesta de Xysti purgatione* 87–8 (ed. Wirbelauer 1993: 268).

of a leading senator at a trial arbitrated by the emperor himself. Drawing on familiar exempla of domestic situations from the Bible and the *Apocryphal Acts* and assimilating these *topoi* with contemporary juridical practices, the authors of the *Gesta de Xysti purgatione* constructs a model of episcopal authority that is seemingly incompatible with the traditional agency exercised by householders. Presented as the emperor's proxy in the city, the man who literally occupies his chair, the bishop appears in unambiguous terms as the city's leading moral, legally constituted authority, whose jurisdiction extends from the *ecclesia* to the *domus*. Indeed, as Rome's ultimate household, the ecclesiastical space of the *basilica Sessoriana* emerges from this narrative as the venue in which episcopal authority is defended and buttressed, and as the new space for the mediation of civic affairs. The private *domus*, by contrast, fades into the background, where it is remembered only as a place of impious (and now seemingly illegal) resistance to the encroaching arm of the bishop. The narrative ends with a chilling warning to any householder who may dare challenge the bishop's presence in the *domus*: protest at the risk of your own soul.

AN ECONOMY OF SALVATION: HOUSEHOLDS AND BISHOPS IN THE EPISCOPAL *GESTA MARTYRUM*

Such a unilateral vision of the householder's relationship to the bishop was not the only one imaginable in late antique Rome. For the writers and readers of the episcopal passions grouped among the *gesta martyrum*, the establishment of episcopal authority within the *domus* involved a process that preserved the householder's agency and restored his house. In these 'papal legends' a very different domestic sphere emerges: here we find the household as the space of a more pious and productive exchange between bishop and householder. Instead of the 'top-down' institutional framework that characterized the relationship between the male protagonists in the *Gesta de Xysti purgatione*, the episcopal passions of the *gesta martyrum* portray a more reciprocal relationship created through participation in rituals of patronage and liturgy.

To examine this alternative model of interaction between bishop and householder, we shall focus upon a *topos* that appears in some half-dozen episcopal passions.[85] Although these narratives culminate in scenes of trials,

[85] See above, n. 26. Although the *Passio S. Marcelli* features the *topos* explored below, the protagonist of the episode is not Pope Marcellus but the deacon Cyriacus. Given its non-episcopal focus, I have omitted the *Passio S. Marcelli* from the present study.

torture, and death (hence their characterization as *passiones*), they formulaicly incorporate tales of 'domestic conversion', episodes in which a Roman bishop and a pagan Roman householder engage in a series of encounters that bring about the householder's personal conversion and the Christianization of his home. What interests me about these encounters is not the act of religious conversion itself, for it is unlikely that these texts functioned as proselytizing documents in the traditional sense. Rather, I am drawn to how the narratives represent conversion as a socially dynamic process of exchange. On the one hand, bishops and householders trade favours in a manner that accords well with our understanding of ancient patronage as an asymmetrical but nevertheless voluntary, reciprocal, and personal relationship between two or more parties.[86] On the other hand, these exchanges also incorporate a more supernatural element, when the bishop proffers his power to heal and baptize. As we shall see, this 'rhetoric of giving' mobilized in the episcopal *gesta matyrum* delineates a discourse of episcopal trust and authority that simultaneously establishes the bishop's authority within the household and shores up the householder's own position within his house and the city at large.

Without suggesting that these passions were created or consumed in concert (indeed both internal differences and independent manuscript histories render such an assumption untenable), the following pages examine this *topos* as an important medium of episcopal and domestic authority in late antique Rome. In order to facilitate our discussion, we shall look closely at a single, paradigmatic example of the *topos*: the *Passio SS. Alexandri, Eventii et Theodoli martyrum*, a sixth- or perhaps early seventh-century account of the martyrdoms of the early second-century Roman bishop Alexander (110–115) and the two priests Eventius and Theodolus.[87] As a potentially late iteration of the *topos*, the passion of Alexander presents an especially detailed and nuanced account of the bishop's interactions within the domestic sphere. Though we shall focus upon this particular text, the reader can compare it with other iterations of the *topos* summarized in the chart included as an appendix to this chapter.

[86] See, for example, the definition of patronage in Wallace-Hadrill 1989: 3.

[87] Dufourcq (1900–10: 1, 14 suggested (via the dating of a seventeenth-century English scholar John Pearson) that the *Passio SS. Alexandri, Eventii, et Theodoli* is an early seventh-century text. In favour of a seventh-century date is the fact that Pope Alexander's *cultus* is entirely literary and late. He does not appear as a martyr, for example, in either the Liberian Catalogue or the *Liber Pontificalis*. See Amore 1975: 83–6.

Before his death at the hands of an evil Roman *comes*, Bishop Alexander was involved in two domestic crises. The first concerned the *domus* of a *vir illustris* and urban prefect named Hermes, whose only son had fallen ill and then died after a group of pagan priests failed to cure him. Following his son's death, Hermes learned from the boy's nurse about the healing powers of Alexander, the outlawed Christian bishop presently hiding from the Roman authorities at the tomb of St Peter. To a late sixth- or seventh-century audience, of course, the *martyrium* of St Peter was not a suburban hideout on the Vatican hill, but where Christians actively worshipped at Constantine's basilica and, moreover, where Roman bishops had been buried since the middle of the fifth century.[88] In imagining Alexander absconding to Peter's tomb, the narrative simultaneously invokes the age of the persecutions and the very post-Constantinian development of the site as a major liturgical and episcopal centre.[89]

Initially dubious and perhaps wary of associating with a Christian, Hermes sends the nurse to Alexander as his proxy, who carries the son on her shoulders to the bishop at St Peter's. Alexander receives the dead boy, says a prayer over his body, and resuscitates him. When the nurse returns with the boy alive, Hermes is overjoyed. He rushes to Alexander, falls to his feet, and asks the bishop to come to his home in order to baptize himself, his wife, his sister, his children, as well as his 1250 slaves, and their wives and children, whom he then proceeds to manumit.[90] The bishop immediately obliges and Hermes responds in a manner fitting to his position as head of the newly restored household: he gives Alexander his wife's *patrimonium*, as well as some of his own property, and names Alexander as the guardian (*tutor*) of his only son.[91]

But in the wake of his household's conversion, Hermes is arrested by the *comes* and entrusted to a tribune named Quirinus, who guards the former prefect in his own home.[92] While interrogating his prisoner, Quirinus learns of Hermes' own tale of domestic woe, and how Alexander restored

88 Krautheimer 1985.

89 The *gesta martyrum* frequently portray Christians living in and around the city's suburban *martyria* and catacombs. While such practices are generally thought to have no historical basis, their frequent portrayal in the martyr narratives warrants closer attention than has been given in the past.

90 *Passio SS. Alexandri, Eventii, et Theodoli martyrum* (ed. Mombritius 1978: 1, 44).

91 *Passio SS. Alexandri, Eventii, et Theodoli martyrum* (ed. Mombritius 1978: 1, 46). The reader should note that Hermes' story is told in two parts, with the initial information about the baptisms given at the very beginning of the passion, and the details of the exchange recounted in a subsequent scene as a later 'flashback'. Such a complex plot structure underlines the literary sophistication of the *gesta martyrum*.

92 Domestic imprisonment was not an uncommon practice in antiquity and late antiquity. See Krause 1996b: 225–6.

his household by bringing his young son back to life. Upon hearing Hermes' story, Quirinus inquires whether Alexander, whom we learn has also been imprisoned in the tribune's *domus*, may be willing to assist his household:

"Let Christ therefore win my soul through you [Alexander and Hermes] in this way: I have an adult daughter and I want to hand her over to a husband. Her appearance is certainly beautiful, but a tumor surrounds her neck. Make her healthy and I shall both grant everything to him [Alexander?] and avow Christ with you." Holy Alexander says to him, "Go and lead her to me in prison at once. Take this collar from my neck, place it on her and have her remain [in prison] together with the collar and by morning you will find her healed."[93]

Yet the negotiations do not end here. For it is then Alexander's turn to make a demand of Quirinus:

"How many people have been shut up in this prison?" And [Quirinus] says, "about twenty." And holy Alexander said to him, "find out if there are any locked up here on account of the name of Christ." And after Quirinus had inquired, he found out and reported to [Alexander] saying, "there is this Eventius, an old presbyter, and Theodolus, whom they say has come from the East and is also a presbyter." Alexander says to him, "Go quickly but escort them to me with honour."[94]

Each makes good on his end of the bargain: Alexander heals Balbina with the collar through the intervention of a mysterious young boy, who appears in the cell with Balbina and demands in return for her healing that she remain a perpetual virgin – an additional request to which Quirinus apparently assents.[95] Quirinus then permits Alexander to have an audience with the two imprisoned Christian priests. But Alexander then ups the ante: 'If you want to offer me a favor (*beneficium*)', he says to Quirinus, 'persuade everyone who is in prison to be baptized too so that they may

[93] *Passio SS. Alexandri, Eventii, et Theodoli martyrum* (ed. Mombritius 1978: 1, 46): 'Lucretur animam meam ergo per vos Christus hoc modo: "Habeo filiam adultam et volo eam tradere viro, cuius aspectum quidem pulchritudo condecorat sed collum eius struma circondat. Hanc vos salvam facite et conferam ei omnia et vobiscum Christum confitear." Dicit ei sanctus Alexander: "Vade et adduc eam ad carcerem ad me cito et tolle boiam de collo meo et impone ei and fac eam simul manere cum boia et mane eam invenes [*sic*] salvam."'

[94] *Passio SS. Alexandri, Eventii, et Theodoli martyrum* (ed. Mombritius 1978: 1, 46): '"Quot sunt in isto carcere clausae personae?" At ille, "Prope viginti." Et dixit ei sanctus Alexander, "Require si sunt hic aliqui pro cristi [*sic*] nomine clausi." Et cum requisset, invenit ac renuntiavit ei dicens, "Est hic Eventius presbiter senex et Theodolus quem dicunt de oriente venisse et idem presbiter." Dicit ei Alexander, "Vade cursim sed cum honore duc eos ad me."'

[95] *Passio SS. Alexandri, Eventii, et Theodoli martyrum* (ed. Mombritius 1978: 1, 46). Later in the narrative (ed. Mombritius 1978: 1, 47) we read that 'his daughter holy Balbina devoted her life to virginity' (*filia eius Balbina sancta in virginitate permansit*).

become Christians.'[96] Quirinus reluctantly agrees and shortly thereafter the prisoners are converted. The entire episode concludes with Alexander's baptism of the tribune, his daughter, and his entire *domus.*

The story of Alexander's interventions in the households of the Roman aristocrat Hermes and the tribune Quirinus combines a number of familiar biblical and hagiographical elements. The healing of a family member and the conversion of a pagan household by a visiting Christian holy man are motifs found in many popular Christian texts, from Christ's raising of Lazarus in the Gospels, to Peter's conversion of Cornelius' household in Acts, to Martin's healing and conversion of a pagan household depicted in his early fifth-century *Vita* by Sulpicius Severus.[97] We might also compare this particular late antique Roman *topos* of domestic conversion to some of the household tales depicted in the *Apocryphal Acts of the Apostles*. For instance, in the *Acts of Andrew* (as known from Gregory of Tours' Latin epitome, *Liber de miraculis beati Andreae apostoli*), we similarly find a nurse acting as a temporary conduit between apostle and householder.[98] But an even closer intertext is the story of Andrew's interactions with Medius of Philippi. In this tale, the apostle is approached by Medius, who asks Andrew to heal his crippled son. Aware that Medius had cruelly imprisoned several other children, Andrew offers him a deal: 'If you want your prayers to come before God, first release the chains of those who suffer, so that your son may also be freed of his disability. For I see that the cruelty which you inflict impedes my prayers.'[99] Medius agrees to the apostle's terms, releases the children, and his son is promptly healed.

To a certain extent, therefore, the basic elements of the domestic conversion episode are not unique to episcopal *gesta martyrum*. Healing commonly encodes spiritual authority and identity in early Christian literature, while conversion is a typical outcome, as both the *Acts of Andrew* and the *Vita S. Martini* attest. Moreover, though Andrew's request of Medius is prompted in part by concerns for spiritual efficacy, the reciprocal structure of their arrangement suggests that the exchange model so prominently featured in

[96] *Passio SS. Alexandri, Eventii, et Theodoli martyrum* (ed. Mombritius 1978: I, 46): 'Dicit ei sanctus Alexandri, "si vis mihi praestare beneficium, suade omnibus qui sunt in carcere baptizari et ut fiant christiani."'

[97] For the raising of Lazarus, see John 11.38–53; Peter's conversion of the household of the soldier Cornelius, Acts 10; and Martin's healing and conversion of a pagan household, see the *Vita S. Martini* 17 (ed. Fontaine 1967: 288–90).

[98] *Acts of Andrew* 30 (ed. MacDonald 1990: 309).

[99] *Acts of Andrew* 15 (ed. MacDonald 1990: 234): 'Et ideo, si praeces tuas ad Deum vis proficisci, absolve prius miserorum catenam, ut et filius tuus a debilitate laxetur; nam video inpedimentus ferre precibus meis malitiam quam exerces.'

the *Passio SS. Alexandri, Eventii et Theodoli martyrum* too has a long literary history.

However, just as the authors of the *Gesta de Xysti purgatione* adapted inherited literary motifs, assimilating them to a definitely post-Constantinian legal framework, so did the authors of the episcopal martyr narratives mobilize these models in new ways. Perhaps the most obvious redirection is the characterization of the householder himself, who regularly appears in these sources not as a wicked and immodest *dominus*, but as a caring and concerned father, who approaches the bishop for assistance.[100] But surely the most striking adaptation engineered by the authors concerns the depiction of the encounter between the householder and the Christian holy man. While in the *Apocryphal Acts* this encounter generally takes the form of a fierce antagonism that literally destroys the household, here we find a more 'domesticated' and socially productive competition, wherein the two exchange favours rather than blows or criminal accusations. The fabled rivalry between apostle and *dominus* has been updated for a seemingly more traditional late antique Christian audience by transposing the relationship between household and bishop onto a thoroughly Roman cultural register.

The 'rhetoric of giving' that characterizes the *topos* of domestic conversion can be gleaned not only from the dialogic narrative form favoured by the authors but also from their use of a socio-economic vocabulary. While we must not press any philological observation too far in the *gesta martyrum* in light of the present state of the published editions, we may draw attention to linguistic patterns of the passion.[101] For example, Quirinus' initial proposition to Alexander opens with the word *lucrari*, a verb meaning 'to win' (as translated here), 'to gain', 'to make a profit', and which also connoted in late Latin 'to persuade' and 'to convert'.[102] Though a more orthodox reading of the sentence may privilege the Christian meaning of *lucrari*, the context makes clear that both connotations are simultaneously operative. Quirinus does not simply offer to be converted by Christ; rather, he proposes to Alexander and Hermes that Christ 'gain' his soul in exchange for the healing of his daughter. Later in the story Alexander too

100 The gendered semantics of this change are intriguing, since most often in the *Apocryphal Acts* it is a female household member who reaches out to the apostle for healing and spiritual instruction, such as Maximilla does in the *Acts of Andrew* 30.

101 For a discussion of various available printed editions of the *gesta martyrum* and their respective problems and merits, see Sessa 2003.

102 *Passio SS. Alexandri, Eventii, et Theodoli martyrum* (ed. Mombritius 1978: 1, 46, text cited above, n. 93). Lewis and Short, s.v. *lucror*, cf. I (a) and II (a).

expressly invokes a language of exchange when he asks Quirinus whether he wants to offer him a *beneficium*, and when he demands that the tribune escort the two priests to him *cum honore*, 'with honour'.[103]

Historians of imperial Rome have frequently drawn attention to such discourses of reciprocity and honour as central to the maintenance of aristocratic agency in an increasingly autocratic society.[104] It is no surprise, therefore, that the traditionalist authors of the *Passio SS. Alexandri, Eventii et Theodoli martyrum* emphasized the agency of the householders in their own conversion. In the case of Hermes, the encounter between bishop and householder centres upon the resurrection of the urban prefect's son, in exchange for whose life Hermes hands over to the bishop some of his most important possessions, including the boy himself. But perhaps the most stunning detail is the 1250 household members whom, at Hermes' express direction, Alexander baptizes. Like nearly all of the other martyr narratives that include the *topos*, the *Passio SS. Alexandri, Eventii, et Theodoli martyrum* presents a precise figure for the size of Hermes' household. For example, in the *Passio S. Callisti papae*, pope Callistus baptizes forty members of the consul Palmatius' household, while in the *Passio S. Clementis martyris et episcopi*, Sisinnius' *domus* of 423 is converted.[105] Such numbers need not necessarily be rejected as fantastic; they evoke the cumulative property of men of elite status, who typically owned several houses as well as properties throughout the empire, as was the case for historical senatorial householders like the Symmachi.[106] In this respect the figures spectacularly underline the householder's own wealth and status within the city: Hermes is no minor *paterfamilias*, but a man who wields control over the social and spiritual lives of a large number of individuals. His consent to engage with Alexander thus buttresses the bishop's status within the city as much as it heightens his own.

In the case of Quirinus, whose *domus* is considerably less impressive (and indeed no figures are given), conversion is also imagined as a process of

103 *Passio SS. Alexandri, Eventii, et Theodoli martyrum* (ed. Mombritius 1978: 1, 46, text cited above, n. 94).

104 Lendon 1997; Daley 1993.

105 Note the similarity of the language denoting the household size among the *gesta martyrum*: cf. *Passio S. Callisti papae* (ed. Mombritius 1978: 1, 269): 'omnem domum Palmatii et uxorum et filios aliosque promiscui sexus numero quadragintuaduos'; *Passio S. Clementis martyris et episcopi* 14 (ed. Funk and Diekamp 1913: 67): 'cum omni domo sua . . . viri cum mulieribus infantibus promiscui sexus numero quadringenti vigenti tres'; *Passio S. Stephani papae* (ed. Mombritius 1978: 11, 496): 'promiscui sexus numero sexaginto'.

106 The fourth-century orator Q. Aurelius Symmachus owned several houses within the city (including the well-known house on the Caelian, cf. *Epp.* 3.12, 14; 7.18), in the *suburbium* (*Epp.* 2.59; 6.66; 7.21), as well as an additional villa at Capua (*Ep.* 1.10).

negotiation between two mutually interested parties.[107] Here *oikonomia*, the *business* of household management, is elaborately stressed by the dialogic parley between the men, who literally barter for body and soul like two well-seasoned buyers in a Mediterranean market. While Quirinus cannot give cash or property to Alexander in exchange for Balbina's healing, he can offer what is perhaps an even more valuable late Roman commodity: bodies. Quirinus signals both his official public power and paternal authority when he agrees to 'hand over' the prisoners incarcerated in his home. And in so doing he inflects his status within the community by showing care for their salvation in a manner that parallels Hermes' agreement to convert his slaves and dependants.

Moreover, that each man elects to hand over his healed child to Alexander (Hermes entrusts his son to Alexander, whom he expressly names as the boy's *tutor*; Quirinus hands over Balbina to Alexander's care as a consecrated virgin) registers a significant shift in values from the pre-Constantinian world reflected in the *Apocryphal Acts* or, for that matter, from the agonistic domestic environment imagined in the *Gesta de Xysti purgatione*.[108] According to the social logic of the *Passio SS. Alexandri, Eventii et Theodoli martyrum*, bishops are eminently trustworthy from the householder's perspective and could play a positive role in critical dimensions of household management, including the rearing of children. Indeed Alexander's relationship to the householders closely parallels that of Paul or even Christ's in the New Testament. In certain respects, the bishop of the *gesta martyrum* is even more apostolic than the apostles.

The exchange of favours between bishop and household culminates in the final scene of the episode, when the bishop ritually converts the *domus* through his performance of the baptismal liturgy. Though we do not typically think of Christian liturgy in terms of the exchange of *beneficia*, it too, our text suggests, could be perceived in late antiquity in this precise way. Although they have received virtually no scholarly attention, the baptismal sequences of the *gesta martyrum* in general and in the episcopal passions in particular are often remarkably detailed. In some texts, like the

[107] The disparities between the two households in terms of status and wealth is intriguing and warrants further study. The *gesta martyrum* characteristically portray a wide socio-economic range of *domus*, from that of the simple *miles* Cerealis in the *Passio S. Cornelii papae* to the more 'middling' household of military tribunes like Quirinus to the *domus* of definitely aristocratic figure like Hermes. In focusing upon the aristocratic households and householders, scholars have tended to elide the remarkable social variation among the *domus* depicted in the *gesta martyrum*.

[108] Is Hermes' son to be understood as an oblate? The text does not elaborate, but Balbina is entrusted to the care of a *foemina religiosa*. See *Passio SS. Alexandri, Eventii, et Theodoli martyrum* (ed. Mombritius 1978: 1, 47).

Passio S. Cornelii papae, the rites are telescoped into a single moment and phrase (*Cornelius baptizavit*), but many other narratives present an elaborate performance that bears a striking resemblance to the ritual reality of the day. For example, in the *Passio SS. Alexandri, Eventii et Theodoli martyrum* Alexander expressly directs his two priests Eventius and Theodolus to catechize the members of the *domus Quirini* through the laying of hands – a gesture that was an element of the historical rite of baptism even as it was practised on infants in the early medieval church.[109]

But the component of the baptismal rite that best exemplifies the dialogic dynamic of liturgy is the final prayer, the three-part, oath-like exchange between celebrant and candidate uttered at the moment of the candidate's immersion into a font of blessed water.[110] While the *Passio SS. Alexandri, Eventii et Theodoli martyrum* does not portray the formula in any detail, it is reproduced with striking realism in two other episcopal martyr narratives. Consider the following synoptic comparison of the baptismal prayer in the passions of popes Stephen and Callistus with the Easter baptismal formulary from the Vatican Gelasian Sacramentary (Vat. Reg. 316), formerly known as the Old Gelasian.[111] This liturgical book, compiled by Frankish nuns at Chelles *c.* 750, is thought to preserve authentic Roman elements from the preceding century, though scholars have recently called into question the degree to which we can isolate the Roman from the later Frankish material.[112] I adduce it not as definitive of 'Roman' practice, but as offering an illustrative and relatively early formulary with which to compare the *gesta martyrum*:

[109] *Passio SS. Alexandri, Eventii, et Theodoli martyrum* (ed. Mombritius 1978: I, 47): 'And [Alexander] instructed Eventius and Thedolous that they lay their hands and make them catechumens' ('et praecepit Eventio et Tehodolo [*sic*] ut manus suas imponerent et cathecuminos eos facerent'). Compare *Actus Silvestri* (ed. Mombritius 1978: II, 512): 'After the emperor Constantine had said these and similar things, Silvester placed his hands upon his head, and, blessing him and making him a catechumen, he left [the palace]' ('Cum haec et his similia Constantinus augustus diceret, imposuit Silvester manus super caput eius et benedicans eum ac faciens cathecuminum abiit'); and *Passio S. Stephani papae* (ed. Mombritius 1978: II, 496): 'And after Stephen had catechized him and his daughter according to the custom of the Christians, he prescribed a fast for them until evening' (*Cumque [Stephanus] cathetizasset eum ac filiam eius secundum consuetudinem christianorum indixit eis ieiunium usque vesperum*). For evidence of laying hands on catechumens in late antique and early medieval practice, see the letter of the Roman Johannes Diaconus to the Roman aristocratic Senarius (dated *c.* 500), *Ad Senarium* 3 (*PL* 59.401) as well as Fisher 1965 and Willis 1994: 116–36.

[110] Whitaker 1965.

[111] *Liber Sacramentorum Romanae Aeclesiae ordinis anni circuli* (Cod. Vat. Reg. Lat. 316/Paris Bibl. Nat. 7193, 41/56) (*Sacramentarium Gelasianum*), ed. C. Mohlberg, L. Eizenhöfer and P. Siffrin 1960. On its textual history, see Vogel 1986: 68–70. One could also compare the fourth-century *Apostolic Traditions* 21.11–18, which resembles the exchange depicted in the biographies (especially the *Passio S. Callisti*).

[112] Vogel 1986: 113. On the problematic use of Vat. Reg. 316 as a witness to earlier Roman practices, see de Jong 2000: 194–5.

Passio S. Stephani	Passio S. Callisti	Cod. Vat. Reg. 316, 449–50
And he placed Nemesius in the water, saying, 'In the name of the Father, the Son and Holy Spirit, I baptize you. Do you believe,' he said, 'in God the almighty Father?' And he responded, 'I believe.' 'And in Christ,' he said, 'our Lord Jesus?' He responded, 'I believe.' 'And in the Holy Spirit?' And he responded, 'I believe.' 'The remission of sins?' He responded, 'I believe.' 'The resurrection of the flesh?' He responded, 'Lord, I believe.'[113]	And the most blessed bishop Callistus blessed the water raised from the well which was inside that same house, and after Palmatius was placed in the tub, [Callistus] said to him, 'Do you believe from your whole heart in God the omnipotent Father, maker of all things seen and unseen?' And Palmatius responded, 'I believe.' And he said to him, 'He who was born of the Holy Spirit from the Virgin Mary?' And Palmatius responded, 'I believe.' And he said to him, 'And in the Holy Spirit, the Holy Church, the remission of sins, the resurrection of the flesh?' And Palmatius shouted and exclaimed in a loud voice with tears, 'Lord, I believe.'[114]	After the font has been blessed, you next baptize each one in this manner, directly after these questions: 'Do you believe in God the Almighty Father?' Response: 'I believe.' 'Do you believe in Jesus Christ Son of our only God, having been born and suffered?' Response: 'I believe,' 'Do you believe in the Holy Spirit, the holy Church, the remission of sins, the resurrection of the flesh?' Response: 'I believe.'[115]
Depositque Nemesium in aquam dicens, 'In nomine patris et filii et spiritus-sancti, baptizo te. Credis,' ait, 'in deum patrem omnipotentem?' Et respondit, 'credo.' 'Et in Christum,' inquit, 'Iesum dominum nostrum?' Respondit, 'credo.' 'Et in spiritum sanctum?' Responditque, 'credo.' 'Remissionem peccatorum?' Respondit, 'credo.' 'Carnis resurrectionem?'	Et allatum aquam de lympho putei qui erat in eadem domo benedixit et deposito Palmatio in pelvim dixit ei beatissimus Calistus episcopus, 'Credis ex toto corde in deum patrem omnipotentem factorem omnium visibilium et invisibilium? Et respondit Palmatius, 'Credo.' Et dixit ei, 'Qui natus est de spiritu sancto ex Maria virgine?' Respondit Palmatius, 'Credo.' Et dixit ei, 'Et in spiritum sanctum	Credis in Deum Patrum omnipotentem? Resp. Credo. Credis in Iesum Christum Filium eius unicum Dominum nostrum, natum et passum? Resp. Credo. Credis et in Spiritum sanctum; sanctam ecclesiam; remissionem peccatorum; carnis ressurectionem? Resp. Credo.

[113] *Passio S. Stephani papae* (ed. Mombritius 1978: II, 496).

[114] *Passio S. Callisti papae* (ed. Mombritius 1978: I, 269) ß.

[115] Cod. Vat. Reg. Lat. 316, *c.* 449–450 (ed. Mohlberg et al. 1960): 'Inde benedicto fonte baptizas unumquemque in ordine suo, sub has interrogations.'

Qui respondit, 'credo domine.'	et sanctam ecclesiam, remissionem peccatorum, carnis resurrectionem?' Et clamare et exclamavit voce magna Palmatius cum lachrymis, 'Credo domine.'

As the comparison illustrates, the writers of the *gesta martyrum* went to great lengths to invoke the experience of baptism in their texts. Though not exactly similar, both passions closely reproduce and expand upon the precise language and form of this stage in the baptismal rite as it was actually practised – a detail that, as Dufourcq first suggested, may reveal the fingerprint of clerical writers in the production of these texts. To be sure, the use of direct speech in this section reflects an aesthetic of realism that was popular among Christian writers in late antiquity, as Erich Auerbach argued long ago.[116] But the dialogue also structurally mirrors the reciprocity that characterizes the relationship between the bishop and the householder in the earlier, more 'earthly' exchanges.[117] Here we find the householder actively participating in his own conversion, his agency once again underlined rather than occluded.

Yet to conclude our analysis on this note would be, I think, to 'misrecognize' the more hierarchical relationship between bishop and householder that these baptismal rites engender.[118] Patronage was, after all, a system predicated upon asymmetry. To be sure, the episcopal *gesta martyrum* do not immediately present the bishop as the patron. In traditional Roman terms, it is the householders who have more to offer by way of resources. Here is where liturgy plays an important role in the texts as a ritual process that could reify a certain relation of power between the bishop and householder in a manner analogous to a judicial pronouncement.[119] Just as the imagined Roman jury of the *Gesta de Xysti purgatione* redefines the boundaries of paternal power in the household through its totalizing defence of the bishop's actions within the domestic

[116] Auerbach 1953 and 1965. See also Pizzaro 1989 and Rapp 1998.

[117] It has even been suggested (Harrill 2001) that early Christian baptismal formulae were modelled on the language of Roman contract law.

[118] For the 'misrecognition' of obligation and hence status between giver and receiver that gift exchange invariably involves, see Pierre Bourdieu's well-known critique of Marcel Mauss on gift exchange economies, first discussed in Bourdieu 1977: 5–7 and developed in later works.

[119] For the idea that liturgy can establish relations of power, see the model of 'ritualization' developed by Bell 1992: 67, 90.

sphere, so does the baptismal sequence of the *gesta martyrum* recalibrate the order of domestic authority by portraying the Roman bishop as the ritual agent of the householder's salvation. According to this tale, it is the bishop's singular ability to invoke God and his supernatural agency that ultimately converts the pagan *domus* and establishes the bishop's presence within the Christian household as its apostle-like founder. The fact that the domestic conversion is presented in the *gesta martyrum* as a distinctly *liturgical* act is highly significant for the rhetorical force of the *topos.* Indeed it is Alexander's distinctly clerical actions within the private home, and not simply his suffering and death, which render him a compelling and constructive exemplum for the exercise of episcopal authority at Rome. For liturgy, unlike other miraculous spectacles of conversion or martyrdom for that matter, is repeatable by all Roman bishops past, present, and future.

As in the *Gesta de Xysti purgatione*, domestic space is highly relevant to the rhetorical programme delineated in the martyr narratives. While our first model of episcopal interaction within the *domus* concluded outside the layman's household in the more definitely ecclesiastical venue of the Sessorian basilica, these episodes of domestic conversion end within the realm of the householder's own *domus*. In presenting the *domus* as an active liturgical site, the authors of the episcopal *gesta martyrum* drew upon a variety of cultural referents, from biblical representations of house-churches to contemporary practices of private piety. In so doing, they asserted the household's very traditional position as the cornerstone of the city. Thus while for some late antique Romans the church had come to monopolize this spatial status, the authors of the *gesta martyrum* brooked no such transposition.

Nevertheless, the *domus* of the episcopal *gesta martyrum* would have been largely unfamiliar to the likes of Cicero or even Paul. For these imagined Roman householders perform their domestic authority through engagement with a distinctly clerical religious 'outsider', whom they welcome into their home and to whom they even entrust the care of their children. And while the baptism of their household is underlined as a paternal prerogative, it is effected only through the spectacular intervention of a supernatural agency that the bishop alone mediates.[120] In this respect,

[120] However, domestic baptismal scenes are found in numerous passions grouped among the *gesta martyrum*, and bishops are not always the celebrants. In both the *Passio S. Laurentii* and the *Passio S. Marcelli*, for example, we find Roman deacons (Laurentius and Cyriacus) and priests (Justinus) taking on this role, while in the *Passio S. Sebastiani*, both the priest Polycarp and the bishop Gaius perform baptisms in private houses.

the *topos* delineates a powerful discourse about the legacy of episcopal authority in the city of Rome: bishops have historically participated in the production and reproduction of Rome's vital domestic resources; their presence within the household is not a sudden, juridical imposition from without, but a socio-ritual development from within, which takes hold through pre-existing social practices and spaces as well as through the cooperation of the householders themselves. Such a discourse gives new meaning and force to Leo's Lenten entreaties to the Roman householders, as to his bi-annual performances of baptism at the Lateran baptistery on Easter and Pentecost. Indeed, they perhaps take on even greater significance when we consider the fact that, by the middle of the fifth century, most Roman Christians (whether children or adults) had most likely been baptized not by the bishop but by their local priests in the numerous baptisteries which archaeologists have discovered amidst the ruins of the *tituli*.[121] For it is precisely this distance between household and bishop that the *gesta martyrum* seek to overcome when they situate baptism within that other prominent ceremonial space of paternal authority in the late antique city, the *domus*, thereby Christening it too as a house of God.[122]

CONCLUSIONS

My lord Hermes *vir illustris*, recover your prefecture! Restore your mind! Take back your fortune! Recover your family and the furniture of your house![123]

Such are the words spoken by the befuddled Quirinus to Hermes upon first learning of the urban prefect's conversion to Christianity and the loss of status and wealth that it apparently entailed. That a man like Hermes,

[121] Most liturologists believe that priests rather than the bishop increasingly performed baptisms in Rome in *tituli* as the numbers of Christians grew. See Fisher 1965: 22. Evidence supporting their position includes the notice in the biography of Marcellus in the *Liber Pontificalis* that the bishop established twenty-five *tituli* in Rome for the express purposes of baptism and penance, and appointed twenty-five presbyters (*Liber Pontificalis*, ed. Duchesne 1886–1957: 1, 164). Material evidence demonstrates that many of the *tituli* were baptismal centres: Saxer 1989: 994–5 and Cosentino 2002: 116–41. Moreover, the practice of stational liturgy physically placed the pope in various churches on some sixty-six days of the year, with only twelve of these masses celebrated on Sundays in *tituli*, as noted by Chavasse 1997: 9–11.

[122] Patristic writers like Cyprian and Augustine frequently employed the term *domus Dei* to denote the community of the church, as found in the Scriptures: Meyer 1998: 189–213. I have been unable to detect any direct borrowing from these writers in the Roman martyr narratives discussed here, nor have I found the phrase *domus Dei*. Nevertheless, I would suggest that the depiction of the *domus* as a place of liturgy and episcopal presence reflects in a diffused manner the patristic, exegetical use of the household as a symbol for God's community on earth.

[123] *Passio SS. Alexandri, Eventii, et Theodoli martyrum* (ed. Mombritius 1978: 1, 44–5): *Domine mi Hermes vir illustris recipe praefecturam tuam. Redi ad mentem tuam. Recipe patrimonium tuum. Recipe familiam tuam tuaeque domus ornatum.*

who had it all according to a Roman calculus of success, would sacrifice his position was unthinkable to the socially inferior tribune. As we have seen, the joke was on Quirinus, who quickly learned that Christianity and a relationship to the bishop of Rome brought a betterment of his domestic situation, not its dissolution. To be sure, the characters of Marinianus and Bassus would have vociferously objected to this characterization of episcopal authority in the domestic sphere, and given the final pronouncement of the bishop's absolute authority, their objections would have been warranted. Their dissenting voices nevertheless deserve our close attention.

If this chapter has done nothing more than simply highlight the significance of the domestic sphere in the history of Roman episcopal authority, then it will have succeeded. But it has also endeavoured to give shape to the interconnections between bishops and households that structured life in late antique Rome. As we have seen, the *Gesta de Xysti purgatione* and the episcopal *gesta martyrum* offer two contrasting ways of seeing the relationship between bishop and householder, the former emphasizing a relationship of coercion grounded in a juridical framework, the latter a more reciprocal system of exchange. As complex refractions of the late antique social imagination, they offer insight into the cultural terms through which late antique men and women perceived and were asked to perceive the presence of episcopal authority in the domestic sphere. In both models, this presence was seen as the amalgamated expression of a traditional and quintessentially Roman social ethics and set of practices fused with an expressly Christian temporality, whereby change is potentially productive so long as it is properly channelled. Changes wrought by bishops within the imagined households of the 'papal legends' are, from the householders' perspectives, a mixed bag. But they are nevertheless significant for the bishop's own standing in the city at large. In the texts explored above, the bishop of Rome is definitively *not* an authority unto himself, the architect of a papal 'machinery', who manages the household exclusively from the bishop's chair (though in the *Gesta de Xysti purgatione* this is a distinct option).[124] Rather his influence within the city is determined, the 'papal legends' imply, by his very connections to men like Bassus, Hermes, and Quirinus. It is their wards he defends, their children he heals, and their property he is entrusted to manage. It is also in their houses that a bishop most dramatically exercises his authority, be it legal or liturgical – a literary *topos* no doubt, but one that illustrates the dangers of writing the history of Roman episcopal authority from an exclusively ecclesiastical angle.

[124] See Llewellyn 1971: 43, who uses this precise terminology.

Appendix: Domestic conversion topos *in the episcopal* gesta martyrum

Passion/Householder	Healing	Confession	Catechism	Baptism
Passio S. Alexandri *et al.*				
Hermes *vir illustris et praefectus urbis*	Alexander resuscitates Hermes' dead son.	Hermes confesses his faith and asks for baptism.	NONE	Alexander baptizes Hermes *cum uxore et sorore et filiis . . . cum mille ducentis quinquaginta servis suis, uxoribus quoque eorum et filiis.*
Quirinus *tribunus*	Alexander heals Balbina's neck tumour.	Quirinus confesses his faith to Alexander after Balbina's healing.	Alexander catechizes Quirinus and Balbina with the other prisoners.	Alexander baptizes Quirinus *cum filia sua Balbina et omni sua domo.*
Passio S. Callisti				
Palmatius *consul*	No healing. But Palmatius witnesses a bacchant miraculously profess Christ's power and truth.	Palmatius confesses belief to Callistus and asks for baptism.	Palmatius fasts for one day and is catechized by the priest Calepodius.	Callistus baptizes *omnem domum Palmatii et uxorem et filios aliosque promiscui sexus numero quadragintuaduos.*
Simplicius *senator*	Callistus heals Simplicius' dependant, Blanda.	No *confessio*; Simplicius asks Callistus for baptism.	Callistus catechizes *omnen domum Simplicii et uxorem et filios et filias eius et animas fere promiscui sexus numero sexagintaocto.*	Baptism of Simplicius' *domus* only implied.
Passio S. Clementis				
Sisinnius *amicus Nervae*	Clement heals a blind and deaf Sisinnius.	Sisinnius confesses belief.	NONE	Clement baptizes Sisinnius *cum omni domo sua,* including *viri cum mulieribus et infantibus promiscui sexus numero quadringenti vigenti tres.*

Appendix: Domestic conversion topos *in the episcopal* gesta martyrum (*cont.*)

Passion/Householder	Healing	Confession	Catechism	Baptism
Passio S. Cornelii Cerealis *miles*	Cornelius heals the paralytic wife of Cerealis, Sallustia.	Sallustia confesses belief; asks for baptism. Cerealis confesses and asks Cornelius for baptism.	NONE	Cornelius baptizes Sallustia and Cerealis with the other soldiers.
Passio S. Stephani Nemesius *tribunus*	Stephen heals Nemesius' blind daughter Lucilla through Nemesius' baptism.	Nemesius and Lucilla confess belief to Stephen.	Stephen catechizes Nemesius and Lucilla.	Stephen baptizes Nemesius, Lucilla and *promiscui sexus numero sexaginto.*
Olympius *tribunus*	No healing; but the family witnesses the miraculous melting of an image of Mars in their home.	Olympius, his wife and son confess Christ's power; Olympius shatters the household idols.	Stephen catechizes the family *ecclesiastica traditione.*	Stephan baptizes *quoquot crediderunt in domo Olympii.*
Actus Silvestri Emperor Constantine	Silvester heals Constantine's leprosy through baptism.	Constantine confesses his faith to Silvester.	Constantine fasts, prays and is catechized by Silvester.	Silvester baptizes Constantine in the baths of his Roman palace.

4

Agnes and Constantia: domesticity and cult patronage in the Passion of Agnes

Hannah Jones

> Let us celebrate the feast day of the most holy Virgin.[1] Here, let psalms echo, there, let sermons resound. Here, let a throng of people rejoice, while there let the poor of Christ be washed . . . At thirteen years[2] old she overcame death, and came into life, since she esteemed only the Creator of life. She was counted as a child in years, but there was boundless wisdom in her mind: young in her body, but wise in her soul; beautiful in appearance, yet more beautiful in faith.[3]

The martyrdom of the Roman virgin Agnes was a sight to behold, according to an impressive group of late Roman narrators, including Bishop Ambrose of Milan, Prudentius, and the anonymous author of the *Passio Agnetis* (*BHL* 156), quoted here. To a greater or lesser degree, these authors revel in conjuring the scene, dwelling on the beauty of the young woman (she is nearly ravished by her persecutors in a brothel), her eagerness to feel the thrust of the executioner's sword, and the intensity of her desire to be joined to Christ. The sexual element in her persecution and death in these narratives has made of Agnes something of a spectacle in modern scholarship, an iconic figure in analyses of the erotics of male ascetic Christianity. It may be, however, that we are the victims of our own interest in contemporary voyeurism. For the late ancient audience of the story of Agnes, we will suggest, the motif of her imperilled virginity worked as a narrative apparatus to concentrate the reader's attention on the social meaning of Agnes' martyrdom – a motif, to be sure, designed to captivate

[1] The present chapter summarizes and develops an argument first put forward in Jones 1998. Warm thanks are due to Lucy Grig, Conrad Leyser, and Kristina Sessa, as well as to the volume's editors Kate Cooper, who also supervised the original dissertation, and Julia Hillner, for unusually generous dialogue; the process of revision has truly been a collaboration. This said, the author bears responsibility for any errors or shortcomings which may remain.

[2] This is in contrast to the twelve years given by Ambrose of Milan, *De virginibus* 1.2.7 (*PL* 16.190).

[3] *Passio S. Agnetis* 1.1 (*AASS Ian. II*, 351 (*BHL* 156)): the *Passio S. Agnetis* appears in numerous editions, listed under *BHL* 156. I have consulted three: *PL* 17.813–21; Mombritius 1, 17–19; and *AASS Ian. II*, 351–4; all three are virtually identical. All references are to the text in the *AASS*.

and beguile the audience, but one whose social meaning was contested by the different writers who took up her tale. If a writer like Ambrose of Milan had seen in Agnes a trophy of female submission to episcopal authority, the virgin's most important role for the anonymous author of the *Passio Agnetis* was as an icon of civic unity. Her feast day is an occasion for the unanimous affirmation of *pax* and *concordia* across the social order.

That the memory of Roman saints was contested, and mobilized, by multiple and sometimes conflicting factions can no longer come as a surprise to modern scholarship, and it has been recongized for some time that the Latin martyr romances known as the *gesta martyrum* offer a particularly rich case study.[4] Among these, the virgin martyr Agnes is among the most interesting, in that an unusual multiplicity of visions of the saint has come down to us. By considering both the evidence for cult patronage and the textual tradition concerning the martyr heroine, the present chapter will attempt to understand the role played by the memory of Agnes in the Roman civic and ecclesiastical landscape from the fourth to the sixth century. In particular, we will analyse the internal rhetorical landscape of a single version of her tradition, the anonymous *Passion of Agnes*, seeking to understand how the *Passio* redirects inherited motifs with respect to martyrdom and virginity.

At different points in the history of her legend, Agnes was sequentially appropriated and reinvented, first as the acceptable face of imperial hegemony, then as the icon of docile submission to episcopal authority, and finally as an exemplum of lay patronage and piety. Building on Kate Cooper's notion of the Lucina motif in the Roman *gesta martyrum*, in which the recurring figure of an aristocratic woman sees to the burial of the martyr, we will ask how the *Passio*'s account of the appearance of Agnes in a healing vision to Constantine's daughter, and the princess' subsequent patronage of the cult, both revised and reasserted an 'imperial' vision of Agnes as against an 'episcopal' memory of the saint, by reconciling the claims of the imperial family with those of the Christian patronage class.

'I, CONSTANTINA': IMPERIAL PATRONAGE AND THE POLYMORPHIC MEMORY OF THE MARTYR AGNES

I, Constantina, venerating God and dedicated to Christ,
Having provided all the expenses with devoted mind

[4] See Cooper 2005b. For introductory discussion of the seminal work of G. B. De Rossi, C. Pietri, P. Llewellyn, and P. Brown, see Cooper 1999.

At divine bidding and with the great help of Christ,
Consecrated this *templum* of Agnes, victorious virgin,
Because she has prevailed over the temples of all earthly works,
[Here] where the loftiest roof gleams with gold.[5]

The recorded history of the cult of Agnes begins with an inscription; unusually, the voice recorded is the feminine first person singular. More specifically, it is the imperial feminine, the voice of Constantina, daughter of the emperor Constantine, the founder of the basilica of Agnes on the Via Nomentana, whose circular mausoleum on the same site became the church now known as S. Costanza. Charles Pietri has shown that despite the claim of the *Liber Pontificalis* that Constantine had built the basilica *ex rogatu filiae suae*, the foundation must have been built after Constantine's death in 337.[6] Pietri's argument is supported by the first person singular of the inscription. The narrative voice of the imperial patroness is all the more vivid in the original Latin because although Constantina as builder is invoked in the first word of the inscription, the main verb – 'sacravi' – is postponed, thus the emphatic 'I' in the translation above. (As with other inscriptions, there is little evidence to judge the relationship between this first person 'voice', the inscription's historical author, and the patroness whose activity is commemorated.)

Important here are a number of points about Constantina as patroness. First is the independence of the imperial family from episcopal influence in this matter. This is a point that died hard in Roman memory. Indeed, the *Liber Pontificalis* remembered that when Pope Liberius had sought refuge with Constantina at Agnes' shrine during the schism with Felix of 355–365, and asked her to intervene on his behalf with her brother Constantius, she had refused to do so.[7] (That Constantina was in fact dead and buried a year before the beginning of the schism – i.e. that the memory of her independence must have been a historical fiction – only underlines the value accorded to the story.) The basilica and mausoleum were founded on land belonging to the imperial family, and after Constantina's death the burial complex continued in use. Ammianus Marcellinus records that in 360 Julian the Apostate sent the body of his Christian wife Helena to be buried

[5] Diehl, *ILCV* 1768, lines 1–6: 'Constantina dm [deum] venerans Xpoque dicata|Omnibus impensis devota mente paratis|Numine divino multum Xpoque iuvante|Sacravi templum victricis virginis Agnes,|Templorum quod vincit opus terrenaque cuncta,|Aurea quae rutilant summi fastigia tecti.' I have followed above the translation given, with discussion, in Curran 2000: 128.

[6] Pietri 1976: 47–50, citing older literature, and Stanley 1994, along with Barberini 2001: 33–6 and Brandenburg 2004: 140–7.

[7] *LP* I, 207 (s.v. Liberius; trans. Davis 1989: 28).

'on his property near the city on the road to Nomentum, where her sister Constantina, once the wife of Gallus, was also buried'.[8]

It must also be remembered that in the 350s the epithets *Christo dicata* and *mente devota*, applied to Constantina, by no means implied status as a virgin of the church. In fact, Constantina was married twice, first to Constantine's nephew Hannibalianus from 335 to 337,[9] and then from 351 to 354 to Gallus Caesar, nephew of her brother Constantius and brother of the emperor Julian. Both marriages seem to have been classic dynastic allegiances designed to support the rule of the Constantinian dynasty by co-opting imperial nephews.[10] She was the mother of at least one daughter by Gallus according to the emperor Julian's *Letter to the Athenians.*[11] Her fertility did not, of course, stop her from acting as patroness to the church, and indeed her religious role as Christian patroness and her civic role as imperial bride may well have been understood as reinforcing one another.[12]

The identities of martyr and princess were soon conflated, however.[13] In the *Passio S. Gallicani*, the *augusta*,[14] like her martyr counterpart Agnes, is pursued in marriage by the general Gallicanus. She converts his two daughters to virginity while her eunuchs, John and Paul, win Gallicanus himself to Christianity.[15] The historical Constantina thus seems to have been submerged into Agnes' virginal identity: both figures conspired in each other's fame at the same time as the inconvenient memory of Constantina's marriage to Gallus was accounted for by the rejected courtship of Gallicanus.

8 Ammianus 21.1.5; again, I have followed Curran's translation. It has recently been argued that the mausoleum to Constantina was in fact built by her brother-in-law, Julian the Apostate, some time after her initial foundation on the site (Mackie 1997), although the argument has not been widely accepted.

9 Hannibalianus 2 (*PLRE* 1.407). He was murdered at Constantinople in 337: Zos. 3.40.3, Julian, *Ep. ad Ath.* 270C.

10 She appears as Constantina 2 in *PLRE* 1.222; the entry also records the proposal of marriage made by Magnentius *c.* 350, possibly to neutralize her support for his rival Vetranio.

11 Julian, *Ep. ad Ath.* 272D; the child is not otherwise attested.

12 Though addressing a different dynasty, Kenneth Holum's discussion of Aelia Flavia Flacilla (d. 387) (Holum 1982: 21–47) discusses the terms on which fertility and Christian *eusebeia* ('zeal for faith') could converge in the person of an imperial consort.

13 An alternate metamorphosis, in the anonymous early medieval *vita Constantinae*, is discussed by Salisbury (1991: 60–8).

14 Constantina was made *augusta* by her father: Philostorgius 3.22.28; in addition, the *LP* s.v. Liberius refers to her as *Constantina augusta* (*LP* 1, 208).

15 *Passio S. Gallicani*: 3 (*AASS Iun V*, 37). I have omitted discussion of the *Passio SS. Joannis et Pauli*, which appears in *AASS Iun V*, 159–60, because, although it is closely related to the traditions of Constantia and Gallicanus, Agnes does not feature in it. See Dufourcq 1988: 1, 145–52, and the contribution of Conrad Leyser to the present volume.

Even Constantina's name was confused in the hagiographical record. Repeatedly, Constantina appears as Constantia, *Constantini augusti filia*. Constantia was in fact the name of Constantine's sister, not his daughter, but both the *Passio Agnetis* and the *Passio Gallicani* assign the aunt's name to her niece.[16] Adding to the confusion was perhaps the memory of another imperial daughter, Flavia Constantia (b. 361/2), the posthumous daughter of Constantius II, who was married to the emperor Gratian before her death in 383.[17]

The legendary associations between Agnes and 'Constantia' continue in two curious traditions in the *Liber Pontificalis*. Under the entry for bishop Silvester (314–335), the *Liber Pontificalis* reports that the emperor Constantine, at the request of his daughter, constructed not only the basilica, but also a baptistery. At the same time, both his daughter Constantina and his sister Constantia were baptized by Silvester.[18] Apart from the *Liber Pontificalis*, however, there is no trace of the involvement of either Silvester or Constantine's sister in the fourth-century building projects.[19] The attempt to link Constantia and Silvester is testimony to a relationship of some kind between the legend of Constantia's cure by Agnes and the tangle of traditions about the conversion of Constantine.

It seems probable, then, that Constantia's appearance as a paradigm of lay patronage in the *Passio* resonated with a mesh of other stories that knew Constantina in this, and other, roles. Constantia's role in the *Passio*, moreover, reverberates with the activities of late antique imperial ladies, whose monument commissions are testimony to a desire to emulate past generations of female benefactors. Leslie Brubaker's discussion of these monuments shows that Constantina was a key link in a chain from Helena to the Theodosian and Anician *matronae* of the fifth and sixth centuries. Constantina emulated Helena through the architecture of her mausoleum, which echoes the mausoleum built by Constantine's mother adjacent to the basilica of SS. Marcellinus and Peter; Constantina's mausoleum in turn

16 *PLRE* I erroneously suggests that the references to 'Constantia' in some versions of the *LP*, and in Sozomen, *HE* 5.2.20, are a mistake for 'Helena'; it is more likely, however, that a hagiographic source confused the *soror Constantini* (Constantia) with the *soror Constantii* (Constantine's daughter Constantina). Salisbury (1991) sees the attribution of pious acts associated with Constantine's daughter, Constantina, to his sister Constantia as an attempt to resolve the discrepancy between the historical Constantina and her legendary persona.

17 Dufourcq 1988: 149. See *PLRE* I.221.

18 *LP* I, 180–1; NB the sixth-century edition of the *LP* seems to have assigned the correct name to Constantina; only manuscripts of the later editions change her name to Constantia, perhaps under the influence of the hagiographical tradition. See Davis 1989: xxxix and 21.

19 See Duchesne 1955: 196–7, nn. 80–1. The archaeological evidence for the construction of an early baptistery (e.g. Leclercq 1907–53: 2612) is no longer widely accepted; see Brandenburg 2004.

became a model of public female patronage.[20] We need not assume, however, that such models spoke only to women. A brickstamp of the Ostrogothic king, Theoderic (492–526)[21] at the basilica of Agnes, can surely be seen as part of an attempt to appropriate Roman authority by emulating the Constantinian dynasty. These suggestions of Constantina/Constantia's role as a paradigm of lay munificence allow us to be more certain in affirming that the *Passio* borrowed her because she offered a vivid emblem of exactly the kind of attention it sought to command for Agnes.

THE 'EPISCOPAL' AGNES

On his return from exile Liberius lived at the cemetery of St Agnes with the emperor Constantius's sister, in the hope that her intervention or request might gain him entrance to the city. Then Constantina Augusta, who was faithful to the Lord Jesus Christ, refused to ask her brother the emperor Constantius, as she had realized what his scheme was. Then Constantius . . . recalled Liberius from St Agnes' cemetery. Immediately on his entry into Rome the emperor Constantius held a council with the heretics including Ursacius and Valens; he ejected the catholic Felix from the bishopric and recalled Liberius. From that day the clergy suffered a persecution which caused the deaths and martyrdom in church of priests and clerics.[22]

With its elements of heresy and conflict among the Christian clergy, of imperial meddling with the affairs of the clergy, and of imperial women meddling with the affairs of imperial men, the above-cited passage from the *Liber Pontificalis* describing the stand-off between rival popes Liberius and Felix in the summer of 358 could stand as an emblem for the troubles of the Roman church in the fourth century. This is even more the case if we remember that the lens through which the *Liber Pontificalis* views the episode is that of the early sixth century, nearly two centuries later, when the story's central lines of tension – between pope and emperor, catholic and Arian – had been realigned dramatically, if not beyond recognition, by the rule of an Arian king.

According to the *Liber Pontificalis*, the crime of Liberius had been to take a 'soft' line on Arianism, allowing the Arian emperor Constantius to compromise the purity of the Roman church's anti-Arian position in exchange for restoring him to his see after three years of exile, during which he had ordained the priest Felix to act as bishop in his stead.[23] Among the many insufficiently understood elements of the story, one that should

[20] Brubaker 1997. [21] Krautheimer 1937–80: 17. [22] *LP* I s.v. Liberius (trans. Davis 1989: 28).

[23] He seems to have allowed restoration of communion as long as the Arians did not rebaptise, according to *LP* I s.v. Liberius (trans. Davis 1989: 28).

concern us in the present chapter is the unwillingness of the emperor's sister Constantina to abet him in his desire to regain communion with the emperor. A triangle is present here involving the emperor, the bishop, and the Christian patron(ess), and much remains to be done to understand the relationship between these parties. The *Liber Pontificalis* places Felix and Constantina on the side of orthodoxy, with the notoriously pro-Arian Constantius and Liberius on the side of heresy.

Constantina had in fact been buried in 354 in her mausoleum in the grounds of the great basilica which she had dedicated to Agnes in the 340s. She could well have known Liberius, who became pope on 17 May 352, before her death, but by his return from exile in 358 she was long dead. It is conceivable that the *Liber Pontificalis* story reflects the tradition recorded in Theoderet that during Constantius' visit to Rome in 357, he had been plagued by noble ladies attempting to persuade him to bring Liberius home.[24] On the other hand, Constantina may have been invoked simply because she was remembered as the patroness of Agnes, and the dramatic setting in the cemetery of St Agnes on the Via Nomentana just outside the city walls was central to the story. If the cemetery of Agnes was associated with imperialist bishops, it was also associated with a member of the imperial family, Constantina, who was remembered as willing to compromise the bonds of family for the sake of loyalty to the Catholic faith.

Already in the mid-fourth century, the cult of Agnes seems to have been the object of interest on the part of both lay elites and the Roman bishop. One of the most widely known Roman martyrs, Agnes was a prize to be fought for, her popularity attested in visual culture by the frequency of her appearance on gold glass bowls,[25] and her appearance in sermons rivalled among martyrs only – at considerable distance – by Laurence and Sebastian.[26] Her cult on the Via Nomentana is attested already by the *Depositio martyrum*, part of a Roman calendar that existed in the 330s and was published in 354, early in the reign of Liberius and before his exile.[27] Dufourcq surmised that before the imperial family acquired land on the Via Nomentana, at an unknown date, there must already have been a humble grave there, understood to be Agnes'.[28] The *Hieronymian*

[24] Theoderet, *HE* 2.14.

[25] Grig 2004a: 203–30, which demonstrates the popularity of Agnes by reference to the frequency of her portrayal on fourth-century gold glasses; see further, on Agnes and her popularity in the city of Rome, Grig 2004b: 79–85 and 2005: all with illustrations.

[26] Dufourcq 1988: I, 28.

[27] Delehaye 1933: 276. For the *Depositio Martyrum*, see Salzman 1990: 42–6.

[28] Constantia's final resting place is attested by Ammianus Marcellinus, see Dufourcq 1988: I, 215.

Martyrology notes her feast day, though not the location of her tomb.[29] The following overview of the evidence for her cult cannot pretend to resolve its complexities, but intends simply to evoke the episcopal interest in Agnes' cult. We will see below that comparable developments took place where her hagiographical tradition was concerned.

The cemetery basilica dedicated to Agnes on the Via Nomentana was decorated by Pope Liberius, presumably after Constantina's death.[30] It became a rallying-point for the party of Ursinus, the rival of Pope Damasus, in 366.[31] Damasus' own intervention, an inscribed poem celebrating the virgin's martyrdom, was established *in situ* in the Nomentana basilica after his success in displacing his rival.[32] Although the inscription to Agnes was only one of a number of similar martyr inscriptions, we can imagine that assertion of episcopal patronage at the Nomentana site was particularly significant.

In the fifth and sixth centuries, we can only glimpse Agnes' role in episcopal liturgy and politics. The *Liber Pontificalis* tells us that Bishop Innocent (401–417) made repairs to the basilica and entrusted its administration and liturgy to two priests of the *titulus Vestinae*, which he was able to found through the legacy of a wealthy laywoman.[33] Following the activities of his predecessor, Bishop Boniface (418–422) used Agnes' basilica for the celebration of Easter.[34] During the Laurentian schism, there was further episcopal activity when Bishop Symmachus (498–514) restored the basilica,[35] plausibly as part of his strategic manipulation of the cult of the saints.[36] His operations were perhaps linked to a convent that may already have existed adjacent to the basilica. A sepulchral inscription of 514 records the death of an Abbess Serena. She may, however, have been the head of another Roman community who wished to be buried near Agnes.[37]

No further renovations were made to the basilica until the major reconstruction by Honorius I (625–638).[38] Peter Llewellyn has shown that Honorius was exceptional among seventh-century bishops as an imitator

[29] *Martyrologium Hieronymianum* (ed. G. B. de Rossi and L. Duchesne, *AASS Nov II*, II). The dating of the *Hieronymian Martyrology* is a labyrinthine issue beyond the scope of the present chapter. It appears that all our extant manuscripts derive from a sixth-century compilation made in Gaul. This was based on fifth-century martyrologies. The *AASS* purports to be an edition of the earliest manuscripts. See Leclercq 1907–53: 2530–63, and also de Gaiffier 1961: 40–59, which sheds light on usage and the Hieronymian attribution.

[30] *LP* I, 208 (s.v. Liberius).

[31] On the need of Damasus to reclaim the site after the schism was concluded, see Sághy 2000: 279–81.

[32] Ferrua 1942: N. 37/*ICUR* VIII, 20753.

[33] *LP* I, 220–2. For the date of the *Liber Pontificalis* see Duchesne 1955: xli–xlviii.

[34] *LP* I, 227. [35] *LP* I, 263. [36] See Townsend 1933: 165–74 and Cooper 1999: 303–5.

[37] Ferrari 1957: 29. [38] *LP* I, 323.

of Gregory the Great.[39] Honorius' patronage of Agnes may have been a concession to Gregory's detractors in Rome, since Gregory conceivably wrote his famous *Dialogues*, if not against, then certainly as an alternative to the cult of the martyrs.[40] These tantalizing suggestions of political context, however, are not resolvable within the present state of scholarship on the *gesta martyrum*. This evidence, nevertheless, is testimony to the substantial efforts invested in the cult of Agnes, of which the *Passio* is only a part.

The literary development of Agnes' legend followed an intersecting, but independent trajectory. The *Passio S. Agnetis* (*BHL* 156) is spuriously attributed to Ambrose of Milan (d. 397), but in fact the text must be later. As P. Allard has shown in detail, the *Passio* developed the writings of Ambrose, Damasus of Rome (d. 384), and Prudentius, who were themselves drawing upon a pre-existing oral tradition.[41] The late fourth-century elaborations of the legend of Agnes emphasize her virginal purity and her vulnerability, attributes which paradoxically enhance her ability to reinforce episcopal power. After meditating on the suffering of the virgin's frail body, Damasus invokes her power as a heavenly intercessor;[42] Marianne Sághy has suggested that visitors might have read this line 'as a warning', given the strong-arm tactics which he had used on the same site during the Ursinian schism in 366.[43] Within a decade or so of Damasus' inscription, Ambrose's *De virginibus*[44] contains the first prose narrative of Agnes' martyrdom. (The martyr is also the subject of a fourth-century hymn[45] attributed to Ambrose, but the attribution has been disputed.) Ambrose and Damasus seem in turn to have served as sources for Prudentius' elaboration of the legend in *Peristephanon* XIV.[46] Again, both Ambrose and Prudentius[47] envision Agnes in terms which emphasize her frailty and the violation of her innocence, a point which has been explored by

39 Llewellyn 1974: 363–80

40 Boesch Gajano 1980 and Boesch Gajano 1979; in English, see Markus 1997: 62, and now Leyser 2000b.

41 Allard 1907–53: 905–18.

42 'I ask you, excellent martyr, to hear favourably Damasus' prayers': Ferrua 1942: N. 71; these verses, already known from manuscript copies, were discovered engraved on the paving of the basilica of Agnes in 1728.

43 Sághy 2000: 281.

44 Ambrose of Milan, *De virginibus* 1.2 (*PL* 16.190–1); on this text, the fundamental study is still Duval 1974.

45 *Hymni S. Ambrosio Attributi, LXV De S. Agnete* (*PL* 17.1249); for discussion see Fontaine 1992.

46 Prudentius, *Peristephanon XIV* (LCL 398.338–45). All translations of Prudentius are from LCL.

47 Prudentius also conferred many of the traditions of Agnes upon Eulalia, virgin-martyr of his native Spain. Petruccione 1990: 81–104.

Virginia Burrus among others.[48] The *Passio S. Agnetis*, we will argue, takes the theme of fragility and violation in a new direction. Drawing on Burrus' approach to the eroticization of Agnes' imperilled virginity in Ambrose and Prudentius, we will suggest that the *Passio* offers a somewhat conservative response to 'eroticized' Agnes. The 'domestic' Agnes of the *Passio* perhaps reflects an attempt to replace the 'episcopal' Agnes with a figure more in keeping with the interests of Roman lay patrons.

Before engaging with the text of the *Passio*, it is worth discussing briefly the problem of its date. As Allard has shown, there are sufficient traces in the *Passio S. Agnetis* of Ambrose, Damasus, Prudentius, and an undated sermon in honour of Agnes, attributed to the fifth-century bishop Maximus of Turin, for us to assume that it post-dates these texts. Allard attempted to assign an early date to the *Passio* on the basis of the sermon ascribed to Maximus of Turin.[49] The direction of influence is fairly clear. The sermon refers only cursorily to names and events, in a manner suggesting that its audience already knew the story, and moreover employs the words *ut legitur* when recounting a detail that we find only in the *Passio*, the prefect's sadness at his inability to protect Agnes from persecution.[50] Allard's hypothesis is undermined, however, by the fact that this sermon, which has also been spuriously attributed to Ambrose,[51] is not necessarily by Maximus.[52] The sermon does, however, lend some weight to Allard's suggestion that the third section of the *Passio*, focused on Agnes' tomb, may, despite stylistic continuity, be the work of a later author.[53] Since the sermon closes with Agnes' death, it could have been composed at a time before the tomb stories had been woven into her legend.

This suggestion would confirm our suspicions of a deliberate effort to bind the story of Agnes to her cult site, but it remains a speculative thesis, and is no help in dating the *Passio*. A number of traditions preserved in the *Liber Pontificalis* indicate that the legendary associations between Agnes and Constantina/Constantia were established by the early sixth century. Even could we untangle the direction of influence between the *Liber Pontificalis* and the *Passio*, however, we would still be unable to account for the possibility of an oral tradition from which both texts might have

[48] On Ambrose and Prudentius, see Burrus 1995b: 25–46, and Grig (above n. 25); on Ambrose, see also Jones 1998 and Burrus 1996: 461–75. On the virgin and 'the gaze', see Castelli 1995 and Cooper 2005b.

[49] Allard 1907–53: 911–12.

[50] Maximus of Turin, *Sermo LVI: In natali S. Agnetis* (*PL* 57.642–8).

[51] The text attributed to Ambrose is identical to that imputed to Maximus of Turin: *Sermo XLVIII: In festo sanctae Agnetis virginis et martyris* (*PL* 17.725–8).

[52] Allard 1907–53: 912 himself notes this problem.

[53] Allard 1907–53: 913.

drawn independently.[54] Nevertheless, the presence of a substantial literary tradition of Agnes by the early fifth century, and the reference to legends of Agnes and Constantia by the sixth, confirm the broad likelihood that the text, like most of the other *gesta martyrum*, was composed, perhaps in stages, during the late fifth and early sixth centuries. One might suspect that a saint whose shrine was known as a site of Arian–Catholic dispute, and for which there is evidence of renovation during the reign of Theoderic, could well have received a new literary treatment of her story at this period.[55] To suggest a more specific date is neither prudent nor necessary to the main point of this contribution.

THE TRANSFORMATION OF DESIRE: AGNES AND THE MOTIF OF IMPERILLED VIRGINITY

We turn now to the *Passio S. Agnetis* itself. As we have seen above, the *Passio* commences with an appeal to celebrate the feast day of its heroine. While enjoining its audience to remember the martyr on her anniversary, the text reserves specific mention for female virgins, who are to be edified by the example of Agnes' suffering. This homiletic opening then immediately gives way to a simple narrative form. The urban prefect's son falls in love with Agnes, and she spurns his advances, claiming that she loves only Christ. Failing to persuade her to abandon her virginity for his son, the prefect condemns her to prostitution. When Agnes enters the brothel, however, it is transformed into a *locus orationis*, a place of prayer. The virgin then narrowly escapes rape at the hands of her predatory suitor, when her guardian angel strikes him dead. She subsequently revives him by her prayers, after which he converts to Christianity. Finally Agnes joins her true betrothed, Christ, through her martyrdom, on 21 January.

After Agnes' death, the *Passio* appends an epilogue, consisting of loosely connected stories set at her tomb. Agnes' parents bury their daughter on the Via Nomentana, and another virgin, Emerentiana, is martyred at her grave. Shortly afterwards, Agnes' parents receive a vision of their daughter while they watch over her tomb. Constantia, daughter of the emperor Constantine, hears of the vision and approaches the tomb for a cure. Receiving this, she converts to Christianity and builds both her own mausoleum and a basilica to Agnes on the Via Nomentana.

As with the fourth-century texts, the *Passio*'s fascination with Agnes' imperilled virginity works here as a rhetorical strategy to lure the audience

[54] The *Liber Pontificalis* is discussed above at pp. 119–21. [55] Dufourcq 1988: 1, 287–92.

into its narrative. On this reading, once Agnes has been established as an erotic figure, the reader is then urged to transform desire into devotion.[56] This extra-textual transformation is encouraged and mirrored through a series of symbolic transformations within the story. But there is an important difference here. In the *Passio*, the process of narrative closure, through which the reader is returned from the world of the text to the world of the everyday, involves the introduction of secondary figures such as Emerentiana, Constantia, and the parents of Agnes. These secondary figures play a crucial role, and their introduction harnesses the story of Agnes to a new social meaning.

The *Passio*'s treatment of the themes of family and civic identity suggests that on at least one level the text was specifically targeted at traditional aristocratic families. Kate Cooper has recently argued that the presence of family clusters in the Roman *gesta martyrum* was an important development reflecting a need to mobilize the support of non-ascetic Christians in the social context of the *gesta*'s production.[57] It will be suggested here that the *Passio* of Agnes represents a specific version of this phenomenon, involving the introduction of parents and princess as exempla for the involvement of the aristocratic laity in sponsoring the martyr cult.

Before turning to examine these themes, we should return to the *Passio S. Agnetis*' opening exhortation to celebrate the feast day of the virgin:

> Let us celebrate the feast day of the most holy Virgin. Here, let psalms echo, there, let sermons resound. Here, let a throng of people rejoice, while there let the poor of Christ be washed . . . At thirteen years[58] old she overcame death, and came into life, since she esteemed only the Creator of life. She was counted as a child in years, but there was boundless wisdom in her mind: young in her body, but wise in her soul; beautiful in appearance, yet more beautiful in faith.[59]

This homiletic opening, with its rhythmic sequence of juxtapositions and paradoxes, places the *Passio* within a broader tradition of sermons preached on the anniversaries of the martyrs.[60] It also echoes Ambrose's treatment of Agnes in *De virginibus*, itself framed as a call to celebrate her feast.[61] The *Passio*'s use of a homiletic formula may be related to its spurious claim to

[56] On cultural-theory approaches to the relationship of reader to protagonist in the *passiones*, see Cooper 2005b: 9–24.

[57] Cooper 2005a and forthcoming.

[58] This is in contrast to the twelve years given by Ambrose of Milan, *De virginibus* 1.2.7 (*PL* 16.190).

[59] *Passio S. Agnetis* 1.1 (*AASS Ian. II*, 351).

[60] See, for example, the series of sermons preached by Maximus of Turin. These are collected in Mutzenbecher 1962. On the use of paradox in the homiletic tradition, see Cameron 1991: 155–88.

[61] Ambrose of Milan, *De virginibus* 1.2.5 (*PL* 16.189–90).

Ambrosian authorship. More importantly, this opening hints both that the interest of the cult of Agnes was at stake in the composition of her *Passio* and that it was expected that the ensuing narrative be read out within a liturgical milieu.

Having briefly dazzled the audience with the paradoxes of age, sex, and suffering, the *Passio* launches into a narrative of sexual peril, as the prefect's son falls dangerously in love with Agnes. She rejects his advances in a highly stylized speech, laden with bridal imagery, telling him that she is 'already constrained by another lover',[62] Christ. She then goes on to describe her relationship with Christ in paradoxically erotic terms:

> At one time I received milk and honey from His mouth, at another I was gathered up in His chaste embraces. Indeed His body was united with my body and His blood adorned my cheeks ... When I love Him, I am chaste; when I touch Him, I am clean; when I receive Him, I am still a virgin.[63]

Agnes is thus established as the object of rivalry between the prefect's son and Christ; a rivalry that is made ambiguously sexual by this speech. By having Agnes introduce herself in these striking terms, the *Passio* compounds its heroine's eroticization: the implicit invitation to view her as an object of desire is put into her own mouth. We might note, moreover, that Agnes employs a persuasively rhythmic sequence of paradoxes to invite this desire; following the same strategy used by the *Passio* to command the celebration of her feast.

We come now to the two main narrative sequences within the text, the challenge to Agnes' virginity and the story of her martyrdom and burial. In the first, on discovering Agnes' rejection of his son, the prefect of Rome at first tries to erode her resolve through both threats and flattery,[64] and, when this fails, sentences her to be led naked to the brothel. This sequence mobilizes a rich tradition of literary motifs centred on the theme of imperilled virginity.

The attempts of the prefect and his son against Agnes' virginity, culminating in her death, can be compared, for example, to Livy's tale of Verginia, in which the virgin heroine is murdered by her father, to save her from sexual subjugation to a Roman magistrate.[65] Agnes' story also echoes the ancient novel, where the heroine preserves her fidelity to an earthly, rather

[62] *Passio S. Agnetis* 1.3 (*AASS Ian. II*, 351). [63] *Passio S. Agnetis* 1.3 (*AASS Ian. II*, 351).

[64] The combination of threats and flattery is a prevailing theme in the *passiones*. For Agnes, see Ambrose of Milan, *De virginibus* 1.2.9 (*PL* 16.190), and Prudentius, *Peristephanon XIV*, lines 16–17 (LCL 398.338).

[65] Livy 3.44–8 (LCL 398.142–60).

than an immortal lover. Stories like Chariton's *Chaereas and Callirhoe*, or Xenophon of Ephesus' *An Ephesian Tale*, where the heroines defend their chastity against all manner of fantastic obstacles, read as convincing ancestors to the legend of Agnes.[66]

This impression is compounded when we consider that Anthia, in *An Ephesian Tale*, is sold to a brothel-keeper during her adventures. By feigning illness, she preserves her fidelity to her true love, Habrocomes, with whom she is eventually reunited.[67] The parallel with Agnes' preservation of her fidelity to Christ in the brothel is striking. Tarsia, heroine of the Latin romance *The Story of Apollonius King of Tyre*, performs an analogous feat in a brothel, extinguishing the ardour of her clients by telling them the tragic story of her life.[68] While direct textual influence is hard to prove, such parallels between Agnes and her classical antecedents add to the widely accepted suggestion that the folk-tale motifs embedded in the ancient novel did not disappear with the demise of the genre, but adapted themselves to become the new cultural myths of hagiography.[69]

In classical literature, these stories of sexual peril often unfold within a rhetorical framework designed to voice civic values. One reading of Livy's story of Verginia has suggested that the articulation of Roman historical identity is at stake in the tale.[70] Parallel concerns shape the ancient novel. The passionate loyalty of heroines like Callirhoe and Anthia to their lovers has been interpreted as an exhortation to the regeneration of the classical city through marriage and offspring.[71] The *Story of Apollonius King of Tyre*, by casting the hero and heroine as father and daughter, makes family continuity, promised in the marriages of couples like Chaereas and Callirhoe, profoundly explicit. Tarsia is sent to Apollonius, in her capacity as prostitute, to console him for the loss of his daughter. While she relates her customary tale of woe, he realizes that Tarsia is the daughter he thought was dead.

The manner in which the motif of sexual peril was taken up by early Christian literature undermined the rhetoric of civic and familial continuity conveyed by the ancient trope. In the apocryphal legend of Thecla, the wealthy and beautiful heroine decides to embrace virginity, rejecting

66 Chariton, *Chaereas and Callirhoe* (ed. Reardon 1989: 21–124); Xenophon of Ephesus, *An Ephesian Tale* (ed. Reardon 1989: 128–69).

67 Xenophon of Ephesus, *An Ephesian Tale* 5.5–7 (ed. Reardon 1989: 161–3).

68 Anonymous, *The Story of Apollonius King of Tyre* 33–6 (ed. Reardon 1989: 759–61).

69 See, for example, Reardon 1989: 3, 12. For a different approach to the meaning of this development, see Cooper 1996: 52.

70 Joshel 1992: 112–30.

71 Cooper 1996: 20–44.

her bridegroom Thamyris to follow Paul. The designs of both Thamyris and an Antiochene aristocrat upon Thecla's virginity propel the plot towards the persecution of both Paul and Thecla.[72] The quasi-love triangle between Thecla, Thamyris, and Paul is often reproduced in the martyr legends, not least that of Agnes, in the form of the virgin-martyr, her mortal suitor, and Christ. In the *Passio S. Agnetis*, the virgin heroine serves to articulate a contrasting view of the city. It almost appears as if the rhetoric of the chaste heroine has doubled back on itself: having been usurped by the refusal of marriage in the *Apocryphal Acts*, it is reappropriated by the author of the *Passio* on behalf of civic tradition.

A related development can be illustrated through the tale of the virgin-martyr Irene, who appears both in the pre-Constantinian *Acta Martyrum* and in the *Passio S. Anastasiae*, one of the Roman *gesta martyrum*.[73] In both accounts of her legend, Irene, like Agnes, is sentenced to the brothel. In the sober narrative of the pre-Constantinian story, however, Irene's condemnation to prostitution is only one incident in an account that invests little in the trope of sexual peril. The faith of Irene and her companions, moreover, is emphasized by their rejection of 'their native city, their family, property and possessions'.[74] In the *Passio S. Anastasiae*, by contrast, the imperilled virginity of Irene and her sisters is the predominant narrative theme. Irene's condemnation to the brothel, therefore, is the apex of an accumulated series of attempts against her virginity; some of which are lavishly baroque.[75] In further contrast to the earlier legend, the elaborated tale of Irene is interwoven into the story of the widowed *matrona* Anastasia, whose *Passio* has been understood in terms of attempts to provide holy exempla for the married civic elite.[76]

There is little doubt that, for an audience steeped in hagiographic culture, Agnes' tale would reverberate with the memory of myriad other saints and their stories. Her *Passio*'s insistence on a purified civic order, and its appeals to family tradition, would have been read as an intervention in an on-going conversation about the social meaning of virginity. It would be unwisely simplistic to suggest that the defiant overtones of the *Acta Apocrypha* and the *Acta Martyrum* were definitively obliterated, as

[72] *Acts of Paul and Thecla* (ed. E. Hennecke and W. Schneemelcher (1992), *New Testament Apocrypha*, II, Cambridge: 239–46); Cooper 1996: 45–67.

[73] *The Martyrdom of Agapê, Irenê and Chionê and Companions* (ed. H. Musurillo (1972), *The Acts of the Christian Martyrs*, 290–1). *Passio S. Anastasiae* 17 (ed. H. Delehaye (1936), *Étude sur le légendier romain. Les saints de Novembre et Décembre*. Brussels: 234).

[74] *The Martyrdom of Agapê, Irenê and Chionê and Companions* (ed. Musurillo, 280–1).

[75] For example, *Passio S. Anastasiae* 12 (ed. Delehaye, 230).

[76] Cooper 1996: 116–43. This is an adaption of the earlier study Cooper 1994.

the motif of the virgin heroine neatly returned to its civic roots in the classical tradition. Nevertheless, we will see below that in the *Passio S. Agnetis*, at least on some level, the virgin heroine was reconscripted into the continuing rhythms of the rhetoric of the city.

It is worth looking in detail at how the theme of imperilled virginity is developed in the *Passio S. Agnetis*. The erotic gaze of the reader is repeatedly invoked, only to be redirected. When Agnes is first exposed naked to the eyes of the bystanders, her hair miraculously grows, veiling her nudity.[77] This miracle recalls other chaste heroines, both Euripides' Polyxena,[78] and the pre-Constantinian *Passio Sanctarum Perpetuae et Felicitatis*, in which Perpetua, being torn apart by beasts in the arena, takes a moment to pull her torn tunic over her thighs, 'thinking more of her modesty than of her pain'.[79] The inclusion of the hair miracle in the *Passio* of Agnes is probably indebted to the *Carmen* of Pope Damasus.[80] In the *Passio*, however, the suggestion of Agnes as sexual spectacle is multiplied by two more miracles. Her guardian angel arrives on the scene, and shrouds her in a dazzling light which blunts the vision of the onlookers. Falling down in prayer, Agnes then receives from the angel a garment to cover herself with.[81] By this trio of miracles, Agnes defends herself against the gaze of two sets of spectators, those in the story and those in the audience of the text.[82] Precisely through these defences, the *Passio* invites contemplation of the tantalizing possibility of Agnes' exposure.

Agnes' miracles achieve only a temporary respite for her modesty. She is still brought to the brothel, where, once inside, the theme of sexual peril reaches its apex and finale as the prefect's son gathers a gang of his companions to rape her. He boldly intrudes into the inner room where Agnes is praying, enveloped in a great light:

> And seeing so great a light around her, he did not give praise to God, but charged into this light, and before he could even seize her by the hand he fell down before her, choked to death by the devil.[83]

[77] Dufourcq (1988: I, 217) notes that this miracle is a 'surnaturalisation' of a point recorded by Damasus: 'Nudaque profusum crinem per membra dedisse', line 7 of Ferrua 1942: N. 37/*ICUR* VIII, 20753.

[78] Dufourcq 1988: I, 29.

[79] *Passio SS. Perpetuae et Felicitatis* 20 (ed. H. Musurillo 1972, *The Acts of the Christian Martyrs*, 128). All translation of the *Acta Martyrum* are from Musurillo.

[80] Ferrua 1942: N. 37/*ICUR* VIII, 20753.

[81] *Passio S. Agnetis* 2.8 (*AASS Ian. II*, 352).

[82] This reading is indebted to Burrus 1995b: 38, and to Leyerle 1993: 159–74.

[83] *Passio S. Agnetis* 2.9 (*AASS Ian. II*, 352). This episode is comparable with Prudentius' *Peristephanon XIV*, lines 40–51 (LCL 398.340), where a youth who dares to look at Agnes' nudity is struck blind.

This final failed assault on Agnes' virginity leads to the conversion of the prefect's son. Upon the discovery of his death, an angry crowd gather at the brothel, accusing Agnes of witchcraft. To prove her innocence to the prefect, Agnes prays for the revival of his son, who emerges from the brothel praising God.[84]

Up to this point, Agnes' desirability to the prefect's son has conspired with the attempts to humiliate, expose, and ultimately rape her, rendering her virginity tantalizing as it stands perpetually on the brink of violation. Once the audience's desire has been built up to this crescendo, however, the *Passio* immediately seeks to subvert its accomplishment. The conversion of the prefect's son can be understood as the key to this process. The *Passio*'s audience, who have been persuaded into voyeuristic complicity with the son's desire for Agnes, should now identify with his new-found Christian piety.

The conversion of the prefect's son is mirrored and anticipated through Agnes' purification of the brothel. Agnes' presence in the brothel transforms it 'into a place of prayer: all who had gone inside . . . were purer when they came outside than they had been when they went in'.[85] An inchoate form of this narrative element first appeared in Prudentius,[86] who in turn may be indebted to Ambrose's story of an anonymous Antiochene virgin in *De virginibus*.[87] In the *Passio* the motif takes on a pivotal role, signalling Agnes' purification of the corrupt desire of the prefect's son and, perhaps more significantly, his father the prefect, who embodies the authority of the city. After the revival of his son, the prefect departs in tears, unwilling to participate in Agnes' persecution. The angry crowds baying for Agnes' blood are thus deprived of the civic sanction of his support. As she goes to her martyrdom, it is Agnes who has the social order on her side.

Before her death, Agnes makes a final speech, confirming that her martyrdom is nothing less than a long-awaited union with her Bridegroom: 'Behold, that which I believed in, now I see; what I hoped for, now I hold; what I longed for, I embrace.'[88] The *Passio*'s actual depiction of Agnes'

[84] *Passio S. Agnetis* 2.10 (*AASS Ian. II*, 352). In *Peristephanon XIV*, lines 57–60 (LCL 398.340), Prudentius reports an oral tradition that Agnes had revived the youth who was struck down for looking lustfully at her.

[85] *Passio S. Agnetis* 2.9 (*AASS Ian. II*, 352).

[86] Prudentius records Agnes' condemnation to the brothel in *Peristephanon XIV*, line 25, and implies that her presence there had a purifying effect, lines 55, 129 (LCL 398.338, 340, 344).

[87] Ambrose of Milan, *De virginibus* 2.4 (*PL* 16.212–16).

[88] *Passio S. Agnetis* 2.11 (*AASS Ian. II*, 353).

martyrdom, however, is a shattering anticlimax. Aspasius,[89] vicarius of Rome, 'ordered that a sword be plunged into her throat. And by this death Christ consecrated His bride and Martyr to Himself, bathed in the ruby redness of her own blood.'[90] The only hint of baroque interest in Agnes' execution is a possible relationship between Agnes' red blood and the *flammeum*, a flame-coloured veil worn by Roman brides.[91] Here the *Passio* is in sharp contrast with Prudentius' flamboyantly eroticized description of Agnes' execution. Agnes, seeing the executioner confronting her with his 'naked sword', rejoices that she has found violent death, rather than dishonour in the brothel:

> I rejoice that there comes a man like this, a savage, cruel, wild man-at-arms, rather than a listless, soft, womanish youth bathed in perfume, coming to destroy me with the death of my honour. This lover, this one at last, I confess it, pleases me. I shall meet his eager steps half-way and not put off his hot desires. I shall welcome the whole length of his blade into my bosom; drawing the sword-blow to the depths of my breast.[92]

There are enough traces of *Peristephanon* XIV in the *Passio* for us to be confident that its author was familiar with the Prudentian traditions. It is possible that the author simply found Prudentius' account somewhat distasteful, and decided to substitute a tamer version of Agnes' death. It is also possible that generic expectations played a part in the different approaches: the *Passio*, whether read aloud as part of the liturgy or not, would not have been expected to include the kind of artful ecphrasis characteristic of elite poetry. But on a rhetorical level, the *Passio* has no need to include a sexualized description of the martyrdom. Desire, as we have seen, has already been sublimated into devotion through the conversion of the prefect's son. Within the rhetorical terms of the story, therefore, desire has been neutralized, and no longer demands satisfaction in a pseudo-erotic climax, as it seems to in Prudentius.

After Agnes' death, as the *Passio* turns to the continuing life of the martyr through her cult, the social agenda behind the text begins to leave clearer clues to its nature. Agnes' parents, rejoicing at her martyrdom, take her body and bury it on their estate on the Via Nomentana. After a second virgin, Emerentiana, has been stoned to death by pagan crowds at

[89] Aspasius Paternus was the judge who exiled Cyprian of Carthage. He may be invoked here in an attempt to link Agnes to the persecution of Cyprian. (See the *Acta Proconsularia Sancti Cypriani* 1 (ed. H. Musurillo, 1972), The Acts of the Christian Martyrs, 169–71).

[90] *Passio S. Agnetis* 2.12 (*AASS Ian. II*, 353).

[91] It is not clear, however, whether the *flammeum* was red, orange, or even yellow. See Treggiari 1991: 163.

[92] Prudentius, *Peristephanon XIV*, lines 69–78 (LCL 342–3).

the tomb, they also lay her body to rest. Watching over her tomb, they see a vision:

in the middle of the silence of the night they saw a host of virgins, who passed by in a great light, all dressed in robes woven with gold. Amongst them they saw the most blessed Agnes, decked out in similar splendour, and at her right hand stood a lamb, shining white as snow.[93]

After telling her parents to be happy that she is joined in Christ's embrace, Agnes disappears. The role of her parents contrasts not only with the prevailing hagiographic trope of familial opposition to the martyrs,[94] but with a pre-existing tradition in both Damasus and the Pseudo-Ambrosian hymn that Agnes had escaped the parental home in order to give herself up to persecution.[95]

The *Passio* therefore appears to have quite deliberately altered the status of her family, to whom she first chooses to reveal the supernatural aspect of her grave. Stripping virginity of its anti-familial connotations, this episode seems to have appealed directly to the traditional Roman laity, embellishing Agnes' cult site in a tale of family continuity. The household is pictured here as playing a central role in the creation and protection of Christian Rome. The *Passio*'s account of the burial of Agnes on her parents' estate acquires further significance when we remember that our earliest sources record the Nomentana site as imperial property rather than the private land of a Roman aristocratic family. The *Liber Pontificalis*, by contrast, refers to the Nomentana complex as an imperial foundation in cooperation with the bishop, eliding the question of pre-Constantinian ownership of the site – lay involvement other than that of the imperial family is not in view.[96]

The *Passio*'s subsequent narrative of Constantia reinforces the holiness of the site of Agnes' burial, establishing it as a place not only of visions, but of cures. When the pagan princess prays for relief from her afflictions

93 *Passio S. Agnetis* 3.14 (*AASS Ian. II*, 353).

94 One well-known example is Thecla's mother in the *Acts of Paul and Thecla*. All comments on Thecla are based on the English translation of the *Acts of Paul and Thecla* in E. Hennecke, W. Schneemelcher (eds.) (1992), *New Testament Apocrypha*, II: 239–46; for Thecla's mother: 242. Although the date at which a Latin version of Thecla's story first appeared in the west is uncertain, there is evidence that her legend was known there by the fourth century. One example is Ambrose of Milan's treatment of Thecla in *De virginibus* 2.3.19–21 (*PL* 16.211–12). A second example of familial opposition to the martyr is Perpetua's father in the pre-Constantinian *Passio SS. Perpetuae et Felicitatis* (ed. Musurillo, 106–31).

95 See *Hymni S. Ambrosio Attributi, LXV De S. Agnete* (*PL* 17.1249), and Damasus of Rome, *Carmen XXIX De S. Agnete Martyre* (*PL* 13.403).

96 *LP* I s.v. Liberius; Dufourcq (1988: I, 215) suggests that the family of Constantine could have acquired the site, thus allowing for previous private ownership.

at Agnes' tomb, the martyr comes to her in another vision, from which she awakens healthy and converts. Constantia's subsequent arrangement for the foundation of the basilica and the mausoleum seems to suggest that sampling the magic of Agnes' tomb is a gift that should be countered with munificent patronage. Her conversion, furthermore, is metaphorically related to the transformation of the ancient city, embodied in the prefect's change of heart.

Agnes' protective relationship to the city of Rome, and of the city's aristocracy, had already been emphasized by Prudentius: 'Laid within sight of their palaces, this maiden watches over the well-being of Rome's citizens.'[97] Constantia's gifts to Agnes show that in the *Passio* this relationship has become reciprocal. It has also been elaborated: the angry crowds who persecuted Agnes and Emerentiana are now transformed into rejoicing citizens, who flock to the tomb of the martyr for cures,

> The whole city was garlanded with wreaths: there was rejoicing among the soldiers, the private citizens and all who listened. The faithlessness of the people was confounded by the princess and faith was praised . . . and as many believers as approached her tomb were cured of whatever infirmity they had been encumbered by. This being done, no one has doubted Christ to this day.[98]

Constantia's story thus not only bestows the glamour of imperial patronage upon the cult, but binds Agnes' legend to the Constantinian Peace of the Church: as we can see in the citation above, it is almost as if the Christianization of the empire was a direct result of Constantia's cure.

The importance accorded to Constantia here would be all the more striking to audiences if they were familiar with the *Actus beati Silvestri*, a text which emphasizes the cooperation of bishop and emperor.[99] This legend, which probably crystallized into written form in the mid-fifth century,[100] relates that Constantine, after a vision of SS. Peter and Paul, was cured of leprosy and baptized by Bishop Silvester. He then founded a church at Peter's tomb on the Vatican hill and another within his own *palatium*; patronage of the Nomentana cult is not attested in this text. The account of Silvester's episcopacy in the *Liber Pontificalis*, by contrast, seems to seek to draw Constantina and Constantia closer to bishop and emperor, recording that '[the emperor] built a basilica to the

97 Prudentius, *Peristephanon XIV*, lines 3–4 (LCL 398.338).

98 *Passio S. Agnetis* 3.16 (*AASS Ian. II*, 353).

99 The *Actus beati Silvestri* is edited in Mombritius 1978: II, 279–93.

100 For the *Actus beati Silvestri* as one of many competing traditions about Constantine, see Fowden 1994: 146–70; the fundamental study is Levison 1924.

martyr St Agnes at the request of his daughter, and a baptistery in the same place, where his sister Constantia was baptized along with the emperor's daughter by Bishop Silvester'.[101]

In the *Passio*, Constantia acquires a role very close to the legendary role of her father – transformer of the Roman empire – as she completes Agnes' efforts to purify the Roman city. At the same time, in her building projects, she offers a paradigm of how the citizens of this new city of devotion may honour the martyr's memory. Looking back over this reading of the *Passio S. Agnetis*, we can appreciate how the legend might have appealed to the concerns of a civic-minded lay patronage class. The vulnerability of Agnes still serves as a narrative hook, but it no longer distances the virgin from the householder class represented by her family. Agnes has been reconciled in more than one respect to traditional Roman values, and the saint can now act in turn as heavenly patron of her city.

THE CIVIC PATRONAGE OF THE MARTYRS

To remark that the cult of the martyrs began to perform a role of civic patronage in post-Constantinian Christianity is not a novel proposal. There has been substantial scholarship on this function of the holy dead.[102] The rise of martyr cult conspired with a paradigm shift in attitudes to death, leading to the transformation of the presence of the dead from a polluting to a protecting force.[103] In Rome, Charles Pietri has shown how Peter and Paul came to symbolize the sacred harmony of the city.[104] At the same time, the ring of martyrs surrounding the city of Rome could be viewed as a menacing presence, ready to act at the bishop's behest.

We have seen that while it contains no explicit announcement of the martyr's role of civic guardianship, the *Passio* of Agnes nevertheless enshrines its heroine in a rhetoric of socially conservative virginity, and it should be clear by now that this tradition was distinct from the notions of virginal heroism present, for example, in the *Apocryphal Acts of the Apostles*. It remains to make clear how the *Passio*'s version of Agnes could

[101] *LP* I s.v. Silverius (trans. Davis 1989: 21). (NB later manuscripts specify 'Constantia' as the name of Constantine's daughter in this passage, but this is not present in the earliest recension, see Davis 1989: xxxix).

[102] For an overview, see Trout 2003.

[103] Brown 1981: 1–10 and Markus 1990: 141–6; for the east, Limberis (1994: 121–30) has explored the protective attributes of the traditional deities of ancient Byzantium which were mobilized in the Constantinopolitan cult of the Theotokos, while Cooper (1995: 7, 12) has discussed Thecla's defence of the city of Seleucia against barbarian invasion.

[104] Pietri 1976: 1554–92; Pietri 1961.

be understood by ancient readers as a reassertion and appropriation of the ancient rhetoric of civic virtue.

In the second half of the fourth century, Athanasius of Alexandria's *Vita Antonii*[105] began to communicate the ascetic ideal of the desert to the Roman aristocracy. In the *Vita Antonii*, the 'world', a hazy notion of corruption which Christians had known they were supposed to flee for centuries, became a tangible *place*: the world was the city, and its rejection now required sharp bodily enactment, the flight to the desert.[106] From the time of the first gusts of asceticism in the west, therefore, the city, which had been the pivot of ancient Mediterranean social organization since the emergence of the classical age, was placed in a position of symbolic ambiguity. In the fifth and sixth centuries, desert spirituality remained an important way of articulating holiness. In the mid-sixth century, the deacons John and Pelagius, identified as the future popes Pelagius I (551–561) and John III (561–575),[107] translated a collection of 'sayings' of the desert fathers. The *Apophthegmata* represent themselves as the written testament of what was essentially an oral culture of spiritual advice. This unaffected style meant that the genre itself could be taken as an implicit critique of the frivolous literary sophistication of the city.[108]

Even the traditions surrounding Thecla, heroine *par excellence* of the rejection of marriage and family, begin to reflect the importance of the marriage ideal. We see this in fifth-century *Life of Thecla*, produced at her cult site at Seleucia in Asia Minor.[109] Early in the text, Paul's opponents, Demas and Hermogenes, protest against the doctrine of Christ's Resurrection, proclaiming that the true resurrection is:

> the succession of children born from us, by which the image of those who begot them is renewed in their off-spring, so that it seems as if those who have passed away a long time ago still move again among the living, as if risen from the dead.[110]

In another episode, Thecla's fiancé, Thamyris, arranges for Paul to appear before a tribunal. Instead of being a silent villain as in the second-century *Acts of Paul and Thecla*, Thamyris in this source makes an impassioned speech against the apostle's denigration of marriage. Marriage, after all, is

105 Athanasius of Alexandria, *Vita beati Antonii* (*PL* 73.125–70).

106 This interpretation is deeply indebted to Brown 1988: 216–17.

107 Petersen 1984: 152.

108 On the tension between 'ascetic' and 'literary' styles in early sixth-century Rome, see Cooper 2001.

109 Scott Johnson's valuable study of this text (2006) came to my attention too late to be taken into consideration here.

110 *Vie de Sainte Thècle* 5 (ed. G. Dagron (1978) *Vie et Miracles de Sainte Thècle Texte grec, traduction et commentaire*. Brussels, 189; trans. Brown 1988: 7).

the 'fountainhead of our nature. From it spring fathers, mothers, children and families. Cities, villages and cultivation have appeared because of it.'[111] Despite the fact that the text is obviously on the side of Paul and Thecla, both famous for a rejection of marriage which the text does not alter, the fifth-century author's grasp of, and willingness to elaborate, the point of view of those who wish to protect the ancient significance of marriage and family is striking testimony to the increasing importance of these ideas once the process of Christianization was well rooted. Marriage and parenthood still represented the regeneration of the ancient city; in the fifth and sixth centuries, the praise of virginity had increasingly to accommodate the traditional values surrounding marriage and family.

In an early fifth-century sermon preached to his congregation on the suffering of the martyrs, Maximus of Turin discussed the civic role of the holy dead:

> Though all the saints are everywhere present and aid everyone, those who suffered for us intervene for us especially. For when a martyr suffers, he suffers not only for himself but for his fellow citizens . . . with these we have a sort of familiarity: they are always with us, they live among us.[112]

The special relationship between the citizens and their martyrs is striking. The local martyr stands as a personal link between his or her community and the spiritual world, as well as a solid bridge between the present and the Christian past. This sense of the martyrs as death-defying links with the community's past, moreover, is not unlike the description of the role of children in the ancient city offered by Paul's opponents in the *Life of Thecla*. The martyrs, like the children begotten through marriage, surround the civic community with tangible manifestations of its continuity.

Returning to the *Passio* of Agnes, we can see how the continuities represented by offspring and martyrs could in fact be conflated. In the vision of Agnes' mother at the grave of her martyred daughter, the martyr is not simply *like* a child, as in Maximus' sermon, she actually *is* a child, depicted in continuing harmony with her family. While it is not necessarily the case that the author of the *Passio* of Agnes sought deliberately to duplicate the civic meanings of marriage and family, it is nevertheless the case that through the enduring family relationships emphasized in the tomb-visions, the *Passio* does appropriate precisely these meanings, by figuring civic continuity explicitly in terms of a child and her parents.

111 *Vie de Sainte Thècle* 6 (ed. Dagron, 191; trans. Brown 1988: 1).

112 Maximus of Turin, *Sermo XII* (ed. Mutzenbecher 1962: 40–1). Translation from Markus 1990: 143.

CONCLUSION: THE VIRGIN AND THE PRINCESS

We have suggested, ultimately, that the motif of imperilled virginity is redirected in the *Passio S. Agnetis*. It still works to captivate and beguile the audience, but the audience, once captivated, is led to explore a new point of identification, that of the auxiliary figures in her entourage. This elaboration of the literary traditions of the martyr could in turn work to ensure that resources of devotion and patronage continued to converge upon the martyr's cult. By weaving an intricate narrative and rhetorical relationship between the motif of imperilled virginity and the themes of civic and familial continuity, the *Passio* sought to tap into and redirect the time-honoured habits of patronage that characterized the Roman aristocracy.

The *Passiones* of female virgin-martyrs tend to have been discussed in detachment from the contexts of cult and patronage, whether as a function of the endeavour to recover women's (and specifically female ascetic) history, or of post-modern inquiry into the dynamics of the gaze. This preliminary attempt to consider the relationship between the *Passio* of Agnes and the evidence for her Roman cult both points to the multiplicity of ways in which gendered rhetoric can be used to persuade, and suggests the methodological principles upon which further studies of virginity in the *gesta martyrum* might proceed.

As a final thought, we might ask what different meanings this relationship between the virgin and the princess might have imparted as it was taken up by the readers on whose continued interest transmission of the text ultimately depended. When the Merovingian queen Radegund of Poitiers (d. 587)[113] separated from her husband, King Clothar, and founded the nunnery of Poitiers with his help, she instituted as its abbess her friend and spiritual daughter, whose name was Agnes. It is not clear whether the abbess took this name upon her accession.[114] For a culture by now steeped in the traditions of the Roman *Passiones*, such a juxtaposition of the holy virgin and the royal lady could surely not have failed to reverberate with the legend of Constantia and the abbess Agnes' namesake.

113 Two *Vitae* of St Radegund were composed soon after her death, one by Venantius Fortunatus and another by Baudonivia, a nun from the convent of Poitiers. These are represented as two books, *De Vita S. Radegundis* (MGH SRM II 364–95). Both *Vitae* are translated in McNamara 1992: 70–105.

114 Radegund mentions Agnes' accession in a letter written to some of the bishops of Gaul, demanding their protection for her foundation and its abbess. This tells us only that Agnes was brought up by the queen from her infancy. The letter is quoted in Gregory of Tours' *Libri Historiarum* 9.42. (trans. O. M. Dalton (1927) *The History of the Franks*, II. Oxford, 418–21).

Radegund's collaborative relationship with Agnes was vividly publicized in the poetry of her long-standing friend and ally, Venantius Fortunatus.[115] Leslie Brubaker has shown how, in the fifth and sixth centuries, imperial women publicly articulated a relationship to the women of Constantine's family in their monument commissions,[116] and Constantina was almost as important as Helena in this matriarchal chain. That Radegund sought to insinuate herself into this strand of imperial memory is clear from her attempt to obtain relics of the True Cross, after which her convent was named: her biographer Baudonivia reminds us that it was Helena who had originally procured the relics of the Cross from Jerusalem.[117] Perhaps Radegund also cultivated an association between herself and her royal predecessor Constantina/Constantia, thus appropriating not only the Constantinian dynasty's matronal authority through Helena, but also its legends of virginal power.

The case of Radegund underscores a final methodological point. Analysis of the rhetoric of the virgin-martyr within the domain of cult and patronage need not exclude historical women. Radegund, after all, was one of the most powerful female players in the blood-stained politics of Merovingian Gaul.[118] Her interest in the cult of Agnes also has profound implications for the study of the *gesta martyrum*. In the case of Roman martyr cult, we have only the most elusive evidence for the nature of the patronage networks that sustained it. The early Frankish transmission of the traditions, however, involves far better-attested figures such as Radegund herself. Since comparably rich evidence may never come to light for the Roman laity, we may have to settle for Radegund, and others like her, as a model of the kind of relationships with the saints that might have been articulated by aristocratic patrons who, though well known in their own day, are now anonymous.

[115] Venantius' *De Virginitate* (*PL* 88.266–76) was dedicated to abbess Agnes. For his relationship with Agnes and Radegund see George 1992.

[116] Brubaker 1997. [117] Baudonivia, *Vita S. Radegundis* 16 (MGH SRM II, 387–9).

[118] Although two other Merovingian queens, Brunhild and Fredegund, are more usually seen in this context, the rebellion that broke out in Poitiers after Radegund's death seems to suggest that the convent was not uninvolved in the feuding between royal kin-groups. For an account of the rebellion, see Gregory of Tours, *Libri Historiarum* 9.39–43 (trans. Dalton, 409–22). On Merovingian queens, see Nelson 1978.

5

'A church in the house of the saints': property and power in the Passion of John and Paul

Conrad Leyser

On the Monte Celio, the transformation of Rome from late ancient to medieval city appears to unfold before our eyes.[1] A short walk from the Colosseum takes one to the *Clivus Scauri*, an exquisitely preserved Roman street running up the hill, and to the formidable redoubt of Christian monuments built around it. To one side, the monastery of S. Gregorio, founded by Gregory the Great on his own property, and its satellite chapels.[2] Immediately adjacent is the so-called 'bibliotheca Agapeti', a reminder of the Christian university planned by Pope Agapetus.[3] Behind this cluster, on the eastern slope of the hill, is the Lateran Palace, commissioned by the emperor Constantine in the fourth century, and the regular residence of popes from the seventh. Archaeologists are now persuaded that Constantine's palatial development was accompanied by interest in the neighbourhood from the most powerful private investors in the city, the Anicians. By 400, the dynasty was well established there, having converted shops and houses into a massive residential complex – the direct or indirect parent of the papal stronghold that took shape in the sixth century.[4]

The shift from private mansion to ecclesiastical redoubt seems still more powerfully enacted on the other side of the Clivus Scauri, in the church of SS. Giovanni e Paolo. According to their *passio*, John and Paul were

[1] I am grateful to the editors and contributors for their comments on drafts of this paper, and also to audiences in Vienna and Oxford for theirs. Kim Bowes, Maximilian Diesenberger, David Ganz, Helmut Reimitz, Claire Sotinel, and Wes Williams have all offered help and advice, ignoring any of which will have been to my cost. My thanks in particular go to Clare Pilsworth for making available a reproduction of the St Petersburg manuscript discussed here, and for generous sight of her work in progress; and to Kate Cooper, who some time ago took aside a monastic historian to draw his attention to the possible significance of the *Passio Iohannis et Pauli*.

[2] See Guidobaldi 1986 and 1995 for further references.

[3] See Marrou 1931, and now Guiliani and Pavolini 1999.

[4] Colini 1944 and Meneghini and Santanegeli Valenzani 2004 are general surveys with further references. I make no attempt here to re-enter the debate on Gregory's kinship to Agapetus and to the Anicians.

executed in the reign of Julian the Apostate (361–363), and buried in their house; under the sponsorship of a senator Byzantius and his son Pammachius, the house became a church.[5] There is, indeed, a *domus* beneath the basilica: from a side entrance on the Clivus Scauri, visitors enter a labyrinth of twenty rooms, many of them stunningly decorated with frescoes, depicting what appear to be Christian scenes. The interpretative challenge of the site has attracted scholarly enthusiasts and sceptics in equal measure, although few of the former would now claim to see here the actual dwelling of John and Paul as described in the *passio*. For much of the twentieth century, debate centred on whether or not we have here a *domus ecclesiae*, a pre-Constantinian dwelling where Christians met in private, subsequently converted to public use after the peace of the church. With scepticism now prevailing on this point, attention has turned to the construction of the basilica directly on top of the domestic complex in the early fifth century, and to the identity of its patron Pammachius. Here, we witness in microcosm, albeit without perfect focus, the process of 'Christianization' in the city.[6]

Our focus is less the site, than the legend of John and Paul. While we must accept that their *passio* gives us no access to domestic Christianity in Rome before Constantine, or under Julian, it is vivid evidence of the uses of the past in the sixth-century city and beyond. The martyrs, we suggest, were the presiding genii loci of the papal *burgo* taking shape on the Caelian hill. Pope Agapetus' father Gordianus had been a priest of the basilica, and his son, reports the *Liber Pontificalis*, had grown up in its precincts.[7] For Gregory, the basilica was a nodal point in the liturgical processions he organized round the city on his accession and later.[8] By the early seventh century, our first Roman pilgrim guide can begin: 'First in the city of Rome, however, lie the bodies of the blessed martyrs John and Paul in a great and very beautiful basilica.'[9] We will seek to trace how the *mythos* of the 'House of John and Paul' took shape in the city, and how it was transmitted to subsequent consumers of Rome, such as the pilgrim guide and his modern scholarly successors.

[5] See Prandi 1953. [6] See Brenk 1995 and 2003: 82–113, and further below. [7] *LP* I, 287.

[8] See Gregory of Tours, *Decem Libri Historiarum* X.1, and Gregory, *Reg.* XIII, 2. For general discussion, see Morin 1940. Note also Gregory, *Reg.* VIII, 5, which arranges for the consecration of an altar at Luni containing the relics of John and Paul, discussed in Leyser 2000b.

[9] *Notitia Ecclesiarum* (Valentini-Zucchetti 1946: 72). 'Primum in urbe Roma beatorum martirum corpora Iohannis et Pauli tamen quiescunt, in basilica magna et valde formosa.' The force of 'tamen' is unclear, and De Rossi emended to 'tantum'.

To match the splendour of the site, we have an unusually early copy of the *passio*. Our witness is to be found in the *vetustissimus* of Corbie, as the Bollandist Papebroch called it, a codex now to be found in two parts in Paris and St Petersburg (Par. Lat. 12634 and St Petersburg Q. v. I 5).[10] The codex is usually dated *c.* 600, with an origin in southern Italy.[11] It is by no means undiscovered, and has been examined by the many scholars involved in the editing of the several texts it presents, above all its monastic Rules.[12] The codex transmits the earliest copies of the Rule of Augustine, and excerpts from *The Rule of the Master* in a florilegium (the so-called 'Rule of Eugippius') which has been at the centre of the debate about the relation between the Master and Benedict.[13] The *Passion of John and Paul*, however, the very last text in the codex, has been somewhat ignored in this discussion: it is, we suggest, a stone unturned.

The *Passion of John and Paul* transmitted in the *vetustissimus* of Corbie is distinctive not only for its early date, but also for the story itself. The narrative of house execution and burial is unusual, both in relation to the other surviving versions of the *passio*, and, more broadly, to the *gesta* corpus as a whole. No other martyrs were said to have been both executed and buried in their own house.[14] Conversely, the other elements commonly in play in the *gesta* – the intergenerational politics of the Roman aristocracy, the ramifying ecclesiastical networks, involving various priests and shrines around the city – are, if not entirely absent here, then certainly a muted presence. The story concerns the *domus* and the emperor, linking the martyrs' ordeal to their defence of their property from the greed of the Apostate.

John and Paul were witnesses, in fact, to the this-worldly force of self-assertion. As icons of autonomy, they lent cultural energy to their papal neighbours at the very moment of institutional self-definition for the Roman church. As we shall see, their example was no less formative for contemporary monastic communities in Campania, and those who came after them. In other words, the significance of the 'house church' of John and Paul lies less in the Roman past than in the medieval future.

10 See *AASS Iun. V*, 159–62 for Papebroch's discussion of the *vetustissimus*, and for his version of the text.

11 A controverted matter: for a summary description and dating of the codex, see Lowe, *CLA* 645–6; at greater length, Masai and Vanderhoven 1953: 42–67; Dunn 1990: 591–2 gives a summary overview of the discussion of date and origin.

12 See e.g. Petitmengin 1971 on Latin Ephrem; Leclercq 1951 on Evagrius; Mutzenbecher 1961 on Maximus of Turin.

13 Verheijen 1967; De Vogüé 1982; and for pioneering comment on the florilegium, Genestout 1946–47. Knowles 1963 remains the classic study of the debate.

14 On other ways in which the *domus* features in the *gesta*, see Sessa in this volume.

THE HOUSE OF JOHN AND PAUL

Like many of the *gesta*, the *Passion of John and Paul* offers, at least initially, some signs of verisimilitude. According to the text, it was in the reign of Julian's successor Jovian that the martyrs' bodies were found by a senator Byzantius and his son Pammachius, who built a church there.[15] Documentary sources confirm the existence in the fifth century of a church initially known as the *titulus Byzantis* or the *titulus Pammachius*, referred to in the early sixth century as the *titulus Iohannis et Pauli*.[16] A probably fifth-century verse inscription preserved in the ninth-century Lorsch *Sylloge* names Pammachius as the founder of the basilica: 'Quis tantas Christo venerandas condidit aedes/Si quaeris cultor Pammachius fidei.'[17] The *cultor* has usually been identified as the Pammachius known from the correspondence of Jerome and Paulinus of Nola, the wealthy Roman aristocrat who converted to the ascetic life after the death of his wife in 397 and who died in 410.[18] At the time of John and Paul's martyrdom, Pammachius would have been beginning his studies in the company of the young Jerome. A church foundation co-sponsored by his father is not an impossibility, although not attested by any other sources. The basilica would seem to date to the late fourth or, more probably, early fifth century, at which point Pammachius' involvement seems extremely plausible.[19] In his thirteen years as a widower (397–410), we know that he busied himself with Christian patronage projects, in particular a *xenodochium* at Porto just outside Rome.[20]

Sustained attempts have been made to mine the site and the *passio* for evidence of Christian cult prior to 400. In the 1880s, excavations at SS. Giovanni e Paolo produced apparently spectacular results.[21] As the Passionist Father Germano di San Stanislao saw it, underneath the basilica, all the elements of the *Passion of John and Paul* were in place: an assembly hall decorated with frescoes showing figures in prayer; a *confessio* with two male martyrs in fresco; an altar containing relics identified (by an early modern plaque) as belonging to John and Paul. In 1913, two graves were found dug into the *confessio* – here, some suggested, was the very ditch

[15] *AASS Iun. V*, 160.

[16] Krautheimer 1937–80: I, 270. The monastery founded by Leo I at the Vatican is attested in the eighth century as 'SS. Iohannis et Pauli', but there is no fifth-century evidence to confirm that this was Leo's original dedication. See Ferrari 1957: 166–72.

[17] De Rossi 1864–77: II, 150. [18] *PLRE* I.663.

[19] See most recently Casti 2004. [20] Jerome, *Ep.* 66. 11 (*PL* 22.645).

[21] Di Stanislao 1894 and 1907. For a reminiscence of the discovery, see Delehaye 1998: 178–9.

into which the martyrs' bodies had been flung.[22] Others made different claims. In an immensely influential article, Richard Krautheimer argued that the site witnessed the transition from pre- to post-Constantinian worship.[23] In the mid-third century, he suggested, the complex, which included houses and shops, began to be used also as a *titulus*, a Christian community house.[24] In the generations after Constantine, the *titulus* and in particular the room that Krautheimer took to be the communal assembly hall were remodelled in 'a strictly hieratic' fashion with the installation of the altar with relics, and the addition of the martyrs' *confessio*.[25] The institutionalization of worship at the site was completed in the early fifth century with Pammachius' construction of the martyrs' basilica.[26]

These grand narratives have been much contested. The Bollandists reacted sceptically to the claims made by excavators of the site. In 1936, summing up a generation's critical work on the cult of John and Paul, Hippolyte Delehaye emphasized that the *Passio Iohannis et Pauli* should not be regarded as a witness to fourth-century realities.[27] It was clearly a fiction spun out of the authentic *passio* of two Antiochene martyrs, Iuventinus and Maximinus, as recounted by John Chrysostom.[28] The occasion for the Roman appropriation of motifs from Chrysostom's text, he suggested, was the change in titular dedication for the church from Pammachius to John and Paul.[29] This shift, for which the *passio* gave narrative legitimation, seems to have occurred between the synod of 499 and the 530s, when the *Liber Pontificalis* refers to the shrine *ad beatum Iohannem et Paulum*, as does the record of the Roman synod of 595.[30]

22 Grossi-Gondi 1914.

23 Krautheimer 1939; see also Krautheimer 1937–80: I, 302, and Krautheimer 1965: 8–9.

24 On the *tituli*, see Hillner and Cooper in this volume.

25 According to Franchi de' Cavalieri 1935, the quite unconnected martyrs Cyprian, Justiniana, and Theoctistus. See also Wilpert 1937, and now Grig 2004a: 120–3.

26 Krautheimer's intervention seems to have inspired those who wished to assert on the one hand a full-blown revival of Father Germanus' position, and on the other, as we shall see below, a deepened attention to the complexities of the literary tradition. See de Sanctis 1962, sceptically reviewed by de Gaiffier 1964b.

27 Delehaye 1936: 124–36, drawing on Franchi de' Cavalieri 1902 and 1915. See also Dufourcq 1886–1910: I, 309–10.

28 John Chrysostom, *In Iuventinum et Maximinum martyres* (*PG* 50.573–8) = *BHG* 975. Whether this sermon circulated in a Latin version is not clear. A sixth-century Latin tradition on these martyrs is established by Cassiodorus *Historia Tripartita* VI.34 (*PL* 69.1054). For comment, see Franchi de' Cavalieri 1902 and de Gaiffier 1956, and on Latin Chrysostom in general, Cooper 1993.

29 Note that this was not a definitive shift: later *LP* entries for Hadrian I, Leo III, and Gregory IV refer to the *titulus Pammachii*: *LP* I, 510; II, 9, 20, 32, 77.

30 *LP* I, 262; Gregory, *Reg.* V.57a (MGH Epp. I, 366).

There was a kernel of historical truth in the legend, argued Delehaye, which pointed to the origins of the cult.[31] In the majority of other later witnesses, the narrative begins not with John and Paul, but with another martyr protagonist, the general Gallicanus. This Gallicanus was a refraction of an historical figure, plausibly identified as Ovinius Gallicanus, consul in 317, and prefect of Rome 316–317.[32] His memory perdures also in the *Liber Pontificalis* notice for Pope Silvester, where Gallicanus appears as a donor to the basilica in Ostia dedicated to Peter, John the Baptist, and St Paul.[33]

Delehaye suggested that the key to the emergence of the cult of John and Paul lay in Ostia. The basilica there supplied the relics on which was founded the Roman cult of John and Paul. On this reading, the characters in the *passio* 'John & Paul, palace attendants of the Emperor Constantine' were, in fact, none other than the Apostle Paul and John the Baptist, whose contact relics were moved inside the city at some point in the fifth century. Delehaye's instinct was to dismiss as fantastical the central event of the story – the house execution and burial. The Roman taboo on corpses inside the city would surely have obtained in the fourth century, he believed. In what follows, we look to build on Delehaye's analysis of the *passio*'s sixth-century context;[34] at the same time, we should note that modern funerary archeology, in Rome and elsewhere, has confounded the assumption that intra-urban burial was unthinkable for late Roman Christians.[35]

Modern archaeology has cast doubt on Krautheimer's view of the site as a *domus ecclesiae.* In 1995 Beat Brenk showed that there was no clear or positive evidence to suggest that the complex had functioned as a 'Christian community centre'; the development of the site in the late third and early fourth centuries could be accounted for in terms of the practical redeployment of the space by a non-Christian owner (although the question must remain open in that a 'house church' is, by definition, invisible).[36] The

[31] Delehaye 1936: 124–36.

[32] The alternative would be Flavius Gallicanus, consul in 330: see Champlin 1982 for a discussion of the issues and the argument for Ovinius Gallicanus. As noted by Champlin, the *passio* may also be carrying (and looking to refract) a memory of Constantina's actual husband Gallus. See further Jones in this volume.

[33] *LP* I, 184. Duchesne suggests *LP*'s Gallicanus in fact transmits a memory of Pammachius: *LP* I, 199, n. 99.

[34] For subsequent work on the literary traditions, see de Gaiffier 1956 and 1957, conceived in dialogue with Grégoire and Orgels 1954. Grégoire's work was to have culminated in a full-length study but this seems never to have appeared; from the mid-1960s the level of scholarly interest in John and Paul seems to have abated. Bundy (1987) attempts a structuralist analysis, although without taking into account the many different recensions of the text.

[35] Costambeys 2001, discussed further below. [36] Brenk 1995, 2000 and 2003: 82–113.

'hieratic remodelling' envisaged by Krautheimer was, more plausibly, a decision by the owner to close down the shop, and to convert the whole site for upscale use as a private and well-appointed residence. Later in the fourth century, Brenk argued, we can speak of 'Christianization', with the installation of the altar and the *confessio* with its three martyrs in fresco. But this remained a private chapel, not a communal meeting place. What the twentieth-century discussion of the 'House of John and Paul' revealed, Brenk adduced in his devastating conclusion, was the tendency of scholars to project what they wanted to see onto the all-but-blank canvas of the evidence.

Brenk's final twist is a masterstroke. Scholars had been working on the assumption that the *passio* of John and Paul was composed to reflect the realities of the house-turned-basilica. Brenk suggested that the reverse may have been the case – that the 'graves of the martyrs' were 'retrofitted' in the sixth century, so as to make the interior space conform to the martyrs' legend. Taken together, the *passio* and the graves represent a none too subtle attempt to launch a cult on the site. The impossibility of dating the *passio* and the trenches with anything like precision will always leave an element of conjecture in this argument. What it invites nonetheless is a return to the study of the tradition of the *passio* and its earliest manuscript witness.

Before turning to this, we may note that in one respect Brenk may have taken his scepticism too far. He argued that the Pammachius who paid for the construction of a basilica on the site in the early fifth century was not the Pammachius known to Jerome and to subsequent scholarship.[37] His thinking was that a man who had taken up the ascetic life, as Pammachius did as a widower, would not have had the funds to complete such an extensive project – and he encouraged scholars to look for another founder of the same name. While it is certainly useful to be reminded that the prosopographical record can be more complex than we would often wish to assume, it is a refrain of this volume that the ascetic lives of the great in Rome often entailed lavish patronage projects of just this sort, Pammachius' relative Melania (he was her mother's first cousin) being a case in point.[38] The decision to instal a basilica athwart an exising residential complex was an astonishingly ambitious venture, but well within the reach, cultural and financial, of a correspondent of Paulinus of Nola,

37 Brenk 1995: 202 and 2004, and Guidobaldi 2004: 1093–5 for lively discussion of the question of two Pammachii. Brenk (2005: 230) signals a *retractatio*.

38 See Cooper in this volume, also Cooper 2006. For Pammachius' relation to Melania, see *PLRE* 1.663, and Harries 1984: 62.

whose own project at Nola was scarcely less ebullient.[39] These men were tycoons of the Christian past for a Christian imperial present. More elusive, but with a legacy all his own, is the author who told the story of the House of John and Paul, and told it for Romans for whom Pammachius was a distant memory.

THE *PASSION OF JOHN AND PAUL*

In the *vetustissimus* of Corbie, the *Passion of John and Paul* opens with astonishing ferocity:

> Therefore after the Emperor Constantine passed away, to be followed by his daughter Constantina, Julian, the very worst of men, was made Emperor by Constantius, nephew of Constantine. At the mercy of his desire for money, he took by force estates belonging to Christians, saying 'Your Christ says in the Gospels, "He who does not give up everything he possesses, cannot be my disciple". For news had reached him that Paul and John every day gave food to crowds of Christian poor, using the riches which the most holy virgin of Christ Constantina had left to them. Julian sent for them to come to him, and said that they should cleave to him. But they said : 'The most Christian men, Constantine of august memory, and Constans, and their kinsman Constantius gloried in being servants of Christ. You have deserted the religion rich in virtue and you pursue those things which you know are never to be possessed without God ... For this wickedness we shun your greeting, and we take ourselves away from your presence: for we are not false Christians, but true ones.'[40]

True belief is yoked here to a discussion of fiscal obligation to the state.

It is usually held that the version transmitted in the Corbie manuscript is a 'late mutation' of the tradition.[41] The original story began, as noted by Delehaye and others, with the general Gallicanus.[42] This may well be

[39] See now Lehmann 2004.

[40] 'Igitur postquam Constantinus Imperator migravit ad caelos, et secuta est filia Constantina, dum esset pessimus Julianus a Constantio, nepote Constantini, effectus Caesar, cupiditate pecuniae captus, patrimonia Christianorum auferens, dicebat, "Christus vester dicit in Evangeliis, Qui non renuntiat omnibus quae possidet, non potest esse meus discipulus." Pervenit namque ad eum, quod Paulus et Iohannis omnibus diebus turbarum Christianorum pauperum recrearent, ex his quas sacratissima virgo Christi Constantina eis reliquerat divitias, et misit qui eos conveniret, dicens debere eos sibi adhaerere. Illi autem dixerunt: "Viri Christianissimi, Augustae memoriae Constantinus et Constans, et nepos eorum Constantinus ... servos se esse Christi gloriarentur ... [R]eliquisti religionem virtutibus plenam, et sequeris ea que optime nosti a Deo penitus non possideri. Pro hac iniquitate a tua salutatione desistimus et a societate Imperii vestri nosmetipsos subtraximus: sumus enim non falsi Christiani, sed veri."' St Petersburg Q v I 5, f. 176r; *AASS Iun. V*, 159.

[41] Franchi de' Cavalieri 1915: 44

[42] Delehaye 1936: 127–8, as noted initially by Papebroch, *AASS, Iun. V*, 159.

the case, but the parallel claim that Gallicanus represents the majority tradition is not based on a systematic survey of the codices.[43] The stratigraphy of the Gallicanus, John, and Paul tradition, and its place in the wider *gesta* tradition, has yet to be properly established. Viewed with less prejudice, what the tradition presents in codicological terms is a number of different text modules which can be abridged and extended, shuffled and reshuffled.[44] The following table may be used as a guide to the dramatis personae, on the understanding that it simplifies what is a bewilderingly complex set of texts.[45]

Passio Gallicani, Iohannis et Pauli (*BHL* 3236, 3237, 3238)	Constantine, Constantina, Gallicanus and daughters, Hilarinus
	Julian, Paul and John, Emperor Julian, Terentianus and son
Passio Iohannis et Pauli (*BHL* 3239, 3240, 3241, 3242; the *vetustissimus* of Corbie transmits *BHL* 3242)	Julian, John and Paul, Terentianus and son
	Crispus and Crispinianus (or Priscus and Priscillianus), priests, and Benedicta *venerabilis femina*
	John and Pigmenius, priests, and Flavianus *illustris*
	Jovian, Byzantius, and Pammachius
Passio Pigmenii/*Passio Bibianae* (*BHL* 6849)	Julian, Flavianus' wife Dafrosa, Faustus
	Bibiana and Demetria (Dafrosa's daughters)
	Olympina and Donatus

In what is usually regarded as the earliest layer of the tradition. Paul and John are 'supporting actors' in the *passio* of Gallicanus. They are introduced as palace attendants of Constantina, daughter of the emperor Constantine, whose hand in marriage is sought by the pagan general Gallicanus.[46] In an attempt to delay the marriage, Constantine sends Paul

[43] *Pace* Grégoire and Orgels 1954: 579 n. 2. In the twenty-one manuscripts captured in the Bollandists' electronic database (http://bhlms.fltr.ucl.ac.be), thirteen contain the conjoined *Passio Gallicani, Iohannis et Pauli*, while eight contain the *Passio Iohannis et Pauli*. That the Corbie manuscript is not included in this census reminds one that the database is not comprehensive in its coverage of manuscript traditions.

[44] See e.g. Par. Lat. 10861, an early ninth-century Anglo-Saxon manuscript, which conflates the *Passio Gervasii et Protasii* with the *Passio Gallicani, Iohannis et Pauli*; discussed by Brown 1986.

[45] Franchi de' Cavalieri (1915) identifies three layers, but as he will have known, this taxonomy is in fact oversimplified. As observed in *AASS Iun. V*, 162, the manuscripts boast an extraordinary diversity of traditions, especially in the closing chapters of the *passio*.

[46] Note that some copies (and the edition printed by Mombritius) have 'Constantia'. Constantina was the daughter of Constantine, Constantia the daughter of Constantius; the Corbie codex has 'Constantina', St Petersburg Q v I 5, f. 176v. For further comment and references, see Grégoire and Orgels 1954: 584, n. 1.

and John on campaign with Gallicanus, while the general's two daughters join Constantina's household. A double conversion ensues: thanks to the intercession of St Agnes, Constantina converts Gallicanus' daughters, while in the field the general himself is persuaded by Paul and John that the Christian God brings greater victory. On his return, Gallicanus duly renounces his marriage to Constantina, and takes up residence in Ostia where he ministers to the poor. All is well until the accession of the pagan emperor Julian, who banishes Gallicanus to Alexandria, where he is eventually martyred for his refusal to sacrifice to the old gods. Julian then turns his attention to Paul and John. Their refusal to cooperate leads to their execution in their home by Julian's *campiductor*, Terentianus. But Terentianus is then converted following his son's exorcism, and, this version ends, he is the narrator of the entire *passio*.

In the next layers, the ending of the *passio* becomes increasingly elaborate, with an increasingly obvious institutional agenda. In some versions, the emperor Jovian sends the senator Byzantius and his son Pammachius to find the bodies and to build a basilica there.[47] Then, in the Corbie codex version (*BHL* 3242), several new characters are introduced. First to enter are the priests Crispus and Crispinianus and the noblewoman Benedicta, who come to John and Paul's aid prior to their martyrdom and are then themselves martyred. They are buried in the house by a further group of three, the priests John and Pigmenius and the nobleman Flavianus. Then follows the discovery of the (now numerous) bodies, and the building of the church by Byzantius and Pammachius.[48] This multiplication of characters did not find favour with the text's Bollandists commentators, concerned as they were to identify an historical core to the legend.

No less striking than the elaboration of the ending, however, is the simplification of the narrative in our Corbie version of the *passio*, and in particular the excision of Gallicanus. Reading the text, it is hard to avoid the impression that its author or editor knew of Gallicanus but decided as a matter of policy to edit him out. The narrative begins *in medias res* with 'Igitur postquam Constantius imperator migravit ad caelos'; Gallicanus is not mentioned, but the narrator shows a concern to remind readers briefly of the imperial succession between Constantine and Julian before moving on with the story.[49] In what follows, we will proceed on the tentatively

[47] Franchi de' Cavalieri 1915: 44, not, however, cross-referenced with *BHL*.

[48] A Greek translation (*BHG* 2191), ed. Halkin 1974, resembles the Corbie version.

[49] 'Igitur postquam Constantinus Imperator migravit ad caelos, et secuta est filia Constantina, dum esset pessimus Julianus a Constantio, nepote Constantini effectus Caesar' (St Petersburg Q v I 5, f. 176r).

held basis that the authors of the *Passio Iohannis et Pauli* transmitted in the Corbie codex have chosen to carve out the story of John and Paul as a free-standing *passio*. On the page, at least, the text is entitled the *Passio Iohannis et Pauli*.[50]

The sense of editorial simplification in the Corbie codex version of the *passio* is confirmed if we see the text in its wider literary genealogy. As de Gaiffier has shown, as literary figures, 'John and Paul' are situated on a cross-roads of two very productive narrative traditions – martyrs under Julian on the one hand, and, on the other, palace eunuchs.[51] Their story is twice spun out of these rich genres. More specifically, their *passio* is an episode in a sequence involving several more dramatis personae besides Gallicanus. As Hannah Jones shows elsewhere in this volume, the *Passio Gallicani* is linked to the *Passio Agnetis*; and the *Passio Iohannis et Pauli* itself acquires 'parental' status, inspiring a series of other *passiones* featuring house burial (but none featuring house execution).[52] Their various grave attendants appear in the *Passio Pigmenii* (also known as the *Passio Bibianae*). In this sequel, Flavianus is sent into exile for taking care of the bodies of Crispus et al. His wife, Dafrosa, is made to remarry, but she converts her new father-in-law, Faustus, who is then martyred. She buries him *in domo sua iuxta domum ss Iohannis et Pauli*.[53] Then she goes back to Flavianus house on the Esquline, where, after her martyrdom, she is eventually buried with her daughters Demetria and Bibiana. As in the case of the *titulus Iohannis et Pauli*, the *titulus Bibianae*, to which we shall return below, is attested in the *Liber Pontificalis*, where it is said to be a foundation of Pope Simplicius (468–483).[54]

Seen from this perspective, the text in the Corbie codex is less of an exercise in elaboration through the addition of extra characters than in the single-minded isolation of John, Paul, and their house as a segment from the wider narrative cycle. The *passio* observes an Aristotelian unity of

This genealogy is not offered in the combined *Passio Gallicani, Iohannis et Pauli*, and its slightly breathless quality could be taken to mean that it is an attempt to smooth off the excision of Gallicanus from the front end of the *passio*.

50 In larger capitals, St Petersburg Q v I 5, f.176r; 51 See de Gaiffier 1956 and 1957.

52 Jones in this volume. See also Grégoire and Orgels 1954 on the way that, just as Constantia merges with Agnes, so Gallicanus merges with Constantine. Further, according to Grégoire and Orgels 1954: 581, n. 1, 592–3, n. 2, John and Paul are part of a narrative group involving Agnes and also Eugenia (with two eunuch attendants, Protus and Hyacinthus), datable to the early fifth century.

53 This *passio* renames Crispus and Crispinianus as Priscus and Priscillianus (see Franchi de' Cavalieri 1915: 54). As noted by de Gaiffier (1956: 27ff), this *passio* leads in turn to that of Donatus of Arezzo, known to Gregory the Great (*Dialogi* I, 37) and to that of Cassian of Autun (see de Gaiffier 1948).

54 *LP* I, 249. Meanwhile, Pigmenius also appears in the *Passio Praxedis*, whose *titulus* was also on the Esquiline. See Llewellyn 1976b for further discussion.

place: the setting is Rome throughout. Gallicanus' story, by contrast, takes in a wide geographical sweep through the empire, from the imperial palace in Rome, to the Persian frontier, back to Rome and Ostia, and thence to Alexandria for Gallicanus' martyrdom. This expansive criss-crossing of the Roman world differs markedly from the claustrophobia of John and Paul in the Corbie codex version. We are taken with our protagonists to an unspecified palace for their interrogation by Julian. Refusing to remain in his service, John and Paul engage in a ten-day flurry of almsgiving activity in the city – and then they are returned in no uncertain terms to their house: *die undecimo sunt constricti intra domum suam.*[55] There they summon the priests and Benedicta to organize their affairs and in particular to continue to give out alms. Their companions are then refused entry. Julian's *campiductor* Terentianus arrives at the house with soldiers, with orders to kill John and Paul on the spot if they refuse to sacrifice. As former palace attendants, public execution is not fitting, he says. Having beheaded them and thrown their bodies into a ditch dug there and then in the house, Terentianus puts out word that they have been sent into exile.

The main character of the story turns out to be the *domus*, as the *passio* devolves into the increasingly desperate attempts of Julian to keep the martyrdom a secret. His attempted ruse briefly confuses Crispus, Crispinianus, and Benedicta. God reveals all to them, whereupon they too are martyred – but not so secretly that the second trio, John and Pigmenius and Flavianus, do not know to bury them *in domo Iohannis et Pauli*, near the saints themselves. It is in the house that Terentianus' son, possessed by a demon, is cured, which prompts his father's conversion. His martyrdom follows, and Terentianus is duly buried in the house by John and Pigmenius. Finally, after the death of Julian, the Christian emperor Jovian orders Byzantius and his son Pammachius to find the bodies in the house; and having done so, to 'make there be a church in the house of the saints'.[56]

The omission of Gallicanus and the dramatization of the house are not simply aesthetic strategies. Their combined effect is to change the character of the story, turning what had been a family drama of parents and marriage alliances into an institutional face off between the imperial government and its subjects. Without Gallicanus and Constantine, the *passio* begins, as we have seen, with a frank discussion of the greediness of the hostile state. The emperor Julian, from the moment of his accession, is seen to be motivated by avarice: seeing that John and Paul are heirs to the wealth of Constantina, he demands that they return to their posts in

[55] St Petersburg Q v I 5, ff. 179v–180r. [56] St Petersburg Q v I 5, f. 183v.

the palace. Committed to a programme of sustenance of the poor, they refuse. Julian taunts them back: 'Et ego etiam clericatum in ecclesia obtinui, et potui, si voluissem, ad primum gradum ecclesiae pervenire.'[57] Instead, Julian says, he chose war and the old gods – a neat moral contrast by the narrator between apostasy and ecclesiastical hierarchy. Of course, the Apostate is presented as a deviation in the development of imperial power: John and Paul assert the true pedigree, citing their loyal service to the good masters Constantine, Constantius, and Constans. But they are not themselves born to the purple. As palace eunuchs, they are by definition men without family: their heirs are the poor and their house, an institutional impression not altogether dispelled by the appearance at the close of the senator Byzantius and his son Pammachius.

To regard to the *Passio Iohannis et Pauli* transmitted by the Corbie codex as an overblown retelling of an earlier story is to miss the point made by this distinctive version. The Corbie *passio* implies a different form of devotional life than its parent text. The *Passio Gallicani*, as Hannah Jones shows elsewhere, encourages a martyr piety of identification. As Gallicanus can assume the attributes of Constantine, and Constantia of Agnes, so the reader can in turn attain heroic status. The *Passio Iohannis et Pauli*, by contrast, suggests that institutional loyalty is the most important aspiration. John and Paul are eunuchs without heirs: their defence of their property is on behalf of the community of faith rather than the biological household. A function of this institutional focus, as Delehaye suggested, may have been to provide a 'back story' for the renaming of the *titulus* in the name of John and Paul over that of Pammachius, and the remodelling of the site as Brenk has suggested; clericalization and 'commercialization' for the purposes of the pilgrim trade are familiar backdrops for the analysis of the *gesta martyrum*. The existence, however, of the early copy of the *passio* allows us to be more specific about this in the context of its monastic transmission in Campania, and from here, back to Rome.

MONKS AS MARTYRS

To the monastic reader, the version of the *Passion of John and Paul* we have been discussing would have struck some familiar chords. The story of their defiance of the emperor ends in triumph: the tormented shrieking of exorcised demons fills the house where the martyrs lie buried. By the late sixth century, monks were accustomed to thinking of themselves as

[57] St Petersburg Q v I 5, f. 177v.

latter-day martyrs; and the analogy between heroism in the arena and the daily struggle of the ascetic round has become a familiar theme of modern scholarship. We see the martyrs as a means by which imperial and post-imperial Christians articulated a connection with the pre-Constantinian past. What the *passio* and, as we shall see, the texts with which it is copied remind us is that the monastic life was orientated relentlessly towards not the past, but the immanent future: death and resurrection in paradise. The ferocity exhibited by the martyrs in anticipation of the world to come could be understood spiritually, in the task of moral purification, but also literally, as an incitement to resist any who sought to infringe their autonomy. Simply put, if monks were martyrs, then the House of John and Paul served as an emblem for the monastery.

The codex in which the *passio* appears is a composite volume. We know from its minuscule annotations that some, at least, of the five sections were at the monastery of Corbie by the mid-ninth century.[58] The key issue for our purposes is to assess the unity of the codex prior to its arrival in Corbie. The five sections are as follows:

(ff. 1–8): the *Rule of the Four Fathers*, and Evagrius' *Sentences for Monks*

(ff. 9–77): the *Rule of Augustine* (this is in fact the *Praeceptum* and *Ordo monasterii* as identified by Verheijen 1967), followed by the florilegium currently identified as the *Rule of Eugippius* (as identified by de Vogüé 1976)

(ff. 78–165): Ephrem the Syrian's *Institutio ad monachos* in Latin and two sermons of a Bishop John on the resurrection

(ff. 166–175): three sermons *De latrone*, attributed in the manuscript to Augustine, but now ascribed to Maximus of Turin

(ff. 176–183): the *Passio Iohannis et Pauli*

Despite (or because of) the attention lavished on the monastic Rule texts in the first two sections, there has been very little work on the codex as a whole. In fact, very few scholars have seen fit to visit both Paris and St Petersburg in order to study all its sections.[59] The assumption has prevailed that the codex is a random assemblage, where the whole is less than the sum of the parts. The reverse, however, may be the case.[60] Like the *passio* itself, the codex has a distinctive profile.

58 See Ganz 1990: 65, 151.

59 Neither Genestout nor Masai and Vanderhoven saw the St Petersburg section: all relied on the descriptions given by Dobias 1929 and 1934 – just before the beginning of the debate over these codices by scholars of monasticism.

60 See further Pilsworth forthcoming.

As Armando Petrucci has emphasized, the copying in sequence of various texts to be read together was something of a revolution in late Roman 'information technology'.[61] In the era of the papyrus roll, texts were copied alone: the rise of the parchment codex, and so the advent of pagination, made possible the juxtaposition of several texts without fear of disorientating the reader. In short, the fifth and sixth centuries saw the development of the Christian miscellany. Arguably, our *vetustissimus* shows the characteristics of a miscellany thus defined.[62] Its contents may have been copied with a view to such an eventual compilation.

The texts in the Corbie codex are selective to the point of idiosyncracy. We have already emphasized the 'stripped down' character of the John and Paul *passio* when compared to the narrative cycle transmitted elsewhere. Other texts in the codex show signs of a similar editorial sensibility. This is obvious in the case of the so-called *Rule of Eugippius*, a series of extracts judiciously culled from other texts, including an abridgement of the compendious *Rule of the Master* which stands comparison to the *Rule of St Benedict*'s feat of compression with the same text.[63] There is a 'chosen' quality also to the Ephrem *Institutio ad monacos* transmitted here; it normally travels with five other sermons of Ephrem, but here is copied as an unusual 'singleton'.[64] The first manuscript in the codex, the *Sentences of Evagrius*, although copied in a later hand than the others, is in keeping with the others in this respect. As its editor has noted, the version transmitted in the Corbie codex does not form part of either of the other main text groups preserved in the manuscript tradition.[65]

The case for regarding the *vetustissimus* as a distinctive and deliberate miscellany can be strengthened by referring to a sister codex, one of Petrucci's key examples of the genre. This is a late sixth-century manuscript, copied most likely in Rome, but with a Corbie provenance (Par. Lat. 12205).[66] The codex contains our earliest full-length copy of the *Rule of the Master*, along with works of Augustine. Scholars of the *Rule of the Master* have been more impressed by the differences between this codex and our *vetustissimus*, but to those outside the immediate field, their

61 Petrucci 1995.

62 Or at least of a 'composito organizzato', as defined by Condello 1994: 75 in discussing St Petersburg Q v I 6–10.

63 See Leyser 2000a: 108–22 and the references there given.

64 See Petitmengin 1971.

65 Leclercq 1951.

66 Petrucci 1995: 15, n. 33, signalling a move away from his earlier agnosticism (Petrucci 1971: 127, n. 160 bis). Suggestive at least of Roman provenance is the eighth-century list of popes contained in this codex: see Masai and Vanderhoven 1953: 36.

similarities may be more striking.[67] I have argued elsewhere that, thanks to the work of the late Caroline Hammond Bammel, it may be possible to delineate with a little more precision the codicological prosopography of the two Corbie codices.[68] Bammel delineates a network of textual exchange reaching from Aquileia to Sicily and north Africa, established during the last ten years of the life of Rufinus – but enduring well into the sixth century, at Castellum Lucullanum near Capua, home to Eugippius and the body of Severinus of Noricum, for example.[69] The Rufinian network had its own conventions for the copying of texts, and an identifiable set of intellectual interests. Manuscripts showing the Rufinian marks typically contain Rufinus' translations of Origen, moral and ascetic instruction (such as the *Sentences of Sextus* and the *Rule of Basil*, both translated by Rufinus), and works of Augustine (linked to Rufinus via Melania and Pinian who, notoriously, came and went from the small-town world of the bishop of Hippo in the early fifth century).[70] In addition, as Kate Cooper has shown, this network could also 'pick up' and transmit martyr tradition.[71] Our two Corbie codices do not carry the distinctive copying marks, but the contents of both codices match the Rufinian profile.[72] They belong to the world of Christian letters evoked by the manuscripts of Donatus of Lucullanum in the late sixth century, for whom late fourth-century scholarship was still a going concern.[73]

The *passio* of John and Paul offers an intriguing perspective on this Rufinian context. As we have seen, the *passio* names Pammachius as the patron of the basilica, which, if we follow out the allegiances of the late fourth century, would appear to give the cult of John and Paul a Hieronymian as opposed to Rufinian genealogy. Pammachius, as we have seen, studied with Jerome, and he was married to Paulina, daughter of Paula, the principal patron of Jerome. What such a schema forgets, however, is that Pammachius was himself related to Melania, the patron of

67 See Masai and Vanderhoven 1953: 27.

68 Hammond Bammel 1977, 1978, 1979, as discussed in Leyser 2000a: 112–17.

69 Bammel (1979: 436) includes Eugippius in her network, but this is disputed by Gorman (1982: 242–4).

70 For recent discussions of Melania and Pinian in Africa, see Brown 2005, O'Donnell 2005: 230–3, and Cooper in this volume.

71 Cooper 1999.

72 Par. Lat. 12205 contains works of Augustine on grace and correction from the late 420s, a series of paranetic works (some now lost), including the *Sentences of Nilus* on the vices, Rufinus' translation of the *Sentences of Sextus*, the First and Second *Rules of the Fathers*, followed by the *Rule of the Master*. See further Masai and Vanderhoven 1953 and Leyser 2000a: 113–15.

73 We have inscribed copies of Ambrosiaster's *Commentary on Romans* (Montecassino 150) and Origen's *Peri Archon* (Metz 225), owned and read by a priest Donatus at Lucullanum in 569/570.

Rufinus.[74] As in parsing the antipathies of the Laurentian schism, we ought not to be overly schematic in our analysis of lines of affiliation.[75] The *passio* is as sure a trace as any that the connections between monastic culture in suburbicarian Italy and its lay patrons in Rome that were taking shape in the world of Rufinus and Jerome were still functional in the era of Cassiodorus and Gregory the Great.

Positing an overall logic to the anthology in the *vetustissimus* of Corbie is clearly a speculative business. With due caution, then, it is suggested that the refrain of this collection is an insistent one, keyed directly to the story of John and Paul. The effect of the sequencing of the texts in the codex is a carefully orchestrated crescendo on the theme of stability. The *Rule of Eugippius* (as identified by de Vogüé), like its cognate the *Rule of St Benedict*, is emphatic that the true monk is one who shows obedience to an abbot and a Rule.[76] The codex then shifts gear to articulate the consequences of obedient *stabilitas* – and of delinquency. Ephrem's *Institutio ad monacos* is a meditation on the need for vigilance and compunction, such is the contrast in the life to come between the rewards of the blessed and the punishment of the reprobate.[77] Next, the sermons of the unknown Bishop John on the resurrection recall the fearless courage of Hannah of the Maccabees as she sacrifices her own children: how much the more should Christians be ready to sacrifice themselves in the certainty of their resurrection.[78] Finally, the three sermons on the robber crucified next to Christ (attributed in the manuscript to Augustine) depart from the premise of human wretchedness, and offer the extraordinary possibility that we will be snatched away from the death that awaits us.[79] Finally, to exemplify the heroism possible in recent times, comes the story of John and Paul.

While no doubt something of a tonic for the reader who has struggled through the unremitting exhortations of the previous three texts, the *passio* should not be thought of simply as a burst of otherworldliness: as we have seen above, this version of the *passio* has a very specific profile, with

[74] Above n. 38. [75] Leyser 2000a: 110. [76] Leyser 2000a: 118–22.

[77] I have consulted the Kilian Fischer imprint of Ephrem's work (Freiburg im Breisgau, not after 1491), held at Chetham's Library in Manchester. There is no modern printed edition; see Petitmengin 1971: 10 and n. 17.

[78] See *PL* 40.1159–68. Note the link to Chrysostom here, one of whose three Sermons *In Maccabeos* (*PL* 50.617–28) circulates in Latin, and bears comparison with the discussion of the Maccabees in the sermons of the otherwise unidentified 'Bishop John' in the Corbie codex. As seen above, Chrysostom's sermon *In Iuventinum et Maximinum* was the original source for the Latin *Passio Iohannis et Pauli*.

[79] Maximus of Turin, *Sermones* 74–6 (CCSL 23.308–11).

a message about the definition of community in the here and now. Once entered, a religious house could not be left. The house arrest under which the martyrs were placed, and then their murder while at supper, recalls the ascetic vocation of the nuns at Arles, according to the *Rule of Caesarius*, composed in the 520s.[80] The *Rule* was the first to legislate for strict enclosure for women. Once the nuns had entered the sacred precinct, they were never to leave: their bodies passed into the graves prepared for them in the floor of their basilica, and the cloister became their mausoleum.[81] Enclosure for men in the Campanian Rules for monks may not have been an absolute requirement as it was for the virgins of Arles, but containment of the body and mind were the watchwords of these texts. What better way to drive the message home than the story of John and Paul, imprisoned in their house, but invincible against imperial and demonic attack.

NEGOTIATING SPACE IN SIXTH-CENTURY ROME

The monks and nuns of Rome – and specifically the inmates of St Andrew's – may well have identified no less strongly than their colleagues in Campania (and later Corbie) with the defiant stability of the eunuchs John and Paul. But here we run up against the familiar conundrum of the sources for monasticism in early medieval Rome. On the one hand, the sixth-century city was awash with monasteries and with relevant texts – witness the parallel production of the *gesta martyrum* and the Latin translation of the *Sayings of the Desert Fathers*. Here, if anywhere, we should be able to say something about the development of the 'monk as martyr' tradition. But, for reasons explored elsewhere in this book, this apparent richness flatters to deceive;[82] and for reasons we have explored on an earlier occasion, our best-placed informant, Gregory, is notoriously reluctant to commit himself to a discussion of Roman martyr piety.[83]

The Roman *Sitz im Leben* of the *passio* was not, or not only, monastic. Taking in a broader view of the city and its church, we may suggest two contexts for what, as we have seen, is a distinctive story of defiance unto death of the emperor. The first concerns urban property in relation to burial.[84] The archaeological record now confirms what Delehaye took

80 See Klingshirn 1990; Leyser 2000a: 84–90; and now Diem 2005.
81 According to Meneghini and Santangeli Valenzani 1995: 284 the same is true of St Andrew's.
82 Costambeys and Leyser, in this volume. 83 Leyser 2000b.
84 Costambeys 2001, and the ample references there given.

to be an impossibility: the intra-urban burial of John and Paul, strictly forbidden by law, was in fact replicated all over the city across the fifth and sixth centuries. Very crudely speaking, as the number of the living diminished in the face of military disaster and plague, the community of the dead in their midst expanded. Where were they to be lodged, and who was to take care of them?

This takes us, as Marios Costambeys has shown, into the midst of the dynamics of property and power in Rome across this period. The haphazard growth of urban cemeteries, usually with ecclesiastical sponsorship, 'was one episode in the Roman Church's appropriation of the disintegrating fabric of the State in Rome'.[85] But the process was far from straightforward. We enter the rebarbative company of Roman gravediggers (*fossores* and *copiatae*) and their *collegia*. Although legally clerical from the start of the fifth century, the stubborn refusal (down to the era of Gregory the Great) of gravedigging corporations to fold in with the rest of the clergy, and their insistence on charging high fees for their services, is one of the great witnesses to the continuing vitality of ancient civic life, and also of its transformation.

Neither *fossores* nor *copiatae* appear in the *Passio Iohannis et Pauli* (although we might wonder if the *campiductor* Terentianus, who buries the martyrs, is not meant to malign the perceived pride and greed of the gravediggers guild).[86] But we cannot miss the connection in the story between burial and control of their property. If we 'follow the money' in the text, it is clear that by turning a house into a virtual urban cemetery, the claims of the state are rebuffed. John and Paul, former palace attendants, are entrusted with *divitiae* by Constantina. Julian attempts unsuccessfully to claw their riches back: the martyrs succeed, effectively, in 'privatizing' their inheritance.[87] In the compromise worked out by Jovian, the state acquiesces in the designation of the house as corporate ecclesiastical property.

The *passio*, then, is a parable of Roman civic development. It does not seem to apply directly to the property on the Caelian hill, to which we turn in a moment. However, exactly this process of alienation of the fisc through ecclesiastical foundation and burial is discernible on the Esquiline at the

[85] Costambeys 2001: 189

[86] A distinctly unflattering image of *fossores* is projected in the *Collectio Avellana*, where they are included in the band of murderous thugs used by Damasus to storm the Liberian basilica. See *CA* 1 (CSEL 35.3), and for discussion, Kate Blair Dixon's paper in this volume.

[87] On this theme in general, see Matthews 1975 and the review of Matthews by Wormald (1976).

tituli of S. Eusebio and, in particular, of Bibiana. As we have seen, the *passio* of Bibiana was a direct literary descendant of John and Paul. It has Bibiana's mother burying her father-in-law in her house, next to the House of John and Paul. Bibiana's church on the Esquiline, meanwhile, and that of S. Eusebio were founded on land which had once been designated gardens. Both had burial plots associated with them, in the case of S. Eusebio an impressively large area. The grounds occupied by Bibiana and her dead were part of the palatial precinct of Constantine, in use as such until the Gothic Wars. Now, the story of Bibiana does not pit the emperor's greed directly against the martyrs' claims to property as does the *passio* of John and Paul – but the invocation of their house in the *Passio Bibianae* may have been enough to register the point that Bibiana's, too, was a story of successful redeployment of imperial resources. As Costambeys notes, the foundation of the *titulus Bibianae* under Pope Simplicius coincided with the abdication of the last Roman emperor in the west. Appealing to the 'House of John and Paul' may have been a way to legitimate claims to property in the post-imperial city.

In the mid-sixth century, of course, the empire struck back in the person of Justinian. Refusing to submit to the emperor became again a political possibility in Rome, and this suggests a second context for our text. The *Passio Iohannis et Pauli* as transmitted by the *vetustissimus* of Corbie may have been produced and also circulated beyond Rome in the context of the increasingly articulate defiance of the emperor by the papacy. There are dangers in such an approach. Patrick Amory has cautioned that the persistent attempts by scholars to parse the Laurentian schism in terms of pro- and anti-imperial parties is misguided.[88] But in the following generation, after the death of Theoderic, Roman and in particular papal politics do start to take this form. Such a view, effectively, restates the findings of Duchesne with regard to the production of the *Liber Pontificalis* (and also the *Liber Diurnus*).[89] These monuments to papal self-definition represent the realization by the bishop of Rome that the emperor's agenda was not in fact his own. In particular, imperial accommodation with monophysite subjects in the east could mean that open confrontation was necessary. Once taken, the stance of independence was difficult to retreat from, as successive occupants of the throne of St Peter were to discover, and at this point the courage of the martyrs was directly and repeatedly relevant. The

[88] Amory 1997: 195–235. [89] *LP* I, xxxiii–lxvii; also Vogel 1975.

genre of the *passio*, suggests Duchesne, bleeds into the second edition of the *Liber Pontificalis*, completed in the last days of Gothic Rome.[90]

One sixth-century pope, in particular, would have had every reason to associate himself with John and Paul: we may return to the Caelian hill, and to the 'Library of Pope Agapetus'. Agapetus' father Gordianus, killed in the street violence of the Laurentian schism, had been a priest of John and Paul's.[91] His son, reports the contemporary account of the *Liber Pontificalis*, had grown up in the precincts of the church.[92] The basilica was something of a 'family church', and it is at least worth speculating that Gordianus and Agapetus were directly responsible for promoting the cult of John and Paul.[93] As pope, Agapetus did not flinch from defying Justinian over the appointment of the monophysite patriarch Anthimus. His encounter here, as staged in the *Liber Pontificalis*, has something of the quality of John and Paul's with the emperor Julian.

> When the dispute occurred between the emperor and Agapetus, Justinian told him: 'Either you will agree with us or I will have you sent into exile'. Then the blessed pope Agapetus made this reply joyfully to the emperor: 'Sinner that I am, I have long waited to come to the most Christian emperor Justinian – but now I have encountered Diocletian: yet I am not in the least afraid of your threats.'

In debate with Anthimus, Agapetus was no less forthright, and succeeded in convicting him of error. 'Then the pious emperor was filled with joy and abased himself before the apostolic see, prostrating himself before the blessed pope Agapetus.'[94]

The memory of Agapetus as a figure of power carried to the end of the century to his neighbour on the Caelian hill. In Gregory's *Dialogues* (written, so a later inscription has it, in the *bibliotheca Agapeti*[95]), Agapetus is shown healing a dumb man in Greece, *en route* to his confrontation with the emperor.[96] The story is freighted with a petrine moral – Agapetus acts *in virtute Dei ex auctoritate Petri* – and forms part of what Vincenzo Recchia has seen as an anti-monophysite dossier in the *Dialogues*, beginning with Pope John I and continuing past Agapetus with Datius of Milan

[90] *LP* I, ccxxx–ccxxxi. See e.g. the entries for John I, who died at the hands of 'the heretic' Theoderic, while his successor Silverius was martyred in the machinations of Vigilius and the imperial family. According to Grégoire and Orgels 1954: 580, n. 2, the *LP*'s account of Gallicanus is drawn from his *passio*.

[91] *LP* I, 261. [92] *LP* I, 287 and 288, n. 1.

[93] Do they in fact feature in the *passio* in the shape of the father and son Byzantius and Pammachius?

[94] *LP* I, 287–8, trans. Davis 1989: 52–3. [95] *ICUR* II, 1, 55, p. 28 vv. 3–6 (= *ILCV* I, 1898).

[96] Gregory, *Dialogi* III, 3 (SC 251.268–70).

and Sabinus of Canosa, both of whom were envoys to Constantinople.[97] Gregory's attitude towards Constantinople was complicated. What he valued, ultimately, was the radical autonomy of divine *virtus* in the face of temporal structures of power. In practice, this afforded a measure of flexibility. On the Three Chapters, which had become a stubborn rallying point for Latin bishops, Gregory conceded gracefully to the imperial position. But as *apocrisarius* in Constantinople, he had refused to be cowed by the patriarch Eutyches in their debate on the resurrection; nor, notoriously, did he accede to the request of the emperor's sister for relics from Rome.[98] In taking these stands, he may have owed more than he might admit (or perhaps his debt was self-evident?) to the example of his Caelian neighbours, John and Paul.

Unwittingly or otherwise, the testimony of the *Dialogues* helps to explain how the *passio* of John and Paul may have travelled south-east from Rome to the monasteries of Lazio and Campania. From Gregory's account of Benedict in Book II of the *Dialogues*, we learn that the patrician Liberius, a papal envoy to Constantinople in 519, also founded a monastery in (probably) Alatri, whose inmate the deacon Servandus was a regular visitor to Montecassino.[99] Servandus was, in fact, with Benedict when he had his so-called 'cosmic vision' of a soul ascending to heaven. The soul thus ascending belonged to none other than Liberius' diplomatic colleague, Germanus, bishop of Capua. As the careers of Liberius and Germanus show, it was possible to span the exalted world of high diplomacy and the local universe of rural monasticism. Either one of these men was perfectly placed to bring a martyr tradition conceived in the thick of Rome and Roman politics out to the monastic scriptorium that produced the codex we have been discussing.

The primary concern of the compiler of the *vetustissimus* of Corbie (and Gregory's in the *Dialogues*) was not papal/imperial politics, but the immanence of the other world. But this theme too relates to the post-imperial world of the Latin west. As Peter Brown has emphasized, from Gregory's epoch on, Latin authors began to imagine in ever more precise detail how God's justice worked in the invisible courts of celestial appeal.[100] In the east, by contrast, no purgatorial space develops: all eyes remain focused on the terrifying power of the imperial amnesty. Precious little such power

97 Gregory, *Dialogi* III, 2–5. See Recchia 1982–83 and 1986 (both collected in Recchia 1996).
98 See Markus 1981 and 1997: 83–96, 125–43, and Markus and Sotinel, forthcoming. Cracco Ruggini 2004.
99 Gregory, *Dialogi* II, 35.4. On Liberius, see O'Donnell 1981, and on his monastery, see now Fentress, Goodson, Laird, and Leone 2005.
100 Brown 2000 and 2003: 248–66.

was available in the west, after 476. The community of the faithful awaited instead divine judgement, and those morally responsible for them developed a profound and potentially aggressive sense of accountability: attack could be the best form of defence of the flock. Accordingly, the development of mechanisms of intercession at the heavenly courts went hand in hand with the elaboration of procedure for dispute settlement, and for the demarcation of institutional property. From the seventh century on, medievalists expect to find narratives of otherworldly journeys and charters of immunity side by side. Those who do not expect to find late Roman precedent for this cosmic disposition of justice high and low might look again at the *Passion of John and Paul* in the *vetustissimus* of Corbie.[101] With its triumph over earthly injustice, and its ferocious vindication of property rights, the *passio* anticipated the claims to sacral autonomy that would be advanced by monasteries in the medieval west – and not least by the monks of Corbie, dedicated as they were to Peter and Paul, and to the foundation of a new Rome north of the Alps.[102]

101 Both Fouracre (1995: 58–9) and Rosenwein (1999: 36) are sceptical of a meaningful late ancient precedent for exemption and the immunity. For the possibility of a different approach (to be explored on another occasion), see the use of Augustine *Sermones* 355 and 356 in the seventh-century Corbie immunity, as observed by Krusch 1906: 358, n. 1. For the common cause made by papal self-assertion and monastic immunity, see Lemarignier 1950b.

102 See Ganz 1990.

PART III

Religion, dynasty, and patronage

6

Poverty, obligation, and inheritance: Roman heiresses and the varieties of senatorial Christianity in fifth-century Rome

Kate Cooper

In 410, Augustine of Hippo had a difficult letter to write to Caeonia Albina, daughter of the Roman *praefectus urbi* Caeonius Rufinus Albinus (*praefectus urbi* from 389 to 391), widow of the senator Valerius Publicola, and mother of the future saint Melania the Younger. Melania had visited Hippo with her husband, Pinian, as part of a tour of visitation to the couple's estates in Italy and Africa. In a pious spree characterized more by enthusiasm than good sense, the pair, both in their mid-twenties, were selling off as many of their extensive land-holdings as the market would bear, and undertaking a one-off bonanza of pious gift-giving to the religious individuals and institutions along their way. Things had evidently gone badly wrong in Augustine's own town of Hippo. Albina had addressed a sharp letter to Augustine, and although her reprimand is now lost, Augustine's letter of reply stands as a record of the tensions and uncertainties in the fifth-century churches regarding the role of aristocratic patrons. In this heady period of experimentation, the 'ground rules' for the direction of aristocratic wealth to pious causes had yet to be established. It is with the fifth-century attempt to develop these ground rules, especially with regard to that most self-possessed group of donors, the senatorial aristocracy, that the present chapter will concern itself.[1]

Melania and Pinian were making their way slowly to Palestine, where, like Melania's grandmother Melania the Elder, who died in 410, they intended to found a monastery and end their days in prayer. Things had not gone well in Rome itself: Pinian's slaves, terrified at the prospect of being sold to dubious owners or manumitted without the traditional

[1] This chapter attempts to offer a new perspective on problems made tractable for English-speaking readers by Brown 1968, Harries 1984, Markus 1990, and Clark 1990, the tip of a veritable iceberg of important work on related subjects by these colleagues, much of it charted in the volume bibliography. I am grateful to Conrad Leyser, Julia Hillner, and Max Diesenberger for their comments, and to Kim Bowes for valuable guidance, although the faults in what follows of course remain my own.

protections due to valued clients,[2] had revolted. Recent studies by Andrea Giardina and Claude Lepelley have demonstrated the context for the anxiety of these dependants, and have shown how profoundly hypocritical the pair's desire to shed worldly ties must have seemed through the eyes of the 'thousands of little people' for whose well-being they were responsible,[3] and how despicable to those of their peers who took these responsibilities seriously. Only the intervention of Pinian's brother Severus, offering to buy the slaves at a self-interested price and promising to act as a proper *dominus*, had calmed the situation.[4] After an equally unpleasant business with the urban prefect over the validity of one of the bequests on which their wealth depended, the pair had been able to set off on their tour.

A stay on the Sicilian estates had been far more satisfactory. Eye-popping largesse was evidently distributed without any unseemliness. In addition, the group had experienced a barbarian raid on one of the littoral islands – probably Lipari – and Melania had had the opportunity to use her funds to redeem a number of captives. In north Africa, they had initially stayed in Thagaste, where they owned extensive estates and the distinguished canon lawyer Alypius, well known in senatorial circles back in Italy, was bishop. But a visit to Hippo, where the intellectually brilliant though less socially established Augustine was bishop, involved an unfortunate incident.

Two of Augustine's letters, the letter to Albina and another to Alypius, tell the story of an uprising potentially even more damaging to the couple's intentions than the problems in Rome.[5] During a Sunday service, the congregation gathered in Augustine's cathedral had begun to shout, 'Pinianus Presbyter!', acclaiming the young senator as priest and thus claiming him as their own. Of course, Augustine himself had been dragooned into ordination by a similar stunt in 391.[6] Claude Lepelley has shown that the congregation were acting on the basis of a long tradition of self-interested public shaming of elites who were seen to be getting off lightly with respect to curial or other responsibilities appropriate to their

[2] Lepelley (1997–98: 22–3, citing Giardina 1988) discusses the obligations of a *dominus* where the sale of slaves was in question.

[3] Lepelley 1997–98; see also Cecconi 1988 and Consolino 1989.

[4] Harries (1984: 67) offers a judicious assessment of Severus' position: 'Far from being "prompted by the devil", Severus was acting . . . in accord with traditional senatorial values. His claims for consideration [that Pinian should sell the slaves to him rather than on the open market] would have been the stronger if, as suggested above, previous sellers like Paulinus had, out of courtesy, offered the first option to their next of kin, as Hilary of Arles was to do.'

[5] The letters are Augustine, *Epp.* 125 (to Alypius) and 126 (to Albina), CSEL 44.3–7 and 7–18.

[6] For contrasting views of Augustine's narrative of this event (our source is his *Sermon* 355, delivered decades later in 425), see Leyser 2005 and O'Donnell 2005: 19–26.

wealth.[7] Had the acclamation succeeded, Pinian would have been bound to Hippo for life, and the city could have made permanent its fleeting status as a convenient object for his – and his wife's – fits of generosity. In the event, Augustine had been able to broker a face-saving resolution. By extracting from Pinian a legally binding undertaking that should he ever seek ordination, he would do so at Hippo, he made it possible for Pinian to demur. It is possible that the congregation failed to appreciate what little danger there was that a man of Pinian's standing would seek ordination in any city where he had not already been elected bishop.

Albina seems to have written a very sharp letter afterwards to Augustine, who as bishop ought, she felt, to have controlled his congregation more successfully. From Augustine's reply it is clear that Albina had accused the crowd of an unseemly greed. Unconvincingly, he tried to reassure her that it had been Pinian's character rather than his wealth that had led the crowd to crave his permanent residence among them. At the same time, Augustine tried to make it clear that the rabble-rousers had included the genuinely destitute. In a city whose poor relief was perpetually under-funded, the hope of a patron who not only meant well but had the wherewithal to act on his good intentions was a matter not of greed but of survival. Augustine's own writings frequently take up the problem of the ethical responsibilities attached to wealth; if having dozens – or thousands – of dependants was perhaps an obstacle to spiritual progress, failing to act in their best interest was a vice to which enthusiastic Christians seemed especially prone. The desire to be freed from responsibilities should not, he repeatedly argued, be misunderstood as a sign of spiritual advancement; indeed, the measure of spiritual achievement was the ability to face unpleasant duties with courage rather than with impatience.[8]

Melania's biographer understandably buried the Hippo episode, if he knew about it at all, although there is a hint that he was aware that Augustine had tried to steer the heiress towards practicality in her benefactions. He remembers the bishop as suggesting that she should establish recurring support for religious foundations instead of making one-off donations: 'The money that you now furnish to monasteries will be used up in a short time. If you wish to have a memorial forever in heaven and on earth, give both a house and an income to each monastery.'[9] The weary

[7] Lepelley 1979: 387–8.

[8] On Augustine's attempts to pressure African *domini* to use their wealth responsibly, see Lepelley 1997–98: 27–32; on Augustine and the ethics of property ownership, see MacQueen 1972.

[9] *Vita Melaniae* 20 (Gorce, *Vie de Mélanie*, 170; trans. Clark, *Life of Melania*, 43).

pragmatism of the suggestion rings true as having indeed come from the bishop of Hippo.[10]

CHRISTIAN PATRONS AND THE PROBLEM OF CHRISTIAN OWNERSHIP

Augustine's letters still stand as the most vivid record of the difficulty often faced by late Roman bishops in trying to steer the exuberant philanthropic gestures of lay men and women who in many cases outranked them. When Christians of the patronage class gave outright gifts to the church, their preference seems to have been for one-off gestures, whether the gifts were modest or extravagant enough to signal an intention of joining the church's poor. The duty of the bishop, for better or worse, was to develop a diocesan strategy for long-term provision of liturgical staff and physical maintenance for the churches, in addition to whatever programme of poor relief was realistic.[11] This made for a tension between the bishop's need for predictable recurrent income, and the donor's tendency to prefer the shortest possible arc of commitment.[12]

Naturally, the members of the community who were in a position to act as benefactors also had their own recurring obligations, toward dependants who might number in the dozens, hundreds or in some cases thousands. As *domini*, senatorial men and women themselves played a role not dissimilar to that of the *episkopoi*. The point gains force when we remember that the author of the anonymous second-century *First Letter to Timothy* preserved in the New Testament among the letters of Paul took successful performance as a Roman head of household as the crucial credential for appointment as an *episkopos*. If a *dominus* wished to support a Christian institution to serve the recurrent fulfilment of obligations to his or her own dependants, as with the establishment of a chapel on a rural estate, an outright gift was unnecessary, since the institution could simply be funded privately. Philanthropic gestures directed outside the sphere of the land-owner's own *dominium*, however, were an entirely different animal.

These extramural gestures were historically about visibility, part of a game played involving honour and the diffusion of envy. They offered a

[10] See Brown 2005 on Augustine's relationship with the Roman exiles in Africa after 410.

[11] Krause (1996a) cautions that we should not overestimate the resources at bishops' disposal for charitable works such as support for widows and poor relief.

[12] Naturally, the really extravagant gifts themselves involved a substantial arc of commitment, a point explored by Allard (1907) with respect to Melania and Pinian.

conspicuous way to display part of the surplus accumulated by an outstandingly prosperous household, which made it possible simultaneously to shame rivals and at the same time to deflect resentment by the less fortunate.[13] Traditionally, two possible modes of extramural benefaction had been available to *domini*. One-off gestures such as the establishment or renovation of a physical building seem to have been the most common.[14] Alternatively, however, the wills of the very rich could include the establishment of endowments to provide for recurring expenses – for example, to distribute largesse on the birthday of the person whose memory was to be kept alive. A piece of land or other investment could also be designated whose income would pay for annual or other periodic gifts to a particular category of person, as long as a bona fide institution such as a *collegium* was willing to receive and administer the payments.

Thus the instruments for the very rich to make the kind of regular, recurring donations that bishops hoped for were in place, at least for as long as Roman law was in force. To be sure, at least some donors did make use of these instruments: a letter of 432 from Pope Celestine to Theodosius II, for example, praises Anicia Faltonia Proba, the widow of Sextus Petronius Probus (cos. 371), for leaving the income of her estates in Asia to support the clergy, the poor, and the monasteries.[15] But if the instruments were available, they were not used as widely as they might have been. The bishop's church could act as the recipient of endowments from the fourth century, and monasteries seem to have been able to do so from the fifth,[16] but single (or indeed multiple) outright gifts and bequests seem to have been far more prevalent than the establishment of endowments. The donation of an investment producing recurring income, such as a farm, offered a compromise between single and periodic transfer,[17] but it lacked the visibility of other kinds of gift.

We have suggested above that the specific role that extramural donations played in the social visibility and estate planning of *domini* was responsible for their preferences, but cultural factors accompanying the rise of senatorial asceticism may have played a part. If the case of Melania and Pinian is anything to go by, ascetic enthusiasm seems to have distracted at least some men and women of the patronage class from finding a way to 'Christianize' their traditional obligations; instead, they seem to have seen it as a force

[13] Douglas and Isherwood (1979) offer a memorable analysis of the mechanics of conspicuous consumption.

[14] Still valuable is Davies 1976, chapter 2, 'Munificence and almsgiving', 11–44, on the continuities and differences between traditional evergetism and Christian almsgiving.

[15] *ACO* 1.2.90. [16] Bitterman 1938: 202. [17] Giardina 1988: 134.

pulling them away – or perhaps freeing them – from those obligations. In the letters of Jerome, for example, we encounter Fabiola, who is praised for wishing to be listed on the widow's roll herself rather than guaranteeing the expenses of the impoverished women already enrolled;[18] it is unlikely that Jerome would have praised her so highly had he been responsible, year-in year-out, for meeting the expenses of the genuinely destitute. Surely Jerome means to praise her for real generosity, but there is a whiff of having one's cake and eating it in the desire to be the heroine of the story rather than the dependable straight-man. Melania and her family illustrate this point; indeed, Melania's biographer crows that Melania herself was registered on the poor roll at Jerusalem,[19] despite the fact that not long afterwards she was rich enough to build a new monastery at her own expense. Although the biographer does not seem to mind the contradiction, it is likely that, like many an aristocratic black sheep before her, Melania's habit was to spend down her revenues as they came in, and then to wait out the lean periods. One suspects that her mother's death in 433[20] explains the ready cash of the late 430s.

The butterfly attitude of a Melania or a Fabiola may not represent the norm, however, at least among the senatorial Christians based in Italy. Ascetic renunciation and personal wealth seem to have sat comfortably together in the minds of senatorial Christians. A case in point is another Anician, the early sixth-century virgin and literary patroness known only as Proba,[21] the probable sister-in-law of Boethius and the dedicatee of the enormously influential *Excerpta Augustini* compiled by Eugippius of Lucullanum.[22] It has been suggested that Eugippius made use of her library in order to prepare the *Excerpta*, which became one of the ubiquitous standards of medieval librarianship.[23] Proba herself lived in Rome, near St Peter's, with the widow Galla, her sister in Christ and possibly her biological sister.[24] It is unclear whether or how their living arrangements were established institutionally, although Gregory the Great's notice of

[18] Jerome, *Ep.* 77, 9, cited in Giardina 1988: 135. [19] *Vita Melaniae* 35 (Gorce, 194).

[20] The date is disputed; on the arguments, see Laurence 2002: 60–1.

[21] Stevens 1982 is still the best introduction to her career and friendship network.

[22] On Proba and Eugippius, see Cooper 2000: 56.

[23] Bammel 1978. Eugippius in turn has been linked by de Vogüé to MS Par. Lat. 12634, the codex containing a late sixth-century copy of the *Passio Iohannis et Pauli*, probably the earliest of the *gesta martyrum* manuscript texts, along with extracts (edited, according to de Vogüé, by Eugippius) from the *Regula Magistri*, the central text for understanding Italian monasticism before the Gothic Wars. This manuscript receives sustained discussion in the contribution of Conrad Leyser to the present volume.

[24] Gregory the Great, *Dialogues* 4.14 (*SC* 265: 56–9).

Galla in his *Dialogues* suggests that she continued to undertake works of charity – and thus disposed of considerable personal means – for some time after she began to live at St Peter's.[25] Eighth-century sources record a *Monasterium S. Stephani cata Galla patricia* in the vicinity of St Peter's, but how it related to the foundation where Galla and Proba had lived is unclear.[26] Proba's status as a professed ascetic could be reconciled with personal possession of a library extensive enough to use as a base for compiling the *Excerpta Augustini*, so we can deduce that the kind of asceticism she was engaged upon did not involve voluntary poverty. Of course, this would have seemed entirely appropriate to a generation for whom the care of what we would now call a rare-book collection was understood to constitute an exalted form of spirituality.[27]

A recent study by Richard Bartlett has argued that for senatorial Italians poverty was not a virtue; ascetic aspirations were no excuse for a failure to perform the traditional duties of a senatorial land-owner. Reviewing the letters of Ennodius during the decade (501–512) when he was a priest of Milan before being consecrated bishop of Pavia in 513, Bartlett has argued that in Italy ascetic virtues were understood as secondary in importance to responsibility for the welfare of others, as seen for example in the *Vita* of Epiphanius, Ennodius' predecessor as bishop of Pavia. His correspondent Arator (evidently the same Arator who wrote the hexameter *De actibus apostolorum* in the early 540s) seems to have lived as an ascetic while holding public office, for example as *comes rerum privatarum* in 526.[28] In Gaul, Bartlett suggests, a man like Arator would be expected to join a monastery, while in Italy he was expected to bring his ascetic aspirations into line with householding and the performance of traditional duties.[29] The present chapter will consider other sources in light of the hypothesis that Italian senatorial asceticism was distinctively conservative in its expectations of how the ascetic should behave. Paying particular attention to the later career of the famous Roman virgin Demetrias, we will suggest that there is indeed reason to believe that embracing the traditional obligations of his or her class was a carefully considered position rather than an oversight for at least some senatorial ascetics.

[25] 'Mox ergo, ut eius coniunx defunctus est, abiecto saeculari habitu, ad omnipotens Dei servitum sese aput Beati Petri apostoli aecclesiam monasterio tradedit, ibique multis annis, simplicitate cordis adque orationi dedita, larga indigentibus aelemosinarium opera inpendit' (*Dialogues* 4.14, cited in Ferrari 1957, 319).

[26] Ferrari 1957: 319–21. See Costambeys and Leyser in this volume on the eighth-century sources.

[27] See Kirkby 1981 and Shanzer 1986. [28] On Arator, see Sotinel 1989.

[29] Bartlett 2001: 207–8.

The idea of a 'traditionalist' senatorial approach to the relationship between virtue and ownership finds additional support from recent scholarship on Italian evergetism. An article by Luce Pietri offering a synthetic overview of the evidence for private foundations in Italy from the fifth and sixth centuries has argued that, up to the Gothic Wars of 535–554, aristocratic Christian donors frequently established private foundations on their own lands, often churches serving their rural estates.[30] What emerges from her study, admittedly based largely on rural rather than urban evidence, is a picture in which rich Christians were reluctant to donate the churches which they established; they often seem simply to have built or reassigned a building and established it informally as a private church. It is not known to what extent these informal arrangements were in use in the cities.

In the case of the Italian private foundations studied by Pietri, which included churches, xenodochia, and monasteries, the evidence for ownership is in fact slim, but there is reason to believe that the donors themselves would retain ownership of the premises, while establishing either an endowment or instructions to their heirs that a certain portion of income should be set aside for staffing and upkeep. It is perhaps in this light that we should understand the *senatusconsultum* of 483, held under the urban prefect Basilius, during which lay donors attempted to stipulate that property donated outright to the Roman church would remain inalienable;[31] if Roman donors were used to maintaining ownership of resources made available for use by the church, it is understandable that they would be tempted to attach conditions to any outright donation. The repercussions of this suggestion are far reaching, in that the assumption has been that in Rome only a small proportion of resources were under private control, an assumption which informs even Charles Pietri's influential argument, challenged by Julia Hillner elsewhere in this volume, that the Roman titular churches were a bastion of lay control in a landscape of predominantly episcopal ownership. Proper consideration of this problem lies beyond the scope of the present chapter, but it is tempting to return to the views espoused by A. H. M. Jones a generation ago, who made an argument very similar to Hillner's about the nature of the *tituli* as churches under the control of the bishop, and left open the possibility that churches *not* designated as *tituli* were in fact *not* under his control. This is a point given force by Krautheimer's (1983) calculation that the combined capacity

[30] Pietri 2002.

[31] The evidence for the *senatusconsultum* is in the *Acta* of the Roman Council of 502 (MGH AA XII, 438–55); for discussion, see Julia Hillner's chapter in this volume.

of the basilicas and parish churches recorded for the fourth and fifth centuries numbered something less than 20,000, 'an astonishingly limited provision for a population, Christian by now, of a few hundred thousand'.[32] Krautheimer suggested that, as late as the fifth century, the majority of Roman Christians worshipped in informal 'community centres', the contemporary incarnation of the ancient, privately owned *domus ecclesiae.*

It is logical enough to imagine that in urban as well as rural environments the wealthy members of the community made space available for Christian purposes on an informal basis. If this was the case in Rome, it may in some ways have set private land-owners in tension with the bishop, but in other ways it would have put them in a position analogous to his own, albeit only with respect to their own dependants. From the late fourth century forward to the time of Pope Leo (440–461), there is copious evidence that private churches were seen by bishops and even emperors as a weak point in the fabric of episcopal control; in the Arian crisis of the 380s imperial legislation explicitly prohibited owners of private churches from making them available for use by heretical priests, evidence that the lay owners were in a position to invite whomever they chose.[33]

Up until the reign of Pope Gelasius (492–496) a *dominus* could expect to appoint the staff of a private foundation, in many cases without episcopal supervision. Reforms under Gelasius required that founders apply for episcopal approval before establishing a foundation, but as late as the reign of Pelagius I (556–561) the custom seems to have been that it was the *dominus* who made the decisions about staffing, albeit subject to episcopal approval of the candidates. Luce Pietri has suggested that the tightening of episcopal control under Pelagius was a response to the breakdown during the Gothic Wars of the old system of senatorial management of distant rural estates.[34]

Where monasteries are concerned, our evidence for their ownership both in Italy and elsewhere in the fifth century is uncertain. This may reflect uncertainty or variety of practice at the time, and almost certainly the problem is compounded by a tendency of medieval and early modern canon lawyers to ignore or suppress ancient evidence which did not contribute to the genealogy of later practice. The first surviving legislation reflecting monasteries established as independent property-holding institutions was not published until 434,[35] but there is reason to believe that at least in Egypt from the mid-fourth century some monasteries had been able

[32] Krautheimer 1983: 102. [33] Colish 2002; see also Maier 1994, 1995a, 1995b.
[34] Pietri 2002: 262. [35] Bitterman 1938: 202, citing *Cod. Theo.* 5.1.1.

to collect rents, and had been responsible for tax returns.[36] The actual ownership basis in these cases, however, is still not fully understood. The *Life of Pachomius* implies at Tabbenisi an institution robust enough to receive bequests of property already in the fourth century, but it should be remembered that Pachomius' immediate successor as abbot, Petronius, was a major benefactor of the monastery, and it is not impossible that he held title to the land. Indeed, this hypothesis could explain the tension surrounding the figure of Petronius, who was not remembered as a man of great spiritual attainments.

Across the twentieth century, historians of canon law attempted to understand whether monasteries were established under Roman law as corporations, or whether the abbot – or even the bishop – was in fact understood to be the legal *possessor* of the monastery's property.[37] Spanish evidence, from the second council of Braga in 572, records that at the death of a bishop, an inventory would be made of his property held individually, along with but distinct from the property which he held on behalf of the church; it is likely that a similar distinction was made in the fifth century, although there could sometimes be confusion.[38] The Italian *Regula Magistri*, produced probably in the first quarter of the sixth century, records that on the death of an abbot a formal *testamentum* would be drawn up recording the gifts brought by the brothers to the monastery, and conveying them to his successor, but discussion of this clause has not shed much light on the ownership of the monastery itself.[39]

In any case, there is no compelling evidence to disallow the hypothesis that ownership of Italian monasteries remained with their founders – whether lay or clerical – and their heirs. In the early fifth century we see that the Jerusalem monastery founded by the Roman aristocrat Paula was taken over on her death by her daughter Eustochium, and on Eustochium's death in turn by Paula's granddaughter Paula the Younger, who was also Eustochium's niece. This could well imply a succession of intra-familial bequests of ownership of the land itself. At the very least it implies an intergenerational handing on of responsibility for the well-being of the institution.[40]

36 Lane Fox 1997: 71, citing Wipsycka 1975.

37 The history of the problem is surveyed in Blecker 1972: 4–5.

38 Ganz 1995: 29 and Blecker 1972: 5.

39 Blecker 1972: 11–12.

40 Gordini 1961: 100, with Harries 1984: 60–1, who deduces the probable contents of the wills of Paula's daughters Iulia (Eustochium), Blaesilla, and Paulina, and of her son Toxotius. Paula the Younger, the daughter of Toxotius, was in fact the second cousin of Melania the Younger, since her mother Laeta's father Publius Caeonius Caecina Albinus, *pontifex* of the cult of Vesta, was the brother of Melania's grandfather, Caeonius Rufius Albinus (*praefectus urbi* 389–391).

I have argued elsewhere that there is evidence in the *Regula Magistri* and the Roman hagiographical legends known as the *gesta martyrum* that Italian monasteries were concerned to establish mutually supportive relations with more traditional households. Explicitly in the *Regula Magistri*, and obliquely in the *gesta*, we find the view that monasteries should take special care to be correct in dealing with the families of new entrants to the community.[41] It is clear from both the *Theodosian Code* and the *Edictum Theoderici* cited by Gaudemet that individual monks in fifth-century Italy were still understood to be owners of property, whose relations would have first call on their property if there was no will.[42] It is unfortunate, however, that no explicit discussion of ownership of the monasteries themselves survives for this period.

FIFTH-CENTURY WRITERS AND THE ANCIENT DEBATE ON RICHES

Before considering further evidence for a specifically Italian attitude to the role of private ownership it is worth reviewing the wider picture in the late Roman west. The fifth-century writers were in fact continuing an ancient debate about the use of riches, and the degree to which the biological family was an appropriate vehicle for accumulating surplus. The consensus among Christian writers had tended to follow a stoic notion of material things as *adiaphora* – morally indifferent[43] – but with the ascetic explosion of the late fourth century, the debate became more heated. This discussion was largely framed as a debate over the significance of advice given in the second-century Pastoral Epistles, as the Letter to Titus and the First and Second Letters to Timothy of the New Testament canon are known. These texts had arisen from the second-century church's attempt to understand whether and how prosperous householders could be assimilated to the Christian church – eventually in a leadership role – as the edge of eschatological expectation began to wane, and the community in its second century began to plan for what might be a long duration of its time on earth.

As for those who in the present age are rich, command them not to be haughty, or to set their hopes on the uncertainty of riches, but rather on God who richly

[41] Cooper forthcoming. [42] The standard discussion for the west is still Gaudemet 1958: 304.

[43] Writing of Clement of Alexandria, William Countryman puts it this: 'The heart of Clement's teaching about wealth was his doctrine of detachment: it is permissible to possess riches, but not to love them' (Countryman 1980: 69).

provides us with everything for their enjoyment. They are to do good, to be rich in good works, generous, and ready to share, thus storing up for themselves the treasure of a good foundation for the future, so that they may take hold of the life that really is life. (1 Timothy 6.17–19)

The problem raised by the Deutero-Pauline epistle to Timothy was its seeming disagreement with one of the sayings of Jesus most popular to the fifth-century church, the advice of Jesus to the rich young man, 'If you wish to be perfect, go, sell your possessions, and give the money to the poor, and you will have treasure in heaven; then come, follow me' (Matthew 19.21). This was the biblical text which had inspired the desert father Antony to take up his life of renunciation, and which, directly and indirectly, was to motivate the desert movement of the late fourth and early fifth centuries and became a central issue in the Pelagian controversy.[44]

The radical Pelagian position, as it is represented by the anonymous treatise *On Riches* from the Caspari corpus, dated to the second decade of the fifth century, is a condemnation not only of the unscrupulous acquisition of riches, but even of the possession of wealth in excess of what is needed to live.

And all the time you convince yourself that it is from God that you receive what, in fact, you either procure with your ill-gotten gains or acquire at the price of shameful sycophancy and oft-repeated acts of obeisance, bowing your head to the ground and addressing as 'Lord' one whom you scorn, while he, the trafficker in offices, also scorns you; and sometimes you glory in being called 'honourable', though the only true honour is that which is paid to moral character, not that acquired by money or shameful servitude.[45]

The problem is not only that the acquisition of riches is necessarily accompanied by dishonesty, but equally that to possess them can only lead either to extravagance or to dishonesty.

But I must not ignore either the excessively subtle and refined ingenuity of those who think themselves religious and are reckoned to be despisers of the world by themselves and by ignorant people, because they go about in more lowly attire, taking no pleasure in possessing ornaments or gold or silver or in display of more

[44] The debate between the saying of Jesus and the saying which the fourth century accepted as having come from the pen of St Paul was central to the dispute between Augustine of Hippo and the radical fringe of the Pelagian movement. Thus Augustine's response to Hilary of Syracuse *c.* 414 rejected the radical Pelagian teaching on the renunciation of wealth precisely because no Christian should accept the idea that the teaching of Paul could possibly contradict the teaching of Jesus; the person who finds such a contradiction must have misinterpreted one or both of the biblical texts. (Augustine, *Ep.* 157.)

[45] *On Riches* 6.3 (trans. Rees, 179–80).

costly metal, and yet keep all their possessions hidden away in their treasuries and, motivated by sheer greed, retain possession of what they disdain to use in the eyes of men merely in order to enjoy a worthless reputation.[46]

What is disputed here is whether it is acceptable to accumulate a surplus beyond what is needed for subsistence. The advice is offered not only to the ascetic but also to the married householder:

But I have sons, you will say, for whom I want to keep all my possessions . . . What then are we saying? That you should completely disinherit your sons? Far from it! Rather, that you should leave them no more than their nature requires. For how can you be said to love them, if you are seen to confer on them something which will only harm them?[47]

This kind of thinking had its roots in a tradition as old as Plato, dwelling on the ethical danger posed by children, the creatures most likely to tempt even a cautious soul to the vice of hoarding.[48]

A passage from the *Ad ecclesiam* of Salvian of Marseilles, written in the late 430s or 440s, reflects a mid-fifth-century Gallo-Roman attempt to elaborate an ideology of Christian ownership that would blur the distinctions between householder and ascetic. For Salvian, all ownership is fundamentally a form of temporary stewardship on behalf of God,

Let us see therefore briefly be it by whom riches themselves are given, for what reason they are given, so that when we have brought to light both the author and the cause of the things given, we may more easily determine to whom they should be given back, and for what use they should be made over. No one, I think, doubts that all earthly substance is given to all as a gift from God . . . So if God gives everything to everybody, no one can doubt that those things which we receive as a gift from God we should bring back to the worship of God . . . For this is to recognize the gift of God . . . that you should honour him in his gifts, from whom you have received the gifts themselves. This is something for which even human affairs sets us an example . . . Surely he is judged the most ungrateful and the most unfaithful of men, he who, forgetful of his most open-handed provider, desires to despoil (by his own master's law) the very man who enriched him with a lease on his own holdings. And so it is for us: we have only use of the things we have . . . we are their possessors as *precarii* only. Whether we like it or not, when we pass out of this world, we leave all of these things here. Why, then, do we try to alienate or embezzle from the *proprietas* of our master goods which we cannot carry away with us, when we only have use of them as usufructuaries?[49]

[46] *On Riches* 20.1 (trans. Rees). [47] *On Riches* 20.2 (trans. Rees).

[48] A useful introduction to this strand of Plato's thinking can be found in Gaca 2003: 23–58.

[49] 'Videamus breviter vel a quo sint datae facultates ipsae vel obquid datae, ut cum auctorem et causam datae rei ostenderemus, facilius ad quem referenda et in quem usum conferenda sint approbare possimus. Omnem substantiam mundialem divino cunctis munere dari nullus homo ut reor,

The individual or family here serves as a steward or tenant, while outright ownership is reserved to God. Salvian's idea that Christians should style themselves *quasi precari possessores* is intended to emphasize that our hold on earthly belongings is through a weak form of tenancy. The bona fide possessor of a property in Roman law was not its owner in the sense of holding title, but he had substantial legal rights; indeed the rich and powerful often held land on this basis.[50] The *precario tenens*, by contrast, did not hold a normal lease: a *precarium* was a grant of property or goods, often by a *dominus* to his client or freedman, conferring *possessio* but only on a provisional basis, revocable at the will of the grantor (Buckland 1950: 524–5). What Salvian means here is that the *possessor* only has use of his or her property through God's favour; the truth is that he or she is merely God's *precarius*. This point must have seemed all too real in mid-fifth-century Gaul, and equally vivid to the senatorial land-owners based in Rome, whose ability to defend *possessio* of estates scattered across a collapsing empire was insecure in the fifth century and may have seemed hopeless in the sixth. The idea of God's ultimate ownership would be given concrete form in the Merovingian and later churches through the development of precarial tenure, according to which families bequeathed or assigned *possessio* of their lands to a monastery while retaining right of use for an agreed period.[51]

The anonymous *Passio Sebastiani* (*BHL* 7543), written in Rome in the fifth or very early sixth century, takes a not incompatible view of riches from the point of view of the wealthy Christian. In a sustained address to the wives and parents of his young protégés Marcus and Marcellianus, Sebastian explains that the true Christian should not allow the love of riches to dissuade him from standing up for the faith.

ambigit ... Igitur si omnia omnibus Deus tribuit, nemini dubium est quod ea quae Dei dono accepimus ad Dei cultum referre debeamus ... Hoc est enim agnoscere munus Dei ... ut datis suis illum honores, a quo data ipsa acceperis: quod quidem etiam humanarum rerum exempla docent ... nonne ingratissimus omnium atque infidelissimus judicetur qui oblitus scilicet hominis benfici ac liberalissimi, spoliare illum jure domini sui velit qui eum ipsum usus possessione ditaverit. Et nos itaque usum tantum earum rerum accepimus quas tenimus ... *quasi precari possessores sumus*. Denique egredientes e mundo isto velimus nolimus hic cuncta relinquimus. Cur ergo cum possessores tantum usufructuarii sumus quod nobiscum auferre non possimus avertere a proprietate domini atque alienare tentamus?' (*Adv. Avaritiam* 1, 5, cited in Monachesi 1921: 93–4).

50 Gaudemet 1958: 304 n. 2, suggests that in fifth-century sources *possidere* and its derivatives are often used in a non-technical sense, as the distinctions between *dominium* (equivalent to the English 'title'), *possessio* (equivalent to the English *seizen*), and the various forms of lease-hold were beginning to blur; in particular the means for obtaining the stronger form of ownership, *dominium*, had already become blurred by Cicero's day (see, e.g., Crook 1967b: 146).

51 See Wood 1995 and Ganz 1995.

> Therefore let it be asked, 'Why were riches given by the Creator if they must be condemned?' Let the riches themselves, made by the creator, address their lovers in this way, saying, 'Thus you love us in the hope that we will never be separated from you. But we are not able to follow you when you die.'[52]

In fact, the *Passio*'s author is here steering close to a motif from the sermons of Augustine, that the poor are *laturarii* – porters – of the rich, who will carry the goods of the rich ahead of them to heaven.[53] We will see below that *Ad Gregoriam*, a conduct manual for a senatorial *matrona*, picks up on Augustine's motif more closely. But the author of the *Passio Sebastiani* offers, in Sebastian's speech, a vision of the rich man's dilemna cast in the vivid imagery of the barbarian invasions.

> Let's say you were crossing through the centre of a battle-line of Barbarians, and came upon a strong man who has always loved you, who had given you a bag of coins, and he said to you, 'Give me the guardianship of the money I gave you, because these barbarians close upon us are threatening to take it from you, and they will steal it from you, killing you with swords.' Would you not, once you had thrown yourself at his feet, ask Him to take them, who were sure would return more than he had received, and even free you from your enemies? From now on you may have Christ as a safe-keeper (*tutor*) for your riches.[54]

How the rich Christian should enact this willingness to trust God as a guardian is not made explicit, but it may be significant that this source encourages the rich Christian to entrust his wealth to 'a strong man who has always loved you' – possibly to a bishop, abbot, or other trusted administrator – instead of placing the burden of riches directly on the backs of the poor. This would be compatible with the view, which I have put forward elsewhere, that the *Passio Sebastiani* was one of a number of texts designed to encourage lay patronage of the Roman monasteries.[55]

[52] *Passio Sebastiani* 15: 'Interrogatur ergo: Cur a Creatore divitiae datae sunt, si contemnendae sunt? Respondemus: Istae divitiae a Creatore factae, alloquuntur quodammodo amatores suos, dicentes: Sic nos amate, ut a vobis numquam separemur. Sequi vos morientes non possumus; antecedere autem vos viuentes possumus: sed si ipsi iubeatis' (*AASS Ian. II*, 265–78).

[53] Augustine, *Serm.* 18, 4; 38, 9; 60, 8 (*Sermo* 18 *De eodem versu Psalmi XLIX, Deus manifestus veniet, etc.*, *PL* 38.129–31, at 130 and 31; *Sermo* 38 *De verbis Ecclesiastici II, 1–5, Fili, accedens ad servitutem Dei, etc. Et de verbis Psalmi XXXVIII, 7, Quanquam in imagine ambulat homo, etc. De continentia et sustinentia.*, *PL* 38.235–41, at 240; *Sermo* 60 *De verbis Evangelii, Matthaei, cap. VI, 19–21, Nolite vobis condere thesauros in terra, etc., exhortatorius ad faciendas eleemosynas*, *PL* 38.402–9, at 406.

[54] *Passio Sebastiani* 16: 'Numquid si transires per medias acies barbarorum, & inuenires fortem virum qui te semper dilexit, qui tibi etiam sacculum pecuniis donauerat plenum, dicentem tibi: Da mihi custodiendas pecunias quas dedi tibi; quia isti barbari insidiantur vt eas tibi auferant, quas dum tibi abstulerint suis te gladiis laniabunt; numquid non pedibus eius aduolutus rogares eum, vt eas ipse susciperet, de quo certus esses quod & ampliora quam acceperat redderet, & te ipsum ab hostibus liberaret? Restat nunc vt diuitiis vestris tutorem possitis habere Christum' (*AASS Ian. II*, 265–78).

[55] Cooper forthcoming.

In a little-read 1922 article attempting to establish the identity of the fifth-century theologian Arnobius the Younger, the Italian scholar Maria Monachesi suggested that the treatment of family relationships in the *Passio Sebastiani* was similar to that reflected in a mid-fifth-century letter addressed to his parents-in-law by Salvian of Marseilles, whom we saw above as the author of *Ad ecclesiam*.[56] It is an intriguing suggestion, given the importance in the *Passio Sebastiani* of the scene in which Sebastian persuades the pagan wives and parents of Marcus and Marcellianus to join them as Christians, first in prison, and ultimately in martyrdom.[57]

In his *Letter* 4, Salvian attempted to dissuade the parents of his wife Palladia, who wished to leave their estate to Palladia and her children. However, after the birth of their first daughter, Auspiciola, the younger couple, Palladia and Salvian, had decided to adopt a life of continence. They had then made known their unwillingness to condone the choice of their own child as a vessel for the inheritance of the grandparents. The grandparents could have circumvented their wishes by adopting Auspiciola directly as the immediate heir, but Palladia and Salvian's decision was an affront to the family honour and to the principle of veneration for forebears and afterlife through progeny.[58] It was precisely the kind of issue over which parents might refuse all contact with treacherous children, an offence far more grave than a difference of religious persuasion. By tradition it was incumbent on the stray children to conform to the wishes of their elders, but Salvian and Palladia instead attempted to explain the reasoning behind their action in hope of winning over the parents, or at least public opinion, to approve their seeming impiety. The letter is a rare example of an attempt to negotiate where religious differences have led family members to disagree over how to fulfil the obligations of *pietas*.[59]

Even though Salvian and the *Passio Sebastiani* agree that children inspired by Christian ideals should invite their families to join them in the faith rather than simply defying parental authority, their views of the

[56] Monachesi 1921: 90–1.

[57] Cooper (2005a) explores the theme of family-centred conversion in the *Passio Sebastiani*.

[58] On the refusal to produce heirs as a criterion for a judgement of filial impiety in the case of the Roman couple Melania and Pinian a generation earlier, see Cooper 2006: 23. An English translation of the Greek *Life of Melania*, with valuable notes and introduction, is offered by Clark 1984.

[59] Another very interesting example is *Honorificentiae tuae* (*PLS* 1, 1687–94; *CPL* 761), one of the early fifth-century letters preserved in the so-called Caspari corpus, a letter from a young father to an older relative, attempting to justify the fact that he wishes to take his daughter, who seems to have been in the older relative's care while the younger man was touring the Mediterranean, and place her in the care of a noble female ascetic whom he has met while visiting Sicily. An English translation is available in Rees 1991: 147–56.

issue of riches and inheritance differ. A passage from *Ad ecclesiam* shows that Salvian's view of inheritance is even more radical than that of the author of *De divitiis*.

> Do I seem to prohibit parents from affection to their children? Certainly not! What is more barbaric, what more inhumane, more inimical to the law: would we then say that one should not love one's children, while we propose that one should love one's enemies? . . . Not at all! Not only do we say that one should love one's children, but that one should love them more than anything, except God alone.[60]

While the author of *De divitiis* had argued that it was in a child's own best interest to be offered only what he needed, Salvian sees the child as essentially competing with God for the parent's affection, even if some children can bring the parent closer to God.

ADVICE TO ROMAN HEIRESSES: DEMETRIAS AND GREGORIA

More attention should be given, we suggest, to an anonymous text written in Rome in the 430s or 440s, which explores the problem of ownership from the point of view of the senatorial ascetic and would-be donor. This text, the *Epistula ad Demetriadem de vera humilitate*, addressed to the Roman virgin Demetrias, tries to theorize a view of riches that acknowledges and accepts the tendency of illustrious households to accumulate wealth, while at the same time encouraging these *domini* to establish bonds of patronage with ecclesiastical and monastic institutions.

Although the views reflected in the text are those of its author rather than of the dedicatee, it is the latter whom we can place firmly in the historical record. Born shortly after 395, Demetrias, granddaughter of Sextus Petronius Probus and Anicia Faltonia Proba, is known to have taken the veil in 413 while her family was in north Africa as refugees from Alaric's invasion of Italy. She is believed to have died in Rome during the reign of Pope Leo (440–461), not long after dedicating a church on the Via Latina to the proto-martyr Stephen, which a surviving inscription commemorates as 'last of her gifts'.[61]

The manuscripts of *De vera humilitate* favour Ambrose of Milan as its author, but this is highly unlikely since Ambrose died in 397, not more than a year or two after the addressee's birth. Since the Renaissance, scholarship

[60] Salvian, *Ad ecclesiam* 15.

[61] On Demetrias and her family in north Africa, see now Brown 2005. The inscription, *ILCV* I, 1765, is preserved in fragments in the Museo delle Terme in Rome; see Krautheimer, *Corpus Basilicarum* IV, 242.

has considered a wide variety of otherwise well-known fifth-century figures as possible candidates for its authorship, but most discussion has centred on Prosper of Aquitaine and Pope Leo the Great. All that can be said with certainty is that the text was written at some time after Demetrias' consecration as a virgin; it seems likely that it was written after the death in 432[62] of her grandmother Anicia Faltonia Proba, when Demetrias was established as an ascetic and patroness.[63]

The author of *De vera humilitate* offers a view of riches rather different from that of Salvian. The same idea of the rich as only temporary holders of wealth is present, but here the emphasis is not on the human being as a dependent tenant, but rather as *procurator*, the actively employed steward who administers the estates of a *dominus*. The important point is the active agency of the rich Christian, and the urgent importance of his or her role; he or she has a crucial job to do and will not be excused for failing to do it.

Not only are Christ's poor sustained by the resources of those who, in order to follow the Lord with less encumbrance, have divested themselves once and for all of their wealth; the same cause is also served by the property of those who administer their possessions exclusively as the goods of the poor, in a kind of stewardship for the Church, each one working according to his resources in order that the household of God may be supplied with what is necessary for food and clothing, and at the same time seeing to it that in their own households all are cherished in kindness and controlled by good discipline under a just and holy management. For as the Apostle says, *If anyone does not take care of his own, and especially of his household, he has denied the faith and is worse than an unbeliever.* (1 Timothy 5.8)[64]

The author continues with a sustained meditation on the metaphor of the community as Body of Christ interpreted through the lens of Augustine's *Praeceptum* and the Acts 4.32 tradition (the 'union of hearts'),[65]

[62] She must have been dead by 15 March 432, when Pope Celestine addressed a letter to Theodosius II referring to her having bequeathed the revenues of her estates in Asia for the support of the clergy, the poor, and the monasteries, *ACO* 1.2.90.

[63] While Krabbe (1965: 47–52) assigns authorship of the text to Prosper of Aquitaine, her arguments seem to my eye to be plausible but not conclusive.

[64] *De vera humilitate* 5, ed. and trans. Krabbe, 158–9: 'non dubium est, et pauperes Christi non eorum tantum facultatibus sustineri qui, ut expeditiores Dominum sequerentur, simul se omnibus suis opibus exuerunt, sed eidem operi etiam illorum substantias deservire qui possessionibus suis non aliter quem rebus pauperum praesunt et ecclesiasticae utilitati sub quaedam procuratione famulantur, elaborantes singuli pro suarum virium portione, ut ad victum atque vestium familiae Dei necessaria conferantur, et simul prospicientes ut in dominus ipsorum sub iusto sanctoque moderamine omnes et benignitas foveat et disciplina contineat, dicente apostolo: Si quis autem suorum, et maxime domesticorum curam non habet, fidem negavit, et est infideli deterior.'

[65] Leyser 2000a: 10–19.

concluding, 'so great is the peace and concord there that even what belongs to the individual cannot exist unless it belongs to all (*non possit esse nisi omnium quod est singulorum*)'.[66] The phrase is intriguingly similar to a phrase in the *Regula Magistri* describing the monastery's property which has been central to scholarly debate about ownership rights among the monks.[67]

A century before the *Rule* of St Benedict, it is clear that a vow of poverty was by no means the *sine qua non* of ascetic identity, at least among the Roman aristocracy. The vision of Demetrias as ascetic and property-holder here is striking to a modern eye. She is clearly not understood to have divested herself of her wealth, and indeed the case is being made that an ascetic is peculiarly well qualified as an administrator of riches. In the event, Demetrias seems to have lived up to the ideal. Her church of St Stephen is recorded as having been founded on her own land on the Via Latina,[68] and indeed there is no evidence that the land was made over to the bishop even after the church's foundation.

In literary terms, the sophisticated marriage of ascetic and householder language in *De vera humilitate* was designed to dissolve the barrier between two distinct traditions. The ascetic householder who retains his or her property and uses it on behalf of the church, rather than selling it off and giving away the proceeds, is confirmed here as the moral equal of the ascetic who, following the rich young man of Matthew 19.21, sells all he or she has and gives the proceeds to the poor. One imagines that this approach to asceticism would have been criticized from at least some quarters. (In the Hippo of early 426, for example, Augustine found himself having to defend the actions of his nephew Patricius, a sub-deacon of the episcopal household, the *monasterium clericorum*, who had not yet been able to divest himself outright of an estate in whose income his ageing mother had an interest.[69])

The author of *De vera humilitate* seems to make every effort to integrate his views into an Augustinian scheme where pride is the root of all sin. A somewhat quirky and paradoxical vision of humility – *vera humilitate* – results from the attempt to explain that, for the rich, retaining control of their resources is a greater demonstration of humility than the splashy

66 *De vera humilitate* 6, ed. and trans. Krabbe, 158 and 160.

67 *omnium est et nullius est* (*RM* 2,48/16,61); Bleker 1972: 16.

68 *Liber Pontificalis* I, 47, ed. Duchesne, 238: 'Leo, natione Tuscius, ex patre Quintiano, sedit ann. XI m. I d. XIII. Huius temporibus fecit Demetria ancilla Dei basilicam sancto Stephano via Latina miliario III, in praedio suo.'

69 Augustine, *Sermo* 356.

gestures of a Melania or a Pinian which may unleash a potentially catastrophic domino effect while glorifying the perpetrator.

The initial approach to the theme of riches shows the writer's care to explain that it is the pride of the rich, not their access to wealth, that is the cause of distress to the poor.

The first concern of humility is with the duties of living together in society, whereby we win divine mercy and forge the bonds of human fellowship. For it is a powerful help in strengthening charity when, according to the teaching of the Apostle, men . . . love to serve as subjects and do not know what it is to be puffed up when they have been placed in authority; when the poor man does not hesitate to give preference to the rich man, and the rich man is glad to make the poor man his equal.[70]

In sections four and five of the treatise the writer makes it emphatically clear that he is not proposing complacency in the possession of riches – far from it. 'At what price is peace in this life more fittingly bought than by giving all riches, all honors, and every worldly desire back to that very same world?'[71] But *how* this should be undertaken is open to debate. A lengthy discussion of Job, the emblematic virtuous householder, leads to a reiteration of the passage from First Timothy cited above. As we saw above, the position being celebrated by the author of *De vera humilitate* is that of rich ascetics such as Demetrias 'who administer their possessions exclusively as the goods of the poor, in a kind of stewardship for the Church'.[72]

Chronologically, *De vera humilitate* is likely to have been written within a decade or so of the completion of Augustine's *City of God*, and Augustine's explication there of the centrality of pride as the origin of other sins may well be reflected here. Certainly, the writer's repeated reminders that the real spiritual danger for the rich is the craving for the grand gesture would have been understood as an appropriation of Augustine's thinking:

Being puffed up, then, and ambitious, and proudly defending one's own gifts and good qualities can cancel out the value of almsgiving, can nullify martyrdom. Such

[70] *De vera humilitate* 3, ed. and trans. Krabbe, 146–7: 'Prima ergo humilitatis ratio in communis vitae versatur officiis, quibus et divina clementia conciliatur et societas humana connectitur. Multum enim ad roborandum dilectionum valet cum, secundum doctrinam apostolicam . . . homines . . . amant servire subiecti et nesciunt tumere praelati; cum et pauper divitem non sibi dubitat anteferre, et dives pauperum sibi gaudet aequare.'

[71] *De vera humilitate* 4, ed. & trans. Krabbe, 150–1: 'Quo autem pretio quies huius temporis aptius comparatur quam ut ipsi mundo omnes divitiae, omnes dignitates et universarum cupiditatum materiae refundantur.'

[72] *De vera humilitate* 5, as above.

is the case if someone pours out great wealth but out of love for human praise, or undergoes cruel suffering, but presuming on his own strength rather than on strength given by God.[73]

Indeed, the passage here could have been written by Augustine at almost any point in his career as a bishop; it echoes closely the caveats against ascetic pride in his treatise *On Holy Virginity* of 401, which Robert Markus has argued was part of a covert effort to reprimand Jerome for his infamous encouragement of ascetics to *sancta superbia*, explicitly in the famous *Letter 22* to Eustochium and implicitly in *Adversus Jovinianum*.[74]

Ad Gregoriam in Palatio, an anonymous conduct manual addressed to a senatorial *matrona* of the fifth or early sixth century, fleshes out the theoretical issues, in that it offers extended advice on the principles of Christian estate management, including a chapter on the humane treatment of slaves.[75] What interests us here, however, is the chapter on avarice, which reprises a number of themes we have already seen. Here is the voice of temptation speaking to the Christian *domina*, encouraging her to believe that as she is a property-owner and patron of the church other Christians will make a play for her money but will not even notice her attempts to live a life of holiness:

All mortals (*omnes homines*), all the mighty and the low, even the bishops of God will venerate you and will be able to honor you only insofar as you have been able to be furnished with money, and not insofar as you have succeeded in being holy. Why do you diminish yourself by wealth (*potestate*) and slip into being prey to your own riches?[76]

In suggesting how she should respond to these taunts, the anonymous author draws on the metaphor of God as a trustworthy guardian which we saw above in the *Passio Sebastiani*.

If the consuls of this world do not fear a vain expenditure of their wealth, to enrich chariot-drivers and actors, and to make brothel-keepers and mimes rich men, but rather glory in these excesses, so long as by this loss of possessions they purchase the favor of the contemptible crowd, why with the praise of all angels do I fear to

[73] *De vera humilitate* 20, ed. & trans. Krabbe 202–3: 'Inflatio ergo et ambitio et propriorum bonorum superba defensio possunt destruere eleemosynas, possunt vacuare martyria, si et magnas opes amore quis humanae laudis effundat et saeva suplicia non ea fortitudine quam Deus tribuit sed ea quam de se praesumpsit excipiat.'

[74] Markus 1990: 45–6; Hunter 1987 is also of great value on the 'silent majority' who disagreed with Jerome.

[75] On this treatise, see Cooper, forthcoming.

[76] *Ad Gregoriam* 12 (CCSL 25A, 209): 'Te omnes homines, te uniuersi sublimes et humiles, te ipsi antistites dei tantum uenerabuntur et praeferre poterunt, quantum nummatus, non quantum sanctus esse potueris. Quid temet ipsum potestate extenuas, et in praedam tuis opibus cedis?'

offer a coin for the relief of the servants of God, which (coin) I trust is to be given back to me a hundred-fold by the right hand of my King (*regis mei dextera*)? And if the earth returns a seed more fruitful than when she received it, why should I not believe that it will be returned to me by the Lord Jesus Christ, especially when I have his bond (*chirografum*) of promise and warning: *Amen, Amen, I say unto you, whatever he has done to the least of those who believe in me, he has done to me*?[77]

He brings home the point by developing Augustine's motif of the poor as the porters who carry the burden of riches forward to heaven. Again, an internal speech is furnished:

For why should I be afraid to give of my own accord what an idle heir (*otiosus heres*) makes off with against my will (*mihi invito*)? For that reason I make over the things that are mine to Him, because I am not able to take them away with me. I will make altogether my own that which in truth is not my own, and I will show my true love for my riches, when I have sent them ahead of me instead of letting them perish. I must press on to reach the most sacred retinue, from which I will no more be allowed to absent myself; there I will build myself a house; in that place I will build storehouses. And because there are no conveyances or beasts of burden, by which I might convey my riches to the other side, will have been able to enter there, I will set all of my belongings on the shoulders (*cervicibus*) of the servants of God.[78] With these porters nothing of mine is allowed to perish; it is necessary that those of whom Christ is the teacher, and the holy angels the protectors, be the ones to carry my riches to the heavens. Let the stomachs of the poor, in which Christ witnesses that he both hungers and is filled, be the storehouses for my crops. Why should an heir mock me with a false blessing, and with lying lips wish [me] life while he grumbles in his soul that [my] death comes slowly?[79]

[77] *Ad Gregoriam* 12 (CCSL 25*A*, 209–10): 'Si huius consules mundi, ut aurigas histriones que locupletent, ut que lenones ac mimos diuites faciant, non metuunt suarum opum inanem subire iacturam, quin immo in his profusionibus gloriantur, dummodo cum damno rerum fauorem contemptibilis uulgi mercentur, ego ad seruorum dei requiem cum fauore omnium angelorum nummum proferre cur timeam, quem mihi centuplatum regis mei dextera reddendum esse confido? Et si terra uberiora semina quam susceperit reddit, cur ego mihi a domino Iesu Christo reddi non credam, praesertim cum eius chirographum teneam pollicentis atque ita cauentis: Amen amen dico uobis, quia qui uni de minimis qui in me credunt fecerit, mihi fecit?' Cf. Matt. 18.5–6, Mark 9.42, Luke 17. 2.

[78] A return to the Augustinian theme of the poor as *laturarii*; see note 53.

[79] *Ad Gregoriam* 12 (CCSL 25*A*, 210–11): 'Cur enim dare sponte timeam, quod mihi otiosus heres tollit inuito? Cui idcirco relinquo quae mea sunt, quia me cum ea auferre non ualeo. Faciam plane meum quod uere meum non est, et uerum meis opibus amorem ostendam, cum meas me diuitias praeire fecero, non perire. Pergendum mihi est ad sacratissimum comitatum, unde me egredi ulterius non licebit; illic mihi domus, illic horrea construam. Et quia illic nulla uehicula, nulla poterint iumenta ingredi, quibus illuc meas possim diuitias transmigrare, famulorum Christi cuncta quae mea sunt ceruicibus ponam. His laturariis nihil mihi perire permittitur; ipsi opes meas ad caelos perferant necesse est, quorum magister Christus est, et sancti angeli protectores. Sint uiscera pauperum horrea frugum mearum, in quibus Christus et esurire se testatur et refici. Cur me heres ficta benedictione inrideat, et cum increpet animo quod tarda mors ueniat, labiis mendacibus uitam exoptat?'

But the *laturarii* here are no longer exclusively the poor, they are 'those of whom Christ is the teacher, and the holy angels the protectors', or again, 'the servants of God'. It is possible that support for monks or clergy, rather than direct benefaction to the poor, is envisaged here as the goal of Gregoria's *benignitas*. But while Gregoria is encouraged to share her surplus, there is no question of her giving up the estate itself. Rather, the intention of the anonymous author is to encourage her to see her benign performance of the role of Christian *domina* as an intrinsically crucial contribution to the well-being of the wider Christian community.

CONCLUSION: SENATORIAL CHRISTIANITY AND THE PROBLEM OF MEMORY

There is reason to believe that the Italian sources we have explored, the letters to Demetrias and Gregoria and the *Passio Sebastiani* and *Regula Magistri*, were produced by writers sponsored by – or in the case of the *Regula Magistri* seeking the sponsorship of – a network of senatorial Christians who had retained *possessio* of their estates despite active engagement with Christian ideals. Numerous small coincidences link the Anician women to circles in Rome that would have been interested in the *gesta martyrum*, and the same is equally true for Gregoria. The sixth-century Proba's protégé, Dionysius Exiguus, addressed his collection of the *Epistulae decretales* of Pope Gelasius (492–496) to Julianus, presbyter of the *titulus Anastasiae* on the Palatine hill in Rome.[80] A fourth-century Proba linked to the gens, the formidable Faltonia Betitia Proba, had been buried in the same *titulus* over a century earlier.[81] *Ad Gregoriam* contains a sustained meditation on the merits of the saint, which seems to reflect a knowledge of her *Passio* (*BHL* 401). And the *Regula Magistri* borrows from both the *Passio Sebastiani* and the *Passio Anastasiae*.[82]

In his *Letter* 130, written to Demetrias shortly after her ascetic profession in 413, Jerome retells the story of her initial approach to her mother and grandmother, distraught in the belief that while she wished to embrace virginity, they were likely to forbid it. According to Jerome, Demetrias fortified herself with the example of the Roman martyr Agnes, and then threw herself at the feet of her mother and grandmother, who astonished her by bursting into tears of happiness.[83] Perhaps it is only a coincidence

80 Dionysius Exiguus, *Praefatio ad Iulianum*. 81 Chastagnol 1962: 132.
82 See Cooper forthcoming, following de Vogüé 1964.
83 Jerome, *Ep.* 30; see the discussion by Anne Kurdock in this volume, pp. 190–224.

that we have here an early witness to imitative piety towards the Roman martyrs, though Demetrias would emerge as the great patron of a Roman martyr basilica, that of St Stephen on the Via Latina. Still, it is perhaps significant that the invocation of Agnes here is precisely as a model for a young ascetic in relation to her biological family, since the *passio* of Agnes, like that of Sebastian, takes care to reconcile the martyr with the parents whom she has initially defied.[84]

Jerome's story of Demetrias and Agnes, of course, reaches back to the early fifth century. Yet aristocratic memory reached across generations. We saw above that in the early sixth Galla and Proba, daughters of the *gens Anicia* young enough to be the granddaughters of Demetrias' brother Anicius Probus, lived in a monastery at St Peter's, which was dedicated to Demetrias' beloved Stephen, although evidence for the dedication is not firm before the eighth century.[85] Whether there was a connection between the sixth-century foundation at St Peter's and the mausoleum there of the grandparents of Demetrias, Sextus Petronius Probus (d. *c.* 388) and Anicia Faltonia Proba (d. before 432), cannot be deduced from the surviving evidence. Hammond-Bammel argued[86] that the later Proba was a direct descendant of the earlier Proba, but here, too, the evidence is inconclusive.

We saw above that these women had the wherewithal to act as powerful literary patrons, both because of their wealth and indeed – in at least Proba's case – because of their ownership of books, over a number of generations. It is tempting to imagine that Proba's fabled collection of Augustine manuscripts was the product of more than one generation's accumulation, remembering always that certain of Augustine's letters had in fact been addressed to Demetrias, her mother, and her grandmother, and there is every reason to suspect that the ladies had returned from their African stay with these and other writings by the controversial bishop. But if there was a systematic attempt to transfer and consolidate an ascetic patrimony among the Anician women, no secure evidence has survived.

In the long term, it is clear that across Europe kin-groups made increasingly innovative use of monasteries as something very like family trusts to abet the consolidation and orderly transfer of access to resources from

[84] On Agnes, see the contribution of Hannah Jones in this volume, pp. 115–39; on reconciliation with the biological family, see Cooper forthcoming.

[85] A gap between the epigraphically well-attested Anicians of the sixth century, and the early sixth-century group, both in Rome and in Constantinople – e.g. Anicia Juliana – was probably caused as much by the economic and political uncertainties of the barbarian invasions as by the choice of some to opt for the ascetic life.

[86] Bammel 1978: 449.

generation to generation. Despite its importance as an intellectual and perhaps ascetic centre, however, this process is virtually untraceable in Rome itself. Even the Italian sources – the *Regula Magistri* or the *gesta martyrum* – have come to us through Frankish libraries, and with rare exception in Frankish copies.[87] In Rome itself, it may well be that the private asceticism of a Demetrias persisted well into the early medieval period, and the low degree of institutionalization would of course have far-reaching repercussions for the later disposition of the books and documents of the ascetics in question, and thus for their visibility in the historical record. We may consider the seemingly marvellous sixth-century library of Proba, of which no trace remains other than a glancing reference by Eugippius, as a case in point.

[87] See Conrad Leyser's contribution to this volume, pp. 140–62.

7

Demetrias ancilla dei: *Anicia Demetrias and the problem of the missing patron*

Anne Kurdock

> How, then, could we so far conceal our true feelings as not to warn you, in whom we feel so deep an interest, to beware of such doctrines, after we had read a certain book addressed to the holy Demetrias? Whether this book has reached you, and who is its author, we are desirous to hear in your answer to this. Augustine, *Epistula* 188.4[1]

Writing in 413 to Anicia Juliana, the mother of the recently dedicated virgin Demetrias, Augustine of Hippo expressed his concern that her daughter had been preyed upon by the author of a dangerous letter containing novel doctrines on divine grace. The letter to which Augustine referred was indeed dangerous: it was none other than the now famous *Epistula ad Demetriam* of Pelagius, the manifesto in which the holy man made known to influential members of the Roman church the ideas on the nature of the soul for which he would eventually be condemned as a heretic. Augustine's implication is that despite or perhaps because of her exalted social standing, Demetrias was in danger of becoming a pawn in a high-stakes game of ecclesiastical authority. Augustine knew – as Pelagius would have known – that by addressing the letter to a figure so exalted as Demetrias, its contents would acquire an aura of respectability for a wider readership that would be difficult, if not impossible, to dispel. The letter is one of the few undisputed works of Pelagius to survive. As Peter Brown put it: 'The long letter which Pelagius wrote to Demetrias, in 413, on the occasion of her declaration to become a nun, was a calculated and widely-publicised declaration of his message.'[2] Equally, the young virgin herself might be affected by its contents. Demetrias had indeed received the letter, and the letter in turn has itself become the primary means by which she is known to modern historiography.

[1] CSEL 57.122; *NPNF* 1.549: 'Quo modo ergo a vobis, quibus tantam dilectionem debemus, admonendis, ut talia caveatis, dissimulare possemus, cum legissemus librum, quem ad sanctam Demetriadem quisnam scripserit vel, utrum ad vos pervenerit, vestris potius rescriptis nosse volumus.'

[2] Brown 2000: 342.

Demetrias has often been understood as the passive recipient of pastoral advice from powerful male ecclesiastical figures – indeed, Jerome too would join the melee of distinguished churchmen seeking to persuade her to their views of the Christian life. For reasons far beyond the scope of this chapter, in the early fifth century it was those who sought patronage, rather than those who conferred it, who left the kind of evidence that would be of interest to the medieval librarians on whom the transmission of evidence largely depends. As a result, the evidence of the same sources for the interests and intentions of their recipients has not sufficiently been explored. Rather, the most ambitious scholarly treatments have tended in recent years to see the female patron as irretrievably hidden from view.[3] The implicit scholarly assumption has tended to be that the figure of Demetrias herself has no bearing on the content of the letters – that she was, so to speak, no more than a *casus scribendi*[4] – and that she carries equally little in our own understanding of the letters.

This is understandable, since the trail of evidence becomes dauntingly thin if we try to follow it far enough to understand the patroness herself, or to assess her own interests and motivations. Yet the extant evidence can allow the historian to present a view in which she figures much more significantly. This view shifts the focus from the letters to the mosaic of briefer references scattered across a variety of sources, documenting Demetrias' own life and the activity of her clan, the *domus Aniciorum*. When the figure of Demetrias is examined within the contemporary social and political context, taking into account the eminent status of her family, an inversion of the previously assumed power structure can be discerned.

What is needed is a methodological model to understand and interpret male presentations of female agency, since male-authored sources predominate in the evidence for late antiquity as it has been transmitted. What I propose to do here is to resituate Demetrias within her own social and familial networks; networks, it should be emphasized, from which her contemporaries, including the men who addressed her, could not have separated her. The correspondence received by Demetrias and the matriarchs of the *gens Anicia* in the period following her dedication as a virgin of the church reflects her status, and that of her mother and grandmother, as patrons who could provide crucial support, both financial and political, at an important turning point.[5] What follows will offer an

[3] Clark 1998 and Jacobs 2000. [4] I owe this appropriate description to Dr Carole Hill.
[5] Layton 2002.

overview of the principal evidence, accompanied by suggestions toward a method for recovering the lost figure of Demetrias.

DEMETRIAS AMNIA VIRGO[6]

Demetrias was numbered among the Roman aristocratic refugees who fled to north Africa upon the sack of Rome in AD 410, transported there by her mother, Anicia Juliana, and her grandmother, Anicia Faltonia Proba. At fourteen years of age, instead of acquiescing to a planned marriage, Demetrias in 413 formally took the veil and was consecrated a virgin of the church by Bishop Aurelius of Carthage. On this occasion, as we have seen, Pelagius wrote to offer his congratulations and advice. Both Jerome and Augustine also wrote to her and to her family, offering their congratulations and words of spiritual guidance regarding her new profession. Through their role as patrons, Demetrias and her kinswomen could lend *gravitas* as well as material assistance to the initiatives of their ecclesiastical protégés.

The centrality of the women of the *gens Anicia*, such as Demetrias' mother Anicia Juliana and her paternal grandmother Anicia Faltonia Proba, to the Christianization of the Roman aristocracy has long been discussed,[7] as has the centrality of its men to Roman political life at the same period.[8] Anicia Faltonia Proba was in many ways the emblematic figure of the Christianity of Roman women of the late fourth century.[9] Praised by Claudian as a mother greater than any in ancient literature[10] and a possible author of the *Cento de laudibus Christi* of biblical stories paraphrased in Virgilian verse,[11] Proba was also the protagonist of perhaps the best-known inscription of Christian Rome, the epitaph at St Peter's dedicated to her husband Sextus Claudius Petronius Probus and celebrating the confluence of Christian and senatorial virtues in his person,[12] and dedicatee of numerous inscriptions by her consul sons. For our purposes, perhaps the most curious of these is a dedication by her son Anicius Hermogenianus Olybrius, and his wife Anicia Juliana, the parents of Demetrias, during Olybrius' term as *consul ordinarius* some

[6] *ILCV* I, 1765. [7] Brown 1961; Cooper 1992; Salzmann 2002, among others.

[8] See, e.g., Matthews 1975. [9] For a full discussion, see Kurdock 2003: 22–64.

[10] Claudian, *Panegyric to Probus and Olybrius* (ed. E. Capps et al., London, 1922).

[11] The two main candidates in modern scholarship have been Faltonia Betitia Proba (d. *c.* 360, see Jones and Martindale 1971–92: I, 732) and Anicia Faltonia Proba; on the problem of authorship see the sources cited in Kurdock 2003: 27–9.

[12] *CIL* 6.1756b. (An English translation can be found in Croke and Harries 1982: 116–17.) Authorship of the epitaph has not been established, but its dramatic situation is that of the newly buried widow expressing her felicity at sharing the same tomb with so great a husband, by extended praise of his merits as consul and Christian. See the discussion in Cooper 1996: 103–4.

time before 395. Although it celebrates Proba as 'a model of preservation and teaching of chastity (*castitatis*)', the terms of the inscription are decidedly neutral as to the religious affiliation of any of the family members. As late as 395, then, it was clearly the case that the Roman church could benefit more from association with the *gens Anicia* than could the *gens* from association with the Roman church.

Demetrias' place within this larger context of the Anician wealth and power dictated both the rhetorical style and the implicit agenda of all the letters addressed to and about her. This focus will be informed by the use of network theory as exemplified by the work of Elizabeth Clark, particularly in her discussion of the Origenist controversy, another ecclesiastical controversy in which lay people were prominently involved, which stressed the centrality of interpersonal allegiances especially at times of political crisis or uncertainty.[13] In considering the texts, we will bear in mind Clark's comment that '"men of letters", like their secular counterparts, sometimes wrote to people whom they knew little, if at all. Such letters cannot always be taken as evidence of close relationships, but perhaps are better understood as a manifestation of ancient patronage systems in a new Christian environment.'[14] The letters themselves are marked both by rhetorical pandering and by an equally rhetorical, if self-conscious, fear of accusations of crass ambition. They may best be understood as attempts by rival parties to secure the patronage not only of Demetrias herself, but of her eminent mother and grandmother. That this was a high-stakes game is clear from the fact that one of the three men, Pelagius, was condemned as a heretic not long afterwards, while another, Jerome, had been expelled from Rome twenty years earlier, on the death of his patron, Pope Damasus, though the accusation seems to have been something closer to malpractice than heresy. Even Augustine was not immune to accusations of heresy, as is evident in his correspondence with the well-connected Julian of Eclanum some years later.[15] We will turn now to consider the three men in their correspondence with Demetrias.

JEROME

I perceive also that I am laying myself open to the attacks of enemies and that I may seem to be flattering a lady of the highest birth and distinction. (Jerome, *Epistula* 130.7)[16]

[13] Clark 1992. [14] Clark 1992: 16–17. [15] Beatrice 1978.

[16] Ed. J. Labourt, Paris 1949–63: VII, 175; *NPNF* 6.264: 'Sentio me inimicorum patere morsibus? Quod adularia videar nobilissimae et clarissimae feminae.'

So Jerome alludes to his concern in his *Epistula* 130, to Demetrias, in which he offers his congratulations and provides advice regarding her new life as a dedicated virgin. Jerome is quick to emphasize that his letter is but the result of a fulfilment of a request from the grandmother and mother, that he should provide spiritual guidance for Demetrias. The care he takes to present his justification for writing the letter invites comment, as we will see below.

The letter can be divided into three sections. The first (chs. 1–6.21) is represented by a lengthy and highly rhetorically stylized introduction on the theme of the greatness of Demetrias and her family; the second section (chs. 6.22–14) discusses spiritual topics which relate directly to Demetrias; and the third (chs. 15–22) consists of advice and exhortation which apply to all virgins. The previous scholarship on Jerome's *Epistula* 130 has focused almost solely on the theological content of the letter and considered its significance only in relation to its author. This has led one scholar to conclude: 'Rhetoric apart, this letter of Jerome's is an unexceptional but quite unremarkable piece of moral instruction, which an old hand like its writer would be able to turn out on demand every day of the week, and I would rate it no higher than beta plus.'[17] This is to under-estimate the letter, however, for an analysis of the rhetorical nuances reveals an implicit agenda of far more significance than its ostensible theological function. In the opening sentences of the letter, Jerome states his intent: 'I am going to write to Demetrias a virgin of Christ and a lady whose birth and riches make her second to none in the Roman world.'[18] In what immediately follows, Jerome bemoans the nature of the difficult position in which he finds himself: 'If, therefore, I employ language adequate to describe her virtue, I shall be thought to flatter her; and if I suppress some details on the score that they might appear incredible, my reserve will not do justice to her undoubted merits.'[19]

One of the most striking initial features of the letter is its highly descriptive and excessive rhetoric, even for Jerome.[20] Having praised members of Demetrias' family, a gesture to which I will shortly return, Jerome

[17] Rees 1991: 32.

[18] Jerome, *Ep.* 130.1: 'Scripturus enim ad Demetriadem virginem Christi, quae et nobilitate et divitiis, prima est in orbe Romano' (ed. Labourt VII: 7, 166; *NPNF* 6.261).

[19] Jerome, *Ep.* 130.1: 'si cuncta virtutibus eius congrua dixero, adularia putabor; si quaedam subtraxero, ne incredibilia videantur, damnum laudabus eius mea faciet verecundia' (ed. Labourt VII, 166; *NPNF* 6.261).

[20] The following descriptions are found in Jerome, *Ep.* 130.4 (ed. Labourt VII: 169): 'Incredibilis animi fortitude, inter gemmas et sericum, inter eunuchorum et puellarum catervas, et adulationem ac ministerial familiae perstrepentis, et exquisitas epulas, quas amplae domus praebebat abundantia,

turns to provide a complete account of the events surrounding Demetrias' decision to take the veil, to become a *virgo dedicata*. In this highly evocative narrative Jerome employs such phrases as 'she admired', 'she longed', 'she thought', and 'she came to hate' in describing Demetrias' innermost thoughts and desires. Jerome finds that the virtue of her final choice of renunciation was all the more enhanced considering her previously luxurious condition:

> Though she had silks and jewels freely at her disposal, and though she was surrounded by crowds of eunuchs and serving-women, a bustling household of flattering and attentive domestics, and though the daintiest feasts that the abundance of a large household could supply were daily set before her; she preferred to all these severe fasting, rough clothing, and frugal living.

Jerome points out that her ascetic discipline only intensified as her impending marriage came closer: 'Demetrias, refusing sheets of linen and beds of down, spread a rug of goat's hair upon the ground and watered her face with ceaseless tears.' Finally, Jerome reports that Demetrias, while in the throes of despair, was comparable to the biblical figure of Esther: 'She came to hate all her fine apparel and cried like Esther to the Lord: "Thou knowest that I abhor the sign of my high estate" ... "and that I abhor it as a menstruous rag [Esther xiv.16]".'

After much mental torment Demetrias had revealed to her grandmother and mother her decision to dedicate herself to perpetual virginity. According to Jerome, the joy felt by all was greater than 'the mind can conceive or speech can interpret'.[21] But the members of Demetrias' family were not alone in their joy at this momentous occasion: Jerome claims that even the tragedy of Rome's destruction had been alleviated. Jerome congratulates Proba and Juliana: 'My words are too weak. Every church in Africa danced for joy ... Then Italy put off her mourning and the ruined walls of Rome resumed in part their olden splendour.'[22] Finally, Demetrias' renunciation has assured her renown, as Jerome proclaimed: 'Meantime in becoming a virgin you have gained more than you have sacrificed. Had

appetisse eam ieiuniorum laborem, asperitatem vestium, victus continentiam ... numquam eam lintamine, numquam plumarum usam mollitie; sed ciliciorum in nuda humo habuisse pro stratu, iugibus faciem rigasse lacrimis ... Oderat ornatum suum; et cum Hester loquebatur ad Dominum: "Tu nosti quod oderim insigne capitis mei"..."et tantae ducam immunditiae, velut pannum mulieris menstruatae".'

[21] Jerome, *Ep*. 130.6: 'quicquid potest cogitare animus, quicquid sermo non potest explicare, illo in tempore factum audivimus' (ed. Labourt VII: 171; *NPNF* 6.263).

[22] Jerome, *Ep*. 130.6: 'Cunctae per Africam ecclesiae quodam exultavere tripudio ... Tunc lugubres vestes Italia mutavit, et semiruta urbis Romae moenia pristinum ex parte recepere fulgorem' (ed. Labourt VII: 172; *NPNF* 6.263).

you become a man's bride but one province would have known of you; while as a Christian virgin, you are known to the whole world.'[23]

De Plinval deprecatingly characterized this narrative as 'somewhat romanticised'.[24] In saying this, he was more correct than he allowed, for Jerome's account is entirely an imagined one. Jerome quietly admitted that he had never met Demetrias personally.[25] Jerome's lavish 'descriptions' of Demetrias, moreover, need also to be assessed in conjunction with his praise of Demetrias' ancestors. Regarding her father, Anicius Hermogenianus Olybrius, Jerome stated:

It is the practice of rhetoricians to exalt him who is the subject of their praises by referring to his forefathers and the past nobility of his race . . . Thus I ought now to recall the distinguished names of the Probii and of the Olybrii, and that illustrious Anician house, the representatives of which have seldom or never been unworthy of the consulship. Or I ought to bring forward Olybrius our virgin's father, whose untimely loss Rome has had to mourn. He was a dutiful son, a lovable husband, a kind master, a popular citizen.[26]

Not only do Demetrias' male ancestors and their consular achievements come in for Jerome's praise. Demetrias' grandmother, Proba, also merits Jerome's accolades for her piety. Jerome then asks:

Who would believe it? That Proba, who of all persons of high rank and birth in the Roman world bears the most illustrious name, whose holy life and universal charity have won for her esteem even among the barbarians, who has made nothing of regular consulships enjoyed by her three sons, . . . is selling off what property she has . . . that these may receive her into everlasting habitations.[27]

Yet Demetrias had even surpassed the achievements of her ancestors.[28]

[23] Jerome, *Ep*. 130.6: 'plus interim recepisti virgo, quam obtulisti. Quam sponsam hominis una tantum provincia noverat, virginem Christi totus orbis audivit' (ed. Labourt VII: 172; *NPNF* 6.263).

[24] de Plinval 1943: 242.

[25] Jerome, *Ep*. 130.2: 'Ignoti ad ignotam scribimus, dumtaxat iuxta faciem corporalem' ('I write as a stranger to a stranger, at least so far as the personal appearance is concerned') (ed. Labourt VII: 167; *NPNF* 6.261).

[26] Jerome, *Ep*. 130.3: 'Rhetorum disciplina est, abavis et atavis, et omni retro nobilitate, onare quem laudes . . . Scilicet nunc mihi Proborum et Olybriorum clara repetenda sunt nomina, et inlustre Anicii sanguinis genus, in quo aut nullus, aut rarus, qui non meruerit consulatum. Aut proferendus Olybrius, virginis nostrae pater, quem inmatura morte subtractum Roma congemuit . . . Pius filius, vir amabilis, clemens dominus, civis affabilis . . .' (ed. Labourt, VII: 168; *NPNF* 6.261).

[27] Jerome, *Ep*. 130.7: 'Quis hoc credit? Proba illa, omnium dignitatum et cunctae nobilitatis in orbe romano nomen inlustrius, cuius sanctitas et in universos effusa bonitas etiam apud barbaros venerabilis fuit; quam trium liberorum . . . non fatigarunt ordinarii consulates . . . nun avitas venundare dicitur possessiones, et facere sibi amicos iniquo mammone, qui se recipient in aeterna tabernacula' (ed. Labourt VII: 173; *NPNF* 6.263–4).

[28] Jerome, *Ep*. 130.6 (ed. Labourt VII: 171; *NPNF* 6.263): 'Agnoscere in illius proposito mentem suam, et gratulari, quod nobilem familiam, virgo virginitate sua nobiliorum faceret' ('In her [Demetrias]

The literary techniques Jerome employs here have direct parallels with contemporary late Roman imperial panegyrics.[29] In addition, Elizabeth Clark has pointed out that of all the letters which Jerome wrote to women, his letter to Demetrias contains the greatest number of classical references.[30] I would argue that the extensive use of classical references represents Jerome's attempt to demonstrate his erudition, imitating the elevated modes of aristocratic discourse to which the women of the Anicii would have been accustomed. Although Jerome extols the virtues Demetrias had newly acquired by her vow of perpetual virginity, it is her worldly social position and wealth, more than any other factor, that dictates the style of his letter.

To ascertain the precise object of Jerome's panegyric we must first examine a revealing aspect of Jerome's counsel to Demetrias. He advises her to 'Follow the example of your Spouse [Luke 11.51]: *be subject* to your grandmother and to your mother', and 'It is a good thing therefore to *defer to one's betters*, to *obey* those set over one, to learn not only from the scriptures but from the example of others how one ought to order one's life, and not to follow that worst of teachers, one's own self-confidence.'[31] Throughout the text Jerome is concerned to sanctify Proba and Juliana's authority over Demetrias. In this way he is attempting not only to please Demetrias' guardians but also, perhaps, to position himself among those who guide Demetrias. Thus, in the metaphor of 1 Corinthians 3.6, in

they [Proba and Juliana] recognized their own mind, and congratulated each other that now a virgin was to make a noble house more noble still by her virginity. She had found, they said, a way to benefit her family and to lessen the calamity of the ruin of Rome.')

29 See MacCormack 1975: 143–205. Examples of these models are provided by the imperial panegyrics that have survived in the Gallic corpus and in manuals of Menander Rhetor. The technique which Jerome employs of praising a subject's ancestors but reserving the highest praise for the subject himself is expressly recommended by Menander Rhetor. See *Treatise* 2.370 (ed. and trans. Russell and Wilson, Oxford, 1981: 80–1).

30 Clark 1979: 74. The references are to Cicero, Virgil, Horace, and Sallust. Clark suggests that in light of Demetrias' relationship to Proba, author of a Christian Virgilian *Cento*, 'perhaps Jerome expected some of her [Proba's] erudition to have rubbed off on Demetrias'. Jerome had found this work of Proba distasteful, however, so his use of classical references in his letter to Demetrias may simply reflect literary conventions when addressing members of the elite society. On Jerome's dislike of Proba's *Cento* see *Ep.* 53.7 (ed. Labourt VII: 15; *NPNF* 6.99) to Paulinus of Nola, which talks of the 'chatty old woman' (*garrula anus*) and others who, 'take in hand the Scriptures, rend them in pieces and teach them before they have learned them' (lacerant, docent, antequam discant). Jerome states that both he and Paulinus have read the *Centos* from Homer and Virgil but would never apply to it Christian meaning and he emphatically concludes that 'all of this is puerile, and resembles the slight of hand of a montebank [i.e. charlatan]' ('puerilia sunt haec et circulatorum ludo similia'). On female aristocratic engagement with Christian teaching see also Rousseau 1995: 116–47.

31 Jerome, *Ep.* 130.12 and 17 respectively (ed. Labourt VII: 182, 190; *NPNF* 6.267, 270): 'Imitare sponsum tuum: esto aviae matrique subiecta; Bonum est igitur oboedire maioribus, parere perfectis, et post regulas scripturarum, vitae suae tramitem ab aliis discere, nec praeceptore uti pessimo, scilicet praesumptione sua.' NB the italic emphases are my own.

which the Lord caused faith to grow, Jerome acknowledges that Proba and Juliana have planted the seed of faith in Demetrias, but he himself is the water which will aid its growth: 'Still these words of mine will not be without their use . . . The grandmother and mother have planted, but it is I that water and the Lord that giveth the increase (1 Cor 3.6).'[32] The attempt to reserve a distinctive role for the independent effort of the expert is characteristic of Jerome.[33]

In his sanctification of Proba's and Juliana's power over Demetrias, he specifically targets the topic of Demetrias' fortune. Jerome warns: 'when your years are riper, and your will steadier, and your resolution stronger, you will do with your money what seems best to you, or rather what the Lord shall command'.[34] While Demetrias is advised to defer always to her elders, especially in the case of her financial affairs, Jerome calls attention to the benevolence of Proba and Juliana as the basis of the very fact of her possessing a fortune.

All Christians are loud in their praises of Christ's holy yokefellows [Proba and Juliana], because they gave to Demetrias when she professed herself a virgin the money which had been set apart as a dowry for her marriage. They would not wrong the heavenly bridegroom; in fact they wished her to come to Him with all her precious riches, that these might not be wasted on the things of this world, but might relieve the distress of God's servants.[35]

Jerome finds this act of mother and grandmother is to be lauded all the more because of its contrast to many other parents, whom he roundly criticizes for providing a 'mere pittance' for ascetic daughters while they give the majority of their fortune to their children who remain 'in the world'.[36] As Jerome points out, Proba's gift to Demetrias can now allow for the burden of 'God's servants' to be lessened. Given Jerome's admission elsewhere of his dire need for money at this time, it seems likely that this could be interpreted as a thinly veiled reference to himself as one of 'God's servants', waiting in hopeful expectation of financial salvation.[37] Taken

[32] Jerome, *Ep.* 130.2 (ed. Labourt VII: 168; *NPNF* 6.261): 'igitur et in opere praesenti auia quidem materque plantauerint, sed et nos rigabimus et dominus incrementum dabit'.

[33] Vessey 1993.

[34] Jerome, *Ep.* 130.14: 'cum aetas maturior fuerit, et voluntas gravior, firmiorque sentential, facies quod tibi visum fuerit; immo quod Dominus imperavit' (ed. Labourt VII: 185; *NPNF* 6.268).

[35] Jerome, *Ep.* 130.7: 'Fertur, et omnium christianorum laude celebratur, quicquid fuerat nuptiis praeparatum, a sancta Christi synoride virgini traditum, ne sponso fieret iniuria; immo ut dotata pristinis opibus veniret ad sponsum; et quod in rebus mundi periturum erat, domesticorum Dei inopiam sustentaret' (ed. Labourt VII: 173; *NPNF* 6.263).

[36] Jerome, *Ep.* 130.6 (ed. Labourt VII: 173; *NPNF* 6.263).

[37] On the admission of his difficult financial situation, see below p. 202.

together with his recommendation to Demetrias to submit herself to the authority of her guardians, among whom, as we have just seen, he sought to number himself, this is a highly significant section of the letter.

This element of Jerome's counsel to Demetrias, to defer to and follow the wishes of her family, falls closer to what seems to have been a late fourth-century norm of the biological family as the key context for female asceticism than we might expect from Jerome.[38] It is all the more striking when we recall that Jerome's typical advocacy of severing all ties with one's family after renunciation is well documented.[39] Jerome's letter to Demetrias reflects the moderated position which he adopted in his later years. Clark suggests that '[n]o doubt Jerome's belated encouragement of familial asceticism resulted from his years of experience with the problems, indeed, the outright dangers, of other ascetic life-styles for women.'[40]

Jerome had early become intimately familiar with the problems that could stem from charges and scandals arising from relationships with ascetic women. The self-consciously circumspect Jerome of AD 414, as we see him writing in *Epistula* 130, was drastically different from the unguarded Jerome of the 380s. The intervening years had been marked by scandals, the most significant of which surrounded his forced abandonment of Rome in AD 384. While other rumours had also circulated, the decisive event which seems to have precipitated his departure from the city was the death of Blesilla, daughter of his patroness Paula. Blesilla, originally an exuberant woman of the world but newly widowed after only seven months of marriage, had died after turning to asceticism and extreme fasting under the guidance of Jerome, and he was widely blamed for her death.[41] Jerome himself later commented on the circumstances of his departure, and

38 See Rousseau 2005 and Cooper 2006 for a discussion of 'domestic asceticism', with close relationships between ascetic family members.

39 See Jerome, *Ep.* 118.4 & 6 (CSEL 55. 439 and 443), *Ep.* 79.4 (CSEL 55.91), and *Ep.* 108.5 (CSEL 55.310). The most striking example of this comes from Jerome's encouragement for Paula to abandon her children and accompany him to the Holy Land. The image (Jerome, *Ep.* 108.6) of Paula's young son Toxotius standing on the dock begging his mother not to leave him also fuelled the fires of Jerome's critics. Palladius complained that Jerome stifled Paula's development and bent her to his own purposes. See Palladius, *Historia Lausiaca* 41.2 (*ACW* 34.118).

40 Clark 1981: 248.

41 On Jerome's letter to Paula after Blesilla's death see *Ep.* 39 (CSEL 54.293–308). Jerome, *Ep.* 39.6 (ed. Labourt VII: 82; *NPNF* 6.304) describes the uproar against him after her death when his enemies demanded to know: 'Quousque genus detestabile monachorum non urbe pellitur . . .?' ('How long must we refrain from driving these detestable monks out of Rome?'), and his consolation to Paula on her daughter's death only consisted of him reminding her that 'too great affection towards one's children is disaffection for God' ('grandis in suos pietas inpietas in Deum est'). Such comments by Jerome must only have further angered his critics. On Jerome and his female patrons in Rome see also Curran 2000: 280–98.

it can be inferred from what he says that the problem stemmed from the scandals surrounding his relationships with aristocratic women.[42]

On the whole, scholars to date have tended to conclude that the charges against Jerome must have been based on sexual misconduct.[43] Accusations of sexual misconduct throughout antiquity afforded an avenue of political attack that was all but routine. But, if we take into account Jerome's careful disclaimers in *Epistula* 130 regarding monetary matters, we can see that misappropriation of funds may have been involved.[44] The social status and wealth of the female aristocrats who comprised Jerome's circle far surpassed his own social position. To Jerome's critics, the danger he represented was not only sexual but financial. In his retrospective challenges to the charges against him, Jerome revealingly states: 'Let them say if they have ever noticed in my conduct anything unbefitting a Christian. Have I taken anyone's money? Have I not disdained all gifts great or small? Has the chink of anyone's coin ever been heard in my hand?'[45]

The significance of the precise nature of the questions Jerome posed lies not only in understanding the events in Rome in AD 384, but, more importantly, in drawing our attention to tensions in the established pattern of a patronage system. Charges of sexual and/or financial misconduct were orientated around a specific notion of abuse for which the Christian clergy had been singled out in AD 370. Valentinian's edict of 370 prohibited the clergy from visiting virgins and prohibited the transfer of private property to clergy.[46] Two of Jerome's letters reveal that he was well aware of this edict in the period immediately preceding his departure from Rome.[47] Even ten years later, in 394, the edict was still present in Jerome's mind.[48] It is the fear of charges of this type of financial abuse that is manifest in Jerome's letter to Demetrias.

42 Jerome discusses this episode in his life in *Ep.* 45 to Asella (CSEL 54.323–8). Note that Jerome's papal patron Pope Damasus also suffered from difficulties surrounding his associations with women. See the following note for details of Damasus' nickname of the 'ear-tickler of married women', *matronarum auriscalpius*.

43 Kelly 1975: 109–13. On the accusations of misconduct levelled against Jerome's own patron, Pope Damasus, see Fontaine 1988: 177–92.

44 See Jerome, *Ep.* 45 (CSEL 54.323–8). In this letter to Asella he describes the circumstances of his departure from Rome. There is an assumed notion of a charge of sexual misconduct, yet an aspect of financial misappropriation is just as apparent. The financial aspect of this scandal, while crucially significant for understanding the anxieties surrounding the patronage system, has often been ignored by scholars such as J. N. D. Kelly when interpreting this event. See Kelly 1975: ch. 11, esp. 113.

45 Jerome, *Ep.* 45.2 (ed. Labourt VII: 97; *NPNF* 6.59): 'Dicant quid umquam in me aliter senserint quam Christianum decebat? Pecuniam cuius accepi? Munera vel parva vel magna non sprevi?' In manu mea aes alicuius insonuit?

46 *CTh* 16.2.4. 47 Jerome, *Ep.* 22.28, 60.11 (CSEL 54.185–6, 562–3).

48 Jerome, *Ep.* 52.6 (CSEL 54.425–6).

Overall then, it seems clear that Jerome's advocacy of Demetrias' subjection to her mother and grandmother serves several functions. In the first place, his counsel serves to ingratiate himself with her family and to neutralize the potential threat he could represent to them by advising that Demetrias should be anything but independent of her family. Jerome thus signals to Proba and Juliana that while he would offer himself as one who would also help guide Demetrias, it is not his intention either to challenge their authority or to supplant them completely. Jerome here portrays himself not as one who will challenge the familial power structure, but rather as one who would hope to join and aid this supervisory group.[49] Jerome also, however, seeks to assure his wider audience, external to the family,[50] that he is not attempting to cultivate an inappropriate relationship motivated by hope of gain. Acutely aware that by writing to Demetrias he has made himself vulnerable to criticism, Jerome emphatically states: 'Let detraction stand aloof and envy give way; let no charge of self-seeking be brought against me.'[51] Nothing could be clearer.

Before his unceremonious departure from Rome thirty years earlier, Jerome had attempted to cultivate a relationship with another female member connected with the *domus Aniciorum*. Even at this early juncture, Jerome was fully alive to the possibility of accusations stemming from his approach to his female social superiors. In his letter to Demetrias' aunt Furia, the daughter-in-law of Sextus Claudius Petronius Probus and Anicia Faltonia Proba, Jerome defended his position by pleading for 'a truce to the envious attack which the tooth of calumny is always making upon the name of Christian, hoping to dissuade men from virtue by fear of abuse. Except by letter we know nothing of one another, and where there is no knowledge in the flesh the only motive for friendship is one of piety.'[52]

It is equally possible, nonetheless, that in 413 Jerome hoped to cultivate the Anician matrons as a source of financial patronage. While Paula's

[49] On ascetic vocation not being necessarily against family strategies see also Sivan 1993a: 81–93.

[50] Letters in late antiquity were often circulated among large groups of people and were not intended to remain solely with the recipient. On letters, see Stowers 1986; on the circulation of texts, see Starr 1987: 213–23; and on the contribution of the literary circle to the process of publication see Gamble 1995: 84–5.

[51] Jerome, *Ep*. 130.2: 'Procul obtrectatio, facessat invidia. Nullum in ambitione sit crimen' (ed. Labourt VII: 167; *NPNF* 6.261).

[52] Jerome, *Ep*. 54.3 (CSEL 54.468; *NPNF* 6.103): 'Facessat invidia, quam nominee Christiano malidicorum semper genuinus infigit, ut, dum probra metuunt, ad virtutes non provocent. Exceptis epistulis ignoramus alterutrum, solaque causa pietatis est, ubi carnis nulla notitia est.' It is possible that Jerome approached Furia because of her marital connection to Paula, one of his strongest female supporters. Furia's brother, Furius, had married Paula's daughter, Blesilla. On Furia, see Jones 1971–1992: I, 375.

fortune had supported Jerome and their endeavours in the Holy Land for the first years of their stay there, it had been necessary for Jerome to sell at least part of his own ancestral property in order to acquire sufficient funds to construct his monasteries.[53] At the time of Paula's death in 404, Jerome reported that not only had Paula's resources been completely depleted but she had in fact left behind a substantial debt.[54] This financial situation may be reflected in his self-conscious awareness of increased vulnerability to charges of abuse we have just examined.

Finally, these manoeuvres demonstrate the true addressee of his letter. On initial appearances, the passage which began this section seems to be a reference to Demetrias, as Jerome wrote: 'I perceive also that I am laying myself open to the attacks of enemies and that I may seem to be flattering a lady of the highest birth and distinction.' The passage continues, however:

> Yet these men will not be able to accuse me when they learn that hitherto I have said nothing about her. I have never either in the lifetime of her husband or since his decease praised her for the antiquity of her family or for the extent of her wealth or power . . . My purpose is to praise the grandmother of my virgin in a style befitting the church, and to thank her for having aided with her goodwill the desire which Demetrias has formed.[55]

More than the simple fear of the inappropriate flattery of a young girl seems to be indicated here. The real point of such an accusation would have been that, through his pastoral counsel to the young virgin, Jerome was in fact attempting to cultivate the doyenne of the *domus Aniciorum*: not Demetrias but Proba should be seen and represented as the object of his 'flattery'.[56] That he was attempting a pre-emptive refutation of such an accusation is evident from his conclusion: 'For the rest, my cell, my food

[53] Jerome stated that it took Paula three years to accumulate the funds to construct the monasteries in Palestine. See Jerome, *Ep.* 108.14 (CSEL 55.324–5), and on the necessity of the sale of Jerome's ancestral land, see Jerome, *Ep.* 66.14 (CSEL 54.665).

[54] Jerome, *Ep.* 108.31 (CSEL 55.349–50).

[55] Jerome, *Ep.* 130.7: 'Sentio me inimicorum patere morsibus? Quod adularia videar nobilissimae et clarissimae feminae; qui accusare non poterunt, si me scierint hucusque tacuisse. Neque enim laudari in ea umquam antiquitatem generic, divitiarum et potentiae magnitudinem, viro vivente vel mortuo, quae alii forsitan mercennaria oratione laudaverint Mihi propositum est stilo ecclesiastico laudare aviam virginis meae, et gratias agree, quod voluntatem eius, sua adiuverit voluntate' (ed. Labourt VII: 175–6; *NPNF* 6.264–5).

[56] One traditional avenue of access to families of the social elite was through the role as educator to their children. For the case of tutors of senatorial children, see Brown 1972: 188 n. 2. While Jerome is fearful of this type of charge being levelled against him, he does not shrink from using it against his enemies.

and clothing, my advanced years, and my narrow circumstances sufficiently refute the charge of flattery.'[57]

The emphatic advice with which Jerome concludes his counsel to Demetrias confirms the dual objects of this strategy:

Let the jewels on your breast and in your ears be the gems of wisdom. Let your tongue know no theme but Christ, let no sound pass your lips that is not holy, and let your words always reproduce that sweetness of which your grandmother and mother set you the example. Imitate them, for they are the models of virtue.[58]

From this standpoint, *Epistula* 130 bears witness not to a *virgo dedicata* seeking advice from an older and very powerful spiritual advisor but, to the contrary, to the advisor's attempts to employ his literary talents to cultivate important and powerful patrons.

PELAGIUS

An easy, simple way to make a speech is to let the very richness of the subject-matter speed it along its course; but we have to proceed along a very different road, since our purpose is to write a manual of instruction for the virgin... (Pelagius, *Ad. Dem.* 1.1[59])

As Jerome had employed his *Epistula* 22 to Eustochium as a manifesto on virginity, Pelagius capitalized on the opportunity of writing to Demetrias to expound his own theological agenda. As noted previously, Pelagius' letter to Demetrias has become renowned for the light it sheds on the otherwise shadowy understanding of Pelagian doctrines. A modern translator of the text aptly summarized its importance: 'because it contains, in the absence of all but a few fragments of his major works of moral theology, our most complete and coherent account of his views on the central Pelagian topics'.[60] One of the most controversial of Pelagius' doctrines was epitomized by his statement to Demetrias that:

Whenever I have to speak on the subject of moral instruction and the conduct of a holy life, it is my practice first to demonstrate the power and quality of human nature and to show what it is capable of achieving, and then to go on to encourage

[57] Jerome, *Ep.* 130.7: 'Alioquin cellula monasterii, vilis cibus, vestisque contempta, et aetas vicina iam morti, brevisque tempori viaticum, carent omni adsentationis infamia' (ed. Labourt VII: 176; *NPNF* 6.265).

[58] Jerome, *Ep.* 130.20 (ed. Labourt VII: 193; *NPNF* 6.271–2): 'haec monilia in pectore et in auribus tuis haereant. Nihil aliud nouerit lingua nisi Chrisum, nihil posit sonare, nisi quod sanctum est. auiae tuae tibi semper ac matris in ore dulcedo uersetur, quarum imitatio forma uirtutis est.'

[59] Pelagius, *Epistula ad sacram Christi virginem Demetriadem* (*PL* 30.15–45, trans. Rees 1991: 29–70).

[60] Rees 1991: 32. On Pelagius and the Pelagian doctrine see Evans 1968; Rees 1988.

the mind of my listener to consider the idea of different kinds of virtues, in case it may be of little or no profit to him to be summoned to pursue ends which he has perhaps assumed hitherto to be beyond his reach.[61]

To Augustine's mind, on reading this statement, Pelagius was denying here the need for God's grace.

As with Jerome's letter, scholarship has tended to recognize Demetrias solely in the role of the passive addressee of Pelagius' letter. As in Jerome's letter also, however, it is more than reasonable to suggest that Pelagius chose Demetrias as the vehicle for his doctrines specifically because of her wealth and power and those of her family. To gain the recommendation of a figure of Demetrias' standing would enhance the possibility of wide acceptance for his views.

While it is true that much of the detailed content of the letters of Jerome and Pelagius is dissimilar, the context for both is evidently much the same. Following the pattern of analysis of Jerome's letter, this section will also turn aside from the theological context of Pelagius' letter and focus not on the apparent differences between the theological positions taken up by Jerome and Pelagius but rather on the similar motivations and fears of the two writers.

Like Jerome, Pelagius praises Demetrias in fulsome terms, insisting that Demetrias' consecration had surpassed all the achievements of her ancestors:

Indeed, you alone have bestowed upon your house an honour which it has not previously possessed throughout its long history: the male members of it have produced memorable consulships, and the register of the most distinguished order in our state has frequently included names from your illustrious house, yet nothing has ever won greater distinction than this honour of yours, which has been inscribed not on a tablet made of earthly material but in the book of immortal memory.[62]

[61] Pelagius, *Ad Dem.* 2 (*PL* 30.17–18, trans. Rees 1991: 36–7): 'Quoties mihi de institutione morum et sanctae vitae conversatione dicendum est, soleo prius humanae naturae vim qualitatemque monstrare, et quid efficere possit, ostendere ac jam inde audientis animum ad species incitare virtutum: ne nihil prosit ad ea vocari, quae forte sibi impossibilia esse praesumpserit.'

[62] Pelagius, *Ad Dem.* 14 (*PL* 30.30, trans. Rees 1991: 50–1): Sola quipped, 'praestetisti generi tuo, quod longa retro aetate non habuit. Licet ediderit virilis sexus memorabiles consulates: et amplissimi ordinis fastus, illustris familiae nomina frequens audierit: nihil unquam tamen in genere vestro hoc tuo honore fuit praestantius, qui non corporali albo, sed in libro memoriae immortalis insertus est.' This same sentiment is echoed by Augustine. See below, p. 207. Note also that the notion that female Christian devotion surpasses the earthly achievements of a hallowed ancestry is also manifest in the case of the late fifth-/early sixth-century Anician *matrona* Anicia Juliana, in her actions as patron.

Secondly, and also like Jerome, Pelagius celebrates Demetrias' choice of perpetual virginity: 'The glorious news of your act of public profession has spread abroad and become the common talk among all men, and the whole world has become so exultant at your conversion that people seem to have waited all along for something to happen which, now that it has happened, they are still scarcely able to credit for all their great joy.'[63]

Opening with a statement of his overt purpose of writing a manual of instruction for one embarking on the ascetic life, Pelagius is careful to counter pre-emptively accusations of self-interest by making clear that his work has not been unsolicited. In the introduction to the letter, he announces:

> nor need we have any fear of exposing ourselves voluntarily to the malicious strings of envy by writing so rashly to such a noble virgin; we write at the request, nay, by the command of her venerable mother, who solicits it from us in a letter sent across the sea and revealing the remarkable force of her heartfelt desire . . . And so, free from any charge of rashness or of vain ambition, let us bend our energies to our appointed task.[64]

Both men's insistence on the claim that the family of Demetrias had requested their work functions as a rhetorical tool to deflect charges of inappropriately addressing themselves to their social superiors for the purpose of self-promotion.

While Pelagius is careful to defend his own actions in writing to Demetrias, he also warns her against false flatterers, when he says:

> Beware of flatterers as your enemies: their speeches are smoother than olive-oil, but they themselves are like poisoned darts; they can corrupt shallow souls with feigned praise and inflict their agreeable wounds on over-credulous minds . . . never giving a thought to what we really are instead of to what we may appear to others to be.[65]

Each of the virgin's would-be advisors, however, would naturally wish to class his rivals in these terms.

[63] Pelagius, *Ad Dem.* 14 (*PL* 30.30, trans. Rees 1991: 51): 'Haec professionis tuae gloria rumore celebri vulgata est per cunctos, et ita ad conversationem tuam totus exsultavit orbis, ut quod prae ingenti gaudio vix adhuc homines credere poterant, id semper videantur optasse.'

[64] Pelagius, *Ad Dem.* 1 (*PL* 30.17, trans. Rees 1991: 36): 'Nec veremur ne temere scribendo, ad tantae nobilitatis virginem, ultro nos morsibus tradamus invidiae. Scribimus enim petente sancta matre eius, imo iubente, idque a nobis transmarinis litteris, miro cum desiderio animi flagitante . . . Remoti igitur a temeritate, et ab ambitione liberi, proposito insudemus operi.'

[65] Pelagius, *Ad Dem.* 21 (*PL* 30.36–7, trans. Rees 1991: 59–60): 'Adulatores ut inimicos cave, quorum sermones super oleum molles, et ipsi sunt iacula. Corrumpunt fictis laudibus leves animas et male credulis mentibus blandum vulnus infligunt . . . nec cogitamus quid ipsi sumus, sed quid alteris esse videamur.'

Both Pelagius and Jerome attempt to take up a position as a spiritual guide for Demetrias while simultaneously defending their own positions and criticizing the attempts and motives of others. In fact, the fiercely competitive atmosphere is revealed in two additional texts of Jerome which criticize Pelagius. First, writing to his friend Ctesiphon, immediately before writing to Demetrias, Jerome gives warning against Pelagius and makes thinly veiled references to Pelagius' involvement with women.[66] This letter criticizes the role of women in the spread of heresy from Simon Magus onwards. Jerome also points out that both Origenism and Priscillianism were well received among women.[67] He concludes this warning by admonishing against the giving of financial support to Pelagius as something which could only assist in spreading the heresy.[68]

Several years later Jerome's criticism of Pelagius and his specific involvement with the Anician women becomes overt. In his *Dialogue against the Pelagians*, Jerome indicates his awareness of Pelagius' correspondence with the Anician women. He pours scorn on Pelagius' blasphemous 'flattery' of Juliana.[69] Jerome's comments may reflect disappointment in his own personal failure to cultivate the women of this family as patrons.

AUGUSTINE

We [Augustine and Alypius] are well aware that you are not ignorant how great Christian affection we consider due to you, and how much, both before God and among men, we are interested in you. For though we knew you, at first by letter, afterwards by personal intercourse, to be pious and Catholic.[70]

[66] Jerome, *Ep.* 133.3 (CSEL 56.244–7; *NPNF* 6.273–5). Orosius states in his *Lib. apol.* 4 (CSEL 5.608–9): 'beatus Hieronymus . . . in epistola sua quam nuper ad Ctesiphontem edidit, condemnavit, similiter et in libro quem nunc scribit, collata in modum dialogi altercatione confutat'. In chapter 7 (CSEL 5.611), Orosius states that the testimony which he gave above was given at the Jerusalem Conference. See also Evans 1968: 126 n.8.

[67] Jerome, *Ep.* 133.3–4 (CSEL 56.244–8). On a group being branded as heretical when female involvement is prominent, see Clark 1993: 128; Burrus 1995a: 7–9, 33–4.

[68] Jerome, *Ep.* 133.13 (CSEL 56.259–60).

[69] Jerome, *Dialogue Against the Pelagians* 3.16 (CCSL 80.119–20; *NPNF* 6.481). Cf. Jerome, *Dialogue Against the Pelagians*, 2.24, 3.14 (CSEL 80.87–9, 116–88; *NPNF* 6.470, 479–80). See also Cavallera 1922: II, 55. NB: Women's involvement in heresies was a commonplace in all the debates surrounding successive heresies. Jerome's strategy here could well be to point to the involvement of women precisely so as to brand Pelagius a heretic.

[70] Augustine, *Ep.* 188.1 (CSEL 57.119–20; *NPNF* 1.548–9): 'scire autem vos optime scimus, quantum vobis debeamus religionis affectum quantaque nobis et apud deum et inter hominess sit cura de vobis. Licet enim vos per litteras primum, deinde etiam praesentia coporali pia et catholica, hoc est vera membra Christi exiguitas nostra cognoverit.'

On Demetrias' consecration, we also find Augustine writing to the Anician women to offer his congratulations on the auspicious event.[71] In this very brief letter he praises Proba and Juliana and warmly thanks them for the token of the veiling ceremony which they have sent to him.[72] In common with Jerome and Pelagius, Augustine too expresses the view that Demetrias' pious action has surpassed the achievement and glory of her ancestors, declaring:

> Who can declare in words, or expound with adequate praises, how incomparably greater is the glory and advantage gained by your family in giving to Christ women consecrated to His service, than in giving to the world men called to the honours of the consulship? For if it be a great and noble thing to leave the mark of an honoured name upon the revolving ages of this world, how much greater and nobler is it to rise above it by unsullied chastity both of heart and of body![73]

In comparison to the twenty chapters of Jerome's letter, the single chapter of Augustine's seems to pale into insignificance. Augustine emphasizes in the brief text only his wish that other women from all social backgrounds will use Demetrias as a model to emulate. He provides no other spiritual advice, and the panegyric style so characteristic of Jerome's letter is entirely absent. Indeed, one can only speculate how the matriarchs received Augustine's counsel, since he writes: 'May it be yours, my daughters, most worthy of the honour due to your rank, to enjoy in her that which was lacking to yourselves.'[74]

At first sight, Augustine's association with Demetrias, represented by this one letter, might seem very different from that of Jerome or Pelagius. In fact, however, *Epistula* 150 is part of a much larger body of correspondence which took place between Augustine and the Anician women as a

[71] Augustine, *Ep.* 150 (CSEL 44.380–2).

[72] Augustine, *Ep.* 150 (CSEL 44.38–381; *NPNF* 1.504): 'For while the consecration of the daughter of your house to a life of virginity is being published by most busy fame in all places where you are known, and that is everywhere, you have outstripped its flight by more sure and reliable information in a letter from yourselves' ('uestrae namque stirpis sanctimoniam uirginalem quoniam quacumque innotuistis ac per hoc ubique fama celeberrima praedicat, uelocissimum uolatum eius fideliore atque certiore litterarum nuntio praeuenistis'); and in conclusion: 'We have received with very great pleasure the gift sent as a souvenir of her taking the veil' ('velationis apophoretum gratissime accepimus').

[73] Augustine, *Ep.* 150 (CSEL 44.381; *NPNF* 1.504): 'quis uerbis explicet, quis digno praeconio prosequatur, quantum incomparabiliter gloriosius atque fructuosius habeat ex uestro sanguine feminas uirgines christus quam uiros consules mundus? nam uolumina temporum si magnum atque praeclarum est nominis dignitate signare, quanto est maius atque praeclarius cordis et corporis integritate transcendere.'

[74] Augustine, *Ep.* 150 (CSEL 44.381; *NPNF* 1.504): 'dominarum honore dignissimae et merito inlustres et praestantissimae filiae, perfruamini in illa, quod defuit uobis, ut nasceretur et uobis'.

group.[75] Not only do six individual letters and works of Augustine to the Anicians survive, but by careful examination of the evidence found in these letters it is possible to reconstruct a pattern of correspondence between the two parties which lasted over a period of at least four years and comprised no fewer than eleven letters.[76] Once again it is the significance of familial and social networks that needs to be emphasized as the larger context in which *Epistula* 150 is best understood. As in the cases of Jerome and Pelagius, it is possible to demonstrate that the varied and lengthy nature of the correspondence between Augustine and the Anician women demonstrates Augustine's desire for and achievement of a lasting relationship with the *gens Anicia*. The real significance of Augustine's letter to Demetrias can only be understood by resituating it within the larger context of the on-going relationship between the Anician women and Augustine.

Augustine's surviving correspondence with the Anician women began *c*. AD 412.[77] Proba seems to have requested, whether in person or by letter, that Augustine write a treatise for her on the subject of prayer.[78] He promised to do so and in consequence he wrote *Epistula* 130. While this letter provides a possible date for the beginning of the relationship between the Anician women and Augustine, both the tone and the style of the letter evidence a sense of familiarity which suggests that the relationship predated this first known correspondence. Augustine himself also indicates this possibility. Reflecting in 416 on his relationship with the Anician women, Augustine notes that in the years before Demetrias' veiling (413) he came to know Juliana at first by correspondence and then by personal

[75] Brown 2005: 9.

[76] Pre-AD 412: Proba's request of Augustine on the subject of prayer, attested in Augustine, *Ep*. 130.1; Augustine's response: *Ep*. 130; AD 412: Proba's question to Augustine regarding the soul and its desires, attested in Augustine *Ep*. 131.1; Augustine's response: *Ep*. 131; AD 413/414: Juliana and Proba's letter to Augustine announcing Demetrias' veiling, attested to by Augustine, *Ep*. 150; AD 413/414: Augustine's congratulatory response, *Ep*. 150; *c*. AD 414: Juliana's personal and written request ('several letters'), to Augustine to write on the topic of widowhood, attested to by Augustine, *De bono vid*. 1; AD 414: Augustine's response, *De bono viduitatis* for Juliana; pre-AD 416: Augustine writes to Juliana, warning against certain men and their dangerous doctrines, attested to by Augustine in *Ep*. 188.2; pre-AD 416: Juliana's response in which she defends her and her family's orthodoxy – Juliana's letter is now lost but excerpts of it are preserved as quotes in Augustine's *Ep*. 188, see esp. chs. 2, 3; AD 416: Augustine's response to Juliana against Pelagius, *Ep*. 188.

[77] NB: It appears that Augustine's initial contact with the larger circle of the members of the *gens Anicia* began with the figure of Italica (sometime before AD 408) and Anicius Auchenius Bassus (see Jones and Martindale 1971–92: I, 465 and 152–3). In Augustine's *Ep*. 99 (ed. T. Page, trans. J. Baxter, LCL. Cambridge, MA, 1965, 178–83) to Italica he criticizes those who have not been informing him of the terrible events at Rome. See also Brown 2000: 290. Bassus composed an epitaph for Augustine's mother, Monica, between 387 and 430, see *Anth. Lat*. I, 670 (ed. Riese).

[78] The existence of this request is found in Augustine, *Ep*. 130.1.1 (CSEL 44.40–1).

acquaintance, and that the 'ministry' he provided to the family in fact aided Demetrias in making her choice of dedicated virginity.[79] Thus it is clear that, while the extant evidence provides a date of 412 for the first attested episode of the relationship, the total evidence demonstrates that it pre-existed this first extant correspondence.

Also around the year 412 Proba commented to Augustine on the tendency of the soul's thoughts and desires to be concerned more with worldly or inappropriate things than with God.[80] Augustine wrote to Proba (*Ep.* 131) briefly responding to her comments and noting his 'gratitude for your most pious care for my welfare'.[81] As mentioned above, after Demetrias' veiling, Augustine again wrote to Proba and Juliana congratulating them on her consecration.

In the period following the veiling, the Anician women continued to request Augustine's guidance regarding spiritual matters. About this time Juliana and Augustine were in personal contact, with Juliana requesting that Augustine write her a treatise on the topic of widowhood.[82] Apparently Augustine did not immediately fulfil the request but, after further entreaties from Juliana in her subsequent letters, he eventually submitted to her

[79] Augustine, *Ep.* 188.1 (CSEL 57.119–20; *NPNF* 1.548–9): 'For though we [Augustine and Alypius] knew you, at first by letter, afterwards by personal intercourse, to be pious and Catholic . . . nevertheless, our humble ministry also was of use to you . . . so great was the fruit arising from this ministry of ours in your family, that when preparations for her marriage were already completed, the holy Demetrias preferred the spiritual embrace of a Husband who is fairer than the sons of men' ('scire autem vos optime scimus, quantum vobis debeamus religionis affectum quantaque nobis et apud deum et inter hominess sit cura de vobis. Licet enim vos per litteras primum, deinde etiam praesentia coporali pia et catholica, hoc est vera membra Christi exiguitas nostra cognoverit, tamen etiam per ministerium nostrum, cum accepissetis verbum auditus dei, sicut dicit apostolus, accepistis non ut verbum hominum, sed, sicut est vere, verbum dei. Cuius ministerii nostri adiuvante gratia et misericordia saluatoris in domo vestra tantus fructus exortus est, ut humanis nuptiis iam paratis sancta Demetrias spiritalem sponsi illius praeferret amplexum, cui specioso prae filiis hominum ad habendam spiritus uberiorem fecunditatem nec amittendam carnis integritatem virgines nubunt.')

[80] Augustine, *Ep.* 131 (CSEL 44.77–9).

[81] Augustine, *Ep.* 131 (CSEL 44.78–9; *NPNF* 1.469): 'Wherefore, in returning the respectful salutation due to your Excellency, and expressing my gratitude for your most pious care for my welfare, I ask the Lord that He may grant to you the rewards of the life to come' ('reddens itaque debitum praestantiae tuae salutationis obsequium agens que gratias, quod salutis nostrae religiosissimam curam geris, posco tibi a domino futurae uitae praemia praesentis').

[82] For personal contact between Augustine and the Anician women, see Augustine, *De bono vid.* 1 (CSEL 41.305; *NPNF* 3.441): 'When I was present, you laded me with entreaty, and, when I had not been able to deny you this, you often by letters demanded my promise' ('praesentem me rogando onerasti et, cum tibi hoc non potuissem negare, saepe meum promissum litteris flagitasti'). In addition it is certain that *De bono viduitatis*, followed Demetrias' veiling, owing to the fact that Augustine refers to Demetrias as a dedicated virgin several times. See chs. 6, 18, 20, 24 & 29 (CSEL 41.309–10; 324–5, 327–8, 334–5, 342–3).

request. In 414, Augustine composed a treatise in the form of a letter to Juliana entitled *De bono viduitatis* (*On the Good of Widowhood*).[83]

What is important to note here is that it is in this work that Augustine first warns Juliana against theological heresy. He cautions her to be wary of the doctrines of certain men which are spreading at the time and which contain notions that are contrary to the doctrine of God's grace. He warns: 'These things I am compelled to admonish by reason of certain little discourses of some men, that are to be shunned and avoided, which have begun to steal through the ears unto the minds of many, being (as must be said with tears) hostile to the grace of Christ.'[84] While Augustine chose not to name this dangerous originator, it can be no other than Pelagius. That this work was composed early in Augustine's involvement against Pelagius is evident from the fact that Augustine still referred to this originator of heresy as one 'most friendly and dear to us, [who] without wilful guilt indeed entangled in this error'.[85] Yet Augustine concludes this warning to Juliana with an interesting note. He counsels: 'But in you let the love of riches grow cold together with the love of marriage, and let a pious use of what property you possess be directed to spiritual delights, that your liberality wax warm rather in helping such as are in want than in enriching covetous persons.'[86] It is possible that this represents a final reference to Pelagius, albeit somewhat cryptically. It seems plain that each of these three outstanding figures of the church is concerned with the possibility that any other of them might receive financial support.

Augustine's respectful tone and vague implications quickly intensify in his subsequent warnings to the Anician women, as, in his own estimation, the threat posed by Pelagius grows greater. From evidence elsewhere in the surviving corpus of letters, we find Augustine writing again to Juliana to warn her against current erroneous doctrines of grace. The exact content of this warning is unknown as Augustine's own letter is no longer extant,

[83] CSEL 41.303–43; *NPNF* 3.437–54. The letter forms an exhortation to Juliana to remain a widow, as the biblical figure of Anna. Yet the notion that widowhood is good and virginity is better remains constant throughout. Augustine writes to Juliana: 'For whilst you are praying as Anna, she [Demetrias] hath become what Mary was' ('dum enim tu oras sicut Anna, facta est illa quod Maria'). See Augustine, *De bono vid.* 20 (CSEL 41.327; *NPNF* 3.449).

[84] Augustine, *De bono vid.* 21 (CSEL 41.328–9; *NPNF* 3.449): 'Haec me admonere conpellunt cavendi atque devitandi quorundam sermunculi, qui per aures ad animas multorum serpere coeperunt, quod cum lacrimis dicendum est, inimici gratiae Christi.' See also ch. 22.

[85] Augustine, *De bono vid.* 22 (CSEL 41.331; *NPNF* 3.450): 'quosdam fratres nostros amicíssimos nobis et dilectíssimos nec malitiose quidem errori huic inplicatos'.

[86] Augustine, *De bono vid.* 26 (CSEL 41.338; *NPNF* 3.452): 'in vobis autem amor divitiarum simul frigescat cum amore nuptiarum, et pius usus rerum, quas possidetis, ad spiritales delicias conferatur, et liberalitas vestra magis ferveat adiuvandis egenis quam ditandis avaris'.

yet it is to be presumed that in it he has implied that Juliana and her family have already been deceived by the heresy. This is clear from Juliana's response to him. For Juliana rigorously and indignantly defends her family's orthodoxy. She writes: 'But your Reverence knows that I and my household are entirely separated from persons of this description; and all of our family follow so strictly the Catholic faith as never at any time to have wandered from it, or fallen into any heresy, I speak not of the heresy of sects who have erred in a measure hardly admitting of expiation, but of those whose errors seem to be trivial.'[87] As Peter Brown comments: 'As a good Christian of the Later Empire, "heresy" to her had meant Greek errors on the Godhead, not African scruples on grace and free will.'[88] Indeed, very shortly after this part of the correspondence Pope Innocent concluded that the accusations of doctrinal heresy against Pelagius were unjustified.[89] Until this point, Augustine's warnings seem to have gone unheeded.

The magnitude of Pelagius' threat to the Anician women has become fully clear to Augustine by the time he composes his response to Juliana's indignant defence.[90] Not only does it appear to Augustine that Juliana has not recognized the significance and seriousness of the Pelagian error but, worse yet, Augustine has learned also that Pelagius has already been in contact with the Anician women. The last letter of the body of correspondence clearly conveys a strong sense of Augustine's vulnerability and of the tenuousness of his position. Augustine carefully suggests that Pelagius is a flatterer;[91] but he rephrases his conviction of the necessity of his advice by arguing that, while Juliana and Demetrias are of course

[87] Augustine, *Ep.* 188.3 (CSEL 57.121; *NPNF* 1.549): 'Sed noverit sacerdotium vestrum longe me ac domunculam meam ab huius modi personis esse discretam; omnisque familia nostra adeo catholicam sequitur fidem, ut in nullam haeresim aliquando deviaverit nec umquam lapsa sit, non dico in eas sectas, quae vix expiantur, sec nec in eas, quae parvos habere videntur errores.' These comments of Juliana's were excerpted by Augustine and written in his subsequent response to her.

[88] Brown 2000: 356.

[89] Pope Innocent, in reviewing the case of Pelagius' condemnation by his predecessor, stated 'this hair-splitting and these pointless debates . . . all pour out of an infectious curiosity, when each and all abuse their intellectual powers and give vent to their uncontrolled eloquence at the expense of the Scriptures. Not even the greatest minds . . . are immune from this. Their writings, in the course of time, are afflicted with the same dangerous lack of judgement. So God has prophesied: "From many words thou shalt not escape sin," and holy David asked for "a gate of prudence before his lips".' (has tendiculas quastionum et inepta certamina . . . ex illa curiositatis contagione profluere, dum unusquisque ingenio suo et intemperanti eloquentia, seu scriptura abutitur, cum in hoc etiam magnorum virorum nonnunquam, cum ipsis auctoribus, scripta periclitentur post permultam temporum seriem interpretantis arbitrio, ut divine praedictum sit, Ex multiloquio non vitari peccatum: et sanctus David postularet circumstantiam labiis suis, orique custodiam). See Zosimus, *Ep. 'Magnum pondus'* 5 (*PL* 45.1720). I owe this reference and translation to Brown 2000: 360.

[90] Augustine, *Ep.* 188 (CSEL 57.119–30).

[91] Augustine, *Ep.* 188.6 (CSEL 57.123–4).

above reproach, his warning will still be useful to their servants, who are more vulnerable to being misled.[92]

In the quotation which began this section, Augustine also carefully reminds Juliana of his own long-standing association with and significance to her family. In the closing paragraph of this letter, Augustine implores Juliana to inform him whether she has read the book addressed to Demetrias, and to confirm to him whether, worse still, it was Juliana herself who had actually commissioned it.[93] If Juliana did feel it necessary to respond to Augustine's pressing concerns, we can only conjecture as to the content of her response since this letter of Augustine's marks the end of the surviving correspondence. Moreover, while the eventual outcome of the Pelagian controversy is well known, another echo of Augustine's disadvantageous position during this time should be noted.[94]

Later that year, Augustine wrote to John of Jerusalem demanding a copy of the proceedings of the Synod of Diospolis at which Pelagius had been exonerated of heresy. His frustration is abundantly plain when he writes: 'I would not for anything venture to cherish resentment that I have not been

[92] Augustine, *Ep.* 188.10 (CSEL 57.127–8).

[93] Augustine, *Ep.* 188.14 (CSEL 57.130; *NPNF* 1.552). Augustine admits to the knowledge of this request in his letter to Juliana. Augustine wrote: 'In this book, though it contain neither his name nor your own honoured name, he nevertheless mentions that a request had been made to him by the mother of the virgin to write to her. In a certain epistle of his, however, to which he openly attaches his name, and does not conceal the name of the sacred virgin, the same Pelagius says that he had written to her' ('in quo libro quamvis nec ipsius nec tuae reverentiae nomen expresserit, tamen a matre virginis, ut ad eam scriberet, a se postulatum esse commemorat. In quadam vero epistula sua idem Pelagius, ubi et nomen suum apertissime ponit nec nomen sacrae virginis tacet, dicit ad eam se scripsisse'). Augustine had made this discovery when he had received a copy of a book addressed to Demetrias which contained doctrines against God's grace. See Augustine, *Ep.* 188.4 (CSEL 57:122; *NPNF* 1.549): 'In this book, were it lawful for such a one to read it, a virgin of Christ would read that her holiness and all her spiritual riches are to spring from no other source than herself, and thus, before she attains to the perfection of blessedness, she would learn – which may God forbid! – to be ungrateful to God' ('in quo libro, si fas est, legat virgo Christi, unde credat virginalem suam sanctitatem omnesque spiritales divitias non nisi ex se ipsa sibi esse, atque ita, priusquam sit plenissime beata, discat deo esse – quod absit! – ingrata').

[94] Augustine also attempted to canvass the support of other aristocrats against Pelagius. After having believed that the Pelagian matter had been resolved, Augustine approached the matter with Paulinus after Pope Zosimus reopened the case against Pelagius. In AD 417, in *Ep.* 186 (CSEL 57.45–80) Augustine warned Paulinus against Pelagius, having been made aware of Paulinus' connections with Pelagius. See Brown 1972: 211–12. In mid-418, Augustine dedicated *De gratia Christi* to Melania and Pinian and therein denounced the Pelagian heresy. This move is especially telling in light of the fact that Augustine was aware of Pelagian supporters among Pinian's group as well as the difficulties the couple experienced with the congregation of Hippo when they had spent a period of time in north Africa. In *Epp.* 126.6 (CSEL 44.7–18), Augustine reveals that he is aware of a Timasius among Pinian's group who is a strong Pelagian supporter. On the difficult episode between Pinian and the congregation at Hippo, see Augustine, *Epp.* 124–6 (CSEL 44.1–18). For this episode, see also Brown 2000: 294.

honoured with letters from your Holiness; for it is better for me to believe that you, my saintly lord and deservedly revered brother, were without anyone to convey them, than to harbour the suspicion that your Grace was scorning me.'[95]

As suggested at the outset of this section, from initial appearances, Augustine's letter to Demetrias is dissimilar to the letters of Jerome and Pelagius. Yet, when Augustine's *Epistula* 150 is recognized as but one piece of correspondence in a larger corpus of work, it does demonstrate his cultivation of a lasting relationship with the Anician matriarchs. At the time of the dissemination of Pelagian doctrines, through reminders of his long-standing relationship with the Anician women, Augustine did all he could to ensure that Pelagius would not benefit from Anician patronage. This may have been an important factor in his eventual success in securing condemnation of Pelagius despite the latter's exoneration at Diospolis. In summary, by writing to the Anician matriarchs, the male authors of these texts hoped to mobilize and benefit from a powerful concentration of female agency. It is this agency that the texts unwittingly but ultimately reveal, albeit in a tantalizingly indirect manner.

Before turning to examine Demetrias in the last stage of her life, a final note of consideration must be made regarding the patronage activities of her mother and grandmother. Scholars have traditionally stressed the freedoms which came with widowhood, as widows could exercise 'greater influence over household and economic resources'.[96] In support of this argument it may be noted that the typically young age of widows, when combined with the legally advantageous rejection of remarriage[97] encouraged by Christian theology, could allow widowhood to represent an extended period of financial and social autonomy.[98] Nevertheless, I would contend that an argument based upon the concept of freedom from familial constraints is largely misleading. The independence or individuality of Roman men and women is strictly a modern concept. As van Bremen has

[95] Augustine, *Ep.* 179.1 (CSEL 44.691, trans. Baxter, 306): 'quod tuae sanctitatis scripta non merui, nihil audeo suscensere; melius enim perlatorem credo defuisse, quam me suspicor a tua ueneratione contemptum, domine beatissime et merito uenerabilis frater'. See also Brown 2000: 358.

[96] Salzman 2002: 148.

[97] Women did not possess legal power (*potestas*) over their children, but in the late fourth century widows could become legal guardians of their children provided that they themselves were of age and refused to remarry. See Arjava 1996: 174, 129. Also on women in control of property see Arjava 1996: 73–5, 132–56, and 84–94 on widows in control of their children's property.

[98] Note Arjava 1996: 169: 'Thus, both literary and inscriptional sources suggest that perpetual widowhood was prized more openly in late antiquity. Christian teaching may have contributed to this although the idea was not totally confined to Christians.' See also Treggiari 1991: 233–6. On the tradition of the *univira* see Lightman and Zeisel 1977: 19–32.

pointed out 'not "independence from" but its diametrical opposite "belonging to" is the criterion we should be applying when measuring status and power'.[99] The *domus* as a source of identity which women drew upon and contributed to did not cease upon widowhood.

Widows' activities as patrons could function as a means by which women were able to keep the family in the public gaze. Through the construction of prominent building projects or through the support of large groups of clerics and the poor, widows could continue to contribute visibly and publicly to the status of a *domus*. This may have involved a similar dynamic to that reflected in the female holding of civic offices in the Greek east in the first century AD when husbands were absent for large periods of time upon entering senatorial careers. In that context, van Bremen has suggested that, '[i]t fell largely to their female relatives – who, it is implied, did not follow their men around the empire – to uphold the family's link with its native (or adoptive) city, to take on local offices and liturgies, and to perpetuate the family's name through generosities and monumental display.'[100] Equally, perhaps a similar balance of autonomy and contribution to the wider group can be discerned in the evidence for virgins of the patronage class. As we turn to focus on Demetrias' activities at the end of her life, we will see that return to her native city, and monumental building there, are indeed in evidence.

THE *VIRGO* IN MATURITY: THE *EPISTULA AD DEMETRIADEM DE VERA HUMILITATE*[101]

Consider now that the faces and eyes of all are turned upon you and that the entire world has settled down to watch the spectacle of your life.[102]

Pelagius' memorable comment proved only half-true. In essence, what the historian confronts in examining the evidence for Demetrias' life amounts to several snapshots during its course, rather than a continuous narrative. The first time Demetrias intersects with the mechanisms for transforming lived experience into historical evidence is around the time of her consecration. Two further instances, neither securely datable, occur when Demetrias returns to Rome and her ancestral estate, and constructs a church dedicated to St Stephen on the Via Latina. Finally, Demetrias

[99] van Bremen 1996: 45. [100] van Bremen 1996: 108.

[101] *PL* 55.161–80. The letter has been dated to *c.* 440, see Krabbe 1965: 5–7.

[102] Pelagius, *Ad Dem.* 14 (*PL* 30.30, trans. Rees, 51): 'In te nunc puta cunctorum ora oculosque converses, et ad spectaculum vitae tuae totum consedisse mundum.'

appears in the historical record through the medium of the advice of one last male ecclesiastic, the author of the *Epistula ad Demetriadem de vera humilitate*, written most likely when she was again ensconced in her native Rome, probably between 435 and 460.

Jerome, Augustine and Pelagius had all quoted the sense of 1 Corinthians 3.6–7 in their letters to Demetrias: 'I planted, Apollos watered, but God gave the growth. So neither the one who plants nor the one who waters is anything, but only God who gives the growth.'[103] All three authors employed this verse as a metaphor by means of which each could cast himself in the role of one who would aid Demetrias' spiritual growth.[104] The author of the *De vera humilitate* too alluded to this passage, commenting:

> So it is understandable that men of the greatest learning encouraged those youthful beginnings of yours by their exhortations. True, the Supreme Husbandman provided for your steady growth and progress, as for His own seedling; nevertheless, those who were working along with God's grace applied themselves to this pious cultivation also, so that the tender plant would become strong and hardy and the tree of your holy resolve would bring forth fruits worthy of its own excellence.[105]

Both the echo of the 1 Corinthians 3 passage and the allusion to the letters of Augustine, Jerome, and Pelagius are clear. In this last surviving *Epistula ad Demetriadem*, however, the underlying theme has become that of 'true humility'. The author explicitly identifies this different purpose in writing in his introductory remarks: 'But what room will there be

[103] 1 Corinthians 3.6–7 (New Revised Standard Version). Verses 8–9 continue: '(8). The one who plants and the one who waters have a common purpose, and each will receive wages according to the labor of each. (9). For we are God's servants, working together; you are God's field, God's building.'

[104] Jerome, *Ep.* 130.2 (CSEL 56.177; *NPNF* 6.261) stated: 'Still these words of mine will not be without their use . . . The grandmother and mother have planted, but it is I that water and the Lord that giveth the increase (1 Cor 3.6).' Pelagius, *Ad Dem.* 1 (*PL* 30.17, trans. Rees, 36) stated: 'quae facile ostendit, quo studio quantaque cura in filia germen coeleste plantaverit, dum illud tam sollicite cupit ab aliis irrigare' ('Thus she [Juliana] shows us with the greatest of ease the zeal and care with which she has planted the heavenly seed in her daughter and how she now desires it to be watered by others just as punctiliously'). Augustine, *Ep.* 188.1 (CSEL 57.120; *NPNF* 1.549) stated: 'This great gift of God, planted and watered indeed by means of His servants, but owing its increase to Himself, had been granted to us as labourers in His vineyard' ('hoc ingens dei donum, quod per servos quidem suos plantat et rigat, sed per se ipsum dat incrementum, nobis operariis provenisse'). NB: It could be argued that in what Augustine says there is an implied criticism of both Jerome, who saw himself as the provider of nourishment, thus showing pride, and Pelagius, who attributed spiritual achievement to the individual, thus denying grace. I owe credit for this observation to Dr Carole Hill.

[105] Ps.-Prosper, *Ep. ad Dem.*1 (ed. and trans. Krabbe, 140–3): 'Illam ergo aetatem tua et illa principia rationabiliter doctissimi viri suis adhortationibus incitarunt. Et licet plantationi suae summus agricola valida ad profectum tuum incrementa praeberet, cooperatores tamen gratiae Dei opportune piam adhibuere culturam, ut germen tenerum fortitudinis robur acciperet et dignos generositate sua fructus propositi tui abor afferret.'

for any words from me?' but to offer counsel to 'beware of pride and earnestly commend to you true humility'.[106] It is to this aspect of the *Epistula ad Demetriadem de vera humilitate*, and its formulation of the role of the wealthy Christian, that we now turn.

And if I discuss the worth of virginity, to suggest this to you now as an ideal would be superfluous, since you yourself, without human prompting, chose it in the very flower of your youth. (Pseudo-Prosper, *Ep. ad Dem.*1)

Modern scholarship has hesitated between Leo the Great and Prosper of Aquitaine as the likeliest suspects for its authorship. The letter was long dated to AD 440 and ascribed to Leo the Great, and has only more recently been redated to 435 and identified as most probably having been written by Prosper.[107] The identification rests largely though not exclusively on the fact that the text is most often found in the manuscript tradition with Prosper's *De vocatione omnium gentium*.[108] Since the discussion of authorship and date has not been conclusive, we will treat the text as an anonymous source. The *De vera humilitate* propounds an anti-Pelagian theological position, with emphasis on an Augustinian doctrine of grace.[109]

The text of the letter itself is divided into twenty-four chapters. The letter can be divided into thematic sections. Section one (chs. 1–6) serves as an introduction. The second section (chs. 7–12) contains the author's direct refutation of the Pelagian notion of the natural ability of the individual to achieve perfection and instead emphasizes the argument that the main hindrance to the acknowledgement of God's grace is the sin of pride. The author argues that the acknowledgement of God's grace is the essence of true humility.[110] The Augustinian, anti-Pelagian stance is further elaborated in chapters 13–15. Finally, chapters 16–24 counsel against pride and discuss true humility and charity. The overall emphasis throughout the text is on the insistence that all gifts stem from God.[111] As before, an analysis of

[106] Ps.-Prosper, *Ep. ad Dem.* 1 (ed. and trans. Krabbe 1965: 142–3): 'Nostris autem paginis quid erit loci? ... cavendae te elationis admoneam et humilitatis tibi sinceritatem fida suggestione commendem.'

[107] See Krabbe 1965: 5–6 and 47–9. The latter reference includes a historical summary of the text's attribution. If Prosper is in fact the author, Krabbe believes that this text was written before his *De vocatione omnium gentium*.

[108] On the figure of Prosper, see Lorenz 1962 and Leyser 1999.

[109] It is important to note that while it is apparent from the context of the letter that the author is denouncing Pelagian doctrine, he never directly names Pelagius or his followers. For the earlier initial reluctance of Augustine and other Pelagian opponents also to name him directly, see Brown 1972: 216–19.

[110] Ps.-Prosper, *Ep. ad Dem.* 7 (ed. and trans. Krabbe 1965: 160–5).

[111] For a theological analysis, see Krabbe 1965: 38–40.

the theological doctrines of this text regarding grace and free will will not be attempted; the focus will instead be on the role of wealthy Christians.

The first chapter of the *De vera humilitate* serves as an introduction and contains several interesting pieces of information, including parallels with the earlier letters to Demetrias by Jerome, Augustine, and Pelagius. While certain of the parallels may indicate only that the author of the *De vera humilitate* was following literary conventions of letter writing, others make it clear that he was aware of the existence of the older letters.[112] Like the previous authors, the author of the *De vera humilitate* also attempts pre-emptively to counter possible accusations of abuse by stressing that Demetrias herself had requested the work. He avers: 'Despite your dignity, O holy virgin Demetrias, you even condescend to the point of urging me to write something to assist your progress.'[113] The author then emphasizes the difficulty of his task. He claims that 'If I proceed to pen your praises and recount the line of noble ancestors to which you add so much distinction, I think I might well be considered annoying and lacking in discretion; either I would be presenting you with the temptation of human glory by my compliments, or I would be presuming that my talents were equal to extolling you and your family.'[114]

Another theme shared by all four authors is the observation that Demetrias' achievements had outstripped those of all her famous ancestors. Finally, the author concludes the introduction by stating his explicit purpose in writing to Demetrias:

> After the eloquent compositions of outstanding masters, what usefulness will you find in the discourse which you have deigned to enjoin upon me? Except, perhaps, that since through their teaching and your own zeal you are advancing in your holy life to higher degrees of virtue, I should counsel you to beware of pride and earnestly commend to you true humility.[115]

The most important thematic section of the letter is that contained in chapters 2–4. It is in these chapters that the author discusses two main

[112] On literary conventions of letter writing, see Stowers 1986.

[113] Ps.-Prosper, *Ep. ad Dem.* 1 (ed. and trans. Krabbe, 138–9): 'o sacra virgo Demetrias, dignationem tuae dignitatis inclinas, ut provectiones tuas etiam meo stilo exigas adiuvari'.

[114] Ps.-Prosper, *Ep. ad Dem.* 1 (ed. and trans. Krabbe, 138–41): 'Si laudes tuas scribere aggrediar, et maiorem seriem quae per te multum illustrator evolvam, onerosum me forte et impudentem videri posse arbitror, qui vel humanae tibi gloriae tentationem adulando ingeram, vel tuis ac tuorum praedicationibus ingenium meum par esse praesumam.'

[115] Ps.-Prosper, *Ep. ad Dem.* 1 (ed. and trans. Krabbe, 142–3): 'Et post ornatissima excellentium magistrorum, quid utilitatis in eo quem indicere indignata es sermone reperies? Nisi forte quia et illorum doctrinis et tuis studiis ad sublimiores gradus virtutum consuetude proficit, cavendae te elationis admoneam et humilitatis tibi sinceritatem fida suggestione commendem.'

themes: the 'law of concord' (*ius concordiae*) and the merits of worldly detachment. Beginning conventionally enough, the author places special emphasis on the attitude of equality that must be engendered between rich and poor, noble and ignoble, and argues for a lack of rivalry for higher rank and honours. However, he goes on to hint at a more unusual and perhaps a more radical view.

The first concern of humility is with the duties of living together ... For it is a powerful help in strengthening charity ... when the poor man does not hesitate to give preference to the rich man, and the rich man is glad to make the poor man his equal; those of high station are not haughty about their illustrious lineage, and the poor are not made proud by the natural endowments in which they share; when, finally, great wealth is not of more account than good character ... From such an equitable and mild law of concord (*modesto iure concordiae*), in which there is no rivalry for higher rank and no one is puffed up by his own good fortune or envious of someone else's, many men make admirable progress toward a humility so strong that it places itself outside all honours and prefers to be fit to receive wrongs rather than able to repel them.[116]

Although here the author is advocating a worldly detachment that includes the notion of despising human glory, and so begins with a conventional evocation of renunciation, in what comes next he goes on to set out a position that is perhaps more radical and certainly more positive for those following a route often seen as being at odds with traditional ascetic withdrawal:

So when the disciples of truth flee human glory and sever themselves from the love of things temporal, that they may savour the things of God rather than those of men, they experience an increase in sensibility, not a decrease; instead of losing vigour of mind, they receive the light of extraordinary understanding. They live in this world, but they detach themselves from the tumult of the world.[117]

The conclusion to this chapter, in which its author reiterates the more traditional notion that it is best to divest oneself of all riches, does little to

[116] Ps.-Prosper, *Ep. ad Dem.* 3 (ed. and trans. Krabbe, 146–9): 'Prima ergo humilitatis ratio in communis vitae versatur officiis ... multum enim ad roborandum dilectionem valet ... cum et pauper divitem non sibi dubitat anteferre, et dives pauperem sibi gaudet aequare; cum et sublimes non superbiunt de claritate prosapiae, et paupers non extolluntur de communione naturae; cum denique non plus tribuitur magnis opibus quam bonis moribus ... Ab hoc aequo et modesto iure concordiae, in quo nullum est de gradu superiore certamen, nec felicitas aut inflate propria at urit aliena, pulchre et mirabiliter a plerisque proficitur ad illam humilitatis fortitudinem quae se extra omnem constituit dignitatem et mavult apta esse iniuriis accipiendis quam idonea repellendis.'

[117] Ps.-Prosper, *Ep. ad Dem.* 4 (ed. and trans. Krabbe, 150–1): 'Cum itaque discipuli veritatis humanam gloriam fugiunt et a temporalium amore desciscunt, ut quae Dei sunt sapient, non quae hominum, proficiunt sensibus, non deficiunt. Neque vigorem cordis amittunt, sed excellentissimae intellegentiae lumen accipiunt, viventes quidem in hoc mundo sed omnes mundi relinquentes.'

erase the strong impression given here that the rightful stewardship of wealth can itself be seen as a form of ascetic practice.[118]

A remark in chapter 2 provides another clue to the author's position, though this is not fully elucidated until chapter 5. While the author counsels that true humility is the ideal, he enters an important caveat: those who in this world are in a naturally humbled position do not necessarily embody true humility. Here, the author states: 'Nor should the general term humility hamper our discreet judgement, making us think that all who are humble, no matter in what way, are worthy of praise . . . Rejoicing over riches well spent is not the same as sighing over riches not acquired, or grieving over those one has lost.'[119] In other words, by defining true humility, already presented by the author as the single most important virtue, as one which all people are able to cultivate and not existing only as the rightful bastion of the poor or deprived, the author points towards his true message for Demetrias: the necessary existence and importance of the good rich man (*bonus dives*).[120] This notion is introduced thus:

> But this virtue [humility], which disregards temporal riches and power and strives to reach eternal life by a road that is steep and narrow, in admitting into the company with Christian humility those who are poor by their choice, *ought not to exclude* those who possess vast estates, rich inheritances, and a great deal of this world's goods. For among the people of God there have always been many eminent examples of men who used their wealth well.[121]

[118] Ps.-Prosper, *Ep. ad Dem.* 4 (ed. and trans. Krabbe, 150–3): 'At what price is peace in this life more fittingly bought than by giving all riches, all honours, and every worldly desire back to that very same world? Through a holy and happy exchange why not purchase Christian liberty, and as sons of God become rich by poverty, strong by suffering, exalted by humility? For to scorn earthly riches, to despise fleeting honours and not to seek glory . . . is not the mark of a cowardly heart or a sluggish spirit, as the lovers of this world fancy' ('Quo autem pretio quies huius temporis aptius comparator quam ut ipsi mundo omnes divitiae, omnes dignitates et universarum cupiditatum materiae refundantur, et sancto beatoque commercio ematur Christiana libertas fiantque filii Dei de paupertate divites, de patientia fortes, de humilitate sublimes? Non enim, ut dilectores huius saeculi putant, parvi cordis aut segnis est animi terrenas opes spernere, honores occiduos fastidire, nec ibi gloriam quaerere').

[119] Ps.-Prosper, *Ep. ad Dem.* 2 (ed. and trans. Krabbe, 144–5): 'Nec generale nomen ita nos a iudicio discretionis excludat ut omnes quoquomodo humiles putemus esse laudabiles . . . quia non idem est gaudere bene expensis divitiis quod aut gemere de non acquisitis aut dolere de perditis.'

[120] For the Christian literary tradition of the 'good rich man', see Clement of Alexandria, *Who Is the Rich Man That Shall Be Saved?* and Cyprian of Carthage, *On Works and Alms*. For an analysis of these texts, see Countryman 1980. For the fourth- and early fifth-century ecclesiastical figures, such as Ambrose and Augustine, on riches see Salzman 2002: 205–8.

[121] Ps.-Prosper, *Ep. ad Dem.* 5 (ed. and trans. Krabbe, 152–5): 'Sed haec virtus, quae temporalis copiae et potentiae negligens ad vitam aeternam angusta et ardua via nititur, non debet voluntarios paupers in consortium christianae humilitatis admttere, eos autem a societate boni huius excludere qui ampla

That this notion is the heart of what he has to say is clear, for the author next goes on to present a threefold validation of the role and existence of the rich Christian like Demetrias, who has not divested herself of her wealth and continues to use it in similar patterns of benevolence and patronage as those employed for centuries by her ancestors. On the good rich man, the author explains that as a matter of fact, wealth and honour can aid the rich man in his quest for humility: as one's whole life is occasion for sin, the temptation and difficulty of sinning with money provides a further challenge for these men to overcome and therefore progress further spiritually. He phrases this argument as follows:

Heaven forbid that the faithful should ever let into their minds such an unholy notion, believing that when God has bestowed wealth and honours on any of His saints, such riches or dignity have stood in the way of their securing the merit of true humility (*vera humilitas*). On the contrary, in their case both wealth and honour furthered progress in this virtue. The whole life of man upon earth is a trial, and need as well as abundance can be an occasion of sin . . . But in every age, and just as much so in our own, as there have been good poor men so also there have been *good rich men* (*boni divites*).[122]

Furthermore, our writer argues that the notion of the good rich man is also supported by his role as steward of the church. In this case, wealth is used wisely for the continued support of the church's needs. In presenting this argument, the author stresses as a corollary the positive effect of this role in terms of the correct administration and support of the good man's household. This emphasis appears very much as an approval of Demetrias' running of a household of virgins and widows similar to the one her grandmother Proba had controlled in north Africa:

Not only are Christ's poor sustained by the resources of those who, in order to follow the Lord with less encumbrance, have divested themselves once and for all of all their wealth; the same cause is also served by the property of those who administer their possessions exclusively as the goods of the poor, in a kind of *stewardship* (*procuratione*) for the Church, each one working according to his own resources in order that the household of God may be supplied with what is necessary for food and clothing, and at the same time seeing to it that in their

praedia, magnifica patrimonia, et multas in hoc saeculo possident facultates, cum in populo Dei multi simper qui divitiis bene uterentur exstiterint.' The author then continues by listing biblical examples, e.g. Isaac, Jacob, Melchisedech, etc. of 'good rich men'.

122 Ps.-Prosper, *Ep. ad Dem.* 5 (ed. and trans. Krabbe, 156–7): 'Absit autem ab animis fidelium tam irreligiosa persuasion, ut cuiquam sanctorum, quibus Deus et divitias est largitus et honores, ad capiendum verae humilitatis meritum credatur vel opulentia obfuisse vel dignitas, cum eis ad huius virtutis provectum utraque profuerint. Quamvis enim tota vita hominis tentatio sit super terram, et tam abundantia quam inopia materia soleant esse peccati . . . exstiterunt tamen in omni tempore, et in nostra quoque aetate non desunt, sicut boni pauperes, ita et boni divites.'

own household all are cherished in kindness and controlled by good discipline under a just and holy management.[123]

Finally, the author of the *De vera humilitate* also gives a positive interpretation of the variety and diversity among the Christian faithful, doing so as a means to justify the rich Christian.[124] He offers the view that 'The Church of God, which is the body of Christ, is with its manifold variety so closely woven together that even disparate elements merge into a single beauty. Every type of man, every station in life, every degree of wealth, every kind of virtue contributes to the indivisible unity and homogeneous beauty of the total edifice.'[125] But by employing true humility as the 'binding force' of the church and the ultimate virtue,[126] this author proffers a palatable role which his addressee can certainly fulfil.

The force of this, and the change of direction it represents from the Augustinian position, is seen most strikingly when we compare this with what Augustine had had to say to Demetrias' grandmother, Anicia Faltonia Proba. Augustine's letter to Proba on the subject of prayer consisted of a twofold answer to Proba's request. He wrote regarding 'what kind of person you ought to be if you would pray, and what things you should ask in prayer'.[127] Augustine instructed Proba that the wealthy too could find a place in heaven through the miracle of Christ but only through the pursuit of becoming truly rich, i.e. rich in good works.[128] Yet Augustine's message is one which provides much less reassurance than does that of the *De vera humilitate* in that he had emphasized the fleeting existence of

123 Ps.-Prosper, *Ep. ad Dem.* 5 (ed. and trans. Krabbe, 158–9): 'et pauperes Christi non eorum tantum facultatibus sustineri qui, ut expeditiores Dominum sequerentur, simul se omnibus suis opibus exuerunt, sed eidem operi etiam illorum substantias deservire qui possessionibus suis non aliter quam rebus pauperum praesunt et ecclesiasticae utilitati sub quadam procuratione famulantur, elaborantes singuli pro suarum virium portione, ut ad victum atque vestitum familiae Dei necessaria conferantur, et simul prospicientes ut in domibus ipsorum sub iusto sanctoque moderamine omnes et benignitas foveat et disciplina contineat.'

124 It is interesting to note that while the author follows Augustine in his rejection of the Pelagian theology primarily regarding the Pelagian notion of free will, consciously or not, he also echoes Augustine's notion of widening the definition of Christian piety to include all varieties of people. On this concept in Augustinian thought, see the evocatively titled chapter 4, 'Augustine: a defence of Christian mediocrity', in Markus 1998: 45–62, and his following chapter on the Pelagian concept of Christian perfectionism, 63–83.

125 Ps.-Prosper, *Ep. ad Dem.* 6 (ed. and trans. Krabbe, 158–9): 'Cum itaque ecclesia Dei, quae est corpus Christi, ita sit multimoda varietate contexta ut in unum decorem etiam quae non sunt paria concurrant, et de omni genere hominum, de omni gradu officiorum, de omni mensuram operum, de omni qualitate virtutum fiat totius aedificationis inseperabilis connexio et indifferens pulchritudo.'

126 Ps.-Prosper, *Ep. ad Dem.* 6 (ed. and trans. Krabbe, 158–61).

127 Augustine, *Ep.* 130.12 (CSEL 44.67; *NPNF* 1.466): 'non solum qualis ores, uerum etiam quid ores'.

128 Augustine, *Ep.* 130.2 (CSEL 44.45–7).

earthly happiness and the truly desolate condition of man no matter how plentiful his earthly life may be.[129] Augustine addressed Proba:

> In saying these things to you, who, being a widow, rich and noble, and the mother of an illustrious family, have asked from me a discourse on prayer, my aim has been to make you feel that, even while your family are spared to you, and live as you would desire, you are desolate so long as you have not attained to that life in which is the true and abiding consolation.[130]

Augustine's counsel, then, was that she must pray ceaselessly, constantly remembering 'however great the temporal prosperity may be which flows around you, you are desolate'.[131] Augustine's concern is clear: Proba, as an extremely wealthy and privileged woman, was at greater risk of not making attempts to achieve true sanctity. For Proba there was no proffered role as stewardess of the church whereby retained wealth was sanctioned in order that it might be slowly distributed to the needy and poor. To Proba, Augustine raised the spectre of the failure to emulate the 'holy men and women' who wisely divested themselves of their riches. He warned that if she were unable to accomplish this because of a sense of duty to her family, then only she knew 'what account you can give to God of your use of riches'.[132] In striking contrast, the message for Demetrias regarding her position and her wealth was entirely more reassuring. According to Elizabeth Clark, the message was clear: 'Those who had been first in the world could rest assured that they were still first in the Kingdom.'[133]

The guidance given to Demetrias in maturity implies that even though she had renounced traditional Roman values such as marriage and children, her form of Christianity was defined neither by extremes of asceticism nor by a complete and immediate divestiture of her fortune. The author of the *De vera humilitate* validates a role for Demetrias as the steward of wealth on behalf of the church: a role which she had seen enacted by her mother and grandmother half a century earlier. Demetrias had not only retained her fortune but she continued to celebrate her elite status and her familial heritage. In her church dedicated to the protomartyr

[129] Augustine, *Ep.* 130.3 (CSEL 44.47–9).

[130] Augustine, *Ep.* 130.2 (CSEL 44.47; *NPNF* 1, 461): 'haec dixi, quoniam sermonem meum uidua diues et nobilis et tantae familiae mater de oratione quaesisti, ut etiam te cum in hac uita permanentibus et obsequentibus tuis te sentias desolatam nondum utique adprehensa illa uita, ubi est uerum certum que solacium'.

[131] Augustine, *Ep.* 130.2 (CSEL 44.47; *NPNF* 1.461): 'quantacumque temporalium bonorum felicitate circumfluas . . . desolatam te esse memineris'.

[132] Augustine, *Ep.* 130.3 (CSEL 44.49; *NPNF* 1.462): 'quam de his rationem reddas deo'.

[133] Clark 1981: 244.

St Stephen, which she built on her ancestral property, Demetrias was proudly proclaimed as '*Demetrias Amnia virgo*'.[134]

DEMETRIAS AND ST STEPHEN

When the Amnian virgin Demetrias leaving this world brought to a close her last day (yet not truly dying) she gave to you, Pope Leo, this last of her vows, that this sacred house arise. The trust of her command is fulfilled, yet it is more glorious to carry out a vow inwardly than outwardly. Stephen, who first in the world was carried away by savage death, and reigns in the height of heaven, had crowned the work. By order of the bishop, the presbyter Tigrinus serves in this hall, sleepless in mind, work, and faith. (*ILCV* I, *1765*, inscription from the church of St Stephen, Via Latina[135])

Leo, born in Tuscia, son of Quintianus, held the see 21 years 1 month 13 days. In his time, God's handmaid Demetrias built a basilica to St Stephen on her estate at the 3rd mile of the Via Latina. (*Liber Pontificalis, Life of Leo the Great (440–461)*[136])

We last glimpse Demetrias during the reign of Pope Leo the Great, living perhaps in Rome, and certainly making a contribution to the city's religious fabric through her construction of a basilica to St Stephen. The two texts above, the Via Latina inscription and the brief notice of Demetrias' foundation in the *Liber Pontificalis*, offer a fleeting trace of commemoration of her own interests and actions as a patron of the Roman church.

The interest of Demetrias in Stephen may have dated to her days in north Africa, since the arrival of Stephen's relics there in 416 had been of great interest to the north African church in general, and to Augustine in particular.[137] Equally, she is likely to have been aware of the interest in Stephen's relics shown by Melania the Younger, the empress Pulcheria, and Pulcheria's sister-in-law Athenais-Eudokia.[138] As Leslie Brubaker has argued, imperial and senatorial women had begun by the end of the fourth century to use the cult of relics as one of their principal media for projecting 'images of dynastic strength'. Perhaps both are significant elements in

[134] Demetrias' grandmother Anicia Faltonia Proba was celebrated as an 'adornment of the *Amnii*'.

[135] *ILCV* I, 1765: 'cum mundum linquens Demetrias Amnia virgo/ clauderet extremum non moritura diem,/ haec tibi, papa Leo, votorum extrema suorum/ tradidit ut sacre surgeret aula domus./ mandati completa fides, sed gloria maior/ interius votum soluere quam propalam./ indiderat culmen Stephanus, qui prius in orbe/ raptus morte truci regnat in arce poli./ praesulis hanc iussu Tigrinus presbyter aulum/ excolit insomnis mente labore fide.'

[136] *LP* I, 47 (ed. L. Duchesne, Paris, 1955: 238): 'Leo, natione Tuscius, ex patre Quintiano, sedit ann. XXI m. I d. XIII. Huius temporibus fecit Demetria ancilla Dei basilicam sancto Stephano via Latina miliario III, in praedio suo.'

[137] See e.g. Augustine, *Sermo* 314–19 (*PL* 38.1425–42); *Civ. Dei.* 10 (CCSL 47.271–314), and Leyser 2005.

[138] The evidence is discussed fully in Kurdock 2003: 125–36.

the hold of Stephen on her imagination. It seems unlikely that if Demetrias herself had possessed relics of Stephen the sources would have failed to record it. Finally, it should be remembered that Stephen was remembered not only as the first of the Christian martyrs, but also as the first deacon of the church at Jerusalem, the steward of its resources.[139] In this he was particularly fitting as a heavenly counterpart for a figure such as Demetrias, whose own claim to stewardship on behalf of the church had been made so emphatically.

With this insight, we have perhaps come as close as we can expect to, to an attestation that the author of the *Epistula ad Demetriadem* knew something about the woman herself. Indeed, we are fortunate to discern even so glancing a profile of her commitments. Without sons or husband, Demetrias was never likely to attract a collection of dedicatory inscriptions like those that commemorate her mother and grandmother. Even her date of death and place of burial are unknown. But in the age of Attila and Geiseric, the habit of self-documentation of the Roman aristocracy was in any event beginning to wane. There is every likelihood that Anicius Olybrius, married to Theodosius II's daughter Placidia in 454/5, consul in 464, and emperor of the western empire in 472, was the son of one of Demetrias' illustrious brothers, yet even in the case of a Roman emperor the epigraphic record is too thin for us to be certain of his parentage.[140] We should perhaps, therefore, be content to know that Demetrias owned an estate in Rome, that she built a church there, that after her death the then pope, Leo, assigned a priest, Tigrinus, to serve its cult, and that nearly a century later the author of the *Liber Pontificalis* still thought her foundation important enough to place it as the head item in Leo's biography. By this time, Olybrius' daughter, named Anicia Juliana after the mother of Demetrias, had built her own great church, that of St Polyeuktos at Constantinople; but that is another story.

139 Leyser 2005.

140 On Olybrius, see Jones and Martindale 1971–92: II, 796–8; Kurdock 2003: 214, and Capizzi 1997: 206–9.

8

Families, patronage, and the titular churches of Rome, c. 300–c. 600

Julia Hillner

Lay patronage of the late antique Roman church presents us with something of an oddity.[1] In the fourth and fifth centuries the Roman church was preparing itself to become one of the most powerful and richest dioceses in the western Roman empire, while in its midst resided the proud members of an extremely wealthy senatorial aristocracy, who were slowly, but inevitably, converting to Christianity.[2] The assumption of interdependency between the two phenomena suggests itself. Yet, for most of the period we have little evidence of where the Roman church got its money from and how far the senatorial aristocracy were involved. In fact, altogether we know of only twelve fairly securely attested interventions by Roman aristocrats on behalf of Roman churches for the fourth and the fifth centuries from the epigraphic and literary evidence.[3]

[1] All translations are my own unless otherwise stated. I would like to thank Kimberley Bowes, Peter Brown, Gillian Clark, Kate Cooper, Marios Costambeys, Kristina Sessa, the members of the Late Antiquity Group at Manchester, and the anonymous readers of Cambridge University Press for their helpful comments and invaluable advice. Responsibility for remaining errors is mine alone.

[2] For a new understanding of the gradual conversion of the traditional senatorial aristocracy in the city of Rome see Salzman 2002.

[3] *ICUR* II, 4097: decoration of St Petrus by a lady called Anastasia and an anonymous man (366–384); De Rossi II: 150, n. 19 = *ILCV* 92: building of a baptistery at an unknown church by the *praefectus urbi* Longinianus (400/402); De Rossi II: 151, n. 25: building of a chapel (?) at S. Lorenzo in Damaso by Attica, *Felicis Magni clarissima coniunx* (fifth century); De Rossi II: 149, n. 17 = *ILCV* 68: decoration of the Lateran basilica by Flavius Constantius Felix and Padusia (428/30); De Rossi II: 55 n. 10 = *ILCV* 1758: decoration of St Petrus by Marinianus, *ex-praefectus urbi*, and Apostasia (440/461); De Rossi II: 148, n. 115 = *ILCV* 1759: decoration of St Petrus or the Lateran basilica by Gallus (mid-fifth century); De Rossi II: 150, n. 20: foundation of a church by a man called Pammachius, also known as the Titulus Pammachii (before the pontificate of Leo (440–461)); De Rossi II: 438, n. 127 = *ILCV* 1637: decoration of St Agatha (dei Goti) by Flavius Ricimer, *magister militum* (459/470); De Rossi II: 24, n. 25: decoration of St Anastasia by Severus and Cassia (461/468); De Rossi II: 436, n. 115 = *ILCV* 1785: bequest of land to the Roman church by a man called Valila. The *Liber Pontificalis* records two cases of aristocratic foundations, one of a lady Vestina, who founded the basilica of SS. Gervasius and Protasius during the pontificate of Innocent (401–417) (*LP* I, 221), and one of the Anician heiress Demetrias, who at the time of Leo I (440–461) founded a church dedicated to St Stephen (*LP* I, 238). The foundation of this church is also confirmed by an inscription: *ILCV* 1765.

Yet, there is one particular type of church foundation in the city of Rome that is often and extensively cited not only to show the involvement of the Roman aristocracy in this matter, but also to provide insight into the legal details of their patronage. In a famous subscription list at a synod held in Rome in 499 the Roman presbyters appear as attached to twenty-nine churches distinguished by the term *titulus* and a personal name in the genitive (for example *titulus Caeciliae*).[4] It is usually assumed that these personal names were for the most part the original founders' names.[5] While the evidence of the subscription list is admittedly obscure,[6] in view of the general lack of sources where patronage in late antique Rome is concerned, the list of 499 provides almost our only opportunity to name a patron.

The list of 499, however, is not our only record for the titular churches. While *tituli* are also mentioned in a number of late antique inscriptions,[7] our main source for the legal context of their foundation is the *Liber Pontificalis*, the book of popes' lives, the first part of which, up to the life of Felix IV (526–530), was written in the 530s.[8] Yet, the information provided by the authors of the *Liber Pontificalis* is inconsistent. On the one hand, the foundation of a system of *tituli* under the control of the Roman bishop is attributed to Pope Evaristus (*c.* 100–110) who divided them among the presbyters.[9] On the other hand, the *Liber Pontificalis* records a number of fourth- and fifth-century foundations of titular churches, which contradicts a well-organized origin of the titular churches. The *Vita* of Pope Silvester (314–335) records that Silvester installed a *titulus*

[4] Acta Syn. a. CCCXCVIII (ed. T. Mommsen, MGH AA XII (1894), 410–15).

[5] See Guidobaldi 2004: 11: 'il *Titulus* veniva in genere intestato al *conditor* che are di norma l'evergete'; see also Saxer 2001: 559.

[6] For a discussion of the onomastic evidence presented by the list see Hillner (forthcoming), where I suggest first that there is no straightforward indication that all the personal names attached to the titular churches in 499 corresponded to the names of founders, and second, that, where these corresponded to founders, these were not necessarily aristocratic. In fact, many of them may have been clerical. See in this regard also Guidobaldi 2004: 10.

[7] *ICUR* IV, 12303 : *T(i)t(ulus) s(an)c(ta)e Anastasiae*; De Rossi II : 322, n. 3: *Titulus Byzantis*; *ICUR* VII, 18160: *Titulus Clementis*, *ICUR* VI, 16002: *Titulus Eusebi*; De Rossi I : 262: *Titulus Fasciolae*; *ICUR* II, 4367 : *Titulus s(an)c(t)i Mar[—]* *ICUR* I, 1816 : *[—]t(itulus?) s(an)c(t)i M[arci?]*; *ICUR* VII, 19991: *Titulus Praxs[edis]*; *ICUR* II, 5160 : *Titulus sanc(tae) Priscae.*

[8] For the composition context of the *Liber Pontificalis* see Duchesne 1955: 7–9; Davis 2000: xii–xvi. For an alternative view of the dating of the first part, attributed to no earlier than the seventh century, see Mommsen 1898: xviii.

[9] *LP* I, 126 (ed. Duchesne 1955). As a note in the *Vita* of Pope Cletus (*c.* 85–95) clarifies that this bishop had ordained twenty-five priests in Rome (*LP* I, 122 (ed. Duchesne)), the number of Evaristus' *tituli* was probably also believed to have been twenty-five. *LP* I, 164 (ed. Duchesne) adds that Pope Marcellus (309–312) organized the twenty-five *tituli* for the administration of baptism, penance, and the burial of the martyrs.

on a *praedium* of the presbyter Equitius.[10] Likewise, Pope Damasus (366–384), according to his *Vita*, founded a titular church.[11] Finally Pope Innocent (401–417) founded a titular church with the money of a *femina illustris* Vestina.[12]

One of the most significant features of the titular churches that appear in these last-mentioned *Liber Pontificalis* texts is the existence of a patrimony of moveable and immoveable property, the rents of which maintained the existence of the church.[13] Scholars have long suspected that this patrimony was what was peculiar to churches called *tituli*.[14] Furthermore, it has been traditionally assumed that this patrimony derived from the founders of these churches. This assumption dismisses any notion of the Roman bishop as organizer of a titular church system, as presented in the *Vita* of Pope Evaristus in the *Liber Pontificalis*, in favour of an aristocratic intervention, as seems to be confirmed by the role of the *femina illustris* Vestina in the *Vita* of Pope Innocent.[15]

This role of the aristocracy was first postulated by Charles Pietri, who has argued that the majority of the titular churches were post-Constantinian lay foundations and that they constituted a particular type of foundation, namely a church provided by its founder with the necessary liturgical instruments and revenues permanently to maintain the building and its clergy. In his magisterial *Roma Christiana* Pietri suggested that the Roman aristocracy, after the example given by Constantine and early fourth-century Roman bishops, who founded and endowed a number of churches in Rome, would start to found and endow churches as well. However, they would have been careful in laying down conditions, which tied the endowment property to their churches. The more the senatorial aristocracy became Christianized the more of these churches would appear, until they numbered twenty-nine at the end of the fifth century, when we have the presbyter subscription list of 499 mentioned above.[16]

[10] *LP* I, 170–1 (ed. Duchesne). [11] *LP* I, 212–13 (ed. Duchesne). [12] *LP* I, 221 (ed. Duchesne)

[13] See Marazzi 1998: 36–43 for an interpretation of the rental figures given by the *Liber Pontificalis*.

[14] See, for example, Guidobaldi 2004: 5: 'È opportuno ricordare, *anche se ormai si tratta di un fatto acquisito*, che i *tituli* sono vere e proprie strutture multifunzionali finanziariamente autonome, poichè dotate di patrimoni propri' (emphasis added).

[15] See, for example, Saxer 2001: 559–60: 'la maggior parte dei tituli fu opera dell'evergesia aristocratica'.

[16] Pietri 1976: 90–6 and 569–73; see also Pietri 1978a: 7; 1981a: 439; 1989: 1043. These works reassess an earlier interpretation of the titular churches developed by Kirsch in his influential book *Die römischen Titelkirchen im Altertum* (1918: 117–137 and *passim*). Kirsch believed that the origin of many of the titular churches, particularly those for which a foundation is not recorded in the *Liber Pontificalis*, lay in the third century. In this period, he claimed, Christians met, and the presbyters of the Roman church were stationed in houses provided by wealthy lay people, which he also calls

Pietri's hypothesis about the nature of the titular churches was surely not meant to be the most important point he made during his life-long study of the late antique Roman church. Yet, it had a remarkable following. The most influential development of his model, perhaps, was made by Peter Llewellyn in two articles which aim at reconstructing the social tension between the senatorial aristocracy, the Roman clergy, and the Roman bishop at the end of the fifth century.[17] Like Pietri, Llewellyn saw the titular churches as lay aristocratic foundations endowed by their founders. However, he envisaged a different legal setting than did Pietri, one in which the presbyters of the individual titular churches formed corporations (*collegia*), tied in client relationships to the aristocratic families who had originally endowed them. While Pietri had understood the bishop's church to be the legal owner of the property assigned to the titular churches, albeit with restrictions, according to Llewellyn it was these priestly *collegia* who owned the *tituli*.

Both Pietri's and Llewellyn's most important case in point was the conflict between the senatorial aristocracy and the Roman bishop at the end of the fifth century, of which we have a reflection in the acts of a synod held in Rome in 502.[18] This synod was primarily concerned with the so-called Laurentian schism, which in turn had its origin in the doctrinal question whether the Roman bishop should accept the *Henotikon* promulgated in 482 by the emperor Zeno. The *Henotikon* was designed to heal the religious divisions between monophysites, who believed that Christ's humanity was absorbed by his divinity, so that he had only one nature, and Chalcedonians, who defined Christ as a single, undivided person, but 'in two natures', one human and one divine. The *Henotikon* condemned monophysitism, but did not mention the christological teaching of Chalcedon, which had been masterminded by the Roman bishop Leo I. This was unacceptable to the Roman see. The question took a political turn, because with the arrival in Italy of the Ostrogoths in 492, imperially orientated members of the senatorial aristocracy would not support a pope

domus ecclesiae. As the Roman church in this period could not officially hold property, the person who provided the house would function as the official owner, although in practice the house had been donated to the church. After the confiscation of these houses in the great persecution at the beginning of the fourth century, Kirsch supposed that Constantine gave them back to the Roman church, now entitled to hold property, which then proceeded to monumentalize some of them as basilicas, but would also found new churches to house presbyters in donated buildings, which were then still called after the original owner.

17 Llewellyn 1976b: 417–27; 1977: 245–75.

18 Acta Syn. a. DII (ed. Mommsen, MGH AA XII (1894), 438–55).

who undermined the authority of the emperor. This in 499 led to a double election of Pope Symmachus, who rejected the *Henotikon*, and Pope Laurentius, who was more conciliatory towards Constantinople.[19]

Pietri suggested that the theological and political problems were only the apparent reasons for the schism. The real concern of the senatorial aristocracy was the bishop's administration of church property.[20] He assumed that at the end of the fifth century members of the senatorial aristocracy started to become worried about the attempts of the Roman bishops to alienate church property, for example to finance episcopal election campaigns. Specifically, the senatorial aristocracy was concerned about the property assigned to the maintenance of the Roman titular churches, that is, mostly their or their ancestors' foundations, and hence the violation of conditions about the use of the property laid down at the time of foundation.[21] Lay opposition to alienation of property for buying votes first arose in the context of the election of Felix III after the death of Pope Simplicius in 483, when the senate ordered that property deriving from lay donations should not be alienated by future popes.[22] Pope Symmachus was accused of alienation of church property in the context of his election in 499, and therefore had to defend his actions in the synod of 502.[23] On this occasion, according to Pietri, he managed to sanction alienation of church property by the bishop in certain cases. Because of Symmachus' triumph regarding the episcopal administration of church property, lay foundations of churches in Rome would start to decline from the late fifth century and aristocrats would turn to their rural estates to found churches, where they could more easily control their donations.[24]

Llewellyn also subscribed to this interpretation of the Laurentian schism, with the variation that he believed the opposition to Symmachus to be organized in the titular churches. He saw the Roman presbyters stationed at these churches as representing their own interests and those of their lay patrons against those of the bishop. Together they tried to defend their control of these institutions' property. Eventually, on this view, it was

[19] On the background of the schism see Chadwick 1967: 200–10. For a discussion of the sources for this schism, and a critical assessment of their manuscript transmission, including the synodal acts, see Wirbelauer 1993.

[20] Pietri 1981b: 425. [21] This is quite clearly spelt out in Pietri 1976: 573; less so in 1981b: 425.

[22] Acta Syn. a. DII (ed. Mommsen, 448).

[23] *Fragmentum Veronese* (ed. Duchesne, 44): 'quod contra decretum a suis decessoribus observatum ecclesiastica dilapidasse praedia et per hoc anathematis se vinculis inretisset'.

[24] Pietri 1981b: 428.

the presbyters who lost out in the synod of 502 when Symmachus established that the Roman bishop could alienate church property.[25]

What Pietri and Llewellyn have in common is the assumption that titular churches were characterized by an endowment to maintain their buildings and clerical personnel, and that this endowment derived from the, often aristocratic, founder of the titular church in question.

While ultimately the precise property relationships of the titular churches may remain shrouded in mystery, I argue that it is worthwhile to contemplate a different context of endowment than that envisaged by Pietri and Llewellyn. This is not to suggest that titular churches were not founded by lay people. However, we need to consider the possibility that the endowment of titular churches with property, which ensured the continuity of the church in question, did not, or at least not always, stem from these founders, but could also be organized by the bishop from ecclesiastical property originating from generic donations, along with personal contributions from both earlier and later donors. An analysis of the foundation stories reported by the *Liber Pontificalis* indeed shows that this is the setting envisaged by their authors. The *Vita* of Pope Silvester (314–335) records that Silvester assigned gifts to the *titulus* he installed on the *praedium* of the presbyter Equitius (*ubi et haec dona constituit*), namely liturgical instruments and a number of rural and urban properties, which are listed with their expected annual income.[26] The majority of the manuscripts of the *Vita* repeat the story of the church foundation towards the end, but with a slightly different angle. Here the presbyter Equitius is not mentioned, but Silvester himself appears as the founder, and the property derived from the generosity of the emperor Constantine (*ubi donavit Constantinus Augustus*). However we interpret these contradictions,[27] the endowment did in one version derive from the pope himself, and in the second version from the emperor, but not from the founder Equitius. Likewise, Pope Damasus (366–384), according to his *Vita*, endowed his titular church with gifts (*ubi et donavit*), including moveable and immoveable property.[28] Also in these cases therefore the pope himself seems to be

[25] Llewellyn 1976b: 424: the priests 'formed a college, were socii, and acted together as a corporation'; and 1977: 248: 'priests . . . organized as a college, liturgically and corporately more isolated'.

[26] *LP* I, 170–1 (ed. Duchesne).

[27] For a possible interpretation of these passages see Krautheimer 1937–80: III, 124; Boaga 1983: 16. Both believe that the second foundation story was a fabrication from the time of Pope Symmachus, who was interested to associate the titular church (which he reconstructed) more with his predecessor Silvester, aided by the emperor, than with an obscure presbyter. For Symmachus' interest in Silvester and the Titulus Equitii see also Wirbelauer 1993: 159–63.

[28] *LP* I, 212–13 (ed. Duchesne).

the source of the endowment. Finally Pope Innocent (401–417) gave liturgical vessels and landed property to the titular church he had founded with the money of a *femina illustris* Vestina (*in eodem dominio optulit*).[29] Again, the pope is the donor, while only one of the rural properties, the *possessio Amandini*, is designated specifically as the property of Vestina.[30]

Yet, when using the *Liber Pontificalis* we of course need to be aware of the sixth-century date of the passages in question, which potentially undermines their reliability, and of the fact that it is a source with a strong episcopal viewpoint. Even if we believe, with Pietri, that the authors of the *Liber Pontificalis* drew for their titular church foundation stories on authentic contemporary documents conserved in the papal archives, which also listed endowed property,[31] this does not have to mean that they accurately reproduced the legal terminology and the legal concepts of the original documents. While this might simply reflect confusion arising from changing usage, we also need to take into account that the authors might have exaggerated any role assigned, be it to the bishop, the emperor, or a lay person. It is therefore necessary to assess to what extent the evidence of the *Liber Pontificalis* can be trusted.

In order to show that it may often be more feasible to regard the Roman bishop as the organizer of the endowment of the titular churches, I shall therefore begin by briefly discussing the use of the term *titulus* in classical and late antique legal discourse. It can be shown that the term denoted the legal rights of the recipient of a donation, rather than those of the donor. As such, it must have been chosen not by the founder of a titular church, but by the subsequent owner, whether this was the bishop or a *collegium* of

29 *LP* I, 221 (ed. Duchesne): 'This lady ordered in her will to build a basilica for the holy martyrs [Gervasius and Protasius] with the money made from the rightful sale of her jewels. And, after the construction of the basilica was finished, the most holy Innocentius established in this place a Roman *titulus* on assignment (*ex delegatione*) of the *inlustris femina* Vestina and transferred into the same property (*dominium*) [here follows a list of liturgical objects and the rents from rural and urban properties]' ('Quae femina suprascripta testamenti paginam sic ordinavit, ut basilica sanctorum martyrum ex ornamentis et margaritis construeretur, venditis iustis extimationibus. Et constructam usque ad perfectum basilicam, in quo loco beatissimus Innocentius ex delegatione inlustris feminae Vestinae titulum Romanum constituit et in eodem dominio optulit').

30 *LP* I, 222 (ed. Duchesne): 'Possessio Amandini quod donavit inlustri feminae Vestinae consubrinae suae.'

31 Pietri 1978b: 318–21. See also Saxer 2001: 499. Pietri's assumption goes back to Duchesne's proposition that the compilers of the Liber pontificalis had access to the papal archives. See also Noble 1985: 353–4. The existence of these documents were, according to Pietri, due to a legal innovation of the emperor Constantine, who, for the first time in Roman law, required written certification, in order to confirm the legitimacy of a donation particularly for tax-reasons. See for a discussion of the law in question (*Fragmenta vaticana* 249, 5–8 (FIRA II 461) = (in part) *CTh* 8.12.1 (ed. T. Mommsen and P. Meyer, 2nd edn, Berlin, 1954: 407–9), Kaser 1975: 281; Evans Grubbs 1995: 117–18).

priests. The term, therefore, does not provide any clues about conditions laid down by a titular church founder about the endowment of his church. In fact, my subsequent investigation into the continuities of traditional evergetical practices of the Roman elite suggests that, given the general reluctance of Roman benefactors to engage in endowment foundations, the endowment of titular churches by their founders was actually something that may rarely have happened. This interpretation would also exclude any property-holding role of corporations of priests separated from the Roman church at the time of foundation.

This new understanding of the endowment of titular churches, in turn, may shed a different light on the nature of the famous conflict between the Roman bishop and the Roman aristocracy at the end of the fifth century, to which I will turn at the end of this chapter. As will become clear from the close analysis of crucial passages in the acts of the synod held in 502, there is no secure evidence that the Roman aristocracy at the end of the fifth century were concerned about their rights as founders of titular churches. Rather, Roman aristocrats were concerned about the fate of single donations they had made to the bishop's church, which the bishop had assigned to the titular churches and other institutions. During the Laurentian schism, the bishop, rather than tightening control over the titular churches, submitted to the aristocracy's wishes of outlawing alienation of episcopal property. In this way, the Laurentian schism could be interpreted not as a defeat, but as a success story for lay benefactors.

The term titulus

Pietri assumed that up to and including the time of Damasus, the Roman bishops, such as Damasus himself, used ecclesiastical property or collections from other donors such as the emperor to endow titular churches they themselves founded, while, with the successive conversion of the Roman aristocracy, members of senatorial families such as Vestina started to found their own titular churches, the property of which they tried to control more tightly, as the conflict during the Laurentian schism shows. In essence, he envisaged a chronological succession of two types of endowment.[32] This assumption, however, is in contradiction with Pietri's own definition of the term *titulus*.

According to Pietri, the term *titulus* reflects a distinctive juridical status limiting the bishop's power vis-à-vis a certain foundation. The founder of

[32] Pietri 1989: 1043; for a similar view see Marazzi 1998: 29–30.

the church gave property to the Roman church, represented by the bishop, with a precise condition on how to use this property, that is, as a patrimony for the foundation. This limited the power of the bishop to use the property for other purposes. The term *titulus* therefore expressed the right of the donor to claim back the property in case of misuse. Pietri founded this explanation on the use of the term *titulus* in classical juridical language as property entitlement on the basis of a legal act, such as donation, acquisition by prescription (*usucapio*), or intestate succession, which could be brought forward in a recovery process.[33] However, Pietri's interpretation of the term only makes sense if the founder of the church also endowed the church, not if the bishop organized the endowment out of ecclesiastical property and various collections. More importantly still, it is also in conflict with what we know about the meaning of the term *titulus* in fifth- and sixth-century Rome.

Leaving aside the sixth-century *Liber Pontificalis* texts, the earliest reference to the term *titulus* is in an inscription of 377 mentioning the Titulus Fasciolae.[34] While we cannot be sure of the exact meaning of the term in this source, a letter of Pope Pelagius I from 558 makes it clear that in the mid-sixth century the term was used to denote a church financially and liturgically dependent on the bishop's church. From this letter we learn that Bishop John of Nola had asked for permission to sell liturgical vessels of the *ecclesia Suessulana*, which was apparently independent of the bishop's church. Pelagius refused to give permission, but advised him to turn the church into a *titulus*, which must mean a church amalgamated to the bishop's church, as it entailed that John could send his presbyters to say mass and to take control of the property.[35] While this case of course postdates the Laurentian schism and the supposed taking control of the titular churches by the bishop, it is often overlooked that a similar situation, at least where liturgy is concerned, is already attested for the early fifth century. Pope Innocent, in a letter to Bishop Decentius of Gubbio, dated 19 March 417, detailed the measures taken in the Roman church when sending out the bread consecrated during the episcopal mass (*fermentum*) in the following way:

33 For the appearance of the term *titulus* in juridical texts Pietri quotes Dig. 5.3.13.1; 23.1.7.7; 28.4.1.9; 28.4.30. Of these, however, only Dig. 5.3.13.1 exists (ed. T. Mommsen and P. Krueger, trans. A. Watson, *The Digest of Justinian*, IV, Pittsburgh, 1985: 184).

34 De Rossi I: 262.

35 Pelagius I, *Ep.* 17 (ed. P. M. Gassò and C. M. Batlle, Montserrat, 1956: 51–2 (Jaffé 976)); for this case see also Jones 1974: 341. For John of Nola see Pietri 2000: 1094.

Concerning the *fermentum*, which on Sundays we sent to the *tituli*, it is superfluous that you ask us, as all our churches are inside the city. The presbyters of these, because they cannot come to us on this day owing to the people assigned to them, receive the *fermentum* produced by us through the acolytes, so that they do not consider themselves separated from our communion on that very day; this we think should not be done for the *parochiae*, because the sacraments should not be brought over a long distance, and we do not send [it] to the presbyters at the various *coemeteria*, and the presbyters of these have the right and the licence to produce it.[36]

We can conclude from this letter that in early fifth-century Rome there were two ecclesiastical zones, an urban district with the bishop's church and the titular churches, and a suburban district with *parochiae* and *coemeteria*. The presbyters of the titular churches should in theory participate in the mass presided by the bishop, but, as they often could not do this because of their obligations for the people assigned to them, they were sent the *fermentum*. This makes clear that there had to be a unity between the mass in the bishop's church and the one in the titular churches and that therefore the *fermentum* had to be the same. This should also be the case with the (rural) *parochiae*, and the *coemeteria*,[37] but these were not sent the *fermentum* because of their distance from the bishop's church, and could produce their own. It is because of this preoccupation about distance that Innocent discouraged Decentius from introducing the Roman rite of *fermentum* in Gubbio, as in Gubbio there was only one bishop's church inside the walls, while all other churches were outside.[38]

This letter in fact makes it clear that already in the early fifth century the term *titulus* was used to denote a church inside the walls of the city of Rome that was dependent on the bishop's church. Yet, according to Pietri, in the fourth century, but also still in the fifth, *tituli* were churches independent from the bishop's church, as this is what the term *titulus* allegedly suggests. This paradox can only be resolved if we accept that Pietri misunderstood

36 Cabié 1973: 26–29: 'De fermento vero, quod die dominica per titulos mittimus, superflue nos consulere voluisti, cum omnes ecclesiae nostrae intra civitatem sint constitutae. Quarum presbyteri, quia die ipso propter plebem sibi creditam nobiscum convenire non possunt, idcirco fermentum a nobis confectum per acolythos accipiunt, ut se a nostra communione maxime illa die non iudicent separatos; quod per parochias fieri debere non puto, quia non longe portanda sunt sacramenta, nec nos per coemeteria diversa constitutis presbyteris destinamus, et presbyteri eorum conficiendorum ius habent atque licentiam.'

37 The term *coemeterium* most likely denoted not a communal cemetery but a martyr tomb and the relevant suburban basilica, see Rebillard 2003: 12–17.

38 Cabie 1973: 50–3; for discussion of the text see also Duchesne 1955: 169, n. 4; Pietri 1989: 1045–6; Saxer 2001: 508.

the use of the term *titulus* in Roman juridical language. An investigation into the meaning of the term *titulus* is therefore appropriate at this point.

In classical literary Latin the term *titulus* was used for a variety of matters, both physical and abstract, which were however closely related.[39] In the first instance it could stand for the material on which a text was inscribed, such as a label, but also for the heading of a book or a chapter. In abstract terms it was used on the one hand as a way to describe the character of somebody or his actions. Often this had a negative connotation, as it was usually made clear that this character might not correspond to reality, and could therefore be just a pretext to mask the real nature of somebody or his actions.[40] On the other hand, it could also denote somebody's fame or glory. The common element of all these cases is that the term *titulus* is used as a tool to classify somebody or something.

Roman jurists used the term often in a similar way as it comes up in literary texts. In a Digest text, for example, the jurist Marcellus deals with a wife who wanted to give property to her son. As the son was still under *patria potestas*, she transfered the property to her husband so that he could leave it to the son after his death. This, according to Marcellus, carried the risk that the order to pass property to the son could be perceived just as a pretext (*titulus*) for something that was really a gift from wife to husband, which was prohibited by law.[41] More often, however, in juridical language the term *titulus* denotes the reason underlying acquisition of property, such as purchase or donation or dowry, and is therefore used as a synonym for *causa traditionis*. Papinian, for example, deals with somebody who acquired something by way of purchase (*titulus emptionis*). Ulpian discusses a case of property reclaim, where the claimant stood a good chance if the defendant had acquired the property for example as a dowry (*titulus pro dote*) at a marriage to a girl under the age of twelve, which was prohibited by law.[42] Again the term is therefore used to classify, in this case the ways to acquire property, and sometimes also in contexts where the acquisition of property was contested. In no way, however, did it define the right to claim back property. In fact, it was the claimant who had to show that the cause of acquisition of property that the defendant brought forward was not a

[39] See Glare 1982, s.v. titulus: 1944–5; Lewis and Short 1963, s.v. titulus: 1875.

[40] See Sen., *Ep.* 45.7 (LCL 75.295): 'temerity is concealed by the name of courage' ('temeritas sub titulo fortitudinis latet'); Liv. 3.67.9 (LCL 133.228) 'under the pretext of equalizing the laws' ('sub titulo legum aequandarum').

[41] Dig. 24.1.49 (Marcellus) (ed. Mommsen and Krueger, trans. Watson, II: 711).

[42] Dig. 20.5.2 (Papinian) (ed. Mommsen and Krueger, trans. Watson, II: 595); Dig. 5.3.13.1 (Ulpian) (ed. Mommsen and Krueger, trans. Watson, I: 184); for this meaning of the term see Heumann and Seckel 1971: 586–7; Kaser 1971: 416, 1975: 282–3; also Berger 1953: 752.

just cause (*iustus titulus*). A donation or a bequest in itself was of course a just cause to acquire property, and, as we will see below, even a donor who laid down conditions on how to use this property did not necessarily have the right to claim it back, if it was not used in the intended way.

In consequence, the term *titulus*, if interpreted as referring to the transfer of ownership in the context of a foundation, would be used only by the acquirer of the property. Interpreted in this way, it was most likely the bishop's church which chose the term *titulus* for a particular church to express that it had acquired the church in question by just means and now was the owner. Significantly, the term appears in an inscription put up in the church of St Andreas Catabarbara that had been built by Pope Simplicius (468–483) on land bequeathed to the bishop's church by a layman called Valila, to show that the church had acquired the ground by way of inheritance.[43] Also significantly, perhaps, in the passages of the *Liber Pontificalis* cited above, it is always the pope who installs (*constituit*) a *titulus*.[44] If the authors of the *Liber Pontificalis* reported the legal terminology of the contemporary foundation documents, this would likewise show that the term *titulus* was used on the ecclesiastical side of the transaction.

The personal names in the genitive in turn, as for example in the case of the *titulus Vestinae*, might express that the church's right of ownership derived from a donation by a particular person, while at the same time honouring this person. In fact, we do not of course have to interpret this polysemantic term exclusively in a legal sense. As we have seen, the term *titulus* could also be used to recall somebody's fame or glory. In this way, the combination of the term *titulus* with other personal names can be interpreted as a reminder of the founder, or somebody else who had been involved with the church.[45] Interestingly, the ninth-century *Liber Pontificalis* uses the term *titulare* to denote the dedication of a monastery to the memory of a saint.[46] Interpreted in a legal way, however, the term

[43] De Rossi II: 436, n. 115 = *ILCV* 1785: 'haec tibi mens Valilae devovit praedia, Christe, | cui testator opes detulit ipse suas, | Simpliciusq(ue) papa sacris caelestibus aptans | effecit vere muneris esse tui | et quod apostolici deessent limina nobis || martiris, Andrae nomine composuit. | utitur haec heres titulis ecclesia iustis | succedensq(ue) domo mystica iura locat. | plebs devota, veni perq(ue) haec commercia disce | terreno censu regna superna peti.'

[44] See Guidobaldi 2004: 6.

[45] That not all personal names were those of founders is most obvious in the case of the *titulus Apostolorum*, founded probably in the late fourth or early fifth century. Originally dedicated to the memory of the apostles, it started to be called *titulus Eudoxiae* from the late sixth century on. Eudoxia is to be identified with Licinia Eudoxia, wife of Valentinian III, who in the 440s had renovated the church; see Krautheimer 1937–80: IV, 179–234; see also Steinby 1993–99: IV, 82–3.

[46] *LP* II, 54 (vita Paschalis) (ed. Duchesne): 'construxit ... cenobium quod et nomine s. Praxedis virginis titulavit.'

titulus must refer to the wish of the bishop's church to show that it had acquired the church in question by just means. It does not provide any clues regarding the origin of the patrimony of a titular church from the honoured founder of the titular church, or indeed any conditions the founder had laid down.

FOUNDATION AND ENDOWMENT: CIVIC EVERGETISM, CHRISTIAN CHARITY, AND THE LAW

Let us now turn to a closer look at the set-up of foundations where a founder both built the church and provided a patrimony, and the probability that this occurred. However, before we examine the actual evidence for endowment foundations in the city of Rome, a number of preliminary points of property law need to be stressed, in order to understand fully the control a founder could exercise over endowment property.

In classical Roman law up to the fourth century there was no concept of an abstract legal personality. That a foundation like a church or a monastery was capable of entering legal relationships, with the right to acquire, own, and alienate property, was recognized by law only in the late fifth century.[47] Legal personalities were either individuals or corporations, which were perceived not as abstract legal personalities, but as communities of individuals, albeit with tenancy in common.[48] What this means is that a church founder who also gave an endowment for its maintenance, or a donor of property to the same church, could not expect that the church itself became the owner of the property he or she endowed it with. Under Roman law a founder could only set up a perpetual foundation by indirect means. The donated object and the endowment supporting its existence (usually called the *tutela*) had to be transferred to an already existing legal personality on condition that the revenue from the property was used for the intended purpose. The same applied to a donor who wanted to give property for the benefit of an already existing church.

[47] For the legal concept of foundations in Roman law see Laum 1914: 1–2, 168 and *passim*; Duff 1938: 168, 194; De Visscher 1955: 197–218; Feenstra 1956: 245–63; Mrozek 1968: 283; Kaser 1971: 310; Goffin 2002: 35. Endowment property could of course also be transferred to an individual, but this rarely happened, as, contrary to corporations, the lifetime of an individual and therefore the unity of his property, was limited, see Laum 1914: 155; Duff 1938: 168. For the fifth century see Duff 1938: 173; Philipsborn 1954: 66–7; Gaudemet 1958: 301–2. See also Jones 1974: 343.

[48] For the Roman concept of legal personality see Schnorr von Carolsfeld 1933; Duff 1938; Philipsborn 1954: 41–70; Kaser 1971: 302–10. These studies show that, probably due to stoic influence, it was alien to the mentality of classical Roman jurists to think about legal personality as an independent entity that was separated from its members.

Under classical Roman law, corporate legal personalities included the *populus Romanus*, cities, and associations (*collegia*).[49] The edict of Constantine and Licinius in 313, which granted legitimacy to Christian institutions and hence transformed Christian possession into lawful ownership, conferred the status of a legal personality also on the bishop's church. The property of the Christians, belonging, according to the edict, to their *corpus idest ecclesiae*, was to be restored to the *corpus* and the *conventicula*. This should be interpreted as the universal church and the individual bishop's churches. Christians conceived the church as an indivisible mystical body on a universal level, which in theory also owned the property of its individual communities. Constantine was keen to express this concept, so alien to Roman legal mentality, with the term *corpus*. However, on a practical level he wanted to make sure that the property could be administered under private law by the bishop's churches, whose representatives had since the third century served as the point of contact with imperial officials.[50] He therefore conferred the same right to own property also on the bishop's church, which in this way became a sort of property guardian. In 321 Constantine issued a constitution which allowed the *sanctissimum catholicae et venerabileque concilium* to receive inheritances.[51] The terminology is not entirely clear, but again seems to subscribe to a notion of the universal church as a property-holder, albeit represented by the council of bishops.[52] Once more the universal church and the bishop's church appear as the two recognized entities, whose legal personality did not need any further explanation.

Constantine's decision meant that a founder of a church could now transfer any endowment property to the bishop's church. Yet, this does not have to mean that the bishop's church was the only Christian group a founder could choose as a recipient of the *tutela* patrimony. As we have seen, Llewellyn suspected that there may have existed *collegia* of presbyters stationed at the titular churches, which the aristocratic founders of the churches entrusted with the endowment property and who were independent from the bishop's church. While it is debated whether Christians used this form of legal personality already in the third century, as a kind of

49 Kaser 1971: 302–10.

50 Duff 1938: 175; Bovini 1949: 162; Gaudemet 1958: 299; Kaser 1975: 156–7. But see also Erhardt (1954: 39), who proposes that the edict of Milan talked of, or was at least understood as, the bishop's church and the single congregations inside the diocesis. However, he argues that this was meant to stress the diocesis as the property-holder, rather than the universal church, which ultimately enabled the bishop to become the most important representative of property administration.

51 *CTh* 16.2.4 (321) (ed. T. Mommsen and P. Meyer, 2nd edn, Berlin, 1954: 836).

52 Pietri 1976: 91; 1989: 322 n. 19.

strategy to be able to own property as a group,[53] we know in fact of Christian groups in the fourth century who were organized as *collegia*. In an anonymous work, the *Praedestinatus* or *Praedestinatorum Haeresis*, a catalogue of heresies probably written in Rome in 435, we read of the Montanist priest Hesperius and his wife Octaviana, who came from north Africa to Rome in the early 390s. They obtained permission from the usurper Eugenius to establish an association outside the walls of the city (*ut sibi collegium extra muros Urbis fabricaret*). Following this, they appropriated the tombs of Processus and Martinianus on the Via Aurelia, and were only expelled from Rome by Theodosius I after his victory over Eugenius.[54]

From this story we can conclude that, when the bishop's church had acquired its own legal personality, the only remedy to hold property corporately outside the bishop's church was via assuming the form of groups that were already recognized as legal personalities. It is in fact quite likely that fourth-century Christian *collegia*, like the one of Hesperius and Octaviana, inherited the model from antiquity. In pre-Christian times the voluntary association, usually called *collegium* or *corpus*,[55] was a common feature in Roman urban life, as individuals organized themselves for a variety of social, professional and religious reasons. Under the Republic there was at first total freedom of association, but owing to the involvement of *collegia* in mob riots, they were suppressed by *senatusconsulta* in 63 BC and again in 56 BC. A probably Augustean *Lex Iulia de collegiis* demanded individual authorization of *collegia* by the senate, which later became a prerogative of the emperor.[56] Officially recognized *collegia*, such as the *populus Romanus*, cities and, later, the bishop's church, had the right to own corporative property and could therefore become the beneficiaries of endowment foundations.[57]

A church founder who wanted to endow his foundation therefore could also have chosen a Christian group other than the bishop's church that was

[53] The legal rights of the Roman church in the third century to own property has been looked at particularly in the context of the development of church-controlled cemeteries in Rome. De Rossi was the first to argue that the Roman Christians, in order to be able to own property such as the first cemeteries, organized themselves as burial *collegia*; see De Rossi 1864–77: I, 101–8. This theory was dismissed a few years later by Duchesne 1906: 381–7. For an overview over the ongoing debate see Rebillard 2003: 55–61.

[54] Praedestinatus 1.86 (*PL* 53.616).

[55] For a discussion of terms see Ausbüttel 1982: 17–19; also Waltzing 1895–1900: I, 339; II, 139, 160; IV, 236–42; De Robertis 1973: 10.

[56] For a short history of the legal standing of *collegia* see Bendlin 2002: 10; also Kaser 1971: 308; Duff 1938: 103–10.

[57] Dig. 34.5.20 (Paulus) (ed. Mommsen and Krueger, trans. Watson, III: 175); Kornemann 1900: 429–37; Kaser 1971: 309.

organized as a *collegium* and hence able to own property, as the recipient of *tutela*-patrimony. Yet, it is doubtful whether this was the case where the foundation of the titular churches was concerned. To begin with, there is no evidence to support the presumption that the presbyters active at the titular churches were organized as *collegia*. Furthermore, the presbyters of the titular churches were, as we have seen, quite clearly at least in the early fifth century liturgically dependent on the bishop's church. This, one would presume, would not have happened if they had originally been organized as associations in antagonism to the bishop's church. Most importantly, in the fourth century we hear of Christian *collegia* only in the context of heretical groups and the evidence for their remit is ambiguous. We should indeed not forget that *collegia* continued, as is shown in the case of Hesperius and Octaviana, to need imperial authorization. Roman emperors, who, as we have seen, only promoted the bishop's church to the level of a legal personality, were interested in the unity of the Roman church and therefore will have been cautious about authorizing groups who might undermine the authority of the bishop. It is therefore unlikely that the presbyters of the titular churches, which numbered at least twenty-nine at the end of the fifth century, were regularly organized by the founders of the churches in the form of *collegia*.[58]

All of this is not to say that the members of late Roman Christian communities always had a clear concept of ownership. After all, according to their own scriptures, the earliest Christian community was supposed to hold property in common, yet at the same time entrusting it to the apostles.[59] David Ganz has shown how this apostolic ideal continued to be a source of legitimization for the holding of property by monks, clerics, and bishops.[60] Yet, according to late Roman law, the perpetual endowment of a church by its founder could only have happened if the founder transferred the endowment property to an officially recognized legal entity, which was most likely the bishop's church. In this case the bishop's church would become the owner of the *tutela*-patrimony, although it would be restricted by any conditions the founder laid down for its use.

When we now take a closer look at the practical situation in the city of Rome, we can note that evidence for endowment foundations is almost non-existent. In fact, reliable sources even reporting just the simple

[58] As Laum (1914: 167) shows in classical times we do not know of any Roman foundation which followed the pattern of a foundation of a *collegium* who was to be the owner of the *tutela*-patrimony, probably owing to the difficulties of obtaining authorisation.

[59] Acts of the Apostles 4. 32; 34–5.

[60] Ganz 1995.

foundation of churches by people other than the bishop are rare in the fourth and fifth centuries. Eight of the twelve interventions by Roman aristocrats mentioned in the introduction can be identified as embellishment of an existing church, most prominently St Petrus in the Vatican and the Lateran basilica.[61] As far as founders of churches are concerned, the *Liber Pontificalis* records two cases of aristocratic foundations, the one of the lady Vestina, and the one of the Anician heiress Demetrias, who at the time of Leo I (440–461) founded a church dedicated to St Stephen. This church, the foundation of which is also confirmed by an inscription, was however situated outside Rome, on the Via Latina.[62] We also know of the foundation of a man called Pammachius. It is recorded in an inscription, supposedly erected at the time of Leo I (440–461) in the vestibule of the titular church of SS. Johannes and Paulus, which reports that one Pammachius *condidit aedes*.[63] As archaeological research has shown that the church itself was erected at the beginning of the fifth century,[64] it has been suggested that the Pammachius in question was the senatorial friend and fellow student of Jerome, who became proconsul in 396, before turning to an ascetic life after the death of his wife Paulina in the same year.[65] This identification has been debated, but hitherto usually accepted.[66] Finally, the already mentioned inscription originating from the church of St Andreas Catabarbara on the Cispian hill records that Valila bequeathed *praedia* to the church on which, at the instigation of Pope Simplicius, the church was built.[67]

Apart from the case of the lady Vestina, which is, as we have seen, hard to interpret, none of these rare texts speaks of any measures of endowment of the new foundation taken by the founder or indeed of any further conditions how to use the property endowed. The silence of the sources both

[61] *ICUR* II, 4097; De Rossi II: 150, n. 19 = *ILCV* 92; De Rossi II: 151, n. 25; De Rossi II: 149, n. 17 = *ILCV* 68; De Rossi II: 55, n. 10 = *ILCV* 1758; De Rossi II: 148, n. 115 = *ILCV* 1759; De Rossi II: 438, n. 127 = *ILCV* 1637; De Rossi II: 24 n. 25 (461/468); compare above n.3.

[62] See above n.3.

[63] De Rossi II: 150, n. 20: 'Antistes Domini[—] celsa sacraria Christi | vestibulum decorat gratia pulchra loci | quae quia compta nitet primaque in fronte renidet | ostendit quantum numinis intus inest | quis tantas Christo venerandas condidit aedes, || si quaeris: cultor pammachius fidei.' The inscription is dated to the time of Leo I as it is believed that the cult of SS. John and Paul, to which the Titulus Pammachii was dedicated, flourished in Rome, particularly under Leo I, because according to *LP* I, 239 (ed. Duchesne) Leo I founded a monastery of SS. John and Paul at the Vatican.

[64] Brenk 1995: 197–9; Steinby 1993–99: III, 106.

[65] See Jones 1991–92: I, 663.

[66] See Brenk 1995: 202.

[67] De Rossi II: 436, n. 115 = *ILCV* 1785 (for the text see above n. 43). In *LP* I, 249 (ed. Duchesne) only Simplicius is mentioned as the founder of the church. See also Cecchelli (1988: 62–76), who raises doubts about the mentioning of Valila in the inscription.

about lay people founding churches in Rome, but more importantly also about lay people endowing their foundations could of course be down to an episcopal viewpoint of the surviving sources and a suppression of other evidence. We know in fact of a case from outside Rome, where a founder did provide a patrimony for his church and laid down precise conditions on what should happen if it was not used for the purpose intended. A man again called Valila, *vir clarissimus et inlustris comes et magister utriusque militiae*, and therefore probably identical with the donor of the land in Rome where St Andreas Catabarbara was built, founded on his property, the *massa Cornutanensis* near Tibur (today's Tivoli near Rome), a church, the *ecclesia Cornutanensis*. For the maintenance of the building, its lighting, and its personnel he gave the bishop of Tibur landed property in Picenum and near Tibur, but declared that he or his heirs would take the property back in the case that it was alienated, even if this was to aid another church in need.[68] The document recording this case, dated 17 April 471, has come down to us in a twelfth-century copy. It is often cited to show that lay contributions for the benefit of the Christian church would come not only in the form of one-off donations, which are so frequently recorded, but also in the form of foundations endowed with a patrimony.[69] However, we need to be aware of the fact that, at least where the city of Rome and its senatorial aristocracy is concerned, it is the only case recorded, and it is a difficult case given the late date of the transmission of the source in question and the fact that it does not concern a church in Rome, and not even an urban church.[70]

We should therefore also look elsewhere to understand the silence of the sources. A text which could shed light on the problem of why so few endowments of churches are recorded is the *Vita Melaniae*, which records the life of the well-known ascetic couple Melania and Pinian, members of the distinguished Roman family of the Valerii, in the first half of the fifth century. Written shortly after Melania's death in 439 by her follower Gerontius, the *Vita* records that when Melania and Pinian left Rome and came to Africa in 408, they set out to give away their property in Numidia, Mauretania, and Africa (proconsularis) without regard, by selling it and

68 *Charta Cornutiana* (ed. Duchesne 1955: cxlvi). For Valila, who is also mentioned on an inscribed seat in the Roman Amphitheatrum Flavium see Jones 1971–92: II, 1147.

69 Duchesne 1955: cxlvi–cxlviii; Gaudemet 1958: 295.

70 On Valila's 'unique' (*singolare*) foundation see also De Francesco (2004: 95–114), who discusses the legal implications of the fact that Valila reserved for himself the usufruct on the donated property during his lifetime, but not those of the prohibition of alienation beyond his death. See also Angrisani 1999 who argues that the document is not authentic, but is dimissed by De Francesco 2004: 99 n. 641.

giving the money to the poor and monks. The African bishops Augustine, Alypius and Aurelius were concerned about this and told them that donations of this kind would be consumed in a short time. To gain eternal merit they should instead found monasteries and endow them with revenues.[71] While Melania and Pinian submitted to this advice, as other lay benefactors from their circle may have done,[72] it is doubtful whether their model was very influential. At the end of the fifth century, Pope Gelasius had to remind lay founders to endow their churches sufficiently to ensure their survival, and still the fourth council of Orleans in 541 prescribed that any church founder had to give sufficient property for the maintenance of his church.[73]

Andrea Giardina, who has studied the case of Melania and Pinian, suggests that the reluctance of late Roman Christian benefactors to make economically reasonable decisions about their fortunes was due to their desire to commit radical acts of asceticism in the eyes of God, rather than to take moderate but more lasting measures. Any suggestions in this regard would have been met with perplexity, as was the case with the Roman lady Fabiola, who, according to Jerome, regarded a careful distribution of her money as a kind of *infidelitas*.[74] Especially, late fourth-century members of the Roman aristocracy were open to contemporary Christian teaching about the inability of the rich to save themselves unless they completely renounced their wealth.[75] While such ideas certainly played a role, especially in the case of fanatic ascetics, it should not be overlooked that in the pre-Christian sphere the frequency of endowment foundations was low as well, if compared with one-off donations.[76] It will therefore be useful to investigate parallels in the practical arrangements of civic *munificentia* and Christian charity.

[71] *Vita Melaniae graec.* 20 (SC 90)

[72] The practice to give rents rather than just money we also find with the Roman lady Anicia Faltonia Proba who in 432 bequeathed the income from her Asian possessions to clerics, poors and monasteries (*Acta conciliorum oecumenicorum*, ed. E. Schwartz, I.2, Berlin, 1914: 90).

[73] Gelasius, *Ep.* 34, fr. 22 (ed. Thiel, *Epistulae Romanorum Pontificum Genuinae*, Brunsberg, 1868, I); Orleans IV (AD 541) can. 33 (ed. J. Gaudemet, *Les canons des concils mérovingiens (VIe–VIIe siècles)*, Paris, 1989: 284). In the east, Justinian laid down a similar rule in NJust. 67.2 (538) (ed. R. Schoell and G. Kroll, *Corpus Iuris Civilis*, III, Berlin, 1972: 345); see Jones 1974: 342; Gaudemet 1958: 304–6; on Gelasius' concerns: Gaudemet 1974.

[74] Jerome, *Ep.* 77.9 (CSEL 55.47): 'Dispensationem pecuniae et cautam distributionem genus infidelitas vocabat'; Giardina 1988: 134–5.

[75] See Brown (2005: 17–20) and his discussion of the circulation of these ideas, going back to Matt. 19.24, among the followers of Pelagius.

[76] See Johnston 1985: 116–17.

Where studies on civic evergetical practice in the first three centuries AD have been undertaken, for example in Baetica, in northern Africa, or in Asia Minor, only a small percentage of endowment foundations are recorded.[77] An exception is northern Italy (Cisalpina) where 14 per cent of all epigraphically recorded donations to cities in the first three centuries were endowment foundations.[78] However, most of these were based on the provision of very modest *tutela*-patrimony. This is also the case with endowment foundations recorded in other regions of the empire. As a general rule we can note that the provision of large *tutela*-patrimonies was rare. The objects of foundations, where they happened, were mostly of a recurrent type. Revenues from the patrimony were used to finance the regular holdings of public banquets, games, and the distribution of *sportulae* and alimentary gifts. As Jean Andreau has shown, the institute of foundations was very often used not to benefit an external party, such as a city or a *collegium*, but to benefit the donor himself directly, especially to finance the upkeep of his tomb.[79] In northern Italy half of the endowment foundations aimed at the distribution of money and food at the tomb of the donor.[80] Financially demanding enterprises, such as the provision for the maintenance of public monuments, are far less frequent. Funds for the upkeep of roads and the heating of public baths sometimes feature, but we hear little about the maintenance of temples.[81] Yet, some foundations in northern Italy were also large scale and focusing on the maintenance of public buildings. The most famous example is certainly that of Pliny the Younger who set aside 200,000 HS for the maintenance of a bath and 100,000 HS for that of a library in his hometown of Comum.[82] He also

77 Wesch-Klein 1990: 13–14; Melchor Gil 1994: 79; Zuiderhoeck 2006. For the concept of foundation being alien to Roman mentality under the republic see Laum 1914: 250–1.

78 For the figure see Goffin 2002: 36. See also Mrozek 1968: 285. Duncan-Jones (1982: 136) provides an explanation for the frequency of foundations in northern Italy, which can be dated almost exclusively to the second century. He thinks that they were influenced by the system of government child support grants introduced in the reign of Trajan, which were organized as perpetual foundations whose capital was underwritten in land. This model was followed by private donors particularly in northern Italy, as it was a very prosperous region where investment in land was beneficial. On the imperial alimentary schemes see Woolf 1990.

79 Andreau 1977: 180–2. Andreau distinguishes between *fondations reflèxes* and *fondations non-reflèxes*.

80 Goffin 2002: 36

81 See Duncan-Jones 1982: 136–7 for the objects of foundations in Italy (171–84 for a list of sources). See also Laum 1914: 60–115 and 1977: 180. In Italy we only hear of two foundations, where the patrimony was used for the upkeep and maintenance of temples: *CIL* 11.6173 (after AD 100, Suasa) and *CIL* 14.2795 = *ILS* 272 (AD 140, Gabii). See Duncan-Jones 1982: 206–7; also Laum 1914: 60–8. See also Goffin 2002: 115 for the lack of foundations for temples.

82 *CIL* 5.5262.

established a foundation for the support and education of free-born children.[83]

The comparatively rare appearance of large endowment foundations is surely surprising, as we would expect them to have been an attractive way to ensure perpetual memory of a donor, which must have been top of the list of motives behind civic *munificentia*.[84] Several explanations for this could be brought forward. First of all, as far as the preference for financing regular festivals and banquets is concerned, patrons may have felt that these guaranteed higher visibility than provision for upkeep. Perpetual upkeep of buildings was also costly, and probably only a few patrons could afford it. Furthermore, those patrons who had families may have been reluctant to make costly foundations that reduced the size of inheritances. However, the patronage behaviour of the just mentioned Pliny the Younger could provide an ulterior explanation as to why benefactors might have been reluctant to venture into such an enterprise. From Pliny, in fact, we learn that it was the legal situation of endowment foundations, which, as we have seen, was based on the transfer of ownership of the *tutela*-patrimony to an existing legal personality, which put off benefactors. In a letter to his friend Caninius, who had asked him for advice on how most feasibly to arrange a foundation for the annual holding of a banquet at Comum, Pliny warned of the high risk that the property made over to the city for this purpose would be misused for other purposes, especially after his death.[85] Suspicion towards the management practices of town magistrates was a recurrent theme with Roman benefactors.[86] The problem of how to keep donations safe from interference posed itself of course also in the case of single donations, but, as long as these were made during the lifetime of the donor, there was a better chance to safeguard the interests of the donor. Legal sources show that problems mostly arose from legacies to cities or *collegia*.[87] Endowment foundations were by nature supposed to exist beyond death of the benefactor and were therefore, as Pliny points out, most vulnerable to misuse. Indeed, as studies have shown, the lifetime of

[83] Pliny, *Ep*. 7.18 (LCL 59.44–46).

[84] Johnston 1985: 106; Goffin 2002: 35; see also Laum 1914: 51–2, whose study shows that *memoria* is the most frequently mentioned motive behind foundations in epigraphical sources.

[85] Pliny, *Ep*. 7.18.1 (LCL 59.44–6): 'Deliberas mecum, quem ad modum pecunia, quam municipibus nostris in epulis obtulisti, post te quoque salva sit. Honesta consultatio, non expedita sententia. Numeres reipublicae summam? Verendum est, ne dilabatur' ('You ask me, in what way the sum of money that you gave to our townsmen for banquets, could be safe also after your death. While this is a honourable question, the answer is not easy. Should you pay the sum to the city? There is the risk that it will be misused').

[86] Galsterer 2000: 353–4. See, for example, Cicero, *Att*. 6.2.5 (LCL 7.446)

[87] Goffin 2002: 52.

foundations, where they occurred, was often very short.[88] This must have been especially disturbing for patrons, where the foundation was a large-scale financial enterprise.

There were of course measures that benefactors could have taken. As David Johnston has shown, problems of misuse could have been anticipated more easily if the cities or *collegia* were prevented from owning the *tutela*-patrimony, for example by using a measure like periodic payment, where the patrimony did not change ownership, but from the rents a certain sum was made over regularly, first by the donor himself and later by his heirs.[89] Pliny the Younger, as he explains in his letter to Caninius, seems to have come up with a plan of his own for his alimentary foundation. He in fact donated real estate to the city of Comum and then rented it back as *ager vectigalis*. The rent paid by him and by any other successive tenant was to be used perpetually to finance the education of the children. While the city of Comum became the owner, it was much harder for magistrates in this way to alienate the land.[90]

Still, we hear surprisingly little of such measures, which shows that they were probably not very popular. Most foundations were set up as legacies of a sum of money or property *sub modo*, that is with a command on how to spend the income from it. Under the institution of a legacy *sub modo*, the legatee obtained ownership directly after the death of the testator without having to fulfil certain conditions first. This made reclaim extremely difficult, as the non-fulfilment of the *modus* did not automatically imply the return of the gift. To safeguard a legacy *sub modo*, a *cautio* could be taken, that is security that the desired action would be performed, but not that the legacy would be restored on breach of condition. If no security was taken, the property could only be claimed back with a *condictio ob rem dati*, not in a vindication process. As the city or the *collegium* had become the owner of the capital, the possibilities to claim property back diminished, especially in successive generations.[91] There existed of course the possibility to petition to the emperor.[92] However, while imperial law at first stressed the obligation of beneficiaries to execute the wish of a donor, therefore safeguarding the donor's interest, the development in the second century

88 Laum 1914: 222–3.

89 Johnston 1985: 117; for this measure see also Laum 1914: 142. This type of foundation of course relied on the goodwill of the heirs and was therefore also vulnerable in a different way.

90 Woolf 1990: 209.

91 For the institution of *modus* see Kaser 1971: 259; Duff 1938: 168. See Laum 1914: 184–7, 191, 238 and Johnston 1985: 117–18 for the inadequacies of Roman private law measures regarding the safeguard of foundations.

92 Duff 1938: 168; Johnston 1985: 119.

was towards also allowing variations of purpose, including alienation of property, if this benefited the situation of the city.[93]

The legal problems surrounding benefactions for cities and *collegia* provide an opportunity for understanding the type of benefactions to the Christian church in later centuries. They show tensions between individuals, reluctant to relinquish their property unconditionally, and the institution, keen to acquire property which could also be used for other purposes. We will meet these tensions again, for example in 483, when the Roman senators accused the Roman bishop of not using their donations in an appropriate way. There is no indication that legal protection for the setting-up of foundations improved in late Roman law.[94] The same problems as before were therefore bound to come up when ownership of the patrimony passed to the bishop's church. In fact, in some ways it may even have been more problematic. In a civic context, members of the patron's family on the city council could have thrown their weight in to support the continuity of their ancestors' foundations against the threats of alienation by their peers. As long as bishops and clerics were not recruited from their circles, which, at least in Rome, did not happen until the sixth century,[95] this was not an option for aristocratic church patrons. Hence many late Roman benefactors may not have behaved in a significantly different way from their pagan predecessors where the practical arrangements of their benefactions were concerned. They will have preferred one-off donations, preferably *inter vivos*, to perpetual maintenance of their donations with *tutela*-patrimony. This may be one of the reasons why in late antique Rome we mostly find evidence for one-off donations of lay benefactors, such as those needed for the decoration of churches.

Still, we can of course note differences between pre-Christian evergetism and Christian charity, and precisely in the behaviour of the beneficiaries. As we have seen, Christian authorities such as the African bishops Augustine, Alypius, and Aurelius, and Pope Gelasius, were not particularly pleased with benefactors' reluctance to set up a *tutela*-patrimony to finance their donations. We do not hear about similar concerns from beneficiaries in classical times. On the contrary, most cities and *collegia* seem to have accepted gifts of all types, as they were led more by social than

[93] Dig. 50.8.6 (Valens) (ed. Mommsen and Krueger, trans. Watson, IV: 923): 'Legatam municipio pecuniam in aliam rem quam defunctus voluit convertere citra principis auctoritatem non licet'; see Laum 1914: 249; Goffin 2002: 40–1; Johnston 1985: 121–4.

[94] Only Justinian ordered the execution of the *modus* in general, see Kaser 1975: 98.

[95] Eck 1978: 581; Rapp 2000: 392–4; see also Pietri 1986: 115–16.

by economic considerations.[96] This, it could be argued, was a luxury that late Roman beneficiaries could not afford anymore. As reinvestment, especially of money into land, and administration of property became increasingly difficult, benefactions had to meet precise economic requirements and beneficiaries such as the church consequently had to become more disciplined about accepting them.[97] Yet, it would be one-sided to suspect only economic motives behind the encouragement of church authorities to establish more lasting ways of patronage, as much as it would be mistaken to attribute solely such motives to the gifts of late Roman church patrons – as we have seen, some, including Melania and Pinian, were anxious to commit an act of giving that would be the safest way to salvation. After all, the nature of the gift, with its ability to expiate sin beyond death, was different in Christian charity than it was in civic evergetism.[98] As Peter Brown has shown, in particular Augustine also tried to encourage more reasonable and longer-lasting use of wealth to prolong its expiatory qualities for the daily sinner.[99]

TITULAR CHURCHES AND THEIR ENDOWMENT: THE LAURENTIAN SCHISM

The synodal acts of 502 have been brought forward as the main piece of evidence supporting the argument that it was lay aristocratic founders who endowed the titular churches with property under strict conditions on how to use it. However, a clearer understanding of the nature of the titular churches and greater insight into the legal problems of controlling property passed to the church can in turn shed light on the patronage relationships reflected in the sources surrounding the Laurentian schism. The synod of 502 assembled to assess a number of accusations made by the anti-pope Laurentius and his followers against Pope Symmachus, amongst others the claim that he had alienated church property during his election campaign. Symmachus' opponents based the legitimacy of their accusations on a ruling of the Roman senate made twenty-odd years earlier, in 483, just before the death of Pope Simplicius, when the election campaign to choose his successor was running high. The clerics present in 502 read and subsequently discussed this senatorial statement. The senate, represented by the *praefectus praetorio*, *patricius*, and *agens vici* of King Odovacer, Flavius Caecina Decius Maximus Basilius Iunior, a member of the highly distinguished Roman

[96] Johnston 1985: 116–17; see also Mrozek 1968: 283–8. [97] Giardina 1988: 133–4.
[98] Brown 2005: 15–16. [99] Brown 2005: 24–6.

family of the Caecinae Decii,[100] had declared that, in the event of Simplicius' death, it wished to be consulted regarding any candidates.[101] Furthermore, the senate ordered in the interest of themselves and their heirs that

> no rural or urban estate, nor ornaments or liturgical vessels of churches, whether they exist now, or whether they, by whatever way, will come into the *ius* of the churches, should be alienated by the bishop who is to be elected now, or by those who will follow in the future, under whatever pretext or invented motive. However, if anybody of these will try to alienate any of these things under any pretext or invented motive, it will be regarded ineffective and invalid, and cursed be who does it, who approves it and who accepts it . . . For it is unjust and equal to a sacrilege that, whatever somebody for the sake of his salvation or the peace of his soul will have donated or securely bequeathed to the venerable church on behalf of the poor, should be transferred to somebody else by those whom it had mostly fitted to safeguard it. However, churches should sell, after rightful evaluation, whatever of the jewels, gold, silver, clothes or equipment will seem to be less appropriate for use, which cannot be kept or remain for long.[102]

What is puzzling, if we follow the models developed by Pietri and Llewellyn, is that in the entire text of the synod there is no mention on either side of violation of the rights of titular church founders (or their heirs) over the property they supposedly endowed their foundations with. On the contrary, there are a number of points which speak against a preoccupation of the senate in this regard. First, it is not clear whether the churches (*ecclesiae*) mentioned by Basilius, the property of which should not be alienated, refer only to titular churches, as he does not use the term. In fact, the only time the term is used in the text of the synod is in Symmachus' own decree where he declares that he wants it to oblige not only the pope, but also the presbyters and past presbyters of the titular

[100] See Jones 1971–92: II, 217.

[101] Acta Syn. a. DII (ed. Mommsen, 445): 'si eum de hac luce transire contigerit, non sine nostra consultatione cuiuslibet celebretur electio'.

[102] Acta Syn. a. DII (ed. Mommsen, 445–6): 'nobis heredibusque nostris Christianae mentis sancimus, ne umquam praedium seu rusticum sive urbanum vel ornamenta aut ministeria ecclesiarum quae nunc sunt vel quae ex quibuslibet titulis ad ecclesiarum iura pervenerint, ab eo qui nunc antistes sub electione communi fuerit ordinandus et illis qui futuris saeculis sequentur quocumque titulo atque commento alienetur. si quis vero eorum earum rerum aliquam sub quocumque titulo atque commento alienare voluerit, inefficax atque inritum iudicetur sitque facienti vel consentienti accipientique anathema . . . quam etiam poenam placuit accipientis heredes proheredesque respicere. in qua re cuilibet clericorum contra dicendi libera sit facultas. iniquum est enim et sacrilegii instar, ut quae vel pro salute vel requie animarum suarum unusquisque venerabili ecclesiae pauperum causa contulerit aut certe reliquerit, ab his, quos hoc maxime servare convenerat, in alterum transferantur. plane quaecumque in gemmis vel auro atque argento nec non et vestibus minus apta usibus vel ornatui videbuntur ecclesiae, quae servari ac diu manere non possunt, sub iusta aestimatione vendantur.'

churches. This sounds as if presbyters would also have been in danger of being accused of alienating the property attached to their *tituli*, which speaks against any alliance between them and lay patrons of the *tituli*, who together supposedly wanted to keep the property where it was.

Furthermore, the property the senate was concerned with in 483 was property that 'by whatever way will come into the *ius* of churches'. Interestingly, Basilius here uses the term *titulus* precisely with the meaning of *causa traditionis* – the way to acquire property. Further on, Basilius becomes more precise about the ways in which the property the senate was thinking about was acquired. It was property 'donated or securely bequeathed to the venerable church on behalf of the poor'. This, in turn, sounds as if there were two steps involved in the way that property would end up in the *ius* of single churches. The first involved a donation or bequest to the bishop's church and a second one the assignment, presumably by the bishop, of this property for a certain purpose, which could have been the maintenance of a church and might have happened according to the specific wish of the donor, but could as well have been just an investment strategy of the bishop in question. The property mentioned by Basilius therefore consisted of gifts or bequests to the church of Rome, which were donated or bequeathed on the assumption that they would be used for the sake of the poor and as such would contribute to the donor's spiritual salvation – which included, but not exclusively, their assignment into the *ius* of single churches. The senators were apparently not concerned about any more direct rights over endowments of their own titular foundations. They spoke as donors, not as founders.

Basilius' statement triggered passionate responses from a number of Italian bishops about the rights of lay people to interfere with papal elections, express anathemata against clerics, or dictate church law, specifically decisions on what to do with church property, all of which, it was viewed, was against the canons, although no evidence was cited. The bishops believed that the ruling of the senate by no means restricted the bishop of Rome, all the more so as no Roman bishop had subscribed to it. In consequence, they rejected the statement, so that no example could be set for any lay person in any city to try and judge about the use of church property, which was the sole prerogative of the bishops.[103] After listening to this discussion, Symmachus issued a final ruling (see Appendix).

[103] Acta Syn. a. DII (ed. Mommsen, 448): 'ne in exemplum remaneret praesumendi quibuslibet laicis quamvis religiosis vel potentibus in quacumque civitate quolibet modo aliquid decernere de ecclesiasticis facultatibus, quarum solis sacerdotibus disponendi indiscusse a deo cura commissa docetur'.

This ruling equally shows that the rights of lay founders over the property of titular churches and the bishop's wish to control this property were not the issues at stake in the conflict. Symmachus in fact practically repeats the senatorial statement of 483 and is even more precise in various respects. He ordered that no bishop of Rome, including Symmachus himself, should be allowed to alienate church property (lines 1–9). Symmachus even extended the definition of alienation to the granting of usufruct, which should only be allowed if the income from the property was used for the maintenance of clerics and pilgrims and for the ransom of captives (lines 11–15). Everything else could constitute an occasion for misuse, which might be an allusion to Basilius' rejection of 'invented motives' for alienation. Still, Symmachus does allow for the alienation of urban houses, if they are in a derelict state and therefore represent an unnecessary financial strain (lines 15–20). This does not, however, have to mean that Symmachus was trying to find a way for the Roman bishop to make some money. Rather, he probably intended to refine the ruling of the senate in 483, as he realized that urban houses did in fact often come as a burden to their owners at a time when the urban property market was declining and especially if these houses were situated in different cities.[104] Therefore Symmachus addressed the senate's grant to sell whatever is 'less appropriate of use', but while the senators were thinking of movable property (which Symmachus also includes among the objects up for sale), the pope added the urban houses to this list. Symmachus also refines the senate's ruling in one other, major respect. He in fact extends the prohibition to alienate church property from the Roman bishop to the presbyters of the titular churches, that is, to other clerics in charge of church property (lines 20–25).

It can therefore not be argued that the synod of 502 presented a landmark regarding the bishop's control over church property. On the contrary, Symmachus accepted the restrictions put on the bishop. The reason for this originates from the precise political context of his situation. The synod had assembled to judge the accusations against him of property alienation during his election campaign, which were based on the senate's ruling of 483. While Symmachus was keen to get rid of these accusations, he could not possibly approve alienation of church property for 'invented motives'. He therefore needed to make clear that lay ruling could not bind the Roman bishop, however acceptable the ruling itself was. As Wirbelauer has shown, the crucial detail of Symmachus' decree was that it was meant to

[104] On the urban property market in Rome at the end of the fifth century see Guidobaldi 1999: 57–60.

come into effect 'from today on' (*a praesenti die*). Therefore, although Symmachus now subscribed to what the senate said in 483, his previous actions could not be judged by it.[105] Furthermore, he even managed to turn the senatorial decree against his opponents. The extention of the prohibition of alienation 'to the presbyters of the churches who are around all the *tituli* of the city of Rome or who have been there' has to be understood as an allusion to his anti-pope Laurentius, a former presbyter of the Titulus Praxedis.[106] Symmachus, who in the course of the schism had lost control over the titular churches to Laurentius, wanted to make sure that if he could not use church property for his own sake, Laurentius could not use it either.

The ruling of the senate in 483, in turn, should also be understood from the precise context of its announcement, the election campaign for a successor to the dying pope Simplicius, which probably saw a high involvement of bribery. The main concern of the senatorial aristocracy might have been to keep in control of papal elections, in view of the accession of many of the candidates to the increased wealth of the church, which was largely due to the senators' own generosity. We can in fact witness the same anxiety in the senate in 532, when Boniface II tried to secure succession for his candidate, the deacon Vigilius (who eventually became pope only in 537).[107] The reference of Symmachus' opponents to the ruling twenty-odd years later should be understood not as an expression of the same concerns of the senatorial aristocracy as in 483, but as a tool to undermine Symmachus' legitimacy. There is in fact in the synodal acts even less evidence that Symmachus' opponents – whoever they were – were concerned about their rights as titular church founders or as heirs of these founders.

In view of this understanding of the synodal acts of 502, we need to ask whether we should also reassess two further pieces of evidence, which have been brought forward to corroborate the point that both the senatorial statement in 483 and Symmachus' decree in 502 were about control over the property of titular churches by either the founders and their peers, or the Roman bishop.

105 Wirbelauer 1993: 24.

106 For Laurence's career at the Titulus Praxedis see Wirbelauer 1993: 425.

107 See Arnaldi 1982: 25–8, cf. 25: 'la pretesa senatoria di interferire in materia di disponibilità dei beni ecclesiastici si tirava dietro l'esigenza di conservare al laicato, e in primo luogo al senato medesimo, un adeguato diritto d'intervento nella scelta stessa del papa, che i canoni, del resto, erano i primi a prevedere'. For the election campaign in 532 see also von Harnack 1924: 24–42.

This regards first the ruling of Pope Gelasius on church foundation in the 490s, which Pietri analysed in the light of the senate's decree in 483 and Symmachus' answer in 502.[108] Gelasius, in fact, in a number of letters to southern Italian bishops, deals with the possible interference of lay people with the business of the churches they founded. According to Pietri this shows that, as a consequence of the senators' opposition to episcopal dealing with church property, the popes started to issue positive legislation against it. The recurrent formula Gelasius uses is that the bishops in whose dioceses lay people founded churches should consecrate these, but also make sure that these founders understood that they could not claim any rights over the respective churches, apart from the right to attend the religious services held there.[109] While this shows that the pope did indeed harbour anxiety about lay foundations, it has been overlooked that Gelasius is referring in his letters to churches in the countryside, situated on the rural estates of their founders, and not to churches in Rome. What does become clear from the letters of Gelasius is that the churches he talks about were founded for the service of the founder and his family, who regarded himself as the owner of the church. One problem that could arise from this was that the heir of the founder would also inherit the church and could decide against its maintenance. In a letter dating from 495/6 Gelasius therefore advised a Bishop Valentinus, before he dedicated a church founded by a lay person, to demand first that it be donated to the bishop's church, that is under a clear transfer of ownership.[110] The preservation of ownership by the founder is however not the situation envisaged by scholars for the titular churches in Rome. The senators in 483 – or Symmachus' opponents in 502 – are not believed to own the titular churches as private chapels. We therefore need to be aware of using sources on patronage in the countryside to describe patronage in the city of Rome.[111]

[108] Pietri 1981b: 430–1; see also Llewellyn 1976: 417; Cooper 1999: 301.

[109] Coll. Brit. Gel. *Ep.* 2 (Jaffé 630) (493/4), to Iustus, bishop of Larinum (Larino in Molise), about a church built by Priscillianus and Felicissimus on their estate called 'Mariana': 'Nihil sibi tamen fundatores ex hac basilica praeter processionis aditum noverint vindicandum'; Thiel, *Epistulae Romanorum Pontificum Genuinae*, Brunsberg, 1868, 1: 448 (Jaffé 679) (492/6) to a Bishop Senecio about a church founded by a *vir honestus* Senilius: 'sciturus praeter processionis aditum . . . nihil ibidem se proprii iuris habiturum'; Thiel, *Epistulae*, 1: 449 (Jaffé 680) (492/6) to Herculentius, bishop of Potentia (Potenza in Basilicata) about a church founded by Trigetius (or Frigentius) on his estate, the *fundus* Sextilianus: 'Nihil tamen fundator ex hac basilica sibi noverit vindicandum, nisi processionis aditum.'

[110] Coll. Brit. Gel. *Ep.* 29 (Jaffé 704).

[111] As a recent Princeton dissertation (Bowes 2002) has shown, lay foundation of villa churches was a very big phenomenon indeed, which has however hitherto received very little scholarly attention in

The second piece of evidence brought forward to stress the concerns of the Roman aristocracy about the titular churches at the end of the fifth century is the *Gesta Praxedis et Pudentianae*, the story of the foundation of two titular churches by an aristocratic lady, Praxedis, and her father Pudens, in collaboration with a priest called Pastor.[112] Llewellyn identified this text as a lay aristocratic pamphlet against the pretensions of the Roman bishop regarding titular church property.

The *Gesta Praxedis et Pudentianae* are part of a cycle of over a hundred fifth- and sixth-century anonymous texts known as the *gesta martyrum*, which record the, mostly fictional, lives and deaths of the martyrs of the city of Rome.[113] Their authorship and production context are generally hard to identify. As a critical edition is lacking for most of the *gesta*, dating is mainly unsatisfying guesswork, often relying on linguistic and stylistic analysis, or on matching their content with specific events to determine a context of composition.[114] Llewellyn's argument of dating the *Gesta Praxedis et Pudentianae* to the time of the Laurentian schism relies heavily on the fact that the text features a prologue, recurrent in other *gesta martyrum*, which tries to defend them against rejection by the Roman church on the basis of inauthenticity. This, according to Llewellyn, is an allusion to the so-called *Decretum Gelasianum de libris recipiendis et non recipiendis*, a document compiled between the end of the fifth and the middle of the sixth century, which enumerates the writings approved and rejected by the Roman church, among others the *gesta sanctorum martyrum*.[115] To Llewellyn the *Decretum* shows that the *gesta* did not constitute an official church line, and that at least some of them were written at the time of the Laurentian schism to defend the expectations of the titular presbyters and their aristocratic patrons.[116]

its own right. In fact, other sources mentioning *ecclesiae privatae* regularly refer to churches in the countryside, see for example *CTh* 16.5.14 (388) (ed. Mommsen, and Meyer, 860); *CTh* 16.2.33 (398) (ed. Mommsen and Meyer, 846); Gaudemet 1958: 303–5.

112 *Gesta Praxedis et Pudentianae* (*AASS Mai IV*, 299–301; repr. in *PG* 11, 1019–24); Llewellyn 1976b: 418–27.

113 For a recent discussion of the *gesta martyrum* see Cooper 2000; the groundwork for the interpretation of the *gesta* was laid by Delehaye (1936) and Dufourcq (1886–1910), who particularly supports a fifth- or sixth-century redaction date.

114 See Pilsworth 2000: 311–17 for a discussion of the various attempts to date the *gesta martyrum*.

115 Decr. Gel. 4.4 (ed. E. von Dobschütz, *Das Decretum Gelasianum de libris recipiendis et non recipiendis*, Leipzig, 1912 (for its dating see ibid. 348)); for a discussion of the prologue, which also recurs in the *Passio Anastasiae*, the *Passio Cantii, Cantiani et Cantianillae* and the *Passio SS. Fidelis, Exanti et Carpophori*, see de Gaiffier 1964b: 341–53.

116 This approach owes a lot to a distinct and well-established strand in historiography, dating back to the days of G. B. De Rossi, and refined by A. Dufourcq and indeed Kirsch, which classifies the *gesta*

We can, however, raise doubts about such an interpretation. To begin with, scholars have brought forward the strong possibility that the prologue was a later interpolation into the *Gesta Praxedis et Pudentianae*.[117] If this was true, the conflict with an offical church line postulated by the prologue might date to a much later time than the original text of the *Gesta Praxedis et Pudentianae*. In this case, even if we accept that the *gesta* were written at the time of the Laurentian schism, their explanation as a direct response to this event would be less easily sustainable. More importantly, however, a look at the *Decretum Gelasianum* shows that this hostility towards the *gesta martyrum* should not be over-emphasized.

While the *Decretum Gelasianum* does discuss whether *gesta martyrum* should be read in church, its wording is far less disparaging than often presumed. The *gesta martyrum* are in fact listed among the books approved, and, although he subsequently classifies them as works not read in the Roman church, the author of the *Decretum* goes to great length to explain that this is due not to disrespect towards the martyrs, but to the anonymity of the texts and hence the problem that they could contain errors. Besides, the examples of *gesta* given, the *Passio Cyrici et Iulittae* and the *Passio Georgii*, do not record the deeds of patrons of titular churches, or indeed of Roman martyrs at all, which raises further doubt whether the *Decretum Gelasianum* was concerned about the promotion of cult sites which could rival episcopal power in the very city of Rome through these texts.[118]

as foundation myths of the Roman churches and sees the intentions of their authors as a wish to promote their respective cult sites; see De Rossi 1864–77: III, xxii. For discussion see Cooper 1999: 299–300.

117 de Gaiffier 1964b: 350–1.

118 Decr. Gel. 4.4 (ed. von Dobschütz): 'item gesta sanctorum martyrum, quae multiplicibus tormentorum cruciatibus et mirabilibus confessionum triumphis inradiant. quis catholicorum dubitet maiora eos in agonibus fuisse perpessos nec suis viribus sed dei gratia et adiutorio universa tolerasse? sed ideo secundum antiquam consuetudinem singulari cautela in sancta Romana ecclesia non leguntur, quia et eorum qui conscripsere nomina penitus ignorantur et ab infidelibus et idiotis superflua aut minus apta quam rei ordo fuerit esse putantur; sicut cuiusdam Cyrici et Iulittae, sicut Georgii aliorumque eiusmodi passiones quae ab hereticis perhibentur conpositae. propter quod, ut dictum est, ne vel levis subsannandi oriretur occasio, in sancta Romana ecclesia non leguntur. nos tamen cum praedicta ecclesia omnes martyres et eorum gloriosos agones, qui deo magis quam hominibus noti sunt, omni devotione veneramur' ('likewise the deeds of the holy martyrs, that gleam from the many tortures on the rack and from wonderful triumphs of confessions. Who of the Catholics doubts that they suffered more in the arenas but would tolerate everything not because of their own strengths, but by the grace and assistance of God? Yet, according to old custom by the greatest caution they are not read in the holy Roman church, because the names of those who wrote are not properly known and [the deeds] through the agency of unbelievers and uneducated are thought to be superfluous or less appropriate than the order of the event was; like the *passio* of Cyricus and Julitta, like that of Georgius and the *passiones* of others which appear to have been composed by heretics. Because of this, as it was said, so that no occasion for trivial mockery can arise,

What this means is that it is difficult to use external evidence to show that the *Gesta Praxedis et Pudentianae* were a late fifth-century pamphlet against the attempts of the Roman bishop to control titular church property. However, this is even more the case if we turn to the content of the text. There is in fact much to be said about its general ambiguity, which makes Llewellyn's interpretation problematic.

Most important for our purposes is the author's report about the legal-set-up of a titular church foundation, as we would expect the *gesta* to reflect the desire of a founder to protect the property from alienation. The *Gesta Praxedis et Pudentianae* propose two different ways to found a *titulus*. The author reports that a layman, Pudens, father to Pudentiana and Praxedis, wanted his house to be consecrated as a church and installed a *titulus nomini nostro*. This *nomini nostro* must refer to the person who tells the story, the presbyter Pastor. It therefore sounds as if Pudens transferred ownership of the house to Pastor. Although it does not seem, therefore, that ownership of the *titulus* was transferred to the bishop's church, the bishop, Pius, was involved in the running of it – when Pastor, Praxedis, and Pudentiana after the death of Pudens planned to build a baptistery, they asked Pius for advice and consecration.

The consecration of the second *titulus* also occurred at the hand of the bishop. Novatus, apparently a layman (but brother of the presbyter Timotheus), had left all his property, including a bath, to Praxedis and Pastor. Praxedis asked bishop Pius whether he could consecrate the bath as a church. Pius did this and installed a *titulus Romanus* there: *(Pius) . . . constituit et titulum Romanum*. What is different from the first foundation story is the reference to a *titulus Romanus*. In light of what we have seen above regarding legal terminology, the use of the term *titulus Romanus* seems to indicate that the church assumed ownership of it, all the more so as the term occurs also in the *Liber Pontificalis* texts.[119]

The *gesta* therefore can surely not be read as stressing either the rights of the lay founder, or the rejection of central church control. Furthermore, the text does not discuss the question of further property assigned to the foundation or preventions against the bishop's control over it. It is therefore doubtful whether this text would have been useful for anybody trying to defend the endowment of his church against episcopal intervention. Significantly, Pietri, who did not subscribe to Llewellyn's notion of the

they are not read in the holy Roman church. However we venerate together with the aforesaid church all the martyrs and their glorious sufferings, which are known more to God than to men, with every devotion').

119 See *LP* I, 170; 221 (ed. Duchesne).

gesta's inspiration by lay politics, argued that the *Gesta Praxedis et Pudentianae* reflect a clerical ideology, as they portray an ideal lay donor submitting to the wishes of the clerics and indeed bishops.[120] This shows clearly that the *gesta*, like so many sources, can be used to argue for entirely different things.

If we consider all of the above, we have to conclude that we need to separate the question of titular church foundation from the conflict between the Roman aristocracy and the pope that arose at the end of the fifth century. The synodal acts of 502 do not provide clues regarding the original set-up of a titular church foundation or the worries of the founders, as they were not particularly concerned with titular church foundation. In turn, we should proceed with caution in using the Laurentian schism as a background against which to interpret evidence such as the letters of Pope Gelasius and *gesta martyrum* texts, as there is the risk that they may have pursued entirely different agendas. Still, the synodal acts do provide an insight into the tensions that arose from the legal nature of benefactions. The senators in 483 were worried that their donations would not be used for their intended purpose and ultimately for the salvation of their souls. Although their motives may have been different, their legal situation was the same as that of earlier civic benefactors. With their donations they had passed ownership of their property to the church and now it proved difficult to influence its appropriate use. This only concerned one-off donations. We can only imagine how they would have felt if they had transformed their property into the highly complicated legal construct of perpetual endowment of their own foundations.

CONCLUSION

This chapter does not suggest that titular churches were not lay foundations or that the names attached to them could not have been those of their founders. However, what it is hoped will have become clear is that we need to separate the institution of foundation – the provision of money and land to erect a church building – from the institution of endowment – the provision of a patrimony, which perpetually maintained the buildings, the liturgy, and the personnel.

This approach allows us, first, to understand the term *titulus* not as a church endowed by its founder, nor even as a church endowed at all with its own patrimony for the maintenance of buildings, liturgy, and personnel.

[120] Pietri 1989: 444, 447.

Rather a *titulus* was a church that the bishop of Rome wanted to be understood, whenever it was legally questioned, as property of the Roman church. Where this property originated from a donation or a bequest, the name of the donor was added to the term *titulus* to make clear that there had been a legitimate way of acquisition of this property from the person in question. This interpretation of course leaves us with the question why only some of the churches owned by the Roman church deserved this special term. After all, we know of churches that the bishop's church owned, for example St Stephen on the Caelian hill[121] and St Andreas Catabarbara, that are not called *tituli* in the sources. Yet, as we have seen, at least in the case of St Andreas Catabarbara, the founding inscription set up by the bishop's church used the term *titulus iustus* to demonstrate that it had acquired the ground by way of inheritance. This should lead us to suspect whether we actually know of all the *tituli* that existed in fourth- and fifth-century Rome. Perhaps scholars have relied too much on the authority of the list of 499, while in fact the completeness of the list could be doubtful. Another possibility, therefore, to understand the nature of the titular churches would be to assume that all the churches the bishop's church owned in the city of Rome were called *tituli*, whether this is transmitted by the sources or not. A confirmation of this assumption is in fact provided by the above-mentioned letter of Pope Innocent to Bishop Decentius of Gubbio, which clearly distinguishes between an ecclesiastical zone inside the walls of the city of Rome, where the churches are called *tituli*, and an ecclesiastical zone outside the walls, where the churches are *parochiae* and martyr basilicas. The letter of Innocent to Decentius of Gubbio, as well as the letter of Pelagius to John of Nola, also seems to indicate that the institution of *tituli*, or at least the awareness of its existence, was not unique to Rome. Yet, we only have evidence of its continuous use in the city of Rome. While a full explanation for this eludes us, it could be argued that such persistent use of a legal term shows either that the bishop's authority in property matters may have been more frequently challenged in Rome or that he had better access to legal expertise to spurn such challenges than most of his peers.

Furthermore, provided that we can presume continuity between traditional and Christian evergetical behaviour, at least where the legal context is concerned, we can conclude that the property of titular churches, where

[121] As S. Andreas Catabarbara, St Stephen on the Caelian hill, according to the *Liber Pontificalis* (*LP* I, 249 (ed. Duchesne)) was dedicated by Pope Simplicius (460–483), but the actual founder may have been a member of the imperial family; see Steinby 1993–99: IV, 373.

it existed, was not necessarily identical with *tutela*-patrimony supplied by the founder. Of course, *a priori* arguments about evergetical behaviour in classical antiquity do not answer all our questions about the endowment context of titular churches. Yet, they make it harder to believe the conventional view that the property was always supplied by the founder. I would argue that in many cases it is safer to envisage the organization of the endowment by the bishop out of ecclesiastical property and with single personal contributions. Intriguingly, this seems to point to the fact that, at least where titular church foundation is concerned, we need to give credit to the accounts of the *Liber Pontificalis*. Of course we need to be aware that the *Liber Pontificalis* is an ecclesiastical source, trying to show the Roman bishop from his best side. The attribution of a foundation of the titular churches to Pope Evaristus in the early second century is a case in point, as it clearly reflects a centralistic sixth-century view on the genealogy of these institutions. It is unquestionable – and indeed corroborated by the other foundation stories the *Liber Pontificalis* provides – that the number of titular churches rather grew organically over the course of centuries. Yet, the very foundation stories in the *Liber Pontificalis* seem to record the circumstances of endowment quite accurately. The *Liber Pontificalis* without doubt provides only the papal side of the patronage history of late antique Rome. However, at least where endowment foundations are concerned, it may not have mentioned lay intervention not because the authors wanted to brush over any lay interests, but because it rarely happened. One could therefore even argue that the sixth-century authors, in this instance, showed a striking sensibility towards lay patronage behaviour.

All of this does not mean, however, that titular churches do not have a story to tell about lay patronage in Rome before the Laurentian schism. Yet the story might hold some surprises. Neither did late antique lay aristocratic benefactors in the fourth and fifth centuries refuse to donate to the bishop's church, preferring their individual and uncentralized Christianity, nor did they donate indiscriminately. On the contrary, the evidence seems to show that lay families did support the bishop's church. After all, as both Valila in his inscription in St Andreas Catabarbara and Basilius in his speech in 483 make clear, lay patrons usually saw the bishop as the impresario of their eternal salvation that they hoped to gain through their gifts. In order to support the bishop's church, however, they chose not endowment foundations with intricate and uncontrollable conditions, but one-off donations, preferably during their own lifetime, when the execution of their wishes could be monitored. In many ways, this must have posed a problem for the bishop's church, as a lack of endowment

foundations put pressure on ecclesiastical property to make up for it. One can imagine, therefore, that bishops would have wished for more lay initiatives.

The crucial issue is that lay aristocratic benefactors simply may not have trusted the Roman bishop, in very much the same way as classical benefactors had not trusted their city councils. The senatorial statement of 483 indeed shows that the bishop was perceived to abuse – however the senators defined this abuse – his ownership of property donated with certain intentions. It is here that the Laurentian schism brought a change in the relationship between lay benefactors and Roman bishops. In 483, the senators demanded from the Roman bishop not to alienate church property donated by lay benefactors. In 502, Symmachus submitted to this wish and turned it into church legislation. The synod of 502 therefore presents a landmark, but not, as is often presumed, of the bishop's control of titular church property. On the contrary, one could argue, it was a landmark in the history of lay benefactions, as the Roman bishop here set a precedent against clerical alienation of church property. This may have led, ultimately, to more rather than less scope for endowment foundations by lay patrons in the following centuries.

APPENDIX

Acta Syn. a. DII (ed. T. MOMMSEN, MGH AA XII, (1894), 449–50.

His ergo perpensis mansuro cum dei nostri consideratione decreto sancimus, ut nulli apostolicae sedis praesuli a praesenti die, donec disponente domino catholicae fidei manserit doctrina salutaris, liceat praedium rusticum, quantaecumque fuerit vel magnitudinis vel exiguitatis, sub qualibet alienatione ad cuiuslibet iura transferre, nec cuiusquam excusemur necessitatis obtentu, quippe cum non sit personale quod loquimur. nec aliquis clericorum vel laicorum sub hac occasione accepta tueatur. se nec in usum fructum rura aliquibus dari liceat nec data retineri praeter clericos et captivos atque peregrinos, ne malae tractationis ministretur occasio, cum liberalitate mille alia itinera reserventur. Sane tantum domus in quibuslibet urbibus constitutae, quarum statum necesse est expensa non modica sustentari, acceptis, si offerri contigerit, sub iusta aestimatione reditibus et divini timore iudicii

After we have, therefore, reflected on these we order in a perpetual decree with the attention of our God that from today on no praesul of the sedes apostolica should be allowed, as long as the doctrine of salvation of the catholic church under the plan of God will have been in place, to transfer a rural piece of land, however big or small, under any alienation whatsoever to the right of anybody, and we will not be excused by any necessity, although what we say is of course not personal. And no cleric or lay person shall be protected under an adopted pretext. But it is neither allowed that rural land is given in usufruct to anybody nor that that already given is held back, except for clerics, captives and pilgrims, so that a pretext does not serve for bad

commutentur. Pari etiam ecclesiarum per omnes Romanae civitatis titulos qui sunt presbyteri vel quicumque fuerint, adstringi volumus lege custodis, quia nefas dictu est obligatione, qua se per caritatem Christi conectit summus pontifex, ea hominem secundi in ecclesia ordinis non teneri. quicumque tamen oblitus dei et decreti huius inmemor, cuius Romanae civitatis sacerdotes volumus religionis nexibus devinciri, in constitutum praesens committens quicquam de iure titulorum vel ecclesiae superius praefatae quolibet modo praeter aurum, argentum vel gemmas, vestes quoque si sunt vel si accesserint, aliaque mobilia ad ornamenta divina minime pertinentia perpetuo iure, exceptis dumtaxat sub praefata condicione domibus, alienare temptaverit, donator, alienator ac venditor honoris sui amissione multetur.

handling, because there are a thousand ways reserved for generosity. However, only houses, in whatever city they are, because of their state of which it is necessary to sustain non modest expenses, should be sold, after the revenues have been accepted, if it happened that they were offered, after rightful estimate, and in the fear of the divine judgement. We want that the presbyters of the churches who are around all the tituli of the city of Rome or who have been there are bound by the same law of the guardian, because it is disgraceful that by the obligation, by which the highest pontifex binds himself for the love of God, a man of the second order in the church is not bound. Whoever still, having forgotten about this degree and God, whose priests in the city of Rome we want to be bound by the binds of religion, turns against present ruling and will have tried to alienate whatever is in the right of the tituli or of aforesaid church in whatever way (except the gold, silver and jewels, and the altar clothes both which there are now and if more will arrive, and the other movables which do not belong to the divine ornaments under perpetual right, also except of course the houses in aforesaid condition), this donor, alienator or vendor will be punished by the loss of his honour.

9

To be the neighbour of St Stephen: patronage, martyr cult, and Roman monasteries, c. *600–*c. *900*

Marios Costambeys and Conrad Leyser

Roman monasticism in the early middle ages presents a paradox. 'No other city in Christendom, save perhaps Constantinople, witnessed the flowering of monastic life as did Rome.'[1] The sources reveal a count of nearly a hundred monasteries founded in the City of Rome between the fifth and the tenth centuries.[2] Forty-nine of these appear in the roll-call of Roman ecclesiastical institutions included in the *Liber Pontificalis* entry for Leo III in 806/7 – suggesting that eighth-century Rome, no less than Skellig Michael off the south-west coast of Ireland or S. Vincenzo al Volturno in the Abruzzi, played a part in the heroic era of monastic foundation in early medieval Europe.[3] And yet, having enumerated the Roman monasteries of this period, there seems to be very little else we can say about them. Thus Guy Ferrari's (still indispensable) *Early Roman Monasteries: Notes towards a History of Monastic Observance in Rome* takes its title advisedly, as a warning to avoid disappointment on the part of those expecting a sustained analysis of the city's monastic life. The *Notes* are set out as a series of institutional biographies, in alphabetical order – but what Ferrari in fact shows is the impossibility of rendering the papal biographies of the *Liber Pontificalis*, and the evidence from other sundry documentary or epigraphic sources, into a coherent and satisfying fulfilment of his own scheme. In the fifty years since the publication of *Early Roman Monasteries*, no one has attempted to write up Ferrari's *Notes*.

This is, in part, a problem of the evidence. The sources which permit us to describe in impressive circumstantial detail the social matrix producing the great houses of, say, Fulda, Lorsch, or Echternach, simply do not exist for Rome. We have no Roman monastic Rules – notoriously, as Ferrari

[1] Ferrari 1957: xix

[2] See Ferrari 1957: 411–19 for a synoptic list of ninety-three foundations.

[3] See *LP* II, 21–5 and below pp. 270–4 for the list in the *Liber Pontificalis*; for an overview of Latin monasticism in this period, see de Jong 1995.

showed, there is no evidence for the monastic use of the Rule of St Benedict in Rome prior to the tenth century – no lives of saintly founders, and, crucially, no collections of charters.[4] While we can list the Roman monasteries, we are remarkably hard pressed to name a single significant Roman abbot or abbess. The canon of the city's ascetic leaders is short – Jerome and his patrons, Gregory the Great and his disciples – and it includes no heads of houses.[5] Not until the tenth century do we find great abbots in Rome, and then they are foreigners: Odo of Cluny and John of Gorze.[6] At this point, the sources for Roman monasticism, its observance and its patrons, do emerge with some clarity – but tenth-century reform does not apparently gather sufficient momentum to allow Roman monasteries to participate fully in the phenomenon of cartulary-making, widespread across western Europe in the eleventh and twelfth centuries. We must look instead in the capacious archives of houses well outside Rome, such as Farfa, Subiaco, and Montecassino for scraps of information about monastic houses inside the city.

But our inability to proceed beyond 'notes' for Roman monasticism is also to do with our assumptions about what monastic history is, and what kind of sources we need in order to be able to write it. Our perspective is most commonly an institutional one: we look habitually for Rules and charters. If the evidence for Roman monasticism is ever to be anything other than a source of frustration, a different approach is called for, and this may be no bad thing. Scholarship on monastic Rules is susceptible to a 'Whig' view of monastic development, a constitutional teleology in which all roads lead to the Rule of St Benedict, which conditions our view of the persistently diverse and ad hoc quality of early medieval ascetic living.[7] Meanwhile, early medievalists have become increasingly aware of the tricks played by the monastic archival memory: few would now seek to rely uncritically on monastic cartularies as 'documentary evidence', given that these collections were usually compiled centuries after matters they purport to document.[8]

In this chapter, we will take it as a working assumption that monastic identities in Rome emerge not through an institutional discourse involving Rules and charters, but associatively, in the patronage and, still more, the narrative of martyr cult. If it is Roman monastic immunities that we seek,

[4] Ferrari 1957: 379–406.

[5] Gregory was not the abbot of the community of St Andrew's which he founded. See Jenal 1995: 1, 268.

[6] See Antonelli 1950: 19–40. [7] See e.g. Dunn 1990: 569.

[8] See Guyotjeannin 1993; Geary 1994; Reuter 1995: 4–5; and now Pohl 2001.

we must go off the piste of the documentary record, and towards the forest of the *gesta martyrum*. As argued elsewhere in this volume, the *gesta* are founded on the post-Constantinian equation of the monastic profession with heroic witness to Christ in the arena. In the martyrs' defiance of the emperor it is possible to discern, sometimes with circumstantial precision, monastic claims to property in defiance of public authority – claims that we see articulated elsewhere in Europe and Byzantium through the medium of the charter.[9] We will suggest that there is, in fact, a patron saint of Roman monasticism in our period: he is the protomartyr St Stephen, deacon of the church at Jerusalem, whose passion is recorded of course in the Acts of the Apostles. The Roman *gesta*'s embellishment of Stephen's story can be used to fill out the lapidary evidence from the *Liber Pontificalis* to tell us what it meant 'to be the neighbour of St Stephen'.[10]

WORKSHOPS OF ROMAN MEMORY

'Institutionalization', in one form or another, is the standard explanation given for the emergence of the sources for monastic history. What we are taught to expect is a Weberian scenario of tension between charisma and institution, in which the oral, bodily evanescence of the former is replaced by the codified permanence of the latter. There are two typical scenarios, one internal, the other external to the community. In the former, the death of the monastic founder is seen to be the classic moment at which his or her disciples are forced to convert an implicit and magical understanding in which all have shared into a written record for future generations. More broadly, we tend to designate the routinization of charisma, and the emergence of an organized institutional memory, as cause and consequence of the passage from eremitism to cenobitism, or again the moulding of a large corporate enterprise like Farfa or Cîteaux from a host of smaller, less well-established communities.[11]

'Prophet versus priest' is the second classic *Sitz im Leben* for the generation of monastic sources. In other words, we expect there to be tension between the monastic movement and the ecclesiastical hierarchy, a dialectic of attraction and competition between a Bishop Athanasius and a St Antony, a Maroveus of Poitiers and a Radegund.[12] The bigger the

[9] See C. Leyser in this volume. [10] Cf. Rosenwein 1989.

[11] For Farfa, to which at least fifty smaller private foundations were given in the eighth and ninth centuries, see Costambeys 2007; for the imperialism of Cîteaux, see H. Leyser 1984.

[12] Brakke 1995; for Radegund's use of Caesarius of Arles' *Rule for Virgins* against the encroachments of Maroveus, see Klingshirn 1990.

place, the greater this confrontation. In Constantinople, as Gilbert Dagron has shown, the contest between great abbots and successive patriarchs dominated the first half of the fifth century, until the victory of the bishops at Chalcedon in 451, which sealed thereafter the power of bishops over monasteries.[13] In the west, it is often argued, bishops exerted stern control over holy men both in the city and in the countryside.[14] Large communities were harder to regulate, and tension between bishops and monasteries is seen to have animated movements for 'reform' through the early medieval centuries, and into the apocalyptic confrontations of the eleventh century.[15] Here, in a final reckoning between rival religious specialists, clerics undertook to observe the standards of sexual continence upheld by exponents of the monastic life, often in an attempt to steal the moral high ground away from monasteries. Conversely, in defence of the encroachment of their property rights by bishops (and lay donors), the inmates of monasteries compiled the cartularies that are our principal source for monastic history.[16]

In Rome, however, neither of these scenarios seems to materialize. The early initiatives in household asceticism at the end of the fourth century do not seem to develop into the formidable presence of urban monks in their thousands as in fifth-century Constantinople. This may serve to remind us that, for all their vocal presence, Jerome and Rufinus were less patrons than clients, an expendable and replaceable resource.[17] By much the same token, there emerged no stark confrontation between the bishop of Rome and any dominant monastic leader to animate the city's documentary or narrative life. In particular, the kind of infrastructure that monastic communities elsewhere in the west developed to fend off the interference of the local bishop did not take shape in Rome. Elsewhere, we find written Rules to vouchsafe the capacity of the community to discipline itself, and charters of immunity to carve out exemption from episcopal jurisdiction.[18] These are largely absent from Rome – and such evidence as we have for Rules and charters reveals a strong papal hand in both.[19] If the pope did not often seek to 'pull rank' with monasteries, it was partly because his own constant and direct involvement as an ecclesiastical

[13] Dagron 1970. [14] Brown 1971 is a *locus classicus* for this point of view.
[15] See e.g. Nightingale 2001. [16] See Lemarignier 1950a; C. Leyser 1997.
[17] See e.g. Layton 2002. [18] On immunities in general, see Fouracre 1995 and Rosenwein 1999.
[19] For the papacy and monastic Rules, see Paul the Deacon, *Historia Langobardorum* 6.40 (ed. L. Bethmann and G. Waitz, MGH SRL (1978), 12–187), but compare Hugeburc of Heidenheim, *Hodoeporicon of St Willibald*, trans. Talbot 1954: 172–4; for immunities, Marazzi 1998: 164–5.

patron undermined the tendency towards confrontation between diocesan authority and monastic autonomy which so preoccupied his episcopal colleagues in the west. The juridical triangle that sustained the development of the immunity – most famously at Cluny – between local bishop, local monastery, and distant pope could not take shape in the city where the local bishop was none other than the elsewhere distant pope.

The Roman record – and the pattern of its selective survival – emerges instead in the city's slow slide away from imperial administration.[20] We know that there were charters in the late Roman period;[21] there are a number of indications that a charter (if defined simply as a single-sheet legal document) was the normal way of doing business. Charters were housed in the municipal archive, the *secretarium*, situated *in vicus Tellure*.[22] Elsewhere in Italy, notably in Ravenna, some of this kind of archive survives.[23] But for Rome, none of it has endured: the fragmentary sources for Roman monasticism are part of a much wider absence in our record for the city. Very few Roman manuscripts of any description survive from before the tenth century.[24] Doubtless the main reason is the fragility of papyrus, which remained the standard writing surface in the city long after its abandonment elsewhere in the west. There was some awareness in the papal *scrinium* of the advantages of parchment. We see priests in the 790s transcribing the papal letters collected in the *Codex Carolinus* from papyrus to the infinitely more durable medium of animal skins.[25] Throughout the ninth century, however, Roman scribes in general followed some of their Byzantine counterparts by persisting with the papyrus of late Roman imperial style – with long-term predictable results.[26]

That said, it is still worth pausing to ask why, apart from the accident of fate, the Roman monastic archives are so poor. A great deal did survive into the modern era, only to be lost: to cite what is perhaps the most egregious case, three thousand documents and three hundred manuscript

20 On the transformation of the documentary practices of the Roman state in this context, see initially von Heckel 1908. On the general theme, see now Brown 2002.

21 The office of *chartularius* is attested in the *Liber Pontificalis*: e.g. *LP* I, 403 (Iordanes), 470 (Gratiosus). Cf. the inscription outside S. Maria in Cosmedin, which takes a charter form: first published and discussed in detail in Bertolini 1947: 143; see now De Rubeis 2001: 119 (n. 11).

22 See Chastagnol 1960: 248. 23 Tjäder 1955–82.

24 The earliest manuscript of Roman provenance of the *Liber Pontificalis*, for example, dates from the eleventh century: Biblioteca Apostolica Vaticana, Vat. Lat. 629.

25 *Codex Carolinus*, ed. W. Gundlach, MGH Epp. III: preface; see Noble 1990: 87–8.

26 On the continued use of papyrus in the Byzantine empire, into the tenth century in some areas, see Mullett 1990: 158.

books from St Andrew's (later St Gregory's) on the Caelian hill may have been dispersed or destroyed in the nineteenth century.[27] Although it is scant consolation, at least this reassures us that some Roman houses did participate in the making of cartularies that proceeded apace elsewhere in the eleventh and twelfth centuries. But (not, perhaps, coincidentally) the great era of 'cartularization' coincided with the high point of the reform papacy, which consumed the documentary energies of the city. In one notorious case, monastic archives were a specific target of Archdeacon Hildebrand. In 1072, a year before his election as Pope Gregory VII, Hildebrand intervened in a dispute between Farfa and the Roman monastery of SS. Cosmas and Damian in Trastevere (also known as S. Cosimato). He ruled against the Roman house, and charged its abbot Odimundus to send the records of the lands concerned in the dispute to Farfa.[28] We should not be altogther surprised, then, to find so many of our sources for Roman monastic history deposited with communities outside the city.

Before the millennium, the papacy had been less assertive, but we should still consider its intervention as the determining factor in explaining why Roman papyri, unlike the Ravenna records, disappear. Countless archival and editorial decisions must have been taken by clergy up and down the ranks of the papal administration. To take the best-documented case: under Pope Hadrian I, the fourteen volumes of correspondence produced by Gregory the Great's chancery – containing 20,000 letters in the (perhaps exorbitant) estimate of one scholar – were compressed into two parchment volumes containing under 700 letters. Hadrian's edition of the *Register* of Gregory immediately became the standard point of reference, even for those with ready access to the archived papyri. Thus in his *Vita Gregorii* (873–876), the bulk of which is composed of extracts from Gregory's letters, John the Deacon boasts of having seen the originals, but every letter he uses comes from the Hadrianic edition. There are traces that his copy of the *Register* differs slightly from those circulating elsewhere in Latin Europe, but John turned his back on the treasure trove of inside information at his disposal. Perhaps the papyri were already

[27] Gustav Hänel had seen over 3000 charters (as well as a *Regestum* dating from 844) at S. Gregorio in 1825 but, according to Ludwig Bethmann's notes as reported by Georg Waitz, these had perished 'in the French period': Waitz 1877: 361. Note that Bartòla (1989) is sceptical of the whole story, but offers an edition of the *Regestum* of S. Gregorio (Bartòla 2003), retrieved from early modern manuscripts. The *Regestum*, however, cannot help us in fill in the early medieval Roman documentary blank: it begins with a forged foundation charter of 590, and continues with documents from the late tenth century.

[28] See Fedele 1898: esp. 478, n. 3; and Fedele 1899.

too fragile to be easily used: all that we know is that, at some point after John wrote, they were lost or discarded entirely.[29]

It was in the sixth century, as argued elsewhere in this volume, that the papacy made the transition 'from memory to written record' and developed its own elaborate bureaucracy.[30] As has long been observed, the branches of its administration took their structure and names (such as the notaries *primicerius* and *secundicerius*), no doubt instinctively, from the later Roman empire. The historical irony is, then, that this profoundly traditional group of men were responsible for the initiation of a text as idiosyncratic as the *Liber Pontificalis*, the serial biography of popes begun in the 530s and kept uninterrupted for over three hundred years, until the 870s.[31] Nothing else like it exists for any other city in Christendom. This is not the place to enter the debates about the origins of the *Liber*, or about which branch of the papal administration was responsible for its composition and maintenance.[32] We would emphasize instead that the *Liber*, like the Hadrianic *Register* of Gregory the Great, represents an extraordinary effort of compression on the part of its compilers. As we comb its apparently capacious inventories of papal beneficence for the shrines of Rome, it is worth recalling that this 'archival' record represents a highly selective fraction of the business in which successive popes were involved.

In this sense, the *Liber* is less of an administrative document, faithfully produced by members of a civil service: we should think of it more as a highly mannered literary, almost liturgical artefact. Whatever its purposes as a training manual for new members of the papal administration, it also served as a public celebration of the bishop of Rome as custodian of the saints of Rome.[33] If the imperial *secretarium* is one context for the *Liber*, another is provided by the Monza papyri, the record of the shipment of ampullae containing oils from the Roman martyr shrines, sent by Gregory the Great to the Lombard queen Theodelinda.[34] This was of course a 'one-off' gift. By contrast, what the *Liber* observes is the inflationary logic of the potlatch – an upward spiral of giving, and then of recording the giving,

[29] Pitz 1990 for the estimate of the size of the orginal *Register*. John the Deacon, *Vita Gregorii, pref.* (*PL* 75.62) records John's knowledge of the originals; Castaldi (2004) identifies hitherto unnoticed features of the copy of the Hadrianic edition he used.

[30] See Cooper and Hillner, 'Introduction' to this volume.

[31] Noble 1985; Bertolini 1970. [32] See e.g. Noble 1985: 354–5 and the references there given.

[33] See Noble 1985 for the suggestion that the *LP* is a training manual.

[34] See *DACL* arts., 'Ampoules' and 'Monza'; Valentini and Zucchetti (1942: 29–47) and CCSL (175: 286–95) give the texts of the *notulae* (the list) and *pittacia* (labels). The letter, traditionally seen as accompanying the gift and ascribed to Gregory, may date from the papacy of Honorius: see Ammannati 2004. For general discussion, see C. Leyser 2000b.

with the notices for each incumbent of the throne of St Peter getting (in general) longer and longer.[35]

As the very emphasis of the *Liber* may betray, the pope did not have complete control of martyr cult in Rome. In what remained throughout the period by far the most populous city in the west, there was instead a dense and bewildering profusion of relics and shrines, monks and nuns, priests and deacons living in close proximity to each other and to the episcopal palaces. The clearest signs of this profusion are provided by the *gesta martyrum*, as jangling and unruly a group of narratives as the notices of the *Liber* seem orderly and (generally) understated. Tempting as it may be to cast the *gesta* as the charisma repressed by the institutional memory of the *Liber*, it would be unwise to overstate the contrast. The *Liber* makes no attempt to hide its interest in schism and defiance;[36] conversely, the *gesta* are not ignorant of the world of the archive from which the *Liber* is drawn. As Chastagnol observed, the *secretarium in Tellure* makes frequent appearances in the narrative world of the Roman martyrs.[37] Here is some encouragement for those, like the present authors, who seek to align the imaginary Rome conveyed by the *gesta* with the itemized inventories of the *Liber Pontificalis*, in order to generate something like a social history of the Roman church and its monasteries.

Overall, the conundrum of the evidence for Roman monasticism is a register of the curious power and weakness of the papacy as an institution. On the one hand, the bishop of Rome exerted an extraordinary degree of control over the media of ecclesiastical commemoration. For over three hundred years, the *Liber Pontificalis* seems to have pre-empted the formation of monastic institutional memories we see elsewhere in the west. Any arguments that there may have been between the bishop and individual houses or their patrons had little resonance in posterity. On the other hand, we should not take this near media monopoly to mean that the papacy reached into every crevice of the city's devotional life – far from it. If foundation charters or grants of immunity have not survived, it may have been because they were not needed by the grandees (such as the future Pope Gregory the Great) who let it be known that henceforth their dwellings should be considered as monasteries – a decision that could be contested by other family members, but over which the bishop had no control whatsoever. In considering 'the rise of the papacy' as an institution, we should

[35] On the potlatch, see Mauss 1967; on the logic of giving to the point of apparent self-destruction, Rosenwein 1999; and on gifts and the sacred, Brown 2003: 31–3.

[36] See Blair-Dixon in this volume. [37] Chastagnol 1960: 248.

remember – here as elsewhere in medieval contexts – that institutionalization was an index, not of surplus, but of a deficit of power.[38] Conversely, if we ask why it is that, after the epoch of Jerome in the late fourth century, we know so little about the institutional development of Roman monasticism, it may be because it continued, untroubled, in a late fourth-century mode – domestic, ephemeral, and beholden to the whim of the great.[39]

PAPAL *LARGESSE* AND ITS LIMITS

Let us return to the 806/7 list of Roman shrines in the *Liber Pontificalis* entry for Leo III; the list gives names, locations, and donations of moveable goods to particular monastic houses, alongside other institutions. It is, however, no Domesday inventory. For example, the list includes monasteries not mentioned in any record since the sixth century, and others appearing for the first time.[40] This should not be taken to mean, of course, that the former had been in continuous existence since the era of Gregory the Great, or that the latter were new foundations. The evidence overall is far too unsystematic to give comprehensive information about which monasteries survived right through the seventh and eighth centuries, which were revived, and which were Leo's own foundations. Yet to view this record as uninformative is perhaps to miss the point: it at least reflects the preoccupations of those who compiled the *Liber Pontificalis*, and the image of the papacy they wished or were able to project. What they did extract from their sources were the dedications of the monasteries of Rome – the cult or cults that each nurtured – and, quite often, the purposes of papal patronage.

The 'processional prose' of the *Liber* evokes a brilliant series of gestures of giving – the unremitting solicitude of the successors of Peter for the shrine of the apostle and the ranks of the saints massed with him in and around the city.[41] 'Brilliant' is in fact the right word for papal generosity: the lighting for churches is a constant in the patronage record of these centuries. Our evidence ranges from epigraphy recording endowments of St Susanna by Sergius I and St Peter's by Gregory II in which *luminaria* are

[38] See e.g. Warren 1984: 113–32.

[39] Rome, therefore, may have been more like Constantinople than Dagron cared to admit: see Dagron 1970: 256. On the powers of lay patrons in this period, see further Hillner in this volume.

[40] The best example of the former is the house known as 'Corsarum': Ferrari 1957: 96–9; Gregory, *Reg. Ep.* 9.191 (probably dedicated to St Symmetrius). In general, see Geertmann 1975: 82–109.

[41] To appropriate K. Leyser's description of the *Quedlinburg Annals*: K. Leyser 1982: 70; see also K. Leyser 1979: 104. Kalas (1999) usefully contributes to our understanding of the development of papal liturgy into the seventh century.

explicitly mentioned, to a donation to the bishopric of Silva Candida by Sergius III requiring that it intercede liturgically for his soul.[42]

The pope's liturgical commitment to the shrines of Rome was the guiding light of his energy as a patron of Roman monasteries. It was the monastic task to light and to give voice to the praise of the saints. This was not a foregone conclusion. The half century following the death of Gregory the Great witnessed the closest Rome came to a Constantinopolitan struggle between bishop and monks for control of the city. Between the brief lines of the *Liber Pontificalis*, Peter Llewellyn has convincingly suggested, can be read the outlines of a near schism on the role monks should play within the Roman church.[43] Gregory, the first monk to be pope, had reorganized the papal curia in such a way as to disrupt the established career structure of the Roman clergy, replacing, for example, the boy attendants at the Lateran with his own ascetic companions. Now, as various scholars have emphasized, this is not to say that Gregory pursued a 'monastic' policy in Rome, or elsewhere.[44] His goal was rather to alert both monks and priests, indeed all who might show moral authority, to the nearness of the end times and the urgency of assuming leadership of the faithful.[45] However, from the perspective of the displaced clerics, Gregory was indeed a disruptive 'monk-pope', and a clerical reaction ensued after his death, led in the first instance by his successor Pope Sabinian. In turn, Gregory's disciples fought to maintain their position, with two of them (Boniface and Honorius) becoming pope. By the accession of Martin I in 649, however, the clerical majority had definitively reasserted itself, and monks were sharply confined to the performance of liturgical duties at the main basilicas.

The Lateran Council of 649 which sees the tacit repression of Latin monks in the city witnesses also the emergence of Greek monks as a presence there.[46] Arriving initially as refugees from the Persian and Arab advances in the east, they cut a distinctive figure in Rome for three centuries. As foreigners, remaining linguistically distinct, their profile in the sources is, ironically, easier to pick out than that of their Latin counterparts. It is clear that they were already established by 649. Thirty-six Greek monks signed the Acts of the Council, including 4 *higoumenoi*; they seem to have been gathered in the first instance at two communities – Renatus on the Esquiline, and Ad Aquas Salvias near the basilica of St Paul's outside the

[42] Sergius I (687–701): *LP* I, 379–80, n. 38 and de Rossi 1870b; Gregory II (715–731): *ICUR* II, 209–10; on both see Marazzi 1998: 151–3 Sergius III (904–911), ed. Zimmerman, 1984: no. 22. On lighting in general, see Fouracre 1995, and further work in progress.

[43] Llewellyn 1974. [44] Jenal 1995: II, 830.

[45] C. Leyser 2000a: 131–87. [46] Sansterre 1983: I, 8–31.

walls. In the 806/7 list, six Greek communities are listed separately.[47] On occasion, they could be troublemakers.[48] However, as Jean-Marie Sansterre has emphasized, in general the Greek monks were keen to assimilate to the liturgical and devotional life of the city and to demonstrate their loyalty to the papacy.[49] In the course of the eighth century, as the papacy parted company with Byzantium, there was no 'Greek protest'. In fact, the iconodule refugees were keen to encourage the cutting of ties with an iconoclastic regime they perceived to be anathema. It may be that the pronounced and well-observed 'anti-Greek' stance of the *Liber Pontificalis* reflects the voice of embittered exiles.[50]

Under the influence of the Greek monks, monastic involvement in the liturgy intensified, in synchronization with the successive phases of papal history: the era of so-called 'Greek' popes (i.e. those between 687 and 752, not counting Benedict II and Gregory II), and the succeeding period, when the Roman aristocracy resurfaces in our evidence in the new political context engendered by Frankish intervention in Italian affairs. That this liturgy had a monastic stripe is confirmed by the *Liber Pontificalis* in relation to the activity both of the Roman Gregory II and of the Syrian-born Gregory III.[51] The former is said to have 'renewed the deserted monasteries alongside St Paul's . . . so that three times by day and night they should recite matins',[52] and with his restoration of St Andrew in Massa Iuliana and SS. Cosmas and Damianus 'arranged for both monasteries to chant praise to God every day and night in the church of God's holy mother' (i.e. S. Maria Maggiore).[53] Gregory III established monks next to the Lateran basilica (at St Pancras) and next to S. Crisogono (at SS. Stephen, Laurence, and Chrysogonus) expressly to sing in those churches, and at a council in 732 specified the liturgical services owed to St Peter's by the three monasteries situated around it, SS. John and Paul, St Stephen 'Maior' and St Martin.[54]

In the 750s, the presence of the martyr saints in the intra-urban liturgy was made newly vivid. Paul I had the bones of saints from the suburban cemeteries brought into the city and placed in '*tituli*, deaconries, monasteries and other churches'.[55] Concerned for their safety at the hands of the Lombards as he may have been, enthusiasm for martyr cult can be seen as

[47] *LP* II, 24–5. [48] *LP* I, 348; trans. Davis 1989: 73. [49] Sansterre 1983: I, 114–62.
[50] See e.g. Noble 1985. [51] Richards 1979: 278–80.
[52] *LP* I, 397; we have not distinguished here between the two recensions of this Life, which do not differ in broad substance here.
[53] *LP* I, 397–8; again, the two recensions differ in wording, though they make the same essential point.
[54] De Rossi 1854: 18. [55] *LP* I, 464.

an equally powerful motive for this move.[56] A wave of new monastic foundations followed, in which Paul took the lead, establishing St Silvester 'in Capite' in July 761. Here, finally, we have a foundation charter, which makes public proclamation of the purpose of the foundation.

Where I have established a congregation of monks for particular commitment in honour and in the names of the blessed pope and martyr Stephen and the blessed pope and confessor of Christ Silvester, in the place where their bodies rest, worthy of veneration. I have decreed it to be a monastery of male monks, that is to say in order to perform melodious psalmody, establishing that unremitting praises be offered in that same place to God our lord redeemer, and that the eternal remembrance of veneration of the same saints reposing there be celebrated to the divine power, and for the embellishment and stability of the *respublica*, not to mention the safety of all faithful Christians; and for the forgiveness of my sins I daily pour forth prayers, and to show the due and fitting honour to the same saints of God.[57]

The monks, then, many of whom were Greeks, were to celebrate 'the eternal remembrance of veneration of the same saints [popes Stephen and Silvester] reposing there'. This charter, one of the very few from Rome in this period, is a monument to the twin motivations of liturgy and cult that lay behind the monastic patronage of eighth-century popes.

By this point, of course, Paul's predecessor and brother Pope Stephen II had also sought external protection against Lombard incursions on the saints, anointing Pippin III as king of the Franks. This new alliance, which as Rosamond McKitterick has shown was a new departure occasioned directly by the Roman–Lombard antagonism of 752–753, immediately registered in the disposition of papal patronage.[58] In 757, Stephen II established six *diaconi* at the monastery of St Denis in Paris to sing

[56] McCulloh (1980) and Osborne (1985) both see Paul's move as a direct response to the Lombard siege of 756; the Lombard threat was not then anything new, however. We should also not dismiss the notion that some motive may have lain in the desire to respond to iconoclasm: Seeliger 1988.

[57] 'Ubi congregationem constitui monachorum speciali censura in honorem et in nomine beatorum Stephani papae et martyris atque Silvestri papae et confessoris Christi, in quo veneranda eorum quiescunt corpora. Monasterium virorum monachorum esse censui, scilicet ad modulationis exercendam psalmodiam, in perpetuum esse decrevi, constituens sedulas ibidem domino Deo redemptori nostro referri laudes, et aeternam eorumdem sanctorum illic quiescentium venerationis memoriam ad gloriam divinae potentiae celebrari, atque pro dilatatione atque stabilitate reipublicae nec non et salute omnium fidelium christianorum, et ob meorum veniam delictorum quotidians fundi preces, et debitum et condecentem eisdem omnibus Dei sanctis exhibere honorem': Federici 1899: 257–8, no. 1, issued 4 July 761 (our trans.); for its reliability, *ibid.* 243–6 and Ferrari 1957: 306.

[58] For a crucial and convincing reinterpretation of the papacy's turn to Pippin III in the 750s, see McKitterick 2004: 133–55, and Becher 2004.

masses,[59] and to its abbot Fulrad, Pippin III's principal Italian envoy, he granted two buildings near St Peter's: a *hospitale* (a pilgrim hostel), and a house that had formerly belonged to a local monk. The *hospitale*, according to the pope's letter, had previously been the property of none other than the Lombard king Ratchis, who had himself retired to a monastery in 749, but who at the time of the pope's grant to Fulrad was making an (ultimately unsuccessful) bid to recover his throne.[60] Under Paul I and Stephen III, martyrs' relics began to leave Rome altogether for the first time, to travel north of the Alps, partly at the behest of Fulrad of St Denis.[61]

The new protectors, however, could go too far. So acquisitive were Frankish relic hunters that a reaction occurred in the pontificate of Hadrian, who declared himself unwilling to see holy bodies further disturbed. A moratorium was imposed, which lasted until 826.[62] Internal translations, into the city from the suburbs (and possibly the other way round), continued. Hadrian, in fact, embarked upon an intensive programme of monastic patronage, outdoing his predecessors in ambition. According to the *Liber Pontificalis*, Hadrian reappointed a community at St Stephen 'Maior' at the Vatican, rebuilt St Eugenia and the monastery of Pope Honorius at the Lateran, restored the house dedicated to St Victor at St Pancras, restored and amalgamated St Laurence in Pallacinis and St Stephen in Vagauda, 'freshly dedicated and established' the monastery of SS. Hadrian and Laurence, and restored St Anastasius after it was destroyed by fire.[63]

In the list of 806/7 (which was independently composed and then tipped into the *Liber* entry) Hadrian's successor Leo sought to establish some kind of hierarchy in the reshuffled sacred geography of the city. The list aspires to cover all ecclesiastical institutions and their sacred patrons; it

59 *Regesta Pontificum Romanorum*, no. 2332 (ed. P. Jaffé, 2nd edn, ed. S. Loewenfeld, F. Kaltenbrunner and P. Ewald, 2 vols., Berlin, 1885–88); a letter not included in the *Codex Carolinus*, dated 757, printed in *PL* 89.1018 (no. XI). For Roman chant in this period, see Bede's report of John the Chanter: *HE* 4.18 (ed. and trans. B. Colgrave and R. A. B. Mynors, Oxford 1969).

60 *Regesta Pontificum Romanorum* no. 2333 (ed. Jaffé), also not included in the *Codex Carolinus*: its full text is in *PL* 89.1013 (no. VIII); see now Schieffer 2000: 287–9. Again, it is tempting to speculate how a Lombard king acquired such property in the heart of papal Rome. His presence there need not be too surprising – the existence of the *schola Langobardorum* shows that he was certainly not the only Lombard in the city – but the context in which the pope deprived him of property suggests that it was orginally granted from the papal patrimony in connection with Ratchis' monachization. Its passing on to Fulrad cannot be unrelated to his closeness to Pippin III.

61 Smith 2000a: 321–2 and 335–6. 62 Smith 2000a: 322–3.

63 *LP* I, 501 (St Stephen 'Maior'), I, 510 (St Eugenia), I, 506 (Honorius), I, 508 (St Victor), I, 507 (St Laurence in Pallacinis and St Stephen in Vagauda), I, 511 (Hadrian and Laurence), I, 512–13 (St Anastasius).

ranks New Testament saints first, and then cults fostered in the monasteries embellished or founded in this period.[64] The ranking principles have bemused modern scholars, who see 'a curious compromise between the importance of the church's status ... and the importance of the saint to whom the building was dedicated'.[65] We would argue that this compromise is far from 'curious', but reflects precisely the balance in the Lateran between the two forces driving patronage: the needs of the administrative hierarchy and the demands of cult veneration. To the papacy, it was ultimately more important to be seen to be giving in profusion than in an orderly way.

The concern of the *Liber Pontificalis* with unbounded papal generosity speaks to an awareness that the reach of the pope as a donor had real and severe limits. There were other monastic influences and patrons from beyond Rome who impinged upon the city in a way the papacy could not control. This is evident from the example of the abbey of Farfa, founded at the end of the seventh century in a political grey area between the Roman *ducatus* and the Lombard duchy of Spoleto. Farfa's eleventh-century chronicle indicates that it already held property in the city in the ninth century, in the 'Scorticlaria' district to the north of the modern Piazza Navona and in the former Thermae Alexandrinae to its east.[66] By the tenth century this area was home to S. Maria Cella Farfae and the neighbouring St Benedict de Thermis.[67] In 998 ownership of these two religious establishments was being contested by the church of St Eustathius in Platana (the modern S. Eustachio).[68] By this point also the abbey was disposing of property in the heart of the Leonine city itself without any intervention by the pope.[69]

64 Geertmann 1975: 82–109. 65 Davis 1992: 175.

66 *Il Chronicon Farfense di Gregorio di Catino* 1.248 (ed. U. Balzani, 2 vols., Rome, 1903) refers to 'infra Romam, terram et campum Agonis cum casis, hortis et criptis ... [followed by list of four named tenants]', part of a list of the properties that (according to Farfa's archivist Gregory of Catino, writing at the end of the eleventh century) had belonged to the abbey before its sack by the Saracens in 897. For the locations, see Fiore Cavaliere 1978, Sanfilippo 1980 and Manselli 1981. Stroll (1997: 32–3) prefers to date the foundation of Farfa's *cella* after the abandonment of the abbey to the Saracens in 897; but Gregory of Catino seems clear that the abbey held properties in the area before that date.

67 Ferrari 1957: 64–5.

68 Gregory of Catino, *Regestum Farfense* 3.426 (ed. I. Giorgi and U. Balzani, *Il Regesto di Farfa*, 5 vols., Rome, 1879–1914) (= *Il Chronicon Farfense di Gregorio di Catino* 2.18 (ed. Balzani), a *placitum* charter of 998: 'duas ecclesias Sanctae Mariae et Sancti Benedicti aedificatas iuxta Thermis Alexandrinis.'

69 *Il Chronicon Farfense di Gregorio di Catino* 1.315 (ed. Balzani) (= *Liber Largitorius vel notarii monasterii Pharphensis*, ed. G. Zucchetti 2 vols., Rome, 1913: 34): 'pro argenti unciis .iiii. dedit foris portam Beati Petri Apostoli, intra civitatem novam quae vocatur Leoniana, iuxta muros ipsius: ab uno latere hortus Sancti Stephani maioris, ab alio Sanctorum iohannis et Pauli, a tertio latere hortus diaconiae Sancti Silvestri et Martini, a quarto murus predictae civitatis'. Given these bounds, it is likely that the land was just behind and to the north of St Peter's.

While it is unclear precisely how Farfa first became established in the city, it need not have done so at papal instigation. The only pope we know to have made grants to Farfa was Hadrian, who made an extensive donation to the abbey at some point in his pontificate, and who had made a grant of land to at least one other landholder in the region of the monastery before January 776.[70] Neither grant was of property in Rome itself. Furthermore, these grants must be seen as part of an attempt by Hadrian to get Farfa to recognize papal lordship through paying an annual *pensio* in return. In other words, they emphasize emphatically that papal 'patronage', in line with early medieval practice, was essentially reciprocal, offering the grantee little hope of vindicating absolute rights of ownership over the property transferred; the papacy was using patronage of Farfa as a vehicle for its rather speculative claims to lordship in Farfa's region, the Sabina.[71] The abbey's ultimate success in resisting those claims means that, whatever their origin, its property in Rome was a conduit of influence from a monastic source that did not bear a papal imprint.

Within the city itself, there are monasteries – distinguished as such in the papal sources – that are recorded in existence in the seventh and eighth centuries without ever being targets of papal largesse. Gregory I's own monastery on the Caelian hill was one; others were the monastery of St Anastasius near St Paul's outside the walls, the *monasterium Corsarum*, St Erasmus, Renatus on the Esquiline, and St Saba.[72] Here we are back in the terrain of the Greek monks, and with the question of their assimilation to the cultic life of the city. While there are some churches, such as S. Maria Antiqua with its lavish fresco cycle, which show continuing devotion to Greek saints, there are others, such as St Saba, where Roman martyr piety was in full flow.[73] The frescoes here depict Sebastian, Laurence, and the protomartyr Stephen. As we shall see, Rome boasted of the translation of Stephen's relics from Constantinople: given the ferocity of some refugees' disdain for the regime they had abandoned, it is not impossible that this was a claim supported or even advanced by Greek monks.

70 Gregory of Catino, *Regestum Farfense* 2.224 (ed. Giorgi and Balzani); *Codice diplomatico longobardo*, V, no. 66 (ed. H. Zielinski, *Fonti per la storia d'Italia* 66, Rome, 1986) for a donation to the abbey by one Lupus of land transferred to him by the pope. For both, see further Costambeys forthcoming: chapter 8.

71 Marazzi 1998: 166–76; Costambeys 2007: chapter 8.

72 Respectively, Ferrari 1975: 33–48, 96–9, 119–31, 276–80, 281–90.

73 Sansterre 1983: I, 155.

CLAIMS ON THE RELICS OF ST STEPHEN

St Stephen may indeed be called the patron saint of Roman monasticism. Six of the forty-nine monastic establishments in the 806/7 list are dedicated to Stephen – more than for any other saint, and one more than the five dedicated to Mary (and this does not include the monastery at S. Crisogono dedicated to Stephen, Laurence, and Chrysogonus, and the amalgamated St Stephen in Vagauda and St Laurence in Pallacinis).[74] Every major basilica has an adjacent monastery of St Stephen's: there is one next to the Lateran, two at St Peter's, one at St Paul's, and one at St Laurence's (and, in the next section of the list, the otherwise unknown St Stephen's oratory in Dulcitius). The *Liber Pontificalis* does not explain why this should have been so, and modern scholars, while noting the phenomenon, have been similarly shy.[75]

Attention to Stephen seems to have been especially concentrated towards the end of the eighth century. Years ago, recalled Pope Hadrian's biographer in the *Liber Pontificalis*, the atrium of the basilica of St Paul's 'had been very desolate, and the grass that grew there was attracting oxen and horses to graze'.[76] Besides these animals, the other inhabitants of the basilica were monks, in a community dedicated to St Stephen. Soon after his accession in 772, Pope Hadrian I made haste to have the atrium paved with marble, so initiating a programme of restoration which was to attract some distinguished patrons.[77] In the early years of the papacy of Leo III, we find Alcuin, Angilbert of St Riquier, Arno of Salzburg, and Charlemagne, king of the Franks, engaged in a lively correspondence on the *causa sancti Pauli*, and specifically the monastery of St Stephen. Described by Ferrari as 'a phase in the monastery's history which is most important for a just appraisal of Roman monasticism', Charlemagne's intervention at St Paul's has been seen as a harbinger of Carolingian monastic reform under Louis

[74] The count of six in the 806/7 list does include two that do not appear earlier: St Stephen at the Lateran (see Ferrari 1975: 315–18) and St Stephen at S. Lorenzo fuori le mura (Ferrari 1975: 182–9).

[75] Llewellyn 1971: 137. [76] *LP* I, 499, trans. Davis: 144.

[77] Similarly at St Peter's, seeing the monastery of St Stephen's had been 'largely inactive, neglected, and uncared for, and no office for worshipping God was being maintained there', Hadrian put the community on a new footing, with a new abbot and a clear set of liturgical duties. Note though that the element of reconstruction may be overdone – a controverted matter. Edmund Thomas and Christian Witschel (1992) have argued that, in classical inscription, the claim to reconstruct is a tendentious one. When it comes to the early middle ages, and in particular to the *Liber Pontificalis*, on the other hand, we find a vocabulary of reconstruction that is corroborated by external evidence. If anything, in fact, recent work has suggested that *LP* authors' depictions of the city's dilapidation were exaggerated, precisely in order to emphasize papal efforts at reconstruction: see Coates Stephens 1997 and now Bauer 2004, with reference to S. Paolo fuori le mura at 190.

the Pious, and, further still into the future, the Cluniac reform movement of the mid-tenth century.[78] Such an ambitious interpretation, however, misses a more immediate point. We will suggest that the 'reform' at St Stephen's has to do with the Roman investment in his cult, and the polite but firm holding at bay of Carolingian outside interest.

Stephen the Protomartyr carried many associations in Carolingian Europe. His relics had come to light in Palestine in 415, at the Synod of Diospolis. Their dramatic discovery was immediately broadcast around the Mediterranean in an eye-witness account, the *Revelatio Stephani*, which we know to have been circulating in the late eighth century. A number of other texts – some of them, like Augustine's *City of God*, very well known at Charlemagne's court – allowed early medieval readers to chart the astonishing impact of Stephen's relics across the late Roman Mediterranean.[79] His cult attracted the attentions of patrons of, literally, the highest order: the empresses Pulcheria and Athenais-Eudokia vied to outdo each other in the construction of shrines to house his relics.[80] In north Africa, we can see that the cult went right down the social scale, to the local dignatories of the churches at Uzalis, Calama, and Hippo, and their dependants. The cures at Stephen shrines across the province caused Augustine to change his mind about the incidence of miracles in the post-apostolic period. His amazement is palpable in the Easter sermons of 426, rewritten within months as a chapter of Book Twenty-Two of the *City of God*, a narrative segment which was to circulate independently of the *City of God* as a whole.[81] It was Augustine who gave a monastic gloss to the cult of Stephen, emphasizing to his audience the connection between Stephen's witness and the Jerusalem community that he served, whose community of property was the model for Augustine's monastery at Hippo and his episcopal household.[82]

At Rome, these various channels of Stephen patronage converged.[83] The first lay founder of a church in Rome recorded in the *Liber Pontificalis* is Anicia Demetrias, a protégé of Augustine and recipient of Augustinian advice well into her career as an independent patron, as Anne Kurdock

[78] Ferrari 1957: 261–3, drawing on Schuster 1904 and 1934: 28–35.
[79] See Saxer 1980: 245–54; also Bradbury 1996.
[80] Clark 1982. [81] BHL 7863–7; Delehaye 1910.
[82] C. Leyser 2005. Stephen's stewardship of the Jerusalem community is noted also by Bruno of Segni in his version of the *Translatio Stephani* (see n. 88 below).
[83] See Toulotte 1902, with due caution for the claim that relics of Stephen came to Rome from north Africa. This rests on the assumption that the Galla ('Galla 3', *PLRE* 2.491) to whom Augustine gave relics of the saint (Augustine, *Ep.* 212) is to be identified with the Symmachan Galla ('Galla 1', *PLRE* 2.490–1).

discusses elsewhere in this volume.[84] Demetrias' church of St Stephen on the Via Latina seems to have started something of a trend. Successive popes followed her lead with the foundations of S. Stefano Rotondo and shrines to Stephen at the basilica of St Laurence (on which, see below).[85] In succeeding generations, it may be that we see the flickers of this Stephen–Augustine–Aniciae nexus in the works of Fulgentius of Ruspe, advisor to Proba and Galla, and of Gregory the Great, who commemorated Galla in the *Dialogues*.[86] As we shall see shortly, Gregory is in turn associated with the memory of Stephen in later *gesta* tradition. The involvement of later popes in the cult of Stephen, and of Hadrian and Leo in particular, therefore represents an investment in 'blue chip' cultural stock.

The relics of St Stephen at Rome are, however, an enigma. Despite their widespread availability in the west, the earliest mention of relics of Stephen at Rome is in the seventh-century *De locis sanctis*, which records the community of St Stephen's at St Paul's as possessing the stone with which the martyr was killed.[87] There is also a tantalizing account of the saint's arrival in Rome. The *Translatio sancti Stephani* purports to be the sermon of an otherwise unknown Roman deacon Lucius celebrating the festival of the saint's translation.[88] This text, which has received relatively little scholarly attention, provides alluring evidence for the meanings of Stephen in eighth- and ninth-century Rome. In offering below a possible, but ultimately unprovable, scenario for its *Sitz im Leben*, our goal is not to 'solve the problem' of the text's date and location, or of the presence of relics of Stephen at Rome; it is rather to use the *Translatio* 'to think with', as a lens through which to view other evidence for papal patronage of Roman monasticism and martyr cult.

84 See Kurdock in this volume. 85 *LP* I, 249; 508.

86 The monastery of St Stephen 'Maior' at the Vatican is probably to be identified with *cata Galla patricia*, the monastery established by Galla *apud beati Petri*, according to Gregory, *Dial* 4.14 (SC 261); see Ferrari 1957: 319–27.

87 *De locis sanctis*, ed. Valentini and Zucchetti 1942: 109.

88 *BHL* 7878–81. Noticing the *Translatio*'s anachronistic conjunction of a daughter of Theodosius with Pope Pelagius, the Bollandists initially dismissed this account: see *AASS Aug. II*, 528–30. The printed text of the *Translatio* must be assembled from *Translatio sancti Stephani protomartyris*, ed. A. Mai, *Spicilegium Romanum*, IV, Rome, 1844: 285–88, which omits the middle section, later supplied by R. Le Chat (ed.) (1931), *Translatio sancti Stephani protomartyris Constantinopoli Romam*, 'Ad Catalogum codicum hagiographicorum bibliothecae publicae Audomaropolitanae appendix', *Analecta Bollandiana* 49: 112–16, from St Omer 716 (thirteenth century; see *Catalogus codicum Audomaropolitanae*, 273). *A terminus post quem* is established by references to Gregory's *Moralia* (see below n. 91); a *terminus ante quem* by the editorial interventions of Bruno of Segni (d. 1123), who added an epilogue (see *Catalogus codicum Parisiensis*, 3 vols., Subsidia Hagiographica 2, Brussels, 1890: I, 130), and made a number of changes to the text itself (classified as *BHL* 7882–4, printed in *Catalogus codicum Bruxellensis*, 2 vols., Subsidia Hagiographica 1, Brussels, 1886–89: I, 70–4, drawn from Brussels Bibl. Reg. 98–100, a probably twelfth-century manuscript).

In Lucius' account, a demon afflicting 'the daughter of the emperor Theodosius' at Rome will only leave if the relics of the protomartyr Stephen are brought to her from Constantinople. Although the people of Constantinople are very reluctant to let the relics of Stephen go, they agree on condition that they receive relics of St Laurence in return. The relics of St Stephen duly arrive in Rome (via Capua)[89] and are carried to the imperial church of St Peter in Chains, but Theodosius' daughter is only healed when they are moved again, to the basilica of St Laurence outside the walls. It transpires, however, that the relics of St Laurence cannot be moved to Constantinople. The parties attempting to move them fall down unconscious, 'as if dead', and the relics stay put. The story is told in a spirit of shameless celebration at the triumph of divine favour for the city of Rome, the pope, and the basilica of St Laurence, which can now boast that it holds the bodies of Laurence from Spain and Stephen from Jerusalem under one roof.[90]

No translation of Stephen to St Laurence's is recorded, which would make for the easy way to date the text. Two explicit references to Gregory's *Moralia in Job* in the *Translatio* establish its *terminus post quem*, while reference to *cardinales episcopi* further suggests that it cannot be before the eighth century, when this term was first used.[91] The anachronistic association of the fifth-century 'daughter of Theodosius' with the late sixth-century Pope Pelagius suggests a date some distance after the events

89 The Capuan context of the *Translatio* is to be explored on another occasion. In support of the late eighth-century date for the *Translatio* suggested here is Hadrian I's insistence in 787 that Capua be placed directly under papal jurisdiction. To be noted also, however, is the late ninth-century reconstruction of the basilica of Stephen at Capua. The *Chronicle of Salerno* (written 974) reports that the relics of Stephen, along with those of Agatha, were brought back from Constantinople by Bishop Germanus of Capua on his return from Constantinople: see *Chronicum Salernitanum* 19 (ed. G. H. Pertz, MGH SS III (1839), 467–561). The early modern chronicler of Capua's religious life, Michele Monaco, recorded the exuberant celebration on the first Sunday in May ('la Domenica delle ghirlande') of the translation from Constantinople: see Bova 2001: 113.

90 The text also claims that Pelagius gave relics of St Stephen to St Peter's. See also the twelfth-century description of the church by Petrus Mallius: 'Supra quam imaginem fecimus loculum tempore domni Alexandri III papae, in quo honorifice cum romano clero posuimus dextrum armum beati Stephani protomartyris, quod domnus Pelagius papa huic basilicae donavit': *Petri Mallii Descriptio Basilicae Vaticanae Aucta atque Emendata a Romano Presbitero*, ed. Valentini and Zucchetti 1946: 388.

91 For cardinals, see *Translatio sancti Stephani* (ed. Le Chat (1931), *Analecta Bollandiana* 49: 115), and in general Kuttner 1945. Gregory citations: see *Translatio sancti Stephani*, (ed. Mai, *Spicilegium Romanum*, IV, Rome, 1844: 286: 'ut beatus refert Gregorius in primo beati Iob' (*Moralia in Iob* 1.1.1, CCSL 143.25) and 'Ait enim Gregorius in libro nono Iob' (*Moralia in Iob* 9.56.100, CCSL 143.527). Neither of the passages cited involves Stephen – even though Stephen makes a number of appearances elsewhere in the *Moralia* (e.g. *Moralia in Iob* 7.35.54; 20.41.79; 23.13.25; 29.20.39). Nor is Stephen invoked by the handful of later authors who cite these Gregory passages (e.g. Hrabanus Maurus, *De universo* 2.1, *PL* 111.33; *Commentaria in Ecclesiasticum* 9.1, *PL* 109.1048).

described. Identifying which of the three possible 'daughters of Theodosius' concerned is a complex matter, explored at greater length elsewhere.[92] In brief, it seems likely that the *Translatio* merges, on the one hand, the Stephen tradition associated with the empress Athenais-Eudokia and, on the other, a Peter in Chains tradition associated variously with her mother-in-law Aelia-Eudoxia and her daughter Licinia-Eudoxia, to produce a composite figure.

A tentative case can be made for dating to the end of the eighth century. The *Translatio*'s memory of 'Eudoxia' might be related to the decision of the *Liber Pontificalis* biographer of Hadrian to name the church of St Peter in Chains as *titulus Eudoxiae*. The passage is worth quoting in full.

> This bountiful Oracle freshly restored this side and that this same basilica of St Laurence the martyr where his holy body is at rest and which adjoins the great basilica this prelate had previously constructed. Also he renewed on all sides St Stephen's church close to them, where the body of St Leo bishop and martyr is at rest, along with St Cyriaca's cemetery and the climb up to it. He also restored the Jerusalem basilica at the Sessorian, and its ancient beams which had decayed replacing them marvellously. Also at the Apostle's titulus, Eudoxia's *ad vincula*, he freshly renewed its whole Church.[93]

In quick succession then, the restoration of the two basilicas of St Laurence, the church of St Stephen, and St Peter in Chains: the shrines involved here are precisely those connected together by the narrative in the *Translatio Stephani*. The *Translatio*, then, may represent a narrative embellishment of the restoration programme of Hadrian, or even, conceivably, a record of a translation of Stephen that actually took place, which the compilers of the *Liber* did not see fit to include in their notice for Hadrian.

A late eighth-century context would fit the polemical tenors of the text. The most obvious target is 'the Greeks'. The *Translatio* reprises the theme better known from Gregory's letter of 594 to Constantina, sister of the emperor Maurice, in which he politely but firmly declined her request for the translation of the head of St Paul from Rome to Constantinople.[94] Moving the martyrs of Rome was taboo, Gregory warned: workmen at the basilicas of St Paul and St Laurence had been struck down for coming too

92 See Cooper, Hillner and Leyser 2006.

93 *LP* I, 508, trans. Davis 1992: 161. For the background, see *LP* I, 245, 249, and Ferrari 1957: 182–5, with n. 3. Ferrari was happy to conclude that this St Stephen' s had its origins in the monastery recorded as having been founded by Pope Hilarius (461–468) at St Laurence's, which he associated with the establishment there by Hilarius' successor Simplicius (468–483) of a 'basilica' of St Stephen (understood by de Rossi and Duchesne to be near the south-east corner of the building of today). The 806/7 list mentions a monastery of St Stephen there, very likely to be identical with what the *Liber Pontificalis*' Life of Hadrian refers to as 'St Stephen's church'.

94 Gregory, *Reg. Ep.* 4.30, discussed with further refs. by C. Leyser 2000b: 302.

close to the tombs of the saints. The *Translatio Stephani* takes this rebuff to the Greeks one step further, by having the body of St Laurence drawing Constantinopolitan relics towards it – while continuing to strike down any with designs on its relocation. It is worth noting here that, since the time of the emperor Theodosius II, the relics of St Stephen at Constantinople had been preserved in a church of St Laurence.[95] At the close of the *Translatio*, Rome and its St Laurence becomes the equal of Byzantium. The story fits glove-like with what we can see of eighth-century Romans' suspicious if not inimical attitude towards Constantinople and its emperor; and as observed above, it may even have been in the interests of iconodule Greek monks to support this kind of Roman claim. One may go still further in observing that St Stephen's capacity to dictate terms to Constantinople, and specifically to female members of the imperial family, may have been exactly what Pope Leo needed as he made his way, with whatever degree of forethought, to defy the empress Irene and to place an imperial crown on Charlemagne's head.

At the same time, the *Translatio* may have carried a coded warning to Charlemagne and his band of northern adventurers not to take their 'protection' of the relics of the Roman martyrs as a licence to command the sacred holdings of the city.[96] If for 'Constantinople' in the *Translatio* we understand 'imperial capital', and hence 'Aachen', then the text would form part of the attempt by Hadrian and Leo to halt the flow of relics north of the Alps, while continuing to countenance and even to promote their redistribution around the city. With this possibility in mind, we might return to what was known in Charlemagne's court as the *causa sancti Pauli*, which in reality was at least as much a *causa sancti Stephani*. What we see here, perhaps, is the attempt by Charlemagne to move in on the relics of Stephen; if so, then like Constantina in the sixth century he was met with decorous but unbending and studious resistance from the Romans.

By the time we encounter it, the 'case of St Paul's' must already have been a subject of discussion both at Charlemagne's court and between the king and Pope Hadrian.[97] Charlemagne's words to Angilbert of St Riquier, whom he proposed to send to Rome in 796 as legate to the newly elected Leo III, imply that in conversation with Pope Hadrian he had offered to 'build' a monastery at St Paul's (which in later letters is named more

[95] For the transfer of the relics of St Stephen from Jerusalem and their deposition in the church of St Laurence see *Marc. Chron.* 439.2 (ed. T. Mommsen, MGH AA XI (1894), 37–108).

[96] Smith 2000a: 318.

[97] Discussions about St Paul's are noted in the *Annales sancti Amandi*, s.a 797 (ed. G. H. Pertz, MGH SS I (1826)).

correctly as St Stephen's).[98] Two years later little progress had been made, and prominent ecclesiastical figures at court were getting anxious. In June 798 Alcuin wrote to Arno of Salzburg, recently returned from Rome, enquiring after news 'de sancti Pauli partibus et Romanorum consiliis'.[99] Around the same time, Angilbert wrote to Arno that a letter had arrived at court from Pope Leo saying that he had 'invested' (*vestisset*) Arno, as representative of the king, with St Paul's and the monastery of St Stephen, a move which had apparently delighted Charlemagne. Nonetheless Pippin, by now king of Italy under his father, had pledged to intercede (presumably with the pope) concerning the case.[100] In August and again in September of that year Alcuin wrote to Arno pressing him to report on the *causa* of St Paul's.[101] If he ever received a reply, we are ignorant of it, as the Frankish evidence ends there.[102] Ferrari comments: 'That the proposed reform and reconstruction of the monastery did not take place is recorded by the silence of the sources on the matter.'[103] For Ferrari, then, the failure to reconstruct St Stephen's at St Paul's implied a failure of monastic observance at Rome as a whole: the Romans' inability or unwillingness to fall into line with Carolingian standards of monastic observance, as represented especially by the Rule of St Benedict.

The problem with this view of a 'failed reform' is that none of the sources above has a word to say about how the monks of St Stephen's should live their lives. This is not simply a question of taciturn evidence: we are dealing here not with curt references condensed out of legal documents but with letters written by a group of men not otherwise known for their silence on the issue of monastic practice. Their correspondence here seems focused on 'building'; also prominent is the use of the term *partes* – which may mean 'boundaries' or 'partitions' and certainly indicates property delineation – and the fact that the whole business is referred to as a *causa*, a word very often used in this period to mean 'dispute'. The language, in other words, is drawn not from the world of regularity and

[98] *Epistolae Karolini aevi* II, no. 92 (ed. E. Dümmler MGH Epistolae IV (1895)): 'de construendo monasterium ad Sanctum Paulum'.

[99] *Epistolae Karolini aevi* II, no. 146 (ed. Dümmler).

[100] *Epistolae Karolini aevi* II, no. 147 (ed. Dümmler).

[101] *Epistolae Karolini aevi* II, nos. 150 and 156 (ed. Dümmler).

[102] The monastery survived – it appears in the 806/7 list – and at some point was felt to be in need of moral correction, because an inscription in the name of a Pope Leo explicitly prohibits thefts of monastic income or bribery of its rector; as Ferrari says, 'evidently such things had been going on'. But since Leo in question could be any between III and VIII it is impossible to know *when* such things had been going on: the measure may well post-date Carolingian activity by a century or more: Ferrari 1957: 264.

[103] Ferrari 1957: 262.

monastic discipline, but from the profane business of the property market. It seems what Charlemagne and his courtiers wanted was the kind of conditional transfer of property that characterized much papal patronage in this period;[104] it is equally clear that Leo was reluctant to make such a grant. Whatever the mechanisms through which these Franks involved themselves in St Stephen's, their reasons for doing so owed little to Ferrari's notion of 'reform'.

We need to turn instead to the politics of martyr cult. As a letter to him from Angilbert of St Riquier makes clear, Arno was interested in the St Paul's project because of his interest in the cult of St Stephen.[105] Corroboration of Arno's interest in Stephen is provided by the presence of an annotated version of the fifth-century *Revelatio Stephani* in a collection of saints' Lives produced in St Amand, where Arno was also abbot (Vienna ÖNB 420). As Max Diesenberger has recently shown, the collection represents a highly self-conscious attempt to impose an ordering principle on the sprawling corpus of Roman martyr narratives. In anticipation of the Bollandist project, Vienna ÖNB 420 abstracts 'individual' *passiones* from the larger cycles in which they unfold. This did not apply to Stephen – unlike, for example, Agnes, he belonged to no such cycle – but the programmatic quality of the codex as a whole lends meaning to his inclusion. In the circle of Arno, Stephen was to be counted among the Roman martyrs whose cults they sought to catalogue. Furthermore, this collection of *vitae* is exactly contemporary with Vienna ÖNB 795 – a justly famous codex containing the patristic commentaries on Romans, and the letters of Alcuin, including the exchange between Alcuin, Angilbert, Charlemagne, and Arno concerning the *causa sancti Pauli*.[106] The book also contains earliest copies of Roman pilgrim itineraries, in particular the *De locis sanctis*, with its description of the stone relic of Stephen at St Paul's.[107]

Our suggestion is that the 'case of St Paul's' may in fact represent a discussion of the relics of St Stephen.[108] Medieval letters, it is well known, do not contain the real content of the exchange between sender and recipient: that went by word of mouth with the bearer. A classic example concerning a dispute over relics comes from the mid-twelfth century. Writing in extravagantly deferential language to the emperor Frederick

[104] Marazzi 1998: 200–6. [105] *Epistolae Karolini aevi* II, no. 147 (ed. Dümmler).

[106] Diesenberger and Wolfram 2004; Diesenberger 2006; for the continuing interest in the *Revelatio* of Stephen in Carolingian court circles, see Reimitz 2000.

[107] As above n. 87. [108] Cf. C. Leyser 2000b.

Barbarossa, Henry II of England concluded that the emperor could hear from the bearer concerning the hand of St James. As Karl Leyser has shown, Henry's flattery of the emperor was intended to lend sweetness to his refusal to let the relic leave the Angevin family mausoleum at Reading abbey.[109] The *causa sancti Pauli* may have had a similar outcome: when we hear no more about it, this may not mean the failure of reform, but Roman success in rebuffing the Carolingian appropriation of the cult. The *Translatio*, conceivably, was intended as a riposte to Arno's circulation of the *Revelatio Stephani*.

If nothing else, the lively energies of the *Translatio* give us a sense of 'Roman' identity, encouraging us to rethink the traditional picture of Rome as the passive recipient of reform from the north. The city was more than capable of speaking for itself. The elements exhibited by the text – pride in Rome, the memory of Gregory the Great, hostility to Greeks, and suspicion of northerners – will emerge with extreme circumstantial clarity in the 870s, in a text of fundamental importance for the emerging profile of Roman monasticism – John the Deacon's *Life of Gregory the Great*.

TENTH-CENTURY REFORM AND ROMAN MONASTICISM

It is often assumed that the late ninth century was the moment at which Rome and its church degenerated into scandal and chaos, only to be rescued by the intervention of outsiders such as Odo of Cluny. 'Tenth-century reform' in Rome is told as a story of normalization of the city's monasticism along the Benedictine lines already in place in western Europe. Viewed from the perspective of Roman martyr cult, however, the tenth century is in many ways continuous with what has come before. Odo's bases in Rome were none other than the two communities dedicated to Stephen – St Laurence's and St Paul's outside the walls. The narrator of his life was the Roman monk John of Salerno, formerly an inmate of St Stephen's at St Paul's. As we have argued elsewhere, across the two generations of apparent chaos and corruption what we can trace is the growing self-confidence of 'Roman' monastic identity.[110] In the early 870s, the procedures of clerical memory which had dominated the city for so long were interrupted: the notice for Hadrian II in the *Liber Pontificalis* breaks off. Briefly resumed in the following decade, the *Liber* spluttered to a close altogether by the end of the ninth century. Long seen as a sign of degeneration, this profound shift in the techniques of memory may in fact have been a choice. By accident or

[109] K. Leyser 1982a. [110] C. Leyser 2004, on which the following paragraphs draw.

design, the ending of the *Liber* represented an opportunity for the self-definition of Roman monasticism, no longer in the shadow of the routinized procedures of the papal *scrinium*.

The clearest voice here is that of John the Deacon, in his *Life of Gregory the Great*, composed 873–876 for his patron Pope John VIII. Like the *Translatio Stephani*, the text is full of animus against both insiders and outsiders. John's *Life of Gregory* is a fierce celebration of its hero as a Latin Christian. John appears to regret that Gregory's monastery of St Andrew was taken over by Greek occupants and looks forward to its restoration to Latin monks.[111] But in that many of his informants were monks of St Andrew's, it would be as well not to overestimate his Hellenophobia.[112] John's real enemies lay closer to home. He finds it a bitter irony that the Lombards, whom Gregory despised, should have written a *Life of Gregory* well before the Romans (Paul the Deacon), and he develops an entire burlesque out of Frankish attempts to follow the Roman liturgy, struggling in vain against their alcohol-bloated barbarian physiognomy.

John's prides and prejudices were those of a brilliant generation who staged a Roman renaissance at the courts of Nicholas I and John VIII – and across the so-called Formosan schism.[113] At one level, the *Life* is a pamphlet seeking to mobilize the memory of Gregory the Great against the party of Formosus, John VIII's great rival and a figure of division in the Roman church for over forty years. Meanwhile, defenders of Formosus, exiled from the city, may have taken up residence with the monks of Montecassino, themselves also exiled thanks to the depredations of the Saracens, and engaged in burnishing the memory of St Benedict.[114] The Formosan schism, indeed, can be seen as an episode in the renaissance, which sought as a whole to take back 'image rights' over the 'Rome brand' so successfully developed by the Carolingians. This is not the place to develop the long overdue rereading of the subsequent rise to power and patronage style of the House of Theophylact – we should simply note that Alberic's invitation to Odo of Cluny was quite of a piece with the cultural patronage of his family.[115]

We should not overestimate the 'normalization' of Roman monasticism in the tenth century. For a balance sheet, let us return to Farfa. The monastery's eleventh-century chronicler uses the terms *cella* and *ecclesia* almost interchangeably when referring to the abbey's establishments in Rome.[116] Blurred institutional boundaries existed even after Odo's reform

[111] John the Deacon, *Vita Gregorii* 4.82 (*PL* 75.229B). [112] As cautioned by Sansterre 1983: I, 143.
[113] Arnaldi 1956; see also Arnaldi 1997. [114] Pohl 2001a and 2001b. [115] See further, C. Leyser 2005.
[116] *Il Chronicon Farfense di Gregorio di Catino* 2.8, 18, 24, 58, 88, 96, 99, 176, 282 (ed. Balzani).

(of Rome and of Farfa): we should continue to foreswear the search for too rigidly defined a monastic observance at any point in this period. We might do better to note the dedications of Farfa's Roman houses, to the Virgin (patron of the abbey itself), and to St Benedict. If we adhere to our opening premise – that monastic identities in Rome were more focused on cult than on observance or institutional structure – then we should, like Gregory the Great, pay more attention in our inquiries to the sanctity of Benedict as perceived by his Roman disciples than to the Rule that bears his name.

Bibliography

Alchermes, Joseph (1989) '*Cura pro mortuis* and *Cultus martyrum*: commemoration in Rome from the second through the sixth century', unpubl. PhD thesis, University of New York.

Alföldi, A. (1970) *Die monarchische Repräsentation in römischen Kaiserreiche*. Darmstadt.

Alföldy, G. (2001) 'Difficillima tempora: urban life, inscriptions, and mentality in late antique Rome', in Burns and Eadie 2001: 3–24.

Allard, P. (1907–53) 'Agnès (Sainte)', *DACL* 1: 905–18.

(1907) 'Une grande fortune romaine au cinquième siècle', *Revue des Questions Historiques* 81: 5–30.

Ammannati, G. (2004) 'La lettera papiracea del Tesoro di Monza attribuito a Gregorio Magno: una nuova ipotesi', *Studi Medievali* 3rd ser., 45: 1051–9.

Amore, A. (1975) *I Martiri di Roma*. Rome.

Amory, P. (1997) *People and Identity in Ostrogothic Italy, 489–554*. Cambridge.

Andreau, J. (1977) 'Fondations privées et rapports sociaux en Italie romaine (Ier–IIIe s. ap. J.-C.)', *Ktema* 2: 157–209.

Andrieu, M. (1948) *Les Ordines Romani du haut moyen âge*, II: *Les textes (Ordines I–XIII)*. Louvain.

Angrisani, M. L. (1999) 'Note di contributo relative al problema dell'autenticità e della datazione della "Charta Cornutiana" conservata nel Regestum Tiburtinum', *Atti e Memorie della Società Tiburtina di Storia e d'Arte* 72: 1–47.

Antonelli, G. (1950) 'L'opera di Odone di Cluny in Italia', *Benedictina* 4: 19–40.

Arena, M. S. and Delogu, P. and others (eds.) (2001) *Roma dall'antichità classica al medioevo: archeologia e storia nel Museo Nazionale Romano Crypta Balbi*. Rome.

Arjava, A. (1996) *Women and Law in Late Antiquity*. Oxford.

(1998) 'Paternal power in late antiquity', *JRS* 88: 147–65.

Arnaldi, G. (1956) 'Giovanni Immonide e la cultura a Roma al tempo di Giovanni VIII', *Bullettino dell'Istituto Storico Italiano per il Medioevo* 68: 33–89.

(1982) 'Rinascita, fine, reincarnazione e successive metamorfosi del senato romano (secoli V–XII)', *Archivio della Società Romana di Storia Patria* 105: 5–56.

(1997) '"Giovanni Immonide e la cultura a Roma al tempo di Giovanni VIII": una *retractatio*', in *Europa medievale e mondo Bizantino: contatti effetive e possibilità di studi comparativi*, ed. G. Arnaldi and G. Cavallo. Rome: 163–77.

Arnheim, M. T. W. (1972) *The Senatorial Aristocracy in the Later Roman Empire*. Oxford.

Auerbach, E. (1953) *Mimesis: The Presentation of Reality in Western Literature*. Princeton.

(1965) *Literary Language and Its Public in Late Antiquity and in the Middle Ages*. London.

Augenti, A. (2000) 'Continuity and discontinuity of a seat of power: the Palatine hill from the fifth to the tenth century', in Smith 2000b: 43–57.

Ausbüttel, F. M. (1982) *Untersuchungen zu den Vereinen im Westen des römischen Reiches*. Kallmünz.

Baldovin, J. F. (1987) *The Urban Character of Christian Worship: The Origins, Development and Meaning of Stational Liturgy*. Rome.

Barberini, P. M. (2001) 'S. Agnese', in LaRegina 2001: 33–6.

Barclay, J. M. G. (1997) 'The family as bearer of religion in Judaism and early Christianity', in *Constructing Early Christian Families*, ed. Halvor Moxnes. London: 66–80.

Barnes, T. D. (1992) 'The capitulation of Liberius and Hilary of Poitiers', *Phoenix* 46: 256–65.

(1995) 'Statistics and the conversion of the Roman aristocracy', *JRS* 85: 135–47.

(1998) *Ammianus Marcellinus and the Representation of Historical Reality*. Ithaca, NY.

(1999) 'Ambrose and Gratian', *Antiquité Tardive* 7: 165–74.

Barnish, S. J. B. (1988) 'Transformation and survival in the western senatorial aristocracy, *c.* AD 400–700', *PBSR* 56: 120–55.

Bartlett, R. (2001) 'Aristocracy and asceticism: the letters of Ennodius and the Gallic and Italian churches', in *Society and Culture in Late Antique Gaul: Revisiting the Sources*, ed. Ralph Mathisen and Danuta Shanzer. Aldershot: 201–16.

Bartòla, A. (1989) 'Prime ricerche sull'antico regesto del monastero dei SS. Andrea e Gregorio al Celio', *Nuovi Annali della Scuola Speciale per Archivisti e Bibliotecari* 3: 39–63.

(2003) *Il regesto del monastero dei SS. Andrea e Gregorio ad Clivum Scauri*, 2 vols. Rome.

Bauer, F. A. (2004) 'Il rinnovamento di Roma sotto Adriano I alla luce del Liber Pontificalis. Immagine e realtà', in Geertman 2004: 189–203.

Bavant, B. (1979) 'Le duché byzantin de Rome: origine, durée et extension géographique', *MEFRM* 91: 41–88.

Beatrice, P. F. (1978) *Tradux Peccat: alle fonti della dottrina agostiniana del peccato originale*. Milan.

Becher, M. (ed.) (2004) *Der Dynastiewechsel von 751: Vorgeschichte, Legitimationsstrategien und Erinnerung*. Münster.

Bell, C. (1992) *Ritual Theory, Ritual Practice*. New York.

Bendlin, A. (2002) 'Gemeinschaft, Öffentlichkeit und Identität: Forschungsgeschichtliche Anmerkungen zu den Mustern sozialer Ordnung in Rom',

in *Religiöse Vereine in der römischen Antike*, ed. U. Egelhaaf-Gaiser and A. Schäfer. Tübingen: 9–40.
Benoist, S. (2005) *Rome, le prince et la cité*. Paris.
Berger, A. (1953) *Encyclopaedic Dictionary of Roman Law*. Philadelphia.
Bertinetti, M. (2000) 'Il Ponte di Valentiniano' in Ensoli and La Rocca 2000: 55–7.
Bertoldi, M. E. (1994) *S. Lorenzo in Lucina. Le chiesa di Roma illustrate*, n. s. 28. Rome.
Bertolini, O. (1924) 'La fine del pontificato di papa Silverio in uno studio recente', *Archivio della Reale Società Romana di Storia Patria* 47: 325–43.
(1947) 'Per la storia delle diaconie romane nell'alto medioevo sino alla fine del secolo VIII', *Archivio della Reale Società Romana di Storia Patria* 70: 1–145, reprinted in Bertolini 1968: 311–460.
(1968) *Scritti scelti di storia medievale*, ed. O. Banti. Livorno, vol. 1: 311–460.
(1970) 'Il Liber Pontificalis', in *La storiografia altomedievale. Settimane di Studio del Centro Italiano di Studi Sull'Alto Medioevo 17*. Spoleto: 387–455.
Bitterman, H. R. (1938) 'The council of Chalcedon and episcopal jurisdiction', *Speculum* 103: 198–203.
Blecker, M. P. (1972) 'Roman law and consilium in the *Regula Magistri* and the *Regula Benedicti*', *Speculum* 47: 1–28.
Boaga, E. (1983) 'Il complesso titolare di S. Martino ai Monti in Roma', *Miscellanea Historiae Pontificiae* 50: 1–17.
Boesch Gajano, S. (1979) '"Narratio" e "expositio" nei Dialoghi di Gregorio Magno', *Bulletino dell'Istituto Italiano per il Medio Evo e Archivio Muratoriano* 88: 1–33.
(1980) 'La proposta agiografica dei "Dialoghi" di Gregorio Magno', *Studi Medievali* 3rd ser., 21: 623–64.
Bourdieu, P. (1977) *Outline of a Theory of Practice*. New York.
Bova, G. (2001) *La vita quotidiana a Capua al tempo della crociate*. Naples.
Bovini, G. (1949) *La proprietà ecclesiastica e la condizione giuridica della chiesa in età preconstantiniana*. Milan.
Bowersock, G. W. (2002). 'Peter and Constantine', in *'Humana Sapit': études d'antiquité tardive offertes à Lellia Cracco Ruggini*, ed. J.-M. Carrié and R. Lizzi Testa. Turnhout: 209–17.
Bowes, K. (2002) 'Possessing the holy: private churches and private piety in late antiquity', unpubl. PhD thesis, Princeton.
Bradbury, S. (ed.) (1996) *Severus of Minorca: Letter on the Conversion of the Jews*. Oxford.
Brakke, D. (1995) *Athanasius and the Politics of Asceticism*. Oxford.
Brandenburg, H. (2004) 'S. Costanza', in LaRegina 2004: 140–7.
Brandt, O. (1994), 'Insc. of Lorenzo in Luc', *RAC* 70: 197–201.
(1995) 'Sul battistero paleochristiano di S. Lorenzo in Lucina', *Archeologia Laziale* 12.1: 145–50.
(1996) 'Field report: la seconda campagna di scavo nel battisterio di S. Lorenzo in Lucina a Roma, rapporto preliminare', *Opuscula Romana* 20: 272–4.

Brenk, B. (1995) 'Microstoria sotto la chiesa dei SS. Giovanni e Paolo: la cristianizzazione di una casa privata', *Rivista dell'Istituto Nazionale di Archeologia e Storia dell'Arte* 18: 169–205.

(1999) 'La cristianizzazione della Domus dei Valerii sul Celio', in Harris 1999: 69–84.

(2000) 'Le costruzioni sotto la chiesa dei SS. Giovanni e Paolo', in Ensoli and La Rocca 2000: 156–8.

(2002) 'L'anno 410 e il suo effetto sull'arte chiesastica a Roma', in Guidobaldi and Guidobaldi 2002: II, 1001–18.

(2003) *Die Christianisierung der spätrömischen Welt: Stadt, Land, Haus, Kirche und Kloster in frühchristlicher Zeit.* Wiesbaden.

(2005) *Architettura e immagini del sacro nella tarda antichità.* Spoleto.

Brogiolo, G. P., Gauthier, N. and Christie, N. (eds.) (2000) *Towns and Their Territories between Late Antiquity and the Early Middle Ages.* Leiden, Boston, and Cologne.

Brogiolo, G. P. and Ward-Perkins, B. (eds.) (1999) *The Idea and Ideal of the Town between Late Antiquity and the Early Middle Ages.* Leiden, Boston, and Cologne.

Broise, H., Dewailly, M. and Jolivet, V. (1999) 'Onorio a Villa Medici', *Archeo* 178: 56–64.

(2000) '*Horti Luculliani*: un palazzo tardoantico a Villa Medici ', in Ensoli and La Rocca 2000: 113–15.

Brown, M. (1986) 'Paris, Bibliothèque Nationale, lat. 10861 and the scriptorium of Christ Church, Canterbury', *Anglo-Saxon England* 15: 119–37.

Brown, P. (1961) 'Aspects of the Christianization of the Roman aristocracy', *JRS* 51: 1–11.

(1967, rev. edn 2000) *Augustine of Hippo: A Biography.* London and Berkeley.

(1968) 'Pelagius and his supporters: aims and environment', *JTS* n.s. 19: 93–114.

(1970) 'The patrons of Pelagius: the Roman aristocracy between east and west', *JTS* n. s. 21: 56–72.

(1971) 'The rise and function of the holy man in late antiquity', *JRS* 61: 80–101; reprinted in Brown 1982: 103–52.

(1972) *Religion and Society in the Age of St. Augustine.* New York.

(1981) *The Cult of the Saints: Its Rise and Function in Latin Christianity.* Chicago.

(1982) *Society and the Holy in Late Antiquity.* London.

(1988) *The Body and Society: Men, Women and Sexual Renunciation in Early Christianity.* New York.

(1992) *Power and Persuasion in Late Antiquity.* Madison, WI.

(2000) 'The decline of the Empire of God: amnesty, penance, and the afterlife from late antiquity to the early middle ages', in *Last Things: Death and Apocalyptic in the Middle Ages*, ed. C. W. Bynum and P. Freedman. Philadelphia: 41–59.

(2002) *Poverty and Leadership in the Later Roman Empire.* Hanover, NH.

(2003) *The Rise of Western Christendom: Triumph and Diversity, AD 200–1000*, 2nd edn. Oxford.

(2005) 'Augustine and a crisis of wealth in late antiquity', *Augustinian Studies* 36: 5–30.

Brown, T. S. (1984) *Gentlemen and Officers: Imperial Administration and Aristocratic Power in Byzantine Italy AD 554–800*. London.
Brown, W. (2002) 'When documents are destroyed or lost: lay people and archives in the early middle ages', *Early Medieval Europe* 11: 337–66.
Brubaker, L. (1997) 'Memories of Helena: patterns in imperial female matronage in the fourth and fifth centuries', in *Women, Men and Eunuchs: Gender in Byzantium*, ed. L. James. London: 52–75.
Bruggisser, P. (2002) 'Constantine aux Rostres', in *Historiae Augustae Colloquium Perusinum*, ed. G. Bonamente and F. Paschoud. Bari: 72–91.
Bruun, P. (1976) 'Notes on the transmission of imperial images in late antiquity', in *Studia Romana in honorem Petri Krarup septuagenarii*, ed. K. Ascani, T. Fischer-Hansen, F. Johansen, S. Skovgaard Jensen, and J. E. Skydsgaard. Odense: 122–31.
Buckland, W. W. (1963) *A Text-Book of Roman Law from Augustus to Justinian*, 3rd edn. Cambridge (2nd edn 1950).
Bundy, D. (1987) '*The Acts of Saint Gallicanus*: a study of the structural relations', *Byzantion* 57: 12–31.
Burgarella, F. (2001) 'Il senato', in *Roma nell'alto medioevo. Settimane de Studio del Centro Italiano di studi sull'alto medioevo 48*. Spoleto: vol. 1, 121–78.
Burns, T. and Eadie, J. (eds.) (2001) *Urban Centers and Rural Contexts in Late Antiquity*. East Lansing, MI.
Burrus, V. (1995a) *The Making of a Heretic: Gender, Authority, and the Priscillianist Controversy*. Berkeley.
(1995b) 'Reading Agnes: the rhetoric of gender in Ambrose and Prudentius', *JECS* 3: 25–46.
(1996) '"Equipped for victory": Ambrose and the gendering of orthodoxy', *JECS* 4: 461–75.
Cabié, R. (1973) *La lettre du pape Innocent I à Decentius de Gubbio*. Louvain.
Cameron, A. (1991) *Christianity and the Rhetoric of Empire: The Development of Christian Discourse*. Berkeley.
(2005) 'The reign of Constantine, AD 306–337', in *The Cambridge Ancient History*, XII: *The Crisis of Empire, AD 193–337*, ed. Averil Cameron and P. Garsney. Cambridge: 90–109.
Capizzi, C. (1997) *Anicia Giuliana: la committente*. Milan.
Caspar, E. (1930–33) *Geschichte des Papsttums von den Anfängen bis zur Höhe der Weltherrschaft*, 2 vols. Tübingen.
Castaldi, L. (2004) 'Il Registrum Epistularum di Gregorio Magno', *Filologia Mediolatina* 11: 55–97.
Castelli, E. (1995) 'Visions and voyerism: holy women and the politics of sight in early Christianity', *Protocol of the Colloquy of the Center for Hermeneutical Studies* 2: 1–20.
Casti, G. (2004) 'Nuovi ossevazioni sulle basiliche di San Pietro in Vincole e dei Santi Giovanni e Paolo. Relazioni strutturali, proposte di cronologia', in Guidobaldi 2004: II, 953–77.
Cavallera, F. (1922) *Saint Jérôme: sa vie et son œuvre*, 2 vols. Louvain and Paris.

Cecchelli, C. (1944) *Monumenti cristiano-eretici di Roma*. Rome.
Cecchelli, M. (1988) 'Valilae o valide? L'iscrizione di S. Andrea all'Esquilino', *Romanobarbarica* 11: 62–76.
Cecconi, G. A. (1988) 'Un evergete mancato: Piniano a Ippona', *Athenaeum* 66: 371–89.
Cerrito, A. (2002) 'Oratori ed edifici di culto minori di Roma tra il IV secolo ed i primi decenni del V', in Guidobaldi and Guidobaldi 2002: 1, 397–418.
Chadwick, H. (1967) *The Early Church*. Harmondsworth.
Champlin, E. (1982) 'Saint Gallicanus (Consul 317)', *Phoenix* 36: 71–6.
(1991) *Final Judgements: Duty and Emotion in Roman Wills, 200 B.C.–A.D. 250*. Berkeley, Los Angeles, and Oxford.
Chastagnol, A. (1960) *La préfecture urbaine à Rome sous le bas-empire*. Paris.
(1962) *Les fastes de la préfecture de Rome au bas-empire*. Paris.
(1966) *Le sénat romain sous le règne d'Odoacre: recherches sur l'épigraphie du Colisée au Ve siècle*. Antiquitas Reihe 3, Band 3. Bonn.
(1996) 'La fin du sénat de Rome', in Lepelley 1996: 345–54.
Chavasse, A. (1997) *Textes liturgiques de l'église de Rome: le cycle liturgique romaine annuel selon le Sacramentaire du Vaticanus Reginensis 316*. Paris.
Chavasse, A. (ed.) (1954) Leo, *Sermones*, CCSL 188a. Turnhout.
Chazelle, C. and Cubitt, C. (forthcoming) *The 'Three Chapters' and the Failed Quest for Unity in the Sixth-Century Mediterranean*. Turnhout.
Christie, N. (2006) *From Constantine to Charlemagne: An Archaeology of Italy AD 300–800*. Aldershot.
Christie, N. and Loseby, S. T. (eds.) (1996) *Towns in Transition: Urban Evolution in Late Antiquity and the Early Middle Ages*. Aldershot.
Christo, S. (1977) 'Notes on the Bonifacian–Eulalian schism', *Aevum* 51: 163–6.
Clanchy, M. (1979) *From Memory to Written Record: England 1066–1307*. London.
Clark, E. (1979) *Jerome, Chrysostom, and Friends: Essays and Translations*. New York and Toronto.
(1981) 'Ascetic renunciation and feminine advancement: a paradox of late ancient Christianity', *Anglican Theological Review* 63: 240–57.
(1982) 'Claims on the bones of St Stephen: the partisans of Melania and Eudocia', *Church History* 51: 141–56.
(1984) *Gerontius, The Life of Melania the Younger: Introduction, Translation, and Commentary*. Lewiston, Lampeter, and Queenston.
(1992) *The Origenist Controversy: The Cultural Construction of an Early Christian Debate*. Princeton.
(1998) 'The lady vanishes: dilemmas of a feminist historian after the "linguistic turn"', *Church History* 67: 1–31.
(2004) *History, Text, Theory*. Durham, NC.
Clark, G. (1993) *Women in Late Antiquity: Pagan and Christian Lifestyles*. Oxford.
Cleary, J. F. (1936) *Canonical Limitations on the Alienation of Church Property: An Historical Synopsis and Commentary*. The Catholic University of America Canon Law Studies 100. Washington, DC.
Coarelli, F. (1999) 'L'edilizia pubblica a Roma in età tetrarchica', in Harris 1999: 23–33.
Coates-Stephens, R. (1996) 'Housing in early medieval Rome', *PBSR* 64: 239–59.

(1997) 'Dark age architecture in Rome', *PBSR* 65: 177–232.

Colini, A. (1944) *Storia e topografia del Celio nell'antichità.* Rome.

Colish, M. L. (2002) 'Why the Portiana? Reflections on the Milanese Basilica crisis of 386', *JECS* 10: 361–72.

Colli, D. (1996) 'Il Palazzo Sessoriano nell'area archeologica di S. Croce in Gerusalemne: ultima sede imperiale a Roma?', *MEFRA* 108: 771–815.

Condello, E. (1994) *Una scrittura e un territorio: l'onciale dei secoli V–VIII nell'Italia meridionale.* Spoleto.

Consolino, F. E. (1989) 'Sante o patrone? Le aristocratiche tardoantiche e il potere della carità', *Studi Storici* 30: 971–91.

Conybeare, C. (2002) 'The ambiguous laughter of Saint Lawrence', *JECS* 10: 174–202.

Cooper, K. (1992) 'Insinuations of womanly influence: an aspect of the Christianization of the Roman aristocracy', *JRS* 82: 150–64.

(1993) 'An(n)ianus of Celeda and the Latin readers of John Chrysostom', *Studia Patristica* 27: 49–55.

(1994) 'Of romance and mediocritas: re-reading the martyr exemplum in the *Passio Sanctae Anastasiae*', in *Modelli di santità e modelli di comportamento*, ed. G. Barone, M. Caffiero, and F. Scorza Barcellona. Turin: 107–23.

(1995) 'A saint in exile: the early medieval Thecla at Rome and Meriamlik', *Hagiographica* 5: 13–20.

(1996) *The Virgin and the Bride: Idealized Womanhood in Late Antiquity.* Cambridge, MA.

(1999) 'The martyr, the *matrona*, and the bishop: the matron Lucina and the politics of martyr cult in fifth- and sixth-century Rome', *Early Medieval Europe* 8: 297–317.

(ed.) (2000) *Early Medieval Europe* 9:3: *The Roman Martyrs and the Politics of Memory.*

(2001) 'The widow as impresario: gender, authority, and legendary afterlives in Eugippius' *Vita Severini*', in *Eugippius und Severinus: der Autor, der Text, und der Heilige*, ed. W. Pohl and M. Diesenberger. Vienna: 53–64.

(2005) 'The household and the desert: monastic and biological communities in the lives of Melania the Younger', in *Household, Women and Christianities in Late Antiquity and the Middle Ages*, ed. A. Mulder-Bakker and J. Wogan-Browne. Leiden: 11–35.

(2005a) 'Ventriloquism and the miraculous: conversion, preaching, and the martyr exemplum in late antiquity', in *Signs, Wonders, and Miracles*, ed. K. Cooper and J. Gregory. Woodbridge: 22–45.

(2005b) 'The virgin as social icon', in *Saints, Scholars, and Politicians: Gender as a Tool in Medieval Studies*, ed. M. Vin Dijk and R. Nip. Leiden: 9–24.

(forthcoming) 'Family, dynasty, and conversion in the Roman gesta martyrum', in *Hagiographische Überlieferung im Frühmittelalter – Zwischen Niederschrift und Wiederschrift*, ed. M. Diesenberger. Vienna.

Cooper, K., Hillner, J., and Leyser, C. (2006) 'Dark age Rome: towards an interactive topography', in *Social and Political Life in Late Antiquity.* Late Antique Archaeology 3.1, ed. W. Bowden, A. Gutteridge and C. Machado. Leiden: 311–37.

Cosentino, A. (2002) 'Il battesimo a Roma: edifici e liturgia', in Guidobaldi and Guidobaldi 2002: I, 109–42.

Costambeys, M. (2000) 'Property, ideology and the territorial power of the papacy in the early middle ages', *EME* 9: 367–96.

(2001) 'Burial topography and the power of the church in fifth- and sixth-century Rome', *PBSR* 69: 169–89.

(2007) *Power and Patronage in Early Medieval Italy: Local Society and the Abbey of Farfa, c.700–900*. Cambridge.

Countryman, L. W. (1980) *The Rich Christian in the Church of the Early Empire*. New York.

Courcelle, P. (1948) *Les lettres grecques en occident: de Macrobe à Cassiodore. Nouv. éd. revue et augmentée*. Paris.

Coustant, P. (1721) *Epistulae Romanorum Pontificum*, vol. 1. Paris.

Cracco Ruggini, L. (2004) 'Gregorio Magno e il mondo mediterraneo', in *Gregorio Magno nel XIV centenario della morte: convegno internazionale, Roma, 22–25 ottobre 2003*. Atti dei convegni Lincei 209. Rome: 11–87.

Croke, B. (1983) 'AD 476: the manufacture of a turning point', *Chiron* 13: 81–119.

Croke, B. and Harries, J. (eds.) (1982) *Religious Conflict in Fourth-Century Rome*. London.

Crook, J. (1967a) '*Patria potestas*', *Classical Quarterly* 17: 113–221.

(1967b) *Law and Life in Rome*. Ithaca, NY.

Cullhed, M. (1994) *Conservator Urbis Suae: Studies in the Politics and Propaganda of the Emperor Maxentius*. Acta Instituti Romani Regni Sueciae (ser. 8) 20. Stockholm.

Curran, J. (2000) *Pagan City and Christian Capital: Rome in the Fourth Century*. Oxford.

Dagron, G. (1970) 'Les moines et la ville', *Travaux et Mémoires* 4: 229–74.

(1978) *Vie et miracles de Ste. Thécle*. Brussels.

(2003) *Emperor and Priest: The Imperial Office in Byzantium*. Cambridge.

Daileader, P. (1993) 'One will, one voice and equal love: papal elections and the *Liber Pontificalis* in the early middle ages', *Archivium Historiae Pontificiae* 31: 11–31.

Daley, B. E. (1993) 'Position and patronage in the early church: the original meaning of "primacy of honour"', *JTS* n.s. 44: 529–53.

Davis, R. (1976) 'The value of the Liber Pontificalis as comparative evidence for territorial estates and church property from the fourth to the sixth century', unpubl. DPhil thesis, Oxford.

(1989, 2nd edn 2000) *The Book of Pontiffs (Liber Pontificalis)*. Translated Texts for Historians 6. Liverpool.

(1992) *The Lives of the Eighth-Century Popes (Liber Pontificalis)*. Liverpool.

Davis, S. J. (2001) *The Cult of Saint Thecla: A Tradition of Women's Piety in Late Antiquity*. Oxford.

De Francesco, D. (2004) *La proprietà fondiaria nel Lazio, secoli IV–VIII: Storia e Topografia*. Rome.

de Gaiffier, B. (1948), 'Les sources de la vie de S. Cassien évêque d'Autun', *Analecta Bollandiana* 66: 33–52.

(1956) '"Sub Iuliano apostata" dans le martyrologe romain', *Analecta Bollandiana* 74: 5–49.

(1957) 'Palatins et eunuques dans quelques documents hagiographiques', *Analecta Bollandiana* 75: 17–46

(1961) 'De l'usage et de la lecture du martyrologe: témoignages antérieurs au XI siècle', *Analecta Bollandiana* 79: 40–59.

(1964a) Review of De Sanctis (1962), *Analecta Bollandiana* 80: 439–40.

(1964b) 'Un prologue hagiographique hostile au décret de Gélase?', *Analecta Bollandiana* 82: 341–53.

de Jong, M. (1995) 'Carolingian monasticism: the power of prayer', in *NCMH*, vol. II, ed. R. McKitterick. Cambridge: 622–53.

(2000) 'Transformations of penance,' in *Rituals of Power from Late Antiquity to the Early Middle Ages*, ed. F. Theuws and J. Nelson. Leiden: 184–224.

de Plinval, G. (1943) *Pélage: ses écrits, sa vie et sa réforme*. Lausanne.

De Robertis, F. (1973) *Storia delle corporazioni e del regime associativo nel mondo romano*, vol. I. Bari.

De Rossi, G. B. (1854) 'Due monumenti inediti spettanti a due concilii romani de' secoli ottavo e undicesimo', *Annali delle Scienze Religiose* 13, 39: 1–46.

(1864–1877) *Roma sotterranea cristiana, descritta ed illustrata*, 3 vols. Rome.

(1870a) 'I monumenti scoperti sotto la basilica di S. Clemente', *BAC* ser. II, 1: 129–69.

(1870b) 'Un insigne epigrafe di donazione di fondi fatta alla chiesa S. Susanna dal Papa Sergio I', *BAC*, ser. II, 1: 89–112.

De Rubeis, F. (2001) 'Epigrafi a Roma dall'età classica all'alto medioevo', in Arena and Delogu 2001: 104–21.

De Salvo, L. (1987) '"Navicularium nolui esse Ecclesiam Christi": a proposito di Aug., *Serm.* 355.4', *Latomus* 46: 46–60.

De Sanctis, G. (1962) *I Santi Giovanni e Paolo, martiri Celimontani*. Rome.

De Spirito, G. (1994a) 'De situ basilica Liberianae', *RAC* 70: 503–7.

(1994b) 'Ursino e Damaso – una nota', in *Peregrina Curiositas: Eine Reise durch den Orbis antiquus*, ed. D. Van Damme. Freiburg and Göttingen: 263–74.

De Visscher, F. (1955) 'Les fondations privées en droit romain classique', *Revue Internationale de Droits de l'Antiquité* ser. 3, 2: 197–218.

de Vogüé, A. (1964) *La Règle du Maître*, 3 vols. Paris.

(1976) *Regula Eugippii*. CSEL 87. Vienna.

(1982) *Les Règles des saints pères*, 2 vols. Sources Chrétiennes 297–8. Paris.

Delehaye, H. (1910) 'Les premiers "libelli miraculorum"', *Analacta Bollandiana* 29: 427–34.

(1921) *Les passions des martyrs et les genres littéraires*. Brussels.

(1933) *Les origines du culte des martyrs*. Brussels.

(1936) *Étude sur le légendier romain: les saints de novembre et décembre*. Brussels.

(1998) *The Legends of the Saints*. Dublin.

Delogu, P. (1988) 'The rebirth of Rome in the eighth and ninth centuries', in *The Rebirth of Towns in the West, AD 700–1050*, ed. R. Hodges and B. Hobley. CBA Research Report 68. London: 32–42.

(1993) 'La storia economica di Roma nell'alto medioevo', in *La Storia economica di Roma nell'alto medioevo alla luce dei recenti scavi archeologici*, ed. P. Delogu and L. Paroli. Florence: 11–30.

(2000) '*Solium imperii – urbs ecclesiae*. Roma fra la tarda antichità e l'alto medioevo', in *Sedes regiae (ann. 400–800)*, ed. G. Ripoll and J. M. Gurt, with A. Chavarría. Barcelona: 83–108.

(2001) 'Il passaggio dall'antichità al medioevo', in *Roma medievale*, ed. A. Vauchez. Rome and Bari: 3–40.

Demandt, A. (1989) *Die Spätantike*. Handbuch der Altertumswissenschaft 3.6. Munich.

Di San Stanislao, G. (1894) *La casa celimontana dei SS. Martiri Giovanni e Paolo*. Rome.

(1907) *La memoria dei SS. Giovanni e Paolo*. Rome.

Diem, A. (2005) *Das monastische Experiment: die Rolle der Keuscheit bei der Entstehung des westlichen Klosterwesens*, Vita regularis. Ordnungen und Deutungen religiösen Lebens im Mittelalter 24. Münster.

Diesenberger, M. (forthcoming) 'Rom als virtueller Raum der Märtyrer. Zur gedanklichen Aneignung der Roma suburbicaria in bayerischen Handschriften um 800', in *Virtuelle Räume: Raumwahrnehmung und Raumvorstellung im Mittelalter*, ed. E. Vavra, vol. II.

Diesenberger, M. and Wolfram, H. (2004) 'Arn und Alkuin – zwei Freunde und ihre Schriften', in *Arn von Salzburg*, ed. M. Niederkorn-Bruck and A. Scharer. Veröffentlichungen des Institut für Österreichische Geschichtsforschung 40. Vienna and Munich: 81–106.

Dixon, S. (1988) *The Roman Mother*. Norman, OK.

Dmitriev, S. (2004) 'Traditions and innovations under Aurelian', *Classical Quarterly* n.s. 54: 568–78.

Dobias, O. (1929) *Les anciens manuscrits latins de la bibliothèque publique de Leningrad*. Leningrad.

(1934) *Histoire de l'atelier graphique de Corbie de 651 à 830*. Leningrad.

Douglas, M. and Isherwood, B. (1979) *The World of Goods: Toward an Anthropology of Consumption*. London.

Duchesne, L. (1877) *Étude sur le Liber Pontificalis*. Paris.

(1906) *Histoire ancienne de l'église*, vol. I. Paris.

(1925) *L'église au VIe siècle*. Paris.

(1955) *Le Liber pontificalis*, 2 vols., 2nd edn. Paris.

Ducloux, A. (1994) *Ad ecclesiam confugere: naissance du droit d'asile dans les églises (IVe–milieu du Ve s.)*. Paris.

Duff, P. W. (1938) *Personality in Roman Private Law*. Cambridge.

Dufourcq, A. (1910, repr. 1988 with a posthumous fifth volume) *Étude sur les gesta martyrum romains*, 4 vols. Paris.

Dufraigne, P. (1994) *Adventus Augusti, Adventus Christi: recherche sur l'exploitation idéologique et littéraire d'un cérémonial dans l'antiquité tardive*. Collection des Études Augustiniennes, Série Antiquité 141. Paris.

Duncan-Jones, R. (1982) *The Economy of the Roman Empire: Quantitative Studies*, 2nd edn. Cambridge.

Dunn, M. (1990) 'Mastering Benedict: monastic rules and their authors in the early medieval west', *EHR* 416: 567–94.

Duval, Y.-M. (1974) 'L'originalité du "De virginibus" dans le mouvement ascétique occidental: Ambroise, Cyprien, Athanase', in *Ambroise de Milan: dix études*, ed. Y.-M. Duval. Paris: 9–66.

Eck, W. (1978) 'Der Einfluß der konstantinischen Wende auf die Auswahl der Bischöfe im 4. und 5. Jahrhundert', *Chiron* 8: 564–5.

(1997) '*Cum dignitate otium.* Senatorial *domus* in Imperial Rome', *Scripta Classica Isralica* 16: 162–90.

Ellis, S. (1988) 'The end of the Roman house', *AJA* 92: 565–76.

(1991) 'Power, architecture and décor: how the late Roman aristocrat appeared to his guests', in *Roman Art in the Private Sphere*, ed. E. Gazda. Ann Arbor: 117–134.

Enciclopedia dei papi (2000), 3 vols. Rome.

Ensoli, S. and La Rocca, E. (eds.) (2000) *Aurea Roma: dalla città pagana alla città cristiana*. Rome.

Erhardt, A. (1954) 'Das Corpus Christi und die Korporation im spät-römischen Recht', *Zeitschrift der Savigny-Stiftung für Rechtsgeschichte, Rom. Abt.* 71: 25–40.

Evans, R. (1968) *Pelagius: Inquirers and Reappraisals*. London.

Evans Grubbs, J. (1995) *Law and Family in Late Antiquity. The Emperor Constantine's Marriage Legislation*. Oxford.

Fedele, P. (1898) 'Carte del monastero dei SS. Cosma et Damiano in Mica Aurea', *Archivio della Reale Società Romana di Storia Patria* 21: 459–534.

(1899) 'Carte del monastero dei SS. Cosma et Damiano in Mica Aurea [2]', *Archivio della Reale Società Romana di Storia Patria* 22: 25–107, and 383–447.

Federici, V. (1899) 'Regesto del monastero di S. Silvestro de Capite', *Archivio della Reale Società Romana di Storia Patria* 22: 213–300.

Feenstra, R. (1956) 'Le concept de fondation du droit romain classique jusqu'à nos jours: théorie et pratique', *Revue Internationale de Droits de l'Antiquité* ser. 3, 3: 245–63.

Fentress, E., Goodson, C., Laird, M., and Leone, S. (2005) *Walls and Memory: The Abbey of San Sebastiano at Alatri (Lazio) from Late Roman Monastery to Renaissance Villa and Beyond*. Disciplina Monastica 2. Turnhout.

Ferrari, G. (1957) *Early Roman Monasteries: Notes for the History of the Monasteries and Convents at Rome from the V through the X Century*. Rome.

Ferrua, A. (1942), *Epigrammata Damasiana*. Vatican City.

(1952–4) 'Nomi di catacombe nelle iscrizioni "in lucinis"', *Rendiconti della Pontificia Accademia Romana di Archeologia* 27: 253–4.

(1953) 'Intorno ad una dedica damasiana', *Rivista di Archeologia Cristiana* 24: 231–5.

Fevrier, P. (1992) 'Un plaidoyer pour Damase: les inscriptions des nécropoles romaines', in *Institutions, societé et vie politique dans l'Empire romain au IVe siècle ap. J. C.*, ed. M. Christol and S. Demougin. Rome: 497–506.

Filson, F. (1939) 'The significance of the early house churches', *Journal of Biblical Literature* 58: 105–12.

Fiore Cavaliere, M. G. (1978) 'Le Terme Alessandrine nei secoli X–XI. I Crescenzi e la "Cella Farfae"', *Rivista dell'Istituto Nazionale d'Archeologia e Storia dell'Arte*, ser. 3, 1: 119–45.

Fisher, J. D. C. (1965) *Christian Initiation: Baptism in the Medieval West*. London.

Fontaine, J. (ed.) (1967) *Vita S. Martini*. Sources Chrétiennes 133. Paris.

(1981) 'Les poèmes épigraphiques expression de la foi: l'ôeuvre de Damase de Rome', in *Naissance de la poésie dans l'occident chrétien*. Paris: 111–25.

(1986) 'Damase poète Théodosien: l'imaginaire poétique des epigrammata', *Saecularia Damasiana, Atti del Convegno Internazionale per il XVI Contenario della Morte di Papa Damaso* I. Vatican City: 113–46.

(1988) 'Un sobriquet perfide de Damase: matronarum auriscalpius' in *Hommage à Henri Le Bonniec: Res Sacra*, ed. D. Porte and J.-P. Néraudau. Brussels: 177–92.

(1992) *Les Hymnes d'Ambroise de Milan*. Paris.

Fouracre, P. (1995) 'Eternal light and earthly needs: practical aspects of the development of Frankish immunities', in *Property and Power in the Early Middle Ages*, ed. W. Davies and P. Fouracre. Cambridge: 53–81.

Fournier, P. (1931) *Histoire des collections canoniques en occident: depuis les Fausses Décrétales jusqu'au Décret de Gratien*. Paris.

Fowden, G. (1994) 'The last days of Constantine: oppositional versions and their influence', *JRS* 84: 146–70.

Franchi de' Cavalieri, P. (1902) 'Nuove note agiographiche', *Studi e Testi* 9: 55–65.

(1915), 'Del testo della *passio SS. Iohannis et Pauli*', *Studi e Testi* 27: 44–61.

(1935) 'Dove furono sepolti i SS. Cipriano, Giustina e Teoctisto?', *Studi e Testi* 65: 341–54.

Francis, J. A. (1995) *Subversive Virtue: Asceticism and Authority in the Second-Century Pagan World*. Philadelphia.

Franklin, C. V. (2001) 'Roman hagiography and Roman legendaries', in *Roma nell'Alto Medioevo (27 aprile–1 maggio 2000)*, 3 vols. Settimane di Studio del Centro Italiano di Studi sull'Alto Medioevo 48. Spoleto: vol. II, 857–95.

Fraschetti, A. (1999) *La conversione: dalla Roma pagana alla Roma cristiana*. Rome and Bari.

Frend, W. H. C. (1984) *The Rise of Christianity*. London.

Funk, F. X. and Diekamp, F. (eds.) (1913) *Patres Apostolici*, vol. II. Tübingen: 51–81.

Gaca, K. L. (2003) *The Making of Fornication: Eros, Ethics, and Political Reform in Greek Philosophy and Early Christianity*. Berkeley, Los Angeles, and London.

Galsterer, H. (2000) 'Local and provincial institutions and government', in *Cambridge Ancient History*, vol. XI, 2nd edn. Cambridge: 341–60.

Gamble, H. Y. (1995) *Books and Readers in the Early Church*. New Haven.

Ganz, D. (1990) *Corbie in the Carolingian Renaissance*. Sigmaringen.

(1995) 'The ideology of sharing: apostolic community and ecclesiastical property in the early middle ages', in *Property and Power in the Early Middle Ages*, ed. W. Davies and P. Fouracre. Cambridge: 17–30.

Garnsey, P. and Saller, R. (1987) *The Roman Empire: Economy, Society and Culture*. London.

Gaudemet, J. (1958) *L'église dans l'empire romain (IV–V siècle)*. Paris.
(1974) 'Histoire d'un texte, les chapitres 4 et 27 de la décrétale du pape Gélase du 11 mars 494', in *Mélanges H.-Ch. Puech*. Paris: 289–98.
Gauthier, N. (1999) 'La topographie chrétienne entre idéologie et pragmatisme', in Brogiolo and Ward-Perkins 1999: 195–209.
Geary, P. (1994) *Phantoms of Remembrance: Memory and Oblivion at the End of the First Millennium*. Princeton.
Geertmann, H. (1975) *More Veterum: il Liber Pontificalis e gli edifici ecclesiastici nella tarda antichità e nell'alto medioevo*. Groningen.
(2003) 'Documenti, redattori e la formazione del testo del Liber Pontificalis', *Meded* 60–61: 267–84.
(ed.) (2004) *Atti del colloquio internazionale 'Il Liber Pontificalis e la storia materiale' (Roma, 21–22 febbraio 2002)*. Mededelingen van het Nederlands Instituut te Rome (Papers of the Netherlands Institute in Rome), Antiquity, 60/61. Assen.
Genestout, A. (1946–47) 'Le plus ancien témoin manuscrit de la Règle du Maître, le Parisinus Latin 12634', *Scriptorium* 1: 129–43.
George, J. W. (1992) *Venantius Fortunatus: A Latin Poet in Merovingian Gaul*. Oxford.
Giardina, A. (1988) 'Carità eversiva: le donazioni di Melania la giovane e gli equilibri della società tardoromana', *Studi Storici* 29: 127–42.
Gillett, A. (2001) 'Rome, Ravenna, and the last western emperors', *PBSR* 69: 131–67.
Giuliani, C. F. and Verducchi, P. (1987) *L'area centrale del Foro Romano*. Il Linguaggio dell'Architettura Romana 1. Florence.
Glare, P. G. W. (ed.) (1982) *Oxford Latin Dictionary*. Oxford.
Goffin, B. (2002) *Euergetismus in Oberitalien*. Bonn.
Gorce, D. (ed.) (1962) *Vie de Sainte Mélanie*. Sources Chrétiennes 90. Paris.
Gordini, G. D. (1961) 'Il monachesimo romano in Palestina nel IV secolo', in *Saint Martin et son temps: memorial du XVIe centenaire des débuts du monachisme en Gaule, 361–1961*. Rome: 85–107.
Gorman, M. (1982) 'The manuscript tradition of Eugippius' *Excerpta Augustini*', *Revue Bénédictine* 92: 242–4.
Gould, G. (1987) 'Basil of Caesarea and the problem of the wealth of monasteries', in *The Church and Wealth*, ed. W. Sheils and D. Woods. Studies in Church History 24. Oxford: 15–24.
Gray, P. T. R. (1979) *The Defense of Chalcedon in the East (451–553)*. Leiden.
Green, M. R. (1971) 'Supporters of the anti-pope Ursinus', *JTS* 22: 531–8.
Grégoire, H. and Orgels, P. (1954) 'S. Gallicanus, consul et martyr dans la Passion des SS. Jean et Paul et sa vision "constantinienne" du crucifié', *Byzantion* 24: 579–601.
Grig, L. (2004a) 'Portraits, pontiffs and the Christianization of fourth-century Rome', *PBSR* 72: 203–30.
(2004b) *Making Martyrs in Late Antiquity*. London.
(2005) 'The paradoxical body of St Agnes', in *Roman Bodies: Antiquity to the Eighteenth Century*, ed. A. Hopkins and M. Wyke. London: 111–22.

Grossi-Gondi, F. (1914) 'Scoperta della tomba primitiva dei SS. Giovanni e Paolo', *Civiltà Cattolica* 3: 579–601.

Guidobaldi, F. (1986) 'L'edilizia abitativa unifamiliare nella Roma tardoantica', in *Società romana e impero tardoantico*, vol. II. Rome and Bari: 165–237.

(1989) 'L'inserimento delle chiese titolari di Roma nel tessuto urbano preesistente: osservazioni ed implicazioni', in *Quaeritur, inventus, colitur: Miscellanea in onore di Umberto Maria Fasola*. Studi di Antichità Cristiana 40. Vatican City: II, 383–96.

(1993) 'Roma. II tessuto abitativo, le domus e i tituli', in *Storia di Roma*, ed. A. Carandini, L. Cracco Ruggini, and A. Giardina. 3 vols. Turin: III, 69–84.

(1995), s.v. 'Domus: Gregorius I (Anicii Petronii?)', *LTUR* 2: 112–13.

(1999) 'Le domus tardoantiche di Roma come sensori delle trasformazioni culturali e sociali', in Harris 1999: 53–68.

(2004) 'La fondazione delle basiliche titolari di Roma nel IV e V secolo. Assenze e presenze nel *Liber Pontificalis*', *Papers of the Netherlands Institute in Rome* 60–61: 5–12.

Guidobaldi, F. and Guidobaldi, A. (2002) *Ecclesiae urbis: Atti del Congresso Internazionale di Studi sulle Chiese di Roma (IV–X secolo); Roma, 4–10 settembre 2000*, 3 vols. Rome.

Giuliani, E. and Pavolini, C. (1999) 'La "Biblioteca di Agapito" e la Basilica di S. Agnese', in Harris 1999: 85–107.

Günther, O. (1895) *Epistulae imperatorum pontificum aliorum Avellana que dicitur collectio*, CSEL 35. Vienna.

(1896) 'Avellana-Studien', *Sitzungsberichte der Philosophisch-Historischen Classe: Akademie der Wissenschaften Wien* 134: 15–134.

Guyotjeanin, O., Morelle, L., and Parisse, M. (eds.) (1993) *Les cartulaires. Actes de la table ronde organisée par l'École nationale des chartes e le G.D.R. 121 du C.N.R.S (Paris, 5–7 décembre 1991)*. Paris.

Halkin, F. (1974) 'La passion grecque des saints Gallican, Jean et Paul (BHG 2191)', *AB* 90: 265–86.

Hammond Bammel, C. P. (1977) 'The last ten years of Rufinus' life and the date of his move south from Aquileia', *JTS* n.s. 28: 372–429.

(1978) 'Products of fifth-century scriptoria preserving conventions used by Rufinus of Aquileia', *JTS* n.s. 29: 366–91.

(1979) 'Products of fifth-century scriptoria preserving conventions used by Rufinus of Aquileia', *JTS* n.s. 30: 430–62.

(1984) 'Products of fifth-century scriptoria preserving conventions used by Rufinus of Aquileia', *JTS* n.s. 35: 347–93.

Harries, Jill (1984) 'Treasure in heaven: property and inheritance among senators of late Rome', in Elizabeth M. Craik (ed.), *Marriage and Property*. Aberdeen, 54–70.

(1999) *Law and Empire in Late Antiquity*. Cambridge.

Harrill, J. A. (2001) 'The influence of Roman contract law on early baptismal formulae (Tertulliam, *Ad martyres* 3)', *Studia Patristica* 36: 275–82.

Harris, W. V. (ed.) (1999) *The Transformations of Urbs Roma in Late Antiquity. JRA* Suppl. 33. Portsmouth, RI.
Hedrick, C. W. (2000) *History and Silence: Purge and Rehabilitation of Memory in Late Antiquity*. Austin, TX.
Henck, N. (2001) 'Constantius Ὁ Φιλοκτίστης ?', *DOP* 55: 279–304.
Heumann, H. and Seckel, E. (1971) *Handlexikon zu den Quellen des römischen Rechts*, 11th edn. Graz.
Hildebrand, H. (1922) 'Die Absetzung des Papstes Silverius (537)', *Historisches Jahrbuch* 42: 213–42.
Hillner, J. (forthcoming) 'Clerics, property and patronage: the case of the Roman titular churches', *Antiquité Tardive*.
Holum, K. (1982) *Theodosian Empresses: Women and Imperial Dominion in Late Antiquity*. Berkeley.
Hülsen, C. (1903) 'Brontotae', *RE Suppl.* 1: 258.
Humfress, C. and Garnsey, P. (2001) *Evolution of the Late Antique World*. Cambridge.
Humphreys, S. C. (1983) *The Family, Women and Death: Comparative Studies*. London.
Humphries, M. (2000) 'Italy, AD 425–605', in *The Cambridge Ancient History, XIV: Late Antiquity: Empire and Successors AD 425–600*, ed. Averil Cameron, B. Ward-Perkins, and Michael Whitby. Cambridge: 525–51.
(2003) 'Roman senators and absent emperors in late antiquity', *Acta ad Archaeologiam et Artium Historiam Pertinentia* 17 (n.s. 3): 27–46.
(2006) *Early Christianity*. London and New York.
(forthcoming) '"The Gracious Favour of the Gods": the mind of the persecutors', in *The Great Persecution, AD 303: A Commemoration. Proceedings of the Fifth Maynooth Patristic Conference*, ed. V. Twomey and M. Humphries. Dublin.
Hunt, D. (1998) 'The Church as a public institution', *The Cambridge Ancient History*, vol. XIII, ed. A. Cameron and P. Garnsey. Cambridge: 238–72.
Hunter, D. (1987) 'Resistance to the ascetic ideal in late fourth-century Rome: the case of Jovinian' *Theological Studies* 48: 45–64.
Jacobs, A. (1999) 'A family affair: marriage, class and ethics in the *Apocryphal Acts of the Apostles*', *JECS* 7: 105–38.
(2000) 'Writing Demetrias: ascetic logic in ancient Christianity', *Church History* 69: 719–48.
Jacobs, A. and Krawiec, R. (2003) 'Father knows best? Christian families in an age of asceticism', *JECS* 11: 257–263.
Jenal, G. (1995) *Italia ascetica atque monastica. Das Asketen- und Mönchtum in Italien von den Anfängen bis zur Zeit der Langobarden (ca. 150/250–604)*, 2 vols. Stuttgart.
John, E. (1962) 'A note on Bede's use of "facultas"', *Revue Bénédictine* 72: 350–5.
Johnson, M. J. (1991) 'On the burial places of the Theodosian dynasty', *Byzantion* 61: 330–8.
(2006) 'Architecture of Empire', in *The Cambridge Companion to the Age of Constantine*, ed. N. Lenski. Cambridge: 278–97.

Johnson, Scott Fitzgerald (2006) *The Life and Miracles of Thekla: A Literary Study*. Hellenic Studies 13. Washington, DC.

Johnson, T. and Dandeker, C. (1989) 'Patronage: relation and system', in Wallace-Hadrill 1989: 219–45.

Johnston, D. (1985) 'Munificence and municipia. Bequests to towns in classical Roman law', *JRS* 75: 105–25.

Jones, A. H. M. (1960) 'Church finance in the fifth and sixth centuries', *JTS* n.s. 11: 84–94.

(1964) *The Later Roman Empire 284–602: A Social, Economic, and Administrative Survey*. Oxford.

(1974) *The Roman Economy: Studies in Ancient Economy and Administrative History*. Oxford.

Jones, A. H. M. and Martindale, R. (1971–92) *Prosopography of the Later Roman Empire*, 3 vols. Cambridge.

Jones, H. I. (1998) 'The desert and desire: virginity, city and family in the Roman martyr-legends of Agnes and Eugenia', unpubl. MA dissertation, Manchester.

Joshel, S. R. (1992) 'The body female and the body politic: Livy's Lucretia and Verginia', in *Pornography and Representation in Greece and Rome*, ed. A. Richlin. New York: 112–30.

Joubert, S. (1995) 'Managing the household: Paul as *paterfamilias* of the Christian household group in Corinth', in *Modelling Early Christianity: Social-Scientific Studies of the New Testament in Context*, ed. Philip Esler. London: 213–23.

Kaegi, W. E. (2003) *Heraclius: Emperor of Byzantium*. Cambridge.

Kalas, G. A. (1999) 'Sacred image – urban space: image, installations, and ritual in the early medieval Roman Forum', unpubl. PhD thesis, Bryn Mawr College.

Kaser, M. (1971) *Das römische Privatrecht*, vol. I, 2nd edn. Munich.

(1975) *Das römische Privatrecht*, vol. II, 2nd edn. Munich.

Kelly, C. (1994) 'Later Roman bureaucracy: going through the files', in *Literacy and Power in the Ancient World*, ed. A. Bowman and G. Woolf. Cambridge: 161–76.

(2003) 'The New Rome and the Old: Ammianus Marcellinus' silences on Constantinople', *Classical Quarterly* n.s. 53: 588–607.

Kelly, J. N. D. (1975) *Jerome: His Life, Writings and Controversies*. London.

Kery, L. (1999) *Canonical Collections of the Early Middle Ages (ca. 400–1140)*. Washington, DC.

Kirkby, H. (1981) 'The scholar and his public', in *Boethius: His Life, Thought, and Influence*, ed. Margaret Gibson. Oxford: 44–69.

Kirsch, J. P. (1918) *Die römischen Titelkirchen im Altertum*. Paderborn.

(1924) 'I santuari domestici di martiri nei titoli romani ed altri simili santuari nelle chiese cristiane e nelle case private di fedeli', *Atti della Pontificia Accademia Romana di Archeologia* 2: 27–43.

Kitchen, J. (1998) *Saints' Lives and the Rhetoric of Gender: Male and Female in Merovingian Hagiography*. Oxford.

Klein, R. (1979) 'Der Rombesuch des Kaisers Konstantius II im Jahre 357', *Athenaeum* n.s. 57: 98–115.

Klingshirn, W. (1990) 'Caesarius' monastery for women in Arles and the composition and function of the *Vita Caesarii*', *Revue Bénédictine* 100: 441–81.
Knowles, D. (1963) 'The Regula Magistri and the Rule of St Benedict', in his *Great Historical Enterprises: Problems in Monastic History*. London: 139–195.
Kornemann, E. (1900) 'Collegia', in *Pauly-Wissowas Realenzyklopädie der Klassischen Alterthumswissenschaften*, vol. IV.1: 380–480.
Krabbe, K. C. (1965) 'Epistula ad Demetriadem De Vera Humilitate: a critical text and translation with introduction and commentary', unpubl. PhD thesis, Catholic University of America, Washington, DC.
Krause, J.-U. (1996a) 'La prise en charge des veuves par l'église dans l'antiquité tardive', in *La fin de la cité antique et le debut de la cité médiévale de la fin du IIIe siècle à l'avènement de Charlemagne*, ed. C. Lepelley. Bari: 115–26.
(1996b) *Gefängnisse im römischen Reich*. Stuttgart.
Krautheimer, R. (1939) 'The beginnings of early Christian architecture', *Review of Religion* 3: 127–48.
(1965) *Early Christian and Byzantine Architecture*. Baltimore.
(1980) *Rome, Profile of a City 312–1308*. Princeton.
(1983) *Three Christian Capitals: Topography and Politics*. Berkeley and Los Angeles.
(1985) *St. Peter's and Medieval Rome*. Rome.
(1995) 'Die Kirche San Lorenzo in Damaso in Rom. Vorläufiger Grabungsbericht', in *Akten des XII. internationalen Kongresses für christliche Archäologie, 1991*. Vatican City: 958–63.
Krautheimer, R. et al. (1937–80) *Corpus Basilicarum Christianarum Romae*, 5 vols. Rome.
Krusch, B. (1906) 'Die Urkunden von Corbie und Levillains letztes Wort', *Neues Archiv* 31: 333–75.
Künzle, P. (1953) 'Del cosidetto "Titulus Archivorum" di papa Damaso', *Rivista di Storia della Chiesa in Italia* 7: 1–26.
(1961) 'Zur basilica Liberiana: basilica Sicinini = basilica Liberiana', *Römische Quartalschift* 56: 1–61.
Kurdock, A. N. (2003) 'The Anician women: patronage and dynastic strategy in a late Roman domus, 350 CE–600 CE', unpubl. PhD thesis, Manchester.
Kuttner, S. (1945) '*Cardinalis:* the history of a canonical concept', *Traditio* 43: 121–214.
Lambert, D. (2003) 'History and community in the works of Salvian of Marseille', unpubl. DPhil thesis, Oxford.
Lane Fox, R. (1997) 'Power and possession in the first monasteries', in *Aspects of the Fourth Century A.D.*, ed. H. W. Pleket and A. M. F. W. Verhoogt. Leiden: 68–95.
Lanzoni, F. (1925) 'I titoli presbiteriali di Roma antica nella storia e nella leggenda', *Rivista di Archeologia Cristiana* 2: 193–257.
LaRegina, A. (2001) *Lexicon topographicum urbis Romae: Suburbium*, vol. I. Rome.
(2004) *Lexicon topographicum urbis Romae: Suburbium*, vol. II. Rome.
Laum, B. (1914) *Stiftungen in der griechischen und römischen Antike: ein Beitrag zur antiken Kulturgeschichte*, vol. I. Leipzig and Berlin.

Laurence, P. (ed.) (2002) *Gerontius, La Vie Latine de Sainte Mélanie: édition critique, traduction et commentaire*. Jerusalem.

Lavan, L. (ed.) (2001) *Recent Research in Late Antique Urbanism*. Portsmouth, RI.

Layton, R. (2002) 'Plagiarism and lay patronage of ascetic scholarship: Jerome, Ambrose and Rufinus', *JECS* 10: 489–522.

Leclercq, H. (1907–53) 'Constance (Baptistère de Sainte)', *DACL* 3.2: 2612.

(1907–53) 'Le Martyrologe', *DACL* 10.2: 2530–63.

(1951) 'L'ancienne version latine des sentences d'Évagre pour les moines', *Scriptorium* 5: 195–213.

Lehmann, T. (2004) *Paulinus Nolanus und die Basilica Nova in Cimitile/Nola. Studien zu einem zentralen Denkmal der spätantiken Architektur*. Wiesbaden.

Lehnen, J. (1997) *Adventus Principis. Untersuchungen zum Sinngehalt und Zeremoniell der Kaiserankunft in den Städten des Imperium Romanum*. Prismata 7. Frankfurt.

Lemarignier, J.-F. (1950a) 'La dislocation du *pagus* et le problème des *consuetudines* (Xe–Xie siècles)', in *Mélanges dédiés à la mémoire de Louis Halphen*. Paris: 401–10.

(1950b) 'L'exemption monastique et les origines de la réforme grégorienne', in *A Cluny. Congrès scientifique 9–11 juillet 1949*. Dijon: 288–340.

Lendon, J. E. (1997) *Empire of Honour*. Oxford.

Lenski, N. (2002) *Failure of Empire: Valens and the Roman State in the Fourth Century AD*. Berkeley, Los Angeles, and London.

Lepelley, C. (1979) *Les cités de l'Afrique romaine au bas-empire*, vol. 1. Paris.

(ed.) (1996) *La fin de la cité antique et le début de la cité médiévale*. Bari.

(1997–98) 'Mélanie la Jeune, entre Rome, la Sicilia, et l'Afrique: les effets socialement pernicieux d'une forme extrême de l'ascétisme', in *Atti del IX congresso internazionale di studi sulla Sicilia antica* [*Kokalos* 43–44], 1.1: 15–32.

Lesne, E. (1910) *Histoire de la propriété ecclésiastique en France*, 2 vols. Paris.

Levison, W. (1924) 'Konstantinische Schenkung und Silvester-Legende', *Miscellanea Fr. Ehrle: Scritti di Storia e Paleografia* 2: 159–247.

(1948) *Aus rheinischer und fränkischer Frühzeit*. Düsseldorf.

Levy, E. (1951) *West Roman Vulgar Law*, 1: *The Law of Property*. Philadelphia.

Lewis, C. T. and Short, C. (1963) *A Latin Dictionary*. Oxford.

Leyerle, B. (1993) 'John Chrysostom and the gaze', *JECS* 1: 159–74.

Leyser, C. (1997) 'Custom, truth, and gender in eleventh-century reform', *SCH* 34: 75–91.

(1999) 'Semi-Pelagianism', in *Augustine through the Ages: An Encyclopedia*, ed. A. Fitzgerald. Grand Rapids, MI: 761–6.

(2000a) *Authority and Asceticism from Augustine to Gregory the Great*. Oxford.

(2000b) 'The temptations of cult: Roman martyr piety in the age of Gregory the Great', *EME* 9.3: 298–307.

(2004) 'Charisma in the archive: Roman monasteries and the memory of Pope Gregory the Great, c.870–c.940', in *Le scritture dai monasteri, II Seminario internazionale di studio 'I monasteri nell'alto medioevo'*, ed. F. de Rubeis and W. Pohl. Rome: 207–24.

(2005) '*Homo pauper, de pauperibus natum*: Augustine, church property, and the cult of Stephen', *Augustinian Studies* 36: 229–37.
Leyser, H. (1984) *Hermits and the New Monasticism: A Study of Religious Communities in Western Europe: 1000–1150*. London.
Leyser, K. (1979) *Rule and Conflict in an Early Medieval Society*. Oxford.
(1982a) 'Frederick Barbarossa, Henry II and the hand of St. James', in his *Medieval Germany and Its Neighbours 900–1250*. London: 215–40.
(1982b) 'Ottonian government', in his *Medieval Germany and Its Neighbours*. London: 69–101.
Liebeschuetz, J. H. W. G. (1996) 'Administration and politics in the cities of the 5th and 6th centuries with special reference to the circus factions', in Lepelley 1996: 160–82.
(2001) *The Decline and Fall of the Roman City*. Oxford and New York.
Lightman, M. and Zeisel, W. (1977) '*Univira*: an example of continuity and change in Roman society', *Church History* 46: 19–32.
Lim, R. (1999) 'People as power: games, munificence, and contested topography', in Harris 1999: 265–81.
Limberis, V. (1994) *Divine Heiress: The Virgin Mary and the Creation of Constantinople*. London.
Lippold, A. (1965) 'Ursinus and Damasus', *Historia* 14: 105–28.
Lipsius, R. A. and Bonnet, M. (1990). *Acta Apostolorum Apocrypha*, 3 vols. Hildesheim.
Lizzi Testa, R. (2004) *Senatori, popoli, papi: il governo di Roma al tempo dei Valentiniani*. Munera 21. Bari.
Llewellyn, P. (1971) *Rome in the Dark Ages*. London.
(1974) 'The Roman church in the seventh century: the legacy of Gregory the Great', *Journal of Ecclesiastical History* 25: 363–80.
(1976a) 'Constans II and the Roman church: a possible instance of imperial pressure', *Byzantion* 46: 120–6.
(1976b) 'The Roman church during the Laurentian schism: priests and senators', *Church History* 45: 417–27.
(1977) 'The Roman clergy during the Laurentian schism (498–506): a preliminary analysis', *Ancient Society* 8: 245–75.
(1986) 'The popes and the constitution in the eighth century', *EHR* 101: 42–67.
Lo Cascio, E. (2000) 'La popolazione', in *Roma imperiale: una metropoli antica*, ed. E. Lo Cascio. Rome: 17–69.
Lorenz, R. (1962) 'Der Augustinismus Prospers von Aquitanien', *ZKG* 73: 217–52.
Maassen, F. (1870) *Geschichte der Quellen und der Literatur des canonischen Rechts im Abendlande bis zum Ausgange des Mittelalters*, vol. I. Graz.
(1877) 'Über eine Sammlung Gregors I. Von Schreiben und Verordnungen der Kaiser und Päpste', in *Sitzungsberichte der philosophisch-historischen Classe der Akademie der Wissenschaften*. Wien: 227–57.
MacCormack, S. (1972) 'Change and continuity in late antiquity: the ceremony of *adventus*', *Historia* 21: 721–32.
(1975) 'Latin prose panegyrics', in *Empire and Aftermath: Silver Latin*, vol. II, ed. T. A. Dorey. London: 143–205.

(1981) *Art and Ceremony in Late Antiquity*. Berkeley, Los Angeles, and London.

McCormick, M. (1986) *Eternal Victory: Triumphal Rulership in Late Antiquity, Byzantium, and the Early Medieval West*. Cambridge.

McCulloh, J. (1980) 'From antiquity to the middle ages: continuity and change in papal relic policy from the 6th to the 8th century', in *Pietas: Festschrift für Bernhard Kötting*, ed. E. Dassmann and K. S. Frank. Jahrbuch für Antike und Christentum, Ergänzungsband 8: 313–24.

MacDonald, D. R. (ed.) (1990) *The Acts of Andrew and the Acts of Andrew and Mattias in the City of Cannibals*. Atlanta.

Machado, C. (forthcoming) 'Building the past: monuments and memory in the Forum Romanum', *Late Antique Archaeology*, ed. W. Bowden and L. Lavan. Leiden: 157–92.

Mackie, G. (1997) 'A new look at the patronage of Santa Costanza, Rome', *Byzantion* 67: 383–406.

McKitterick, R. (2004) *History and Memory in the Carolingian World*. Cambridge.

McLynn, N. (1992) 'Christian controversy and violence in the fourth century', *Kodai* 3: 15–44.

(2004) 'The transformation of imperial churchgoing in the fourth century', in *Approaching Late Antiquity: The Transformation from Early to Late Empire*, ed. S. Swain and M. Edwards. Oxford: 235–70.

McNamara, J. A. (ed.) (1992) *Sainted Women of the Dark Ages*. London.

MacQueen, D. J. (1972) 'St. Augustine's concept of property ownership', *Recherches Augustiniennes* 8: 187–229.

McSheffrey, M. (2004) 'Place, space and situation: public and private in the making of marriage in late medieval London', *Speculum* 79: 960–90.

Magi, L. (1972) *La sede romana nella corrispondenza degli imperatori e patriarchi bizantini (VI–VII sec.)*. Bibliothèque de la Revue d'Histoire Ecclésiastique 57. Rome and Louvain.

Maier, H. O. (1994) 'Private space as the social context of Arianism in Ambrose's Milan', *JTS* 45: 72–93.

(1995a) 'The topography of heresy and dissent in late fourth-century Rome', *Historia* 44: 232–49.

(1995b) 'Religious dissent, heresy and households in late antiquity', *Vigiliae Christianae* 49: 49–63.

(1996) '"Manichee!": Leo the Great and the orthodox panopticon', *JECS* 4: 441–60.

Manacorda, D. (2001) *Crypta Balbi: archeologia e storia di un paesaggio urbano*. Milan.

Manselli, R. (1981) 'Dalla cella farfense a San Luigi de'Francesi: storia di un angolo di Roma', in *Les fondations nationales dans la Rome pontificale*. Collections de l'École Française de Rome 52. Rome: 75–81.

Marazzi, F. (1998) *I 'Patrimonia Sanctae Romanae Ecclesiae' nel Lazio (secoli IV–X): strutture amministrative e prassi gestionale (dal IV agli inizi del X secolo)*. Rome.

(2000) 'Rome in transition: economic and political change in the fourth and fifth centuries', in Smith 2000: 21–41.

Markus, R. (1970, 2nd edn 1988) *Saeculum: History and Society in the Theology of Saint Augustine*. Cambridge.

(1981) 'Gregory the Great's Europe', *Transactions of the Royal Historical Society* 31: 21–36.

(1990, 2nd edn 1998) *The End of Ancient Christianity*. Cambridge.

(1997) *Gregory the Great and His World*. Cambridge.

Markus, R. and Sotinel, C. (forthcoming) 'Introduction', in Chazelle and Cubitt, forthcoming.

Marrou, H.-I. (1931) 'Autour de la bibliothèque du pape Agapit', *MEFRA* 48: 124–69.

Masai, F. and Vanderhoven, H. (1953) *La Règle du Maître: édition diplomatique des manuscrits latins 12205 et 12634 de Paris*. Brussels and Paris.

Mathews, T. F. (1962) 'An early Roman chancel arrangement and its liturgical function', *RivAC* 38: 73–95.

Matthews, J. (1975, 2nd edn 1990) *Western Aristocracies and Imperial Court, AD 364–425*. Oxford.

(1989) *The Roman Empire of Ammianus*. London.

(2000) *Laying Down the Law: A Study of the Theodosian Code*. New Haven.

Mauss, M. (1967) *The Gift: Forms and Functions of Exchange in Archaic Societies*, trans. I. Cunnison. New York.

Meeks, W. (1983). *The First Urban Christians: The Social World of the Apostle Paul*. New Haven.

Melchor Gil, E. (1994) *El mecenezago civico en la Bética: la contribución de los evergetas al desarrollo de la vida municipal*. Cordoba.

Mendels, D. (1999) *The Media Revolution of Early Christianity: An Essay on Eusebius's 'Ecclesiastical History'*. Grand Rapids, MI.

Meneghini, R. and Santangeli Valenzani, R. (1995) 'Sepolture intramuranee a Roma – aggiornamenti e considerazione', *Archeologia Medievale* 22: 283–90.

(1996) 'Episodi di trasformazione del paessaggio urbano nella Roma altomedievale attraverso l'analisi di due contesti: un isolato in Piazza dei Cinquecento e l'area dei Fori Imperiali', *Archeologia Medievale* 33: 53–99.

(2001a) 'La trasformazione del tessuto urbano tra V e IX secolo', in Arena and Delogu 2001: 20–33.

(2001b) 'I Fori Imperiali nell'alto medioevo', in Arena and Delogu 2001: 34–9.

(2004), *Roma nell'alto medioevo. Topografia e urbanistica della città dal V al X secolo*. Rome.

Meyer, U. (1998) *Soziales Handeln im Zeichen des 'Hauses': zur Öikonomik in der Spätantike und im frühen Mittelalter*. Göttingen.

Millar, F. (1992) *The Emperor in the Roman World (31 BC–AD 337)*, 2nd edn. London.

Miller, M. C. (2003) 'The Florentine bishop's ritual entry and the origins of the medieval episcopal *adventus*', *Revue d'Histoire Ecclésiastique* 98: 5–27.

Mohlberg, C., Eizenhöfer, L. and Siffrin, P. (eds.) (1960) *Liber Sacramentorum Romanae Aeclesiae ordinis anni circuli* (Cod. Vat. Reg. lat. 316/Paris Bibl. Nat. 7193, 41/56) (*Sacramentarium Gelasianum*). Rome.

Mombritius, B. (ed.) (1978) *Sanctuarium seu Vitae Sanctorum*, 2 vols. New York.

Mommsen, T. (ed). (1894) Monumenta Germaniae Historica AA XII. Berlin.

(1898) *Gesta Pontificum Romanorum*, I: *Liber Pontificalis, pars prior*. MGH. Berlin.

Mommsen, T. and Meyer, E. (eds.) (1954) *Theodosiani Libri cum Constitutionibus Sirmondianis*. Berlin.

Monachesi, Maria (1921) 'Arnobio il Giovane ed una sua possible attività agiografica' *Bolletino di Studi Storici-religiosi* 1: 96–109.

Moorhead, J. (1992) *Theodoric in Italy*. Oxford.

Morin, G. (1940) 'La part des papes du sixième siècle dans les développement de l'année liturgique', *Revue Bénédictine* 52: 3–14.

Mrozek, S. (1968) 'Zur Frage der Tutela in römischen Inschriften', *Acta Antiqua Academiae Scientiarum Hungaricae* 16: 283–8.

Mullett, M. 'Writing in early medieval Byzantium', in *The Uses of Literacy in Early Medieval Europe*, ed. R. McKitterick. Cambridge: 156–85.

Munier, C. (1998) 'Exemption monastique et conciles africains (526–536)', *Revue Bénédictine* 108: 5–24.

Mutzenbecher, A. (1961) 'Bestimmung der echten Sermones des Maximus Taurinensis', *Sacris Erudiri* 12: 197–293.

(ed.) (1962) *Maximi Episcopi Taurinensis Sermones* (Corpus Christianorum. Series Latina 23). Turnhout.

Näf, B. (1995) *Senatorisches Standesbewußtein in spätrömischer Zeit*. Freiburg.

Nelson, J. L. (1978) 'Queens as Jezebels: the careers of Brunhild and Balthild in Merovingian history', in *Medieval Women*, ed. D. Baker. Oxford: 31–78.

Nightingale, J. (2001) *Monasteries and Patrons in the Gorze Reform: Lotharingia, c. 850–1000*. Oxford.

Niquet, H. (2000) *Monumenta virtutum titulique: senatorische Selbstdarstellung im spätantiken Rom im Spiegel der epigraphischen Denkmäler*. Stuttgart.

Noble, T. F. X. (1984) *The Republic of St. Peter: The Birth of the Papal State 680–825*, Philadelphia.

(1985) 'A new look at the Liber Pontificalis', *Archivum Historiae Pontificiae* 23: 347–58.

(1990) 'Literacy and papal government in late antiquity and the early middle ages', in *The Uses of Literacy in Early Medieval Europe*, ed. R. McKitterick. Cambridge: 82–108.

(2001) 'Topography, celebration, and power: the making of a papal Rome in the eighth and ninth centuries', in *Topographies of Power in the Early Middle Ages*, ed. M. de Jong and F. Theuws, with C. Van Rhijn. The Transformation of the Roman World 6. Leiden: 217–41.

North, H. (1966) *Sophrosyne: Self-knowledge and Self-restraint in Greek literature*. Ithaca, NY.

O'Donnell, J. (1981) 'Liberius the Patrician', *Traditio* 37: 31–72.

(2005) *Augustine: Sinner and Saint*. New York.

Orlandi, S. (2004) *Roma. Anfiteatri e strutture annesse con una nuova edizione e commento delle iscrizioni del Colosseo*. Epigrafia Anfiteatrale dell'Occidente Romano 6 = 15. Rome.

Osborne, J. (1985) 'The Roman catacombs in the middle ages', *PBSR* 53: 278–328.

Packer, J. E. (1997) *The Forum of Trajan*. Berkeley and Los Angeles.

Pani Ermini, L. (2000) *Christiana Loca: lo spazio cristiano nella Roma del primo milennio*. Rome.

Perkins, J. (1995) *The Suffering Self: Pain and Narrative Representation in the Early Christian Era*. London.

Petersen, J. M. (1984) *The Dialogues of Gregory the Great in their Late Antique Cultural Background*. Toronto.

(1987) '"Homo omnino Latinus?": the theological and cultural background of Gregory the Great', *Speculum* 62: 529–51.

Petitmengin, P. (1971) 'Notes sur des manuscrits patristiques latins', *Revue des Études Augustiniennes* 17: 3–10.

Petrucci, A.(1971) 'L'onciale romana: origini, sviluppo e diffusione di una stilizzazione grafica altomedievale (sec. VI–IX)', *Studi Medievali* 3rd ser. 12: 75–134, +20 pls.

(1995) *Writers and Readers in Medieval Italy: Studies in the History of Written Culture*, ed. and trans. C. Radding. New Haven. Originally published as Petrucci, A. (1986) 'Dal libro unitario al libro miscellaneo', in *Società romana e impero tardoantica*, vol. IV, ed. A. Giardina. Rome and Bari: 173–87, 271–4, pls. 40–8.

Petruccione, J. (1990) 'The portrait of St. Eulalia of Mérida in Prudentius' Peristephanon 3', *AB* 108: 81–104.

Philipsborn, A. (1954) 'Der Begriff der juristischen Person im römischen Recht', *Zeitschrift der Savigny-Stiftung für Rechtsgeschichte (Rom. Abt.)* 71: 41–70.

Pietri, C. (1961) 'Concordia apostolorum et renovatio urbis (cult des martyrs et propagande pontificale)', *MEFRA* 73: 275–322.

(1976) *Roma christiana: recherches sur l'église de Rome, son organisation, sa politique, son idéologie de Miltiade à Sixte III* (311–440). Rome.

(1978a) 'Recherches sur les domus ecclesiae', *Revue des Études Augustiniennes* 24: 3–21.

(1978b) 'Évergétisme et richesses ecclésiastiques dans l'Italie du IVe à la fin du Ve s.: l'exemple romain', *Ktema* 3: 317–37.

(1981a) 'Donateurs et pieux établissements d'après le légendier romain (Ve–VIIe s.)', in *Hagiographie: cultures et sociétés IV–XII siècle. Actes du Colloque organisé à Nanterre et à Paris 2–5 mai 1979*. Paris: 435–53.

(1981b) 'Aristocratie et société cléricale dans l'Italie chrétienne au temps d'Odoacre et de Théodoric', *MEFRA* 93.1: 417–67.

(1986) 'Clercs et serviteurs laïcs de l'église romaine au temps de Grégoire le Grand', in *Grégoire le Grand. Actes du colloque, Chantilly Centre culturel Les Fontaines, 15–19 septembre 1982*, ed. J. Fontaine. Paris: 107–22.

(1989) 'Régions ecclésiastiques et paroisses romaines', in *Actes du XIe Congrès d'archéologie chrétienne, Lyon 1986*. Rome: 1035–67.

Pietri, C. and Pietri, L. (eds.) (1999–2000) *Prosopographie de l'Italie chrétienne (313–604)*, 2 vols. Prosopographie chrétienne du Bas-Empire 2.1 and 2.2. Rome.

Pietri, L. (2002) 'Évergétisme chrétien et fondations privées dans l'Italie de l'antiquité tardive', in *'Humana Sapit': études d'antiquité tardive offertes à Lellia Cracco Ruggini*, ed. R. Lizzi Testa and J.-M. Carrié. Turnhout: 253–63.

Pilsworth, C. (2000) 'Dating the *gesta martyrum*: a manuscript based approach', *EME* 9: 309–24.

(forthcoming) 'Vile scraps: "booklet" style manuscripts and the transmission and use of the Italian martyr narratives in early medieval Europe', in *Hagiographische Handschriften im Mittelalter zwischen Wiederschrift und Niederschrift*, ed. M. Diesenberger and M. Niederkorn-Bruck. Vienna.

Pisani Sartorio, G. (2000) 'Il Palazzo di Massenzio sulla via Appia', in Ensoli and La Rocca 2000: 116–19.

Pitz, E. (1990) *Papstreskripte im frühen Mittelalter: Diplomatische und rechtsgeschichtliche Studien zum Brief-Corpus Gregors des Großen*. Sigmaringen.

Pizzaro, J. (1989) *A Rhetoric of the Scene: Dramatic Narrative in the Early Middle Ages*. Toronto.

Pohl, W. (2001a) 'History in fragments. Montecassino's politics of memory', *EME* 10.3: 343–74.

(2001b) *Werkstätte der Erinnerung: Montecassino und die Gestaltung der langobardischen Vergangenheit*. Mitteilungen des Instituts für Österreichische Geschichtsforschung, Erg.-Band 39. Vienna.

Pomares, G. (ed.) (1959) Gelasius, *Adversum Andromachum et ceteros Romanos qui Lupercalia secundum morem pristinum colenda constituunt*, Sources Chrétiennes 65. Paris.

Poulin, J.-C. (2006) 'Les libelli dans l'édition hagiographique avant le XIIe siècle', in *Livrets, collections et textes: études sur la tradition hagiographique latine*, ed. M. Heinzelmann. Ostfildern: 15–193.

Prandi, A. (1953) *Il complesso monumentale della basilica celimontana dei SS. Giovanni e Paolo*. Rome.

Prinz, F. (1965) *Frühes Mönchtum im Frankenreich: Kultur und Gesellschaft in Gallien, den Rheinlanden und Bayern am Beispiel der monastischen Entwicklung (4. bis 8. Jahrhundert)*. Vienna.

Rapp, C. (1998) 'Storytelling as spiritual communication in early Greek hagiography: the use of *diegesis*', *JECS* 6.3: 431–48.

(2000) 'The elite status of bishops in late antiquity in ecclesiastical, spiritual and social contexts', *Arethusa* 33: 379–99.

(2005) *Holy Bishops in Late Antiquity: The Nature of Christian Leadership in an Age of Transition*. Berkeley.

Reardon, B. P. (1989) *Collected Ancient Greek Novels*. London.

Rebillard, E. (2003) *Religion et sépulture: l'église, les vivants et les morts dans l'antiquité tardive*. Paris.

Recchia, V. (1982–83) 'San Benedetto e la politica religiosa dell'Occidente nella prima metà del secolo VI dai *Dialogi* di Gregorio Magno', *Romanobarbarica* 7: 201–52.

(1986) 'I protagonisti dell'offensiva romana antimonofisita tra la fine del quinto e i primi decenni del sesto secolo dai Dialoghi di Gregorio Magno', in

Grégoire le Grand: Colloque international sur Grégoire le Grand, Chantilly 1982, ed. J. Fontaine, R. Gillet, and S. Pellistrandi. Paris: 159–69.
(1996) *Gregorio magno papa ed esegeta biblica*. Bari.
Rees, B. R. (1988) *Pelagius: A Reluctant Heretic*. Woodbridge.
(1991) *The Letters of Pelagius and His Followers*. Woodbridge.
Reimitz, H. (2000) 'Ein karolingisches Geschichtsbuch aus St Amand: Der *Codex Vindobonensis* palat. 473', in *Text–Schrift–Codex: quellenkundliche Arbeiten aus dem Institut für Österreichische Geschichtsforschung*, ed. C. Egger and H. Weigl. Vienna: 43–90.
Reuter, T. (1995) 'Introduction: reading the tenth century', in *NCMH*, vol. III, ed. T. Reuter. Cambridge: 1–24.
Rich, J. (ed.) (1992) *The City in Late Antiquity*. London and New York.
Richards, J. (1979) *The Popes and the Papacy in the Early Middle Ages, 476–752*. London.
Riché, P. (1976) *Education and Culture in the Barbarian West*. New York.
Riggsby, A. (1997) '"Public" and "private" in Roman culture: the case of the *cubiculum*', *JRA* 10: 36–55.
Rosenwein, B. (1989) *To Be the Neighbor of St Peter: The Social Meaning of Cluny's Property, 909–1049*. Ithaca, NY.
(1999) *Negotiating Space: Power, Restraint, and Privileges of Immunity in Early Medieval Europe*. Manchester.
Rousseau, P. (1985, 2nd edn 1999) *Pachomius: The Making of a Community in Fourth Century Egypt*. Berkeley.
(1995) '"Learned women" and the formation of a Christian culture in late antiquity', *Symbolae Osloenses* 70: 116–47.
(2005) 'The pious household and the virgin chorus: reflections on Gregory of Nyssa's Life of Macrina', *JECS* 13.2: 165–86.
Sághy, M. (2000) '*Scinditur in partes populus*: Pope Damasus and the martyrs of Rome', *EME* 9: 273–87.
Salisbury, J. E. (ed.) (1991) *Church Fathers, Independent Virgins*. New York.
Saller, R. (1999) '*Paterfamilias* and *materfamilias* and the gendered semantics of the Roman household', *CP* 94: 184–99.
Salzman, M. R. (1990) *On Roman Time: The Codex-Calendar of 354 and the Rhythms of Urban Life in Late Antiquity*. Berkeley and Los Angeles.
(2002) *The Making of a Christian Aristocracy: Social and Religious Change in the Western Empire*. Cambridge, MA.
Sanfilippo, I. L. (1980) 'I possessi romani di Farfa, Montecassino e Subiaco, secoli IX–XII', *Archivio della Società Romana di Storia Patria* 103: 13–39.
Sansterre, J.-M. (1983) *Les moines grecs et orientaux à Rome aux époques byzantine et carolingienne (milieu du VIe s.–fin du IXe s.)*. 2 vols. Brussels.
Santangeli Valenzani, R. (1997) 'Edilizia residenziale e aristocrazia urbana a Roma nell'altomedioevo', in *I Congresso nazionale di archeologia medievale, Pisa 29–31 mai, 1997*. Florence: 64–70.
(2000) 'Residential building in early medieval Rome', in *Early Medieval Rome and the Christian West: Essays in Honor of Donald A. Bullough*, ed. Julia M. H. Smith. Leiden: 101–12.

Saxer, V. (1980) *Morts, martyrs, reliques en Afrique chrétienne aux premiers siècles*. Paris.
(1989) 'L'utilisation par la liturgie de l'espace urbain et suburbain: l'example de Rome dans l'antiquité et le haut moyen âge', in *Actes du XIe Congrès international d'archéologie chrétienne (21–28 sept. 1986)*. Rome: 917–1033.
(2001) 'La chiesa di Roma dal V al X secolo: amministrazione centrale e organizzazione territoriale', in *Roma nell'alto medioevo*, vol. II. Spoleto: 493–632.
Scalia, G. (1977) 'Gli *archiva* di papa Damaso e le biblioteche di papa Ilaro', *Studi Medievali* 18.1: 39–63.
Schieffer, R. (2000) 'Charlemagne and Rome', in Smith 2000b: 279–96.
Schlinkert, D. (1996) *Ordo senatorius und nobilitas: die Konstitution des Senatsadels in der Spätantike*. Stuttgart.
Schnorr von Carolsfeld, L. (1933) *Geschichte der juristischen Person*. Munich.
Schuster, I. (1904) 'L'oratorio di santo Stefano sulla via Ostiense dal secolo sesto all'undecimo', *Nuovo Bollettino di Archeologia Cristiana* 10: 185–204.
(1934) *La Basilica e il Monastero di S. Paolo fuori le Mura: note storiche*. Turin.
Seeck, O. (1919) *Regesten der Kaiser und Päpste*. Stuttgart.
Seeliger, H. (1988) 'Einhards römische Reliquien: zur Übertragung der heiligen Marcellinus und Petrus ins Frankenreich', *Römische Quartalschrift für Christliche Altertumskunde und Kirchengeschichte* 83: 38–75.
Selb, W. (1967) 'Episcopalis audientia von der Zeit Konstantins bis zu Novelle XXXV Valentinians III', *Zeitschrift der Savigny-Stifung für Rechtsgeschichte* 84: 162–217.
Sessa, K. (2003) 'The household and the bishop: establishing episcopal authority in late antique Rome', Unpubl. PhD thesis, Berkeley.
Shanzer, D. (1986) *A Philosophical and Literary Commentary on Martianus Capella's De Nuptiis Philologiae et Mercurii Book 1*. Berkeley and Los Angeles.
Shaw, B. D. (1987) 'The family in late antiquity: the experience of Augustine', *Past and Present* 115: 3–51.
Sivan, H. (1993a) 'On hymens and holiness in late antiquity', *JAChr* 36: 81–93.
(1993b) 'Anician women, the Cento of Proba, and aristocratic conversion in the fourth century', *Vigiliae Christianae* 47: 140–57.
Smith, J. M. H. (2000a) 'Old saints, new cults: Roman relics in Carolingian Francia', in Smith 2000b: 317–40.
(ed.) (2000b) *Early Medieval Rome and the Christian West: Essays in Honour of Donald A. Bullough*. Leiden.
Smith, R. (2003), '"Restored utility, eternal city": patronal imagery at Rome in the fourth century AD', in *Bread and Circuses: Euergetism and Municipal Patronage in Roman Italy*, ed. T. Cornell and K. Lomas. London and New York: 142–66.
Sotinel, C. (1989) 'Arator, un poète au service de la politique du pape Vigile', *MEFRA* 101: 805–20.
(1992) 'Autorité pontificale et pouvoir imperial sous le règne de Justinien: le pape Vigile', *MEFRA* 104: 439–63.
(2000a) 'Silverio', in *Enciclopedia dei papi*, vol. I: 508–11. Rome.

(2000b) 'Vigilio', in *Enciclopedia dein papi*, vol. 1: 512–29. Rome.

(2002) 'Chronologie, topographie, histoire: quelques hypothèses sur S. Felix in Pincis, église disparu', in Guidobaldi and Guidobaldi 2002: 1, 449–72.

(2005) 'Emperors and popes in the sixth century: the Western view', in *The Cambridge Companion to the Age of Justinian*, ed. M. Maas. Cambridge: 267–90.

Stanley, S. J. (1994) 'New discoveries at Santa Costanza', *DOP* 48: 257–61.

Starr, R. (1987) 'The circulation of literary texts in the Roman world', *Classical Quarterly* 37: 213–23.

Steinby, E. M. (1993–99) *Lexicon Topographicum Urbis Romae*, 6 vols. Rome.

Stevens, S. T. (1982) 'The circle of bishop Fulgentius', *Traditio* 38: 327–41.

Stowers, S. (1986) *Letter Writing in Greco-Roman Antiquity*. Philadelphia.

Stroll, M. (1997) *The Medieval Abbey of Farfa: Target of Papal and Imperial Ambitions*. Leiden.

Stutz, U. (1895) *Geschichte des kirchlichen Benefizialwesens von seinen Anfängen bis auf die Zeit Alexanders III*. Stuttgart.

(1938) 'The proprietary church as an element of medieval Germanic ecclesiastical law', in *Medieval Germany, 911–1250*, ed. G. Barraclough, 2 vols. Oxford.

Susman, F. (1961 [1964]) 'Il culto di S. Pietro a Roma dalla morte di Leone Magno a Vitaliano (461–672)', *Archivio della Società Romana di Storia Patria* 84 (ser. 3, vol. 15): 1–193.

Syme, R. (1939) *The Roman Revolution*. Oxford.

Talbot, C. H. (1954) *The Anglo-Saxon Missionaries in Germany*. London and New York.

Teitler, H. (1985) Notarii *and* Exceptores*: an inquiry into role and significance of shorthand writers in the imperial and ecclesiastical bureaucracy of the Roman Empire; from the early Principate to c. 450 A.D.* Amsterdam.

Thomas, E. and Witschel, C. (1992) 'Claim and reality of Roman rebuilding inscriptions', *PBSR* 60: 135–77.

Thomas, P. (1906) *Le droit de propriété des laïques sur les églises et le patronage laïque au moyen âge*. Paris.

Tjäder, J.-O. (1955–82) *Die nichtliterarischen lateinischen Papyri Italiens aus der Zeit 445–700*, 2 vols. Uppsala and Stockholm.

Toulotte, M. (1902) 'Le culte de saint Étienne en Afrique et à Rome', *Nuovo Bollettino di Archeologia Cristiana* 8: 211–16.

Townsend, W. T. (1933) 'The so-called Symmachan forgeries', *Journal of Religion* 13: 165–74.

Treggiari, S. (1991) *Roman Marriage: Iusti Coniuges from the Time of Cicero to the Time of Ulpian*. Oxford.

Troncarelli, F. (1988) 'I codici di Cassiodoro: le testimonianze più antiche', *Scrittura e Civiltà* 12: 47–99.

Trout, D. (2001) 'The verse epitaph(s) of Petronius Probus: competitive commemoration in late fourth-century Rome', *New England Classical Journal* 28.3: 157–76.

(2003) 'Damasus and the invention of Early Christian Rome', *Journal of Medieval and Early Modern Studies* 33.3: 517–36.

Twyman, S. (2002) *Papal Ceremonial at Rome in the Twelfth Century*. Henry Bradshaw Society, Subsidia 4. London.

Uhalde, K. (2007) *Expectations of Justice in the Age of Augustine*. Philadelphia.

Ullmann, W. (1970) *The Growth of the Papal Government in the Middle Ages: A Study in the Relation of Clerical to Lay Power*, 3rd edn. London.

Valentini, R. and Zucchetti, G. (1942) *Codice topografico della città di Roma*, vol. II. Rome.

(1946) *Codice topografico della città di Roma*, vol. III. Rome.

van Bremen, R. (1996) *The Limits of Participation: Women and Civic Life in the Greek East in the Hellenistic and Roman Periods*. Amsterdam.

Verheijen, L. (1967) *La Règle de S. Augustin*, 2 vols. Paris.

Verrando, G. N. (1983) 'Osservazioni sulla collocazione cronologica degli apocrifi Atti di Pietri dello Pseudo-Lino', *Vetera Christianorum* 20: 391–426.

(1987) 'Note sulle tradizioni agiografiche su Processo, Martiniano e Lucina', *Vetera Christianorum* 24: 351–75.

Vessey, M. (1993) 'Conference and confession. Literary pragmatics in Augustine's "Apologia contra Hieronymum"', *JECS* 1: 175–213.

Veyne, P. (1990) *Bread and Circuses*. London.

Vielliard, R. (1928) 'Les titres romains et les deux éditions du *Liber Pontificalis*', *Rivista di Archeologia Cristiana* 5: 89–103.

Vitiello, M. (2004) 'Teoderico a Roma. Politica, amministrazione e propaganda nell' *adventus* dell'anno 500 (considerazioni sull' "Anonimo Valesiano II")', *Historia* 53: 73–120.

Vogel, C. (1975) 'Le "Liber Pontificalis" dans l'édition de Louis Duchesne', in *Monseigneur Duchesne et son temps*, Collections de l'École Française de Rome 23. Rome: 100–27.

(1986) *Medieval Liturgy: An Introduction to the Sources*, rev. and trans. W. G. Story and N. K. Rassmussen. Washington, DC.

von Harnack, A. (1924) 'Der erste deutsche Papst (Bonifatius II. 530/2) und die beiden letzten Dekrete des römischen Senats', *Sitzungsberichte der Preussischen Akademie der Wissenschaften* 5: 24–42.

von Heckel, R. (1908) 'Das päpstliche und sicilische Registerwesen in vergleichender Darstellung mit besonderer Berücksichtigung der Ursprünge', *Archiv für Urkundenforschung* 1: 394–424.

von Savigny, F. K. (1884) *Jural Relations or the Roman Law of Persons as Subject of Jural Relations*, trans. W. H. Rattigan. London.

Waitz, G. (1877) 'Reise nach Italien im Frühjahr 1876', *Neues Archiv für Ältere Deutsche Geschichtskunde* 2: 325–81.

Wallace-Hadrill, A. (1988) 'The social structure of the Roman house', *PBSR* 56: 43–97.

(ed.) (1989) *Patronage in Ancient Society*. London.

(1994) *Houses and Societies in Pompeii and Herculaneum*. Princeton.

Waltzing, J. P. (1895–1900) *Étude historique sur les corporations professionnelles chez les Romains*, 4 vols. Brussels.

Ward-Perkins, B. (1984) *From Classical Antiquity to the Middle Ages: Urban Public Building in Northern and Central Italy, AD 300–850*. Oxford.

Warren, W. L. (1984) 'The myth of Anglo-Norman administrative efficiency', *Transactions of the Royal Historical Society* 5th ser., 34: 113–32.

Wesch-Klein, G. (1990) *'Liberalitas in rem publicam': private Aufwendungen zugunsten von Gemeinden im römischen Afrika bis 284 n. Chr.* Bonn.

Whitaker, E. C. (1965) 'The history of the baptismal formula', *Journal of Ecclesiastical History* 16: 1–12.

White, L. M. (1990) *Building God's House in the Roman World: Architecture and Adaptation among Pagans, Christians and Jews*. Baltimore.

Wickham, C. (2005) *Framing the Middle Ages: Europe and the Mediterranean, 400–800*. Oxford.

Willis, G. G. (1994) *A History of Early Roman Liturgy to the Death of Gregory the Great*. London.

Wilpert, J. (1937) 'Le pitture della *confessio* dei SS Giovanni e Paolo', in *Scritti in onore di Bartolemeo Nogara*. Rome: 517–23.

Wirbelauer, E. (1993) *Zwei Päpste in Rom: Der Konflikt zwischen Laurentius und Symmachus (498–514)*. Munich.

Wood, I. N. (1995) 'Teutsind, Witlaic and the history of Merovingian precaria', *in Property and Power in the Early Middle Ages*, ed. W. Davies and P. Fouracre. Cambridge: 31–52.

Wood, S. (2006) *The Proprietary Church in the Medieval West*. Oxford.

Woolf, G. (1990) 'Food, poverty and patronage: the significance of the epigraphy of the Roman alimentary schemes in early imperial Italy', *PBSR* 58: 197–228.

Wormald, P. (1976) 'The decline of the Western empire and the survival of its aristocracy', Review of Matthews (1975), *JRS* 66: 217–36.

Wipszycka, E. (1975) 'Les terres de la congrégation Pachomienne dans une liste de payements pour les Apora', in *Le monde grec: hommages à Claire Préaux*, ed. J. Bingen et al. Brussels: 625–36.

Zecchini, G. (1980) 'I "Gesta de Xysti purgatione" e le fazioni aristocratiche a Roma alla metà del V secolo', *Rivista della Storia della Chiesa in Italia* 34: 60–74.

Zimmerman, H. (ed.) (1984) *Papsturkunden 896–1046*, I: *896–996*. Vienna.

Zuiderhoeck, A. (2006) 'Citizens, elites and benefactors: the politics of public generosity in Roman Asia Minor', unpubl. PhD thesis, Groningen.

Index

Aachen 282
Abruzzi 262
Abundantius of Traianopolitanus, bishop 62
Acacian schism 62, 63, 67–8
Acacius, patriarch of Constantinople 67
acclamations 21, 34, 49
Achilleus, pope 66
Acta martyrum 89
Actus Silvestri 98
Ad Gregoriam in Palatio 179, 187
adventus 21–58
Aelia Eudoxia, empress 281
Aelia Flavia Flacilla 118
Aëtius, general 41
Africa 2, 31, 40, 47, 57, 62, 64, 69, 155, 165, 166, 168, 181, 188, 192, 195, 212, 220, 223, 239, 242–4, 247, 278
Agapetus, pope 52, 61, 65, 67–70, 140–1, 160
Agatho, pope 55
Agilulf, Lombard king 23
Agnellus of Ravenna 24
Agnes, Frankish abbess 138, 139
Agnes, saint 115–39; *see also gesta martyrum*, Rome: churches and monasteries
Agrippa, prefect 96
Alaric, Visigothic king 33, 181
Alatri 161
Alberic, 286
Albinus 96
Alcuin 277, 283–4
Alexander, pope 87, 100–3
Alexandria 44, 151
alienation of church property 91–2, 229–60
almsgiving 219
Alypius, bishop of Thagaste 166, 243–7
Amalasuintha, Ostrogothic regent 3, 4
Ambrose, bishop of Milan 5, 10, 28, 38, 93, 115–16, 123–4, 133, 181, 219
  De virginibus 115, 123, 126, 131–3
Ambrosiaster
  Commentary on Romans 155
Ammianus Marcellinus 27, 29, 30, 32, 35, 37, 52, 72, 117, 121
Anastasia, saint; *see gesta martyrum*; Rome: churches and monasteries
Anastasius I, emperor 45
Angilbert of St Riquier 277, 282–4
Anicia Demetrias 10, 16, 17, 18, 171, 181–3, 187, 188, 190–224, 241, 278
Anicia Faltonia Proba 37, 169, 181–2, 188, 192, 195–6, 197–8, 201, 202, 207–8, 209, 220, 221–2, 223, 243
Anicia Juliana 188, 190–224
Anicii 16, 37, 119, 140, 170, 187, 188, 191, 192–3, 197, 201, 202, 206, 207–13, 241
Anicius Acilius Glabrio Faustus, consul 45
Anicius Auchenius Bassus, consul 208
Anicius Faustus Junior Albus, prefect 63
Anicius Hermogenianus Olybrius, consul 192, 196
Anicius Olybrius, emperor 224
annona (food supply, food distribution) 2, 42, 46, 48
Anthemius, emperor 41, 43–4
Anthimus, patriarch of Constantinople 67, 160
Antioch 64, 69
Antony, saint 176, 264
Apocrisarius 55, 161
Apocryphal Acts of the Apostles 82, 89, 95–9, 103–6, 129, 135
  Acts of Andrew 82, 103, 104;
  Acts of Paul and Thecla 89, 90, 95, 128, 133, 136–7;
  Acts of Peter 82, 89, 90, 95–6;
  Acts of Thomas 82
Apophthegmata 136
Aquileia 155
Arator 171
  De actibus apostolorum 171
Arcadius, emperor 36
archaeology 24, 26, 71–2, 83–4, 111, 119, 140–1, 145, 241

archives 8, 62, 74–6, 231, 263, 266–7, 268, 269, 275; *see also* libraries
Arianism 4, 60, 75, 120–1, 125, 173
aristocracy 5, 7, 13, 14, 15, 22, 79, 84, 105, 116, 126, 134, 139, 142, 165, 183, 192, 197, 212, 224, 226–60; *see also* Senatorial aristocracy
Arles 40, 157
Arno of Salzburg 277, 283–5
Arnobius the Younger 180
asceticism 9–11, 13, 15, 18, 96, 136, 138, 143, 146, 153, 169, 171–89, 195, 199, 201, 205, 219, 222, 243, 263, 271
Asia 169, 243
Asia Minor 136, 244
Aspasius Paternus, judge 132
Athalaric, Ostrogothic king 47
Athanasius, bishop of Alexandria 264
  Vita Antonii 136
Athaulf, Visigothic king 47
Athenais-Eudokia, empress 223, 278, 281
Attila, Hunnic king 224
Augustine of Hippo 9–10, 47, 111, 153, 154, 155, 156, 162, 165–85, 186, 190, 192, 193, 204, 207–13, 215, 216–22, 223, 243–7, 248, 278
  City of God 184, 278
  De gratia Christi 212
  On Holy Virginity 185
  On the Good of Widowhood 210
  Praeceptum 182
Augustus, emperor 32, 71, 81
  Lex Julia de adulteris 81
  Lex Julia de collegiis 239
Aurelian, emperor 52
Aurelius of Carthage, bishop 192, 243–7
Auspiciola, daughter of Salvian of Marseilles 180–1
authority 4, 13, 14, 17, 40, 43, 49, 54, 56, 58, 85–112, 116, 139, 180, 199, 201, 264
avarice 96, 177, 185
Avitus, emperor 41, 43

Baetica 244
baptism 14, 72, 85, 87, 94, 100, 101–3, 105, 106–11, 119, 120, 134
Barcelona 47
Basilius, urban prefect 172
Bassus 93–7
Baudonivia 138, 139
Belisarius, general 3, 67
Benedict I, pope 66
Benedict II, pope 55, 272
Benedict of Nursia 15, 161, 286–7
beneficia 85, 105, 106
bequests 166, 174, 178; *see also* donations
Bibiana, saint; *see gesta martyrum*; Rome: churches and monasteries
bishop 21–58, 59–76, 79–112, 225–60, 262–86; *see also* authority; references to individual popes
  extra legal authority 82–112
Blesilla, daughter of Paula 199
Bobbio 8
Boethius 170
Boniface I, pope 52, 63, 66–7, 73, 122
Boniface II, pope 48, 52, 64, 65, 66, 252
Boniface IV, pope 54
Boniface V, pope 271
Bonifatian schism 62–3, 66
book collections 188
bribery 252
Brontotae 44
brothels 115, 125, 127, 128, 131
Brunhild, Frankish queen 139
Bruno of Segni 278
burial 143–5, 146, 150, 157, 158, 226
Byzantium 23, 24, 50, 54, 61, 135, 264, 266, 272, 279, 282; *see also* Ravenna, *exarch* of

Caecina Decius Maximinus Basilius, praetorian prefect 92
Caecius Decius Maximus Basilius Iunior, praetorian prefect 97
Caeonia Albina 165, 166–7
Caeonius Rufinus Albinus, urban prefect 165
Caesarius of Arles
  Rule for Virgins 264
  see also monastic rules
Calama 278
Calendar of 354 11, 33
Callistus, pope 87, 105
Campania 17, 152, 161
Caninius, friend of Pliny the Younger 245–6
canon law collections 59; *see also Collectio Avellana*
Capua 105, 155, 280
cartularies 263, 265; *see also* charters
Caspari corpus 180
Cassian of Autun 150
Cassiodorus Senator 9, 47, 156
  Chronicle 44
  Historia Tripartita 144
Castellum Lucullanum 155
catacombs 101
Celestine, pope 169, 182
celibacy 95, 96
cemeteries 11, 121, 158, 272

ceremony 13–14, 21–58, 80
Chalcedon, council of 68–9, 90, 228, 265
Chariton, *Chaereas and Callirhoe* 128
charity 216
Charlemagne, Frankish king 277–8, 282–4
charters 8, 162, 263, 265–7, 269, 273
Chelles 107
Chronicle of Salerno 280
churches, titular, *see* Rome: churches and monasteries; titular churches; *titulus*
Cicero 80, 110, 178, 197, 245
Cîteaux 264
civilitas 3
Claudian, poet 27, 30, 43, 46, 192
Clement, pope 86
Clement of Alexandria 175
  Who Is the Rich Man That Shall be Saved? 219
Cletus, pope 226
Clothar I, Frankish king 138
Cluny 17, 266, 278
Codex Carolinus 266, 274
codices, *see* manuscripts
coemeteria 234
Collectio Avellana 5, 7, 14, 59–76, 158
Collectio Italica 64, 76
Collectio Sanblasiana, see Collectio Italica
collegia 169, 228, 231–2, 237–40, 240, 244–7
Comum 244–5, 246
concordia 218
Constans I, emperor 27, 35
Constans II, emperor 55, 56, 58
Constantina, 117–39
Constantina, sister of emperor Maurice 281–2
Constantine I, emperor 22, 26–57, 81, 116–17, 119, 133, 134, 135, 140–1, 145, 159, 228, 230, 231, 238, 262
Constantine IV, emperor 55
Constantine VII Porphyrogenitus, emperor
  Liber de Caeremoniis 44
Constantinople 21, 22, 41, 44–5, 46, 49–50, 55, 57, 58, 64, 67–9, 118, 135, 161, 188, 224, 229, 265, 270, 271, 276, 280, 281–2
  second council of 69
  St Polyeuktos, church 224
Constantius II, emperor 27–8, 32, 36, 60, 70, 73, 117–18, 119, 120–1
  equestrian statue of 36;
  obelisk of 36;
Corbie 17, 142, 147–56
Cornelius, pope 86
corporations, *see collegia*
councils 28, 48, 71
  of Braga (second) 174
  of Diospolis (415) 212–13, 278
  of Orleans
  of Rome (499) 49, 226
  of Rome (502) 172, 228–60
  of Rome (595) 144
  of Rome (649) 271
  see also Chalcedon, council of; Constantinople, second council of; Nicaea, council of
court, imperial 22, 49, 55
Crimea 56
Ctesiphon, correspondent of Jerome 206
Cyprian of Carthage 111, 132
  On Works and Alms 219

Dalmatia 41
Damasus I, pope 22, 28, 38, 59–60, 64–5, 70–5, 122, 123, 130, 133, 158, 193, 200, 227, 230, 232
  Carmen 130
damnatio memoriae 39, 46
Datius of Milan 160
Decentius of Gubbio, bishop 233–4, 258
decretals 85
Decretum Gelasianum de libris recipiendis et non recipiendis 254–5
De divitiis, see On Riches
De locis sanctis 279, 284
demography 24
depositio martyrum 121
Digest 235
Diocletian, emperor 22, 30, 52
Dionysius Exiguus 59, 63–4, 90, 187
  Epistulae decretales 187
Dioscorus, opponent of Pope Boniface II in 530 66
Dioscorus of Tyre, bishop 62
divorce 81
domestic space, *see domus*
dominus 94, 166, 168–9, 173, 181, 185–7; *see also paterfamilias*
domus 14, 37, 79, 80, 80–111, 141, 142, 151, 153, 214
domus Dei 111
domus ecclesiae 83, 141, 145, 173, 227
donations 16, 83, 165–6, 167–74, 225–60
Donatism 9
Donatus of Arezzo 150
Donatus of Lucullanum 155
dynasty 17

Echternach 262
economy 24, 26, 50
edict of Constantine and Licinius (313) 238
Edictum Theoderici 175
Egypt 173
Eigenkirche 7

elections, papal 55, 252
embassies 50
emperor 1, 3, 4–5, 13, 14, 15, 18, 21, 22–58, 61, 98, 134, 142, 159, 173, 246
endowment 227, 230–1, 232, 237–60; *see also* bequests; donations
Ennodius of Pavia 63, 171
  Vita of Epiphanius of Pavia 171–89
Ephrem the Syrian, *Instituto ad monachos, see* monastic rules
Epifanius 92–5
epigraphy 5–6, 11, 32, 36, 37, 38, 39, 48, 75, 91, 117, 122, 143, 181, 188, 192, 213, 224, 225, 233, 241, 242, 244, 258, 259, 262, 266, 270
Epiphanius of Constantia 62
Epistula ad Demetriadem de vera humilitate 15, 181–4, 187, 215–24
Equitius, presbyter 227, 228, 230
Eugenius, usurper 39, 239
Eugippius of Lucullanum 15, 155, 170, 189
  Excerpta Augustini 170
Eulalia, Spanish martyr 123
Eulalius, anti-pope 63
eunuchs 150
Euripides 130
Eusthatius, *dux* 5
Eustochium 174, 185, 203
Eutyches, patriarch of Constantinople 76, 161
Evagrius, *Sentences for Monks, see* monastic rules
Evaristus, pope 226–7, 259
Eventius, priest and *gesta* character 100
evergetism 169, 172, 232, 243–5; *see also* donations
exemplum 110, 116, 125–6, 129, 197
exemption 162, *see also* immunities
Ezekiel 23

Fabian, pope 11, 74, 76
Fabiola 170, 243
Facundus of Hermiane 62
Faltonia Betitia Proba 187, 192
family 10, 15, 16, 17, 18, 80–112, 126, 133, 137, 138, 174–88, 191, 194, 195, 199, 201, 202, 213–14, 222
Farfa 263, 264, 267, 275–6, 286
Felix II, pope 70, 73, 117, 120–1
Felix III, pope 97, 229
Felix IV, pope 4, 62, 64–5, 70, 226
festivals 33–4
financial misconduct 200
First Letter to Timothy 168
Flavia Constantia 119
Flavia Hilarina 72
Flavian, patriarch of Constantinople 76
Flavius Caecina Decius Maximus Basilius Iunior, patrician 248, 249–51, 259
Flavius Messius Phoebus Severus, consul 43
Fonte Avellana, St Romuald's 61
food distribution, *see annona*
food supply, *see annona*
Formosan schism 286
Formosus, pope 286
Franks 13, 17, 107, 138, 139, 178, 189, 273, 277, 283, 284, 286
Fredegund, Frankish queen 139
Frederick Barbarossa 284
Fulda 262
Fulgentius of Ruspe 279
Fulrad of St Denis 274
funerals 47
Furia 201

Galla 170, 279
Galla Placidia 43, 47
Gallus Caesar 118
games 5, 34, 48
Gaul 40, 64, 71, 122, 138, 139, 171, 178
Geiseric, Vandal king 224
Gelasian Sacramentary (Reg. Vat. 316) 107
Gelasius I, pope 52, 62, 76, 79, 173, 187, 243–7, 253, 257
Germanus of Capua, bishop 161, 280
Gerontius 242
  Vita Melaniae 242
Gesta Alexandrii 76
Gesta de absolutione Miseni 70, 76
Gesta de nomine Acaci 70
Gesta de Xysti purgatione 14, 86, 87–99, 112
Gesta Liberii 71
gesta martyrum 11–13, 14, 15, 17, 86, 87–90, 99–112, 116–39, 142, 148, 157, 170, 175, 187, 189, 254–7, 264, 269
  Passio S. Agnetis 14, 115–38, 150
  Passio SS. Alexandri, Eventii, et Theodoli martyrum 86, 100–7
  Passio S. Anastasiae 129, 187
  Passio S. Bibianae 159
  Passio S. Callisti papae et martyris 86, 105, 107
  Passio S. Clementis martyris et episcopi 105
  Passio S. Cornelii papae 106
  Passio SS. Cyrici et Iulittae 255
  Passio S. Gallicani 118–19, 147–52
  Passio S. Georgii 255
  Passio SS. Iohannis et Pauli 15, 140–62, 170
  Passio SS. Perpetuae et Felicitatis 130, 133
  Passio S. Pigmenii, see Passio S. Bibianae
  Passio S. Polychronii 42
  Passio SS. Praxedis et Pudentianae 84, 254–7

Passio S. Sebastiani 178–80, 185, 187;
Passio S. Stephani papae et martyris 86, 107;
Gesta Senatus 45
gifts, *see* donations
gold glass 121
Gordianus, priest 141, 160
Gothic Wars 3, 4–5, 24, 54, 159, 170, 172–3
Goths 33, 37, 67, 160; *see also* Ostrogoths
Gratian, emperor 30, 35, 119
gravediggers 59, 158
Greece 160, 214
Greeks 273, 285; *see also* monks, Greek
Gregorius, *notarius* 6
Gregory I, pope 15, 21–57, 74, 79, 84, 91, 123, 140–1, 156, 157–8, 263, 267, 268, 269, 270–1, 276, 279, 281, 285, 286–7;
Dialogues 123, 160–1, 170, 279;
Moralia in Job 280;
Registrum 21, 267–8;
Gregory II, pope 270, 272
Gregory III, pope 272
Gregory IV, pope 144
Gregory VII, pope 267
Gregory of Catino 275
Gregory of Tours
Liber de miraculis beati Andreae apostoli 103
Libri Historiarum 22, 138, 139
guardianship 92–3, 94
Gubbio 234

Hadrian I, pope 144, 267, 274, 276, 277, 280, 281, 282
Hadrian II, pope 285
hagiography 11, 103, 128, 129, 133, 175
Hannah of the Maccabees 156
Hannibalianus 118
healing 87, 100–3, 134, 160, 278
Helena 119, 139
Henotikon, see Zeno, emperor
Henry II, English king 285
Heraclius, emperor 55, 57
Herperius, Montanist priest 239–40
Hieronymian Martyrology 121, 122
Hilarius, pope (461–8) 281
Hilary of Syracuse 176
Hildebrand 267; *see also* Gregory VII
Hippo 155, 165, 166, 183, 212, 278
Homer 197
homilies 126
Honorius, emperor 30, 31, 33, 36–7, 39, 47, 52, 62, 63–4, 66, 73
Honorius I, pope 54–5, 66, 122, 268, 271, 274
Horace 197
Hormisdas, pope 62, 68, 91
household 79–112, 220
Christian 157
lay 14, 17
management 80
see also domestic space, *domus*
humility 215–16, 219–20; *see also Epistula ad Demetriadem de vera humilitate*

Ibas of Edessa 69
iconoclasm 273
icons, *see* images
Illyricum 52, 69
images of emperors 21, 25, 44–5
immunities 162, 263, 265, 269
inheritance 42, 96, 169, 180, 188, 238, 246, 258
Innocent, pope 62, 122, 211, 227, 231, 233, 258
inscriptions, *see* epigraphy
Ireland 262
Irene, empress 282
Italica, member of Anician family 208
Iunius Bassus 38
Iuventinus, Antiochene martyr 144

Jerome 10, 60, 72, 75, 143, 146, 155, 170, 185, 187, 191, 192, 193–206, 207, 215, 217, 241, 243, 263, 265, 270
Adversus Jovinianum 185
Dialogue Against the Pelagians 206
Jerusalem 139, 170, 174, 206, 224, 264, 278, 280
Jews 71
John I, pope 160
John II, pope 47, 61, 65, 66, 68–70
John III, pope 136
John V, pope 28
John VIII, pope 286
John Chrysostom 144, 156
John of Gorze 44
John of Jerusalem 212
John of Nola, bishop 233, 258
John of Salerno 285
John the Deacon 107, 267, 285–6
Vita Gregorii 267, 285–6
Jovian, emperor 143
Julian (the Apostate), emperor 117, 118, 141, 143, 151, 160
Letter to the Athenians 118
Julian of Eclanum 193
Julianus, presbyter 187
Julius Nepos, emperor 41
Justinian, emperor 3, 40, 50, 54, 55, 60, 61, 62, 65, 67–9, 73, 93, 159, 160, 243, 247
Judicatum of 69

Laurence, saint 71, 280–2
Laurentian Fragment 66, 96
Laurentian schism 12, 63–4, 76, 83, 85, 87–8, 122, 156, 159–60, 228–9, 232–59, 260
Laurentius, anti-pope 28, 63, 66, 83, 87, 229, 248, 252; *see also* Laurentian schism
law 35, 41, 42, 44–5, 46, 51, 52, 85, 92, 93–9, 104, 109–11, 112, 158, 169, 178, 213, 227, 228, 231–60, 283; *see also* canon law collections; *Digest*; *Theodosian Code*
Lazarus 103
Lazio 17, 161
legal affairs, *see* laws
Leo, emperor 44
Leo I, pope 22, 34, 47, 62, 76, 79, 82, 111, 143, 173, 181–2, 216, 223, 224, 228, 241, 279
Leo III, pope 144, 262, 270, 274, 277, 282–4
Leontia Augusta, 21, 44
letters 5, 16, 47, 53, 61–5, 85, 94, 165, 166–7, 171, 180, 187, 190–1, 193–206, 207–24, 233–4, 245–6, 253, 257, 258, 267, 268, 274, 283, 284
Lex Iulia de collegiis, *see* Augustus, emperor
Liber Diurnus 159
Liber Pontificalis 4–5, 7, 11–13, 14, 17–18, 28–9, 38, 54–5, 59–76, 79, 85, 86, 87, 90, 91, 96, 100, 111, 117, 119, 120–2, 124, 125, 134, 141, 144, 150, 159–60, 223–4, 226–7, 230–1, 233, 236, 241, 256, 258, 259, 262, 264, 266, 268–77, 278, 281, 285
  Cononian epitome 70
  Felician epitome 70
Liberian Catalogue 11, 100
Liberius, patrician 8–9, 161
Liberius, pope 27, 28, 38, 51, 64, 70, 73, 93, 117, 120–1
libraries 5, 8, 170, 189, 191, 244; *see also* Rome: *Bibliotheca Agapeti*; book collections
Licinia Eudoxia, empress 236, 281
Lipari 166
liturgy 14, 38, 53, 56, 81, 82, 84, 85, 88, 90, 99, 106–11, 122, 127, 132, 141, 168, 214, 227, 230, 231, 233, 240, 257, 268, 271, 272–3, 286; *see also* stational liturgy
Livy, historian 127–8
Lombards 23, 24, 50, 272, 273, 274, 286
Longinus, praetorian prefect 24
Lorsch 143, 262
Louis the Pious, Frankish king 277
luminaria 270–1
Lupercalia 79

Magnentius, usurper 32, 36, 39, 118
Magnus Maximus, usurper 32–3, 36, 38–9, 44, 62
Majorian, emperor 41–2
  fourth *Novella* of (458) 42
Manichaeism 9, 52, 75
manuscripts 13, 15, 60–5, 75, 100, 119, 122, 123, 135, 142–62, 181, 229, 230, 266, 284
Marcellus, jurist 235
Marcellus, pope 74, 111, 226
Marcian, emperor 44–5, 76
Marcus Aurelius, emperor 30, 52
Marinianus 91–7
Maroveus of Poitiers 264
marriage 95, 137, 177, 192, 213, 222, 235
Martin I, pope 56, 271
Martin of Tours 103
martyr cults 14, 18, 38
martyrdom 15
Martyrium beati Petri conscriptum a Lino episcopo 90
matrona 165–88, 190–224
Mauretania 242
Maurice, emperor 281
Maxentius, emperor 29–30, 31–2, 34–5, 43, 44
Maximinus, Antiochene martyr 144
Maximus of Turin 124, 126, 137
  De latrone 153
mediocritas 9–10
Melania the Elder 165
Melania the Younger 10, 146, 155, 165–70, 212, 223, 242–3, 248
memory 4–5, 90, 116, 117, 135, 139, 145, 188, 264, 268, 269, 285, 286
Menander Rhetor 197
Menas, patriarch of Constantinople 69
Mercurius, titular priest 91; *see also* John II, pope
Milan 28, 38
  basilica Ambrosiana 38
Milvian bridge 51
  battle 30, 31, 35
miracles 110, 130
miscellanies 154
monastic Rules 15, 142–57, 262, 263, 265
  of Augustine 142, 153
  of Basil 155
  of Benedict 154, 156, 183, 263, 283
  of Caesarius 157
  Ephrem the Syrian, *Institutio ad monachos* 153, 154, 156
  of Eugippius 142, 153, 154, 156
  Evagrius, *Sentences for Monks* 153, 154
  of the Fathers 155
  of the Four Fathers 153
  of the Master (*Regula Magistri*) 142, 154, 155, 170, 174–5, 183, 187, 189
monasticism 8, 17, 262–87
  Campanian 142
  Italian 15, 170

rural 15, 17, 161
suburban 79, 156
urban 79, 265
Monica, mother of Augustine 208
monks
Greek 271–2, 276, 281–2
Scythian 62, 68
monophysitism 159–60, 228
Montanism 239
Montecassino, 161, 263, 286
Monza 268
motif 15, 96, 116, 127–8, 138
munificence, civic 2, 43; *see also* euergetism
Mursa, battle of 36

Narses, general 54
Nepotianus, usurper 30, 39
Nestorius 76
Nicaea, council of 90
Nicholas I, pope 286
Nicomachus Flavianus, senator 39, 46
Nola 146
Nonantola 61
Notitia Dignitatum 52
novels, ancient, *see* romance, ancient
Numidia 242

Octaviana, Montanist 239–40
Odimundus, abbot 267
Odo of Cluny 263, 285–6
Odovacer, king of Italy 41, 248
Old Testament 23
Olybrius, emperor 41
On Riches 176, 181
Onesimus 94–5
Ordo Romamus 53
Origen 155
Peri Archon 155
Origenism 206
Origenist controversy 193
Orosius 206
Ostia 145, 151
basilica of Peter, John the Baptist, and St Paul 145
Ostrogoths 25, 40, 41, 46, 47–9, 54, 61, 87, 228, 267; *see also* Goths
Ovinius Gallicanus, consul and prefect 145

Pacatus, orator 32, 39
Pachomius, *Life* of 174
paganism 38
Palestine 165, 202, 278
Palladia, wife of Salvian of Marseilles 180
Palladius 199
Pammachius 143–4, 146, 155, 241
panegyric 27, 30, 32–3, 39, 43–4, 197, 207
Papinian, jurist 235
Paris 142, 153
St Denis
parochiae 234
Passio Silverii 65, 67
passiones, see gesta martyrum
Pastoral Epistles 175
paterfamilias 80–1, 82, 92–3, 105
patria potestas 80–1, 97, 235
Patricius, nephew of Augustine 183
Paul, saint 80, 82, 95, 106, 110, 176
Letters 9, 82, 94–5
Paul I, pope 272
Paul the Deacon, 286
Historia Langobardorum 23
Paul the Younger 174
Paula, founder of Jerusalem monastery 155, 174, 199, 201
Paulina, wife of Pammachius 155, 241
Paulinus of Milan, 93
Paulinus of Nola 143, 146, 197
Pelagianism 9, 176, 203, 211–13, 216, 221
Pelagianist controversy 176
Pelagius 190, 192, 193, 203–6, 207, 210–13, 214, 215, 216–17, 243
Epistula ad Demetriadem 190
Pelagius I, pope 136, 173, 233, 258, 280
Persia 151
Peter, saint 4, 74, 82, 96; *see also gesta martyrum*; Rome: churches and monasteries
Petronius, abbot of Tabbenisi 174
Petronius Maximus, emperor 41
Philemon 94–5
Philostorgius 118
Phocas, emperor, 21, 44, 54, 57
Picenum 242
Pinian 155, 165–7, 169, 184, 212, 242–3, 248
Pippin, king of Italy 283
Pippin III, Frankish king 273, 274
Pius, bishop
Placidia, wife of Anicius Olybrius 224
plague 2, 158
Plato 177
Pliny the Younger 244–6
Poitiers 138, 139
Pollentia, battle 37
poor, *see* poverty
Porto 143
portraits, *see* images
Postumianus, official 42
potlatch 268, 269

poverty 92, 152, 168, 169–70, 171, 176, 179, 184, 186–7, 219, 222, 243, 250
precarium 178, 182
Praedestinatus / Praedestinatorum Haeresis 239
Praxedis, saint; *see gesta martyrum*; Rome: churches and monasteries
precarial tenure 178
pride 184, 216
primicerius 74, 268
Priscillianism 206
Priscus Attalus, usurper 33, 37, 39
Proba 15, 170, 187, 279
  Cento de laudibus Christi 192, 197
processions 141
Procopius 3
Procopius of Gaza 45
Proiectus 91
Prosper of Aquitaine 182, 216
  Chronicle 43, 44, 47
  De vocatione omnium gentium 216
prostitution 46, 125, 129
Prudentius 36, 115, 123–4, 131–2, 134
  Contra Symmachum 5
  Peristephanon 123, 130, 131
Pudens, saint; *see gesta martyrum*; Rome: churches and monasteries
Pudentiana, saint; *see gesta martyrum*; Rome: churches and monasteries
Pulcheria, empress 223

Radegund of Poitiers 138–9, 264
Ratchis, Lombard king 274
Ravenna 36, 40, 42, 49, 55, 266–7
  exarch of 54, 55–6
Reading Abbey 285
reciprocity 109, 112
record keeping 4; *see also* archives; libraries
relics 141, 144, 145, 223, 269, 274, 276, 278–9, 280, 282, 284
Revelatio Stephani 278, 284–5
Ricimer 43
ritual 25–57, 74–6
romance, ancient 89, 127–8
Rome
  Gothic sack of 33, 37, 40
  population of 2, 26; *see also* demography
  prefect of 22, 39, 48, 51, 52, 62, 63, 93, 145, 165, 166, 172
  Vandal sack of 40
Rome: churches and monasteries 276, 277
  Ad Aquas Salvias, monastery 271
  basilica Agnetis 117, 120, 123
  basilica Constantiniana 38, 101
  basilica Heleniana 97
  basilica Liberiana 38, 59, 71–2, 158
  basilica Laurentiana 279, 281
  basilica SS. Marcellini et Petri 119
  basilica S. Pauli (extramural) 36, 271
  basilica Sicinini 72
  basilica Sessoriana 110
  capella Liberiana 38
  Lateran (basilica constantiniana) 21, 25, 27, 28, 38, 52, 56–7, 74, 111, 140, 241, 271, 272, 274, 275
  Renatus, monastery (Esquiline hill) 271
  S. Adriano 55
  SS. Adrianus et Laurentius 274
  S. Agata dei Goti 43
  S. Anastasius 274
  S. *Andreas Catabarbara* 236, 241–2, 258, 259
  S. *Andreas (Massa Iuliana)* 272
  S. *Andreas* (later S. Gregorio) (Caelian hill) 47
  S. Balbina 83
  S. Benedictus de Thermis 275
  S. Bibiana 159
  S. Caesarius 21, 56
  S. Cosimato (= SS. Cosma e Damiano, Monastery) 267, 272
  SS. Cosma e Damiano 51
  S. Costanza 117
  S. Crisogono 272
  S. Croce in Gerusalemme 43
  S. Eugenia 274
  S. Eusebio 159
  S. Eustachio (= St Eustathius in Platana) 275
  SS. Giovanni e Paolo 140–62,
  S. Gregorio, monastery 140
  S. Iohannes in Laterano 27, 35, 51
  SS. Iohannes et Paulus, monastery (Vatican) 241
  S. Laurentius in Pallacinis 274
  S. Lorenzo in Damaso 75
  S. Lorenzo in Lucina 71, 72
  S. Lorenzo fuori le mura 71, 279, 281
  SS. Marcellinus et Petrus
  S. Maria Cella Farfae 275
  S. Maria Antiqua 51
  S. Maria in Cosmedin 5, 266
  S. Maria Maggiore 28, 38, 52, 72, 272
  S. Martinus, monastery 272
  S. Pancras 272
  S. Paulus (= S. Angelo in Pescheria) 5
  S. Petrus, martyrium 101
  S. Petronilla 47
  S. Pietro in Vaticano 27, 35, 47, 48, 51, 52, 53, 55, 56, 170, 241, 270
  S. Pietro in Vincoli 43, 272
  S. Sabina 72
  S. Silvestro 'in capite' 273
  S. Stephanus cata Galla patricia, monastery 171
  S. Stefano Rotondo 279

SS. Stephanus, Laurentius et Chrysogonus 272
S. Stefano in Vagauda 274
S. Stephanus 'Maior', monastery 274
S. Stephanus (Via Latina) 181–3, 188, 223, 241, 279
S. Stephanus (Caelian hill) 258
S. Susanna 270
S. Victor at S. Pancras 274
titulus Anastasiae 187
titulus Apostolorum 236
titulus Byzantis 143
titulus Clementis 83, 91
titulus Equitii 230
titulus Eudoxiae 236, 281
titulus Fasciolae 233
titulus Iohannis et Pauli 241
titulus Iulii 71
titulus Lucinae 71
titulus Marcelli 52
titulus Pammachii 143, 144, 241
titulus Praxedis 252
titulus Vestinae 122, 236
Vatican 143, 274
Rome: civic topography
Amphitheatrum Flavium 242
Ara Pacis 71
arch of Septimus Severus 36
atrium of Minerva 46
basilica of Maxentius 55
Baths of Diocletian and Maximian 34
Bibliotheca Agapeti 140, 160
Caelian hill 81, 91, 105, 140, 141, 158, 160–1, 258, 267
Campus Martius 6, 71
Capitoline hill 31
Circus Maximus 27, 34, 36
Cispian hill 241
Clivus Scauri 140–1
Colosseum 27, 42, 140
'Corsarum', house 270
Crypta Balbi 6
Esquiline hill 38, 158, 271
Forum
of Augustus 46
of Caesar 34
of Trajan 27, 46, 48
Romanum 30, 34, 35, 37, 51, 54, 57
horologium Augusti 71
house of the Valerii 81
imperial palaces 21, 30, 34, 37, 48, 57, 94, 151
Palatine hill 21, 30, 34, 37, 56, 187
Pantheon 27, 54–5
Pincian hill 37
Pons Aurelius 35
temple of Jupiter Optimus Maximus 31
temple of Venus and Rome 55
Templum Pacis 46
'templum Romae' 54
Trastevere 93, 267
Vatican hill 27, 134
Via Appia 29, 34
Via Aurelia 239
Via Latina 181–3, 188, 223, 241
Via Nomentana 117–18, 121–2, 125, 132–3
Via Ostiensis 36
Via Sacra 29, 35, 36, 37
Via Salaria 54
Via Triumphalis 35
Viminal hill 34
Romulus Augustulus 40
Rufinus of Aquileia 75, 155–6, 265
Rules, *see* monastic Rules

S. Vincenzo al Volturno 262
Sabina, region 276
Sabinian, pope 51, 271
Sabinus of Canosa 161
sacrifices 31
Sallust 197
Salventius, prefect of Rome 48
Salvian of Marseilles 180, 182
Ad Ecclesiam 15, 177–8, 181
Sayings of the Desert Fathers 157
schism 62, 66, 117, 122; *see also* Acacian schism; Bonifatian schism; Formosan schism; Laurentian schism; Ursinian schism
Scythia 62
Seleucia 135, 136
senate 2, 21, 23–4, 25–33, 248–60
curia 30, 34, 55, 57
house 36, 37, 39
of Constantinople 32
senatorial aristocracy 1, 2–3, 4–5, 9–10, 12, 23, 80, 88, 105, 171–88, 214, 223, 225
Sentences of Nilus 155
Sentences of Sextus 155
Septimius Severus, emperor 93
Serena, abbess 122
Sergius I, pope 28, 56, 270
Sergius III, pope 271
Servandus, deacon 161
Severinus of Noricum 155
Severus, brother of Pinian 166
sex, extra-marital 80
Sextus Claudius Petronius Probus, consul 38, 169, 181, 188, 192, 201
sexual misconduct 86, 96
allegations of 98, 200, 206
Sicily 155
Sidonius Apollinaris 43–4
Silva Candida 271

Silverius, pope 65, 67, 160
Silvester, pope 64, 86, 119, 134, 226, 230
Simon Magus 206
Simplicius, pope 62, 67, 150, 159, 229, 236, 241, 248, 252, 258, 281
Sisinnius 105
Skellig Michael 262
slavery 81, 93, 97, 106, 165, 166
  manumission 93
Smaragdus 54, 57
Socrates, historian 72
Sozomen, historian 72, 119
Spain 40, 71, 123, 280
Spoleto 275
St Amand 284
St Denis 273
St Petersburg 142, 153
stational liturgy 53, 56, 111
Stephen I, pope 87
Stephen III, pope 274
Stephen, saint 17, 223, 264–85
Stilicho, general 37, 39
Story of Apollonius King of Tyre 128
Subiaco 263
Sulpicius Severus, *Vita S. Martini* 103
Symmachan Apocrypha 64, 66; *see also Collectio Italica*; *Collectio Sanblasiana*; Symmachan forgeries
Symmachan forgeries 85–6, 88, 89, 90, 97; *see also Collectio Italica*; *Collectio Sanblasiana*; *Symmachan Apocrypha*
Symmachi 105
Symmachus, pope 28, 48, 52, 62, 63, 66, 83, 87–8, 92, 96, 98, 122, 229, 230, 248–53, 260; *see also* Laurentian schism
Symmachus, Quintus Aurelius 5, 32, 34, 35, 36, 39, 105
synods, *see* councils

Tabbenisi 174
tax 1–2, 55, 174, 231
temperantia 10
Tetrarchy 30, 34
Themistius, orator 32
Theodahad, Ostrogothic king 3
Theodelinda, Lombard queen 268
Theoderic, Ostrogothic king 3, 4, 15, 48–9, 54, 60, 81, 85, 125, 159, 160
Theodolus, priest and *gesta* character 100
Theodora, empress 67
Theodore, exarch 56
Theodore of Mopsuesta 69
Theodoret, historian 27, 28, 69, 121
Theodosian Code 45, 175
Theodosius I, emperor 28, 32–3, 36, 38–9, 44, 46, 56, 239
Theodosius II, emperor 2, 42, 45, 169, 182, 224, 280, 282
Theodosius, *primicerius notariorum* 42
Theodosius, son of Galla Placidia and Athaulf 47
Theodotus, *primicerius* 5
Theotokos 135
Three Chapter Controversy 55, 67–9, 161
Tibur 242; *see also* Tivoli
Tigrinus, priest 224
titular churches 16, 70, 83, 84, 88, 91, 111, 144, 152, 172, 225–60, 272; *see also* Rome: churches and monasteries
titulus, *see* titular churches
titulus, legal terminology 235–6
Tivoli 242
  ecclesia Cornutanensis 242
topos 96, 99–100, 105, 110
Toxotius, son of Paula, Jerome's patroness 199
Trajan 244
Translatio Sancti Stephani 278, 279–82, 285, 286
trials 85, 86, 99
Trier 35
triumphs 31, 32

Ulpian, jurist 235
Ursinian schism 62
Ursinus, pope 28, 59, 70–3, 122
Uzalis 278

Valens, emperor 35
Valentinian I, emperor 35, 96, 200
Valentinian II, emperor 36, 73
Valentinian III, emperor 37, 40–3, 45, 46, 47, 48, 66, 71, 86, 93, 96, 97, 236
Valentinus, bishop 253
Valerius Publicola, senator 165
Valila, donor to St Andreas Catabarbara 236, 241–2, 259
Vatican Gelasian Sacramentary 107–9
Venantius Fortunatus 138, 139
  De Virginitate 135
Vestina, *femina illustris* 227, 231, 232, 241
Vetranio 118
Vigilius, pope 55, 61, 65–6, 67–70, 160, 252
  Constitutum 69
Virgil 197
virginity 15, 115–39, 168, 170, 187, 194, 195, 197, 200, 203, 205, 209
Vita Siricii 75

Vitalian, pope 56
Vitruvius 80

wardship, *see* guardianship
wealth 16, 18
widowhood 210–14

xenodochia 143, 172
Xenophon 80
Xenophon of Ephesus, *An Ephesian Tale* 128
Xystus III, pope 64, 71, 72, 86, 91–8

Zeno, emperor 41, 67
  Henotikon 228
Zosimus, historian 44
Zosimus, pope 62, 212

Lightning Source UK Ltd.
Milton Keynes UK
UKHW041355211218
334365UK00001B/107/P